Advanced Software Testing—Vol. 1

About the Author

With a quarter-century of software and systems engineering experience, **Rex Black** is President of RBCS (www.rbcs-us.com), a leader in software, hardware, and systems testing. For over a dozen years, RBCS has delivered services in consulting, outsourcing, and training for software and hardware testing. Employing the industry's most experienced and recognized consultants, RBCS conducts product testing; builds and improves testing groups; and hires testing staff for hundreds of clients worldwide. Ranging from Fortune 20 companies to start-ups, RBCS's clients save time and money through improved product development, decreased tech support calls, improved corporate reputation, and more.

As the leader of RBCS, Rex is the most prolific author practicing in the field of software testing today. His popular first book, Managing the Testing Process, has sold over 30,000 copies around the world, including Japanese, Chinese, and Indian releases. His three other books on testing, Critical Testing Processes, Foundations of Software Testing, and Pragmatic Software Testing, have also sold tens of thousands of copies, including Hebrew, Indian, Chinese, Japanese and Russian editions. He has written over twenty-five articles, presented hundreds of papers, workshops, and seminars, and given about thirty keynote speeches at conferences and events around the world. Rex is the President of the International Software Testing Qualifications Board (ISTQB) and a Director of the American Software Testing Qualifications Board (ASTQB).

Rex Black

Advanced Software Testing—Vol. 1

Guide to the ISTQB Advanced Certification as an Advanced Test Analyst

rockynook

Rex Black
rex_black@rexblackconsulting.com

Editor: Jimi DeRouen
Copyeditor: Judy Flynn, Santa Barbara, USA
Layout and Type: Gerry Ichikawa, Santa Barbara
Cover Design: Helmut Kraus, www.exclam.de

Printed in the United States of America

ISBN-13: 978-1-933952-19-2

1st Edition © 2009 by Rex Black (3rd Printing, March 2014)
17 16 15 14   3 4 5

Rock Nook Inc.
 802 E. Cota Street, 3rd Floor
Santa Barbara, CA 93103

www.rockynook.com

Distributed by O'Reilly Media
1005 Gravenstein Highway North
Sebastopol, CA 95472-2811

Acknowledgements

A complete list of people who deserve thanks for helping me along in my career as a test professional would probably make up its own small book. Here I'll confine myself to those who had an immediate impact on my ability to write this particular book.

First of all, I'd like to thank my colleagues on the American Software Testing Qualifications Board and the International Software Testing Qualifications Board, and especially the Advanced Syllabus Working Party, who made this book possible by creating the process and the material from which this book grew. Not only has it been a real pleasure sharing ideas with and learning from each of the participants, but I have had the distinct honor of being elected president of both the American Software Testing Qualifications Board and the International Software Testing Qualifications Board twice. As I approach the end of my statutory last term as president, I look back with pride at our accomplishments so far, I look forward with pride to what we'll accomplish together in the future, and I hope this book serves as a suitable expression of the gratitude and professional pride I feel toward what we have done for the field of software testing.

Next, I'd like to thank the people who helped me create the material that grew into this book. The materials in this book, our Advanced Test Analyst instructor-lead training course, and our Advanced Test Analyst e-learning course were reviewed, re-reviewed, and polished with the hours of dedicated assistance by José Mata, Judy McKay, Jamie Mitchell, Paul Jorgensen, and Pat Masters.

Now, once the materials were created, the task of assembling the first rough draft of this book from scripts, slides, the syllabus, and a rough framework fell to Dena Pauletti, RBCS' extremely competent and meticulous technical administrator. This book would have taken literally months longer to prepare without her intrepid and timely assistance.

Of course, the Advanced syllabus could not exist without a foundation, specifically the ISTQB Foundation syllabus. I had the honor of working with that Working Party as well. I thank them for their excellent work over the years, creating the fertile soil from which the Advanced syllabus and thus this book sprang.

In the creation of the training courses and the materials that make up this book, I have drawn on all the experiences as I have had an author, practitioner, consultant, and trainer. So, I have benefited from individuals too numerous to list. I thank those of you who have bought one of my previous books, for you contributed to my skills as a writer. I thank those of you who have worked with me on a project, for you have contributed to my abilities as a test manager, test analyst, and technical test analyst. I thank those of you who have hired me to work with you as a consultant, for you have given me the opportunity to learn from your organizations. I thank those of you who have taken a training course from me, for you have collectively taught me much more than I taught each of you. I thank my my readers, colleagues, clients, and students, and hope that my contributions to you have repaid the debt of gratitude that I owe you.

For over a dozen years, I have run a testing services company, RBCS. From humble beginnings, RBCS has grown into an international consulting, training, and outsourcing firm with clients on six continents. While I have remained a hands-on contributor to the firm, over 100 employees, subcontractors, and business partners have been the driving force of our ongoing success. I thank all of you for your hard work for our clients. Without the success of RBCS, I could hardly avail myself of the luxury of writing technical books, which is a source of great pride but not a whole lot of money. Again, I hope that our mutual successes together have repaid the debt of gratitude that I owe each of you.

Finally, I thank my family, especially my wife, Laurel, and my daughters, Emma and Charlotte. The hectic work schedule entailed in running a global testing services company means little time enough for my family, and my insatiable habit of writing books reduces that time further. To Laurel, Emma, and Charlotte, know that I am aware that I can never fully repay the debt that I owe you for all that you give to me, but also know that my love for each of you is much greater than the time we get to share together.

Table of Contents

Appendix

Introduction

This is a book on advanced software testing for test analysts. By that I mean that I address topics that a practitioner who has chosen software testing as a career should know. I focus on those skills and techniques related to test analysis, test design, test execution, and test results evaluation. I assume that you know the basic concepts of test engineering, test design, test tools, testing in the software development lifecycle, and test management. You are ready to mature your level of understanding of these concepts and to apply these mature, advanced concepts to your daily work as a test professional.

This book follows the International Software Testing Qualifications Board's (ISTQB) Advanced Level Syllabus, with a focus on the material and learning objectives for the advanced test analyst. As such, this book can help you prepare for ISTQB Advanced Level Test Analyst exam. You can use this book to self-study for those exams or as part of an e-learning or instructor-lead course on the topics covered in those exams. If you are taking an ISTQB-accredited Advanced Level Test Analyst training course, this book is an ideal companion text for that course.

However, even if you are not interested in the ISTQB exams, you will find this book useful to prepare yourself for advanced work in software testing. If you are a test manager, test director, test analyst, technical test analyst, automated test engineer, manual test engineer, programmer, or in any other field where a sophisticated understanding of software testing is needed, then this book is for you.

This book focuses on test analysis. The book consists of 11 chapters, addressing the following material:

1. Basic aspects of software testing
2. Testing processes
3. Test management

4. Test techniques
5. Testing of software characteristics
6. Reviews
7. Incident (defect) management
8. Standards and test process improvement
9. Test tools and automation
10. People skills (team composition)
11. Preparing for the exam

Since that structure follows the structure of the ISTQB Advanced Syllabus, some of the chapters address the material in great detail, as they are central to the test analyst role. Some of the chapters address the material in less detail, as the test analyst need only be familiar with it. For example, I cover test techniques in detail in this book because that is central to what a test analyst does, while I spend less time on test management.

If you also read the companion volume to this book, which is for test managers, you'll find parallel chapters that address the material in detail but with different emphasis. For example, test analysts need to know quite a bit about incident management. Test analysts spend a lot of time creating incident reports, and you need to know how to do that well. Test managers also need to know a lot about incident management, but they focus on how to keep incidents moving through their reporting and resolution lifecycle and how to gather metrics from such reports.

What should a test analyst be able to do? Or, to ask the question another way, what should you have learned to do—or learned to do better—by the time you finish this book?

■ Implement the test strategy with a focus on business domain requirements
■ Analyze the system based on user quality expectations and apply that analysis to the testing to be done
■ Evaluate the system requirements to determine whether the business objectives can be met by that system
■ Prepare and execute adequate testing activities, and report on the progress of these activities
■ Provide the necessary evidence and data to support evaluations and findings
■ Implement the necessary tools and techniques to achieve the defined goals

In this book, we focus on these main concepts. I suggest that you keep these high-level objectives in mind as we proceed through the material in each of the following chapters.

In writing this book and the companion volume on test management, I've kept foremost in my mind the question of how to make this material useful to you. If you are using this book to prepare for an ISTQB Advanced Level Test Analyst exam, then I recommend that you read chapter 11 first, then read the other 10 chapters in order. If you are using this book to expand your overall understanding of testing to an advanced level but do not intend to take an ISTQB Advanced Level Test Analyst exam, then I recommend that you read chapters 1 through 10 only. If you are using this book as a reference, then feel free to read only those chapters that are of specific interest to you.

Each of the first 10 chapters is divided into sections. For the most part, I have followed the organization of the ISTQB Advanced Syllabus to the point of section divisions, but subsections and sub-subsection divisions in the syllabus might not appear. You'll also notice that each section starts with a text box describing the learning objectives for this section. If you are curious about how to interpret those K2, K3, and K4 tags in front of each learning objective, and how learning objectives work within the ISTQB syllabus, read chapter 11.

Software testing is in many ways similar to playing the piano, cooking a meal, or driving a car. How so? In each case, you can read books about these activities, but until you have practiced, you know very little about how to do it. So I've included practical, real-world exercises for the key concepts. I encourage you to practice these concepts with the exercises in the book. Then, make sure you take these concepts and apply them on your projects. You can become an advanced software testing professional only by doing software testing.

ISTQB Copyright

This book is based on the ISTQB Advanced Syllabus version 2007. It also references the ISTQB Foundation Syllabus version 2007. It uses terminology definitions from the ISTQB Glossary version 2.0. These three documents are copyrighted by the ISTQB and used by permission.

1 Test Basics

"Who am I? Why am I here?"

> Admiral James Stockdale, United States vice presidential
> candidate in 1992, at a vice presidential debate.

The first chapter of the Advanced Syllabus is concerned with contextual and background material that influences the remaining chapters. There are five sections:

1. Introduction
2. Testing in the Software Lifecycle
3. Specific Systems
4. Metrics and Measurement
5. Ethics

Let's look at each section and how it relates to test analysis.

1.1 Introduction

Learning objectives
Recall of content only

This chapter, as the name implies, introduces some basic aspects of software testing. These central testing themes have general relevance for testing professionals.

There are four major areas:

- Lifecycles and their effects on testing
- Special types of systems and their effects on testing

> **ISTQB Glossary**
>
> **software lifecycle:** The period of time that begins when a software product is conceived and ends when the software is no longer available for use. The software lifecycle typically includes a concept phase, requirements phase, design phase, implementation phase, test phase, installation and checkout phase, operation and maintenance phase, and sometimes, retirement phase. Note that these phases may overlap or be performed iteratively.

- Metrics and measures for testing and quality
- Ethical issues

Many of these concepts are expanded upon in later chapters. While you might suspect this material and the material in the Foundation syllabus to be redundant, based on the name of this chapter, it actually expands on ideas introduced there.

1.2   Testing in the Software Lifecycle

Learning objectives
Recall of content only

Chapter 2 in the Foundation Syllabus discusses integrating testing into the software lifecycle. As with the Foundation Syllabus, in the Advanced Syllabus, you should understand that testing must be integrated into the software lifecycle to succeed. This is true whether the particular lifecycle chosen is sequential, incremental, iterative, or spiral.

Proper alignment between the testing process and other processes in the lifecycle is critical for success. This is especially true at key interfaces and handoffs between testing and lifecycle activities such as these:

- Requirements engineering and management
- Project management
- Configuration and change management
- Software development and maintenance

- ◼ Technical support
- ◼ Technical documentation

Let's look at two examples of alignment.

In a sequential lifecycle model, a key assumption is that the project team will define the requirements early in the project and then manage the (hopefully limited) changes to those requirements during the rest of the project. In such a situation, if the team follows a formal requirements process, an independent test team in charge of the system test level can follow an analytical requirements-based test strategy.

Using such a strategy in a sequential model, the test team would start—early in the project—planning and designing tests following an analysis of the requirements specification to identify test conditions. This planning, analysis, and design work might identify defects in the requirements, making testing a preventive activity. Failure detection would start later in the lifecycle, once system test execution began.

However, suppose the project follows an incremental lifecycle model, adhering to one of the agile methodologies like Scrum. The test team won't receive a complete set of requirements early in the project, if ever. Instead, the test team will receive requirements at the beginning of each 30 day "sprint."

Rather than analyzing requirements at the outset of the project, the best the test team can do is to identify and prioritize key quality risk areas; i.e., they can follow an analytical risk-based test strategy. Specific test designs and implementation will occur immediately before test execution, potentially reducing the preventive role of testing. Failure detection starts very early in the project, at the end of the first sprint, and continues in repetitive, short cycles throughout the project. In such a case, testing activities in the fundamental testing process overlap and are concurrent with each other as well as with major activities in the software lifecycle.

No matter what the lifecycle—and indeed, especially with the more fast-paced agile lifecycles—good change management and configuration management are critical for testing. A lack of proper change management results in an inability for the test team to keep up with what the system is and what it should do. A lack of proper configuration management, as was discussed in the Foundation Syllabus, leads to loss of changes, an inability to say what was tested at

> **ISTQB Glossary**
>
> **system of systems:** Multiple heterogeneous, distributed systems that are embedded in networks at multiple levels and in multiple domains and are interconnected, addressing large-scale interdisciplinary common problems and purposes.

what point in time, and severe lack of clarity around the meaning of the test results.

The Foundation Syllabus cited four typical test levels:

- Unit or component
- Integration
- System
- Acceptance

The Foundation Syllabus mentioned some reasons for variation in these levels, especially with integration and acceptance.

Integration testing can mean component integration testing—integrating a set of components to form a system, testing the builds throughout that process. Or it can mean system integration testing—integrating a set of systems to form a system of systems, testing the system of systems as it emerges from the conglomeration of systems.

Acceptance test variations, discussed in the Foundation Syllabus, included user acceptance tests and regulatory acceptance tests.

Along with these four levels and their variants, at the Advanced level you need to keep in mind additional test levels that you might need for your projects. These would include the following:

- Hardware-software integration testing
- Feature interaction testing
- Customer product integration testing

You should expect to find most, if not all, of the following for each level:

- Clearly defined test goals and scope
- Traceability to the test basis (if available)

■ Entry and exit criteria, as appropriate both for the level and for the system lifecycle

■ Test deliverables, including results reporting

■ Test techniques that will be applied, as appropriate for the level, for the team, and for the risks inherent in the system

■ Measurements and metrics

■ Test tools, where applicable and as appropriate for the level

■ And, if applicable, compliance with organizational or other standards

When RBCS associates perform assessments of test teams, we often find organizations that use test levels but that perform them in isolation. This is often inefficient and confusing. While these topics are discussed more in the companion volume on advanced test management, test analysts should keep in mind that using documents like test policies and frequent contact between test-related staff can coordinate the test levels to reduce gaps, overlap, and confusion about results.

Let's take a closer look at this concept of alignment. We'll use the V-model shown in figure 1-1 as an example. We'll further assume that we are talking about the system test level.

In the V-model, with a well-aligned test process, test planning occurs concurrently with project planning. In other words, the moment of involvement of testing is at the very start of the project.

Once the test plan is approved, test control begins. Test control continues through to test closure. Analysis, design, implementation, execution, evaluation of exit criteria, and test results reporting are carried out according to the plan. Deviations from the plan are managed.

Test analysis starts immediately after or even concurrently with test planning. Test analysis and test design happen concurrently with requirements, high-level design, and low-level design. Test implementation, including test environment implementation, starts during system design and completes just before test execution begins.

Test execution begins when the test entry criteria are met. More realistically, test execution starts when most entry criteria are met and any outstanding entry criteria are waived. In V-model theory, the entry criteria would include successful completion of both component test and integration test levels. Test

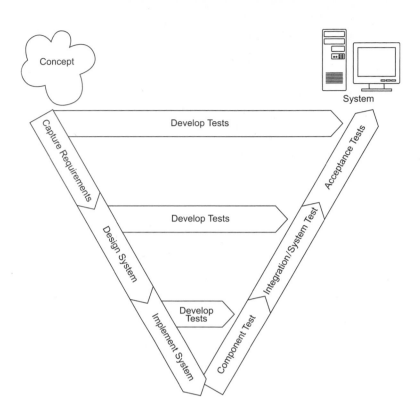

Figure 1–1   *V-model*

execution continues until the test exit criteria are met, though again some of these will often be waived.

Evaluation of test exit criteria and reporting of test results occur throughout test execution.

Test closure activities occur after test execution is declared complete.

This kind of precise alignment of test activities with each other and with the rest of the system lifecycle absolutely *will not* just happen. Nor can you expect to be able to instill this alignment continuously throughout the process, without any forethought.

Rather, for each test level, no matter what the selected software lifecycle and test process, the test manager must perform this alignment. Not only must this happen during the test and project planning, but test control includes acting to ensure on going alignment.

No matter what test process and software lifecycle are chosen, each project has its own quirks. This is especially true for complex projects such as the systems of systems projects common in the military and among RBCS's larger clients. In such a case, the test manager must plan not only to align test processes, but also to modify them. Off-the-rack process models, whether for testing alone or for the entire software lifecycle, don't fit such complex projects well.

1.3 Specific Systems

Learning objectives
Recall of content only

Systems of systems are independent systems tied together to serve a common purpose. Because they are independent and tied together, they often lack a single, coherent user or operator interface, a unified data model, compatible external interfaces, and so forth.

Such projects include the following characteristics and risks:

- The integration of commercial off-the-shelf (COTS) software along with some amount of custom development, often taking place over a long period.
- Significant technical, lifecycle, and organizational complexity and heterogeneity. This organizational and lifecycle complexity can include issues of confidentiality, company secrets, and regulations.
- Different development lifecycles and other processes among disparate teams, especially—as is frequently the case—when insourcing, outsourcing, and offshoring are involved.
- Serious potential reliability issues due to intersystem coupling, where one inherently weaker system creates ripple-effect failures across the entire system of systems.
- System integration testing, including interoperability testing, is essential. Well-defined interfaces for testing are needed.

At the risk of restating the obvious, systems of systems projects are more complex than single-system projects. The complexity increase applies organizationally, technically, process-wise, and team-wise. Good project management, formal development lifecycles and process, configuration management, and quality assurance become more important as size and complexity increase.

Let's focus on the lifecycle implications for a moment.

As mentioned before, with systems of systems projects, we are typically going to have multiple levels of integration. First, we will have component integration for each system, and then we'll have system integration as we build the system of systems.

We will also typically have multiple version management and version control systems and processes, unless all the systems happen to be built by the same (presumably large) organization and that organization follows the same approach throughout its software development team. This is not something my associates and I commonly see during assessments of large companies, by the way.

The duration of the project tends to be long. I have seen them be planned for as long as five to seven years. A system of systems project with five or six systems might be considered relatively short and relatively small if it lasted "only" a year and involved "only" 40 or 50 people. Across this project, there are multiple test levels, usually owned by different parties.

Because of the size and complexity of the project, it's easy for handoff and transfers of responsibility to break down. So, we need formal information transfer among project members, especially at milestones.

Even when we're integrating purely off-the-shelf systems, these systems are evolving. That's all the more likely to be true with custom systems. So, we have the management challenge of coordinating development of the individual systems and the test analyst challenge of proper regression tests at the system of systems level when things change.

Especially with off-the-shelf systems, maintenance testing can be triggered—sometimes without much warning—by external entities and events such as obsolescence, bankruptcy, or upgrade of an individual system.

If you think of the fundamental test process in a system of systems project, the progress of levels is not two-dimensional. Instead, imagine a sort of pyramidal structure, as shown in figure 1-2.

At the base, you have component testing. A separate component test level exists for each system.

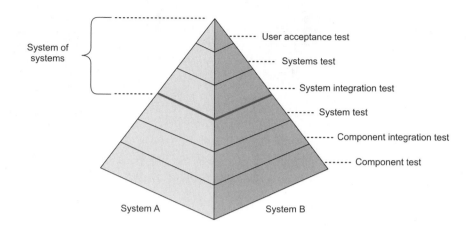

Figure 1–2   *Fundamental test process in a system of systems project*

Moving up the pyramid, you have component integration testing. A separate component integration test level exists for each system.

Next, you have system testing. A separate system test level exists for each system.

Note that, for each of these test levels, you have separate organizational ownership if the systems come from different vendors. You also probably have separate team ownership, because multiple groups often handle component, integration, and system test.

Continuing to move up the pyramid, you come to system integration testing. Now, finally, we are talking about a single test level across all systems. Next above that is systems testing, focusing on end-to-end tests that span all the systems. Finally, we have user acceptance testing. For each of these test levels, while we have single organizational ownership, we probably have separate team ownership.

Simply put, safety-critical systems are those systems upon which lives depend. Failure of such a system—or even temporary performance or reliability degradation or undesirable side effects as support actions are carried out—can injure or kill people, or, in the case of military systems, fail to injure or kill people at a battle-critical juncture.

Safety-critical systems, like systems of systems, have certain associated characteristics and risks:

> **ISTQB Glossary**
>
> **safety-critical system:** A system whose failure or malfunction may result in death or serious injury to people, loss or severe damage to equipment, or environmental harm.

■ Because defects can cause death, and deaths can cause civil and criminal penalties, proof of adequate testing can be and often is used to reduce liability.

■ For obvious reasons, various regulations and standards often apply to safety critical systems. The regulations and standards can constrain the process, the organizational structure, and the product. Unlike the usual constraints on a project, though, these are constructed specifically to increase the level of quality rather than to enable trade-offs to enhance schedule, budget, or feature outcomes at the expense of quality. Overall, there is a focus on quality as a very important project priority.

■ There is typically a rigorous approach to both development and testing. Throughout the lifecycle, traceability extends all the way from regulatory requirements to test results. This provides a means of demonstrating compliance. This requires extensive, detailed documentation but provides high levels of audit ability, even by non-test experts.

Audits are common if regulations are imposed. Demonstrating compliance can involve tracing from the regulatory requirement through development to the test results. An outside party typically performs the audits. So, the traceability gathering up front and the audit/compliance activities at the back end affect management, development, testing, and the competent authorities, both from a people and a process point of view.

During the lifecycle—often as early as design—the project team uses safety analysis techniques to identify potential problems. Single points of failure are often resolved through system redundancy.

In some cases, safety-critical systems are complex systems or even systems of systems. In other cases, non-safety-critical components or systems are integrated into safety-critical systems or systems of systems. For example, networking or communication equipment is not inherently a safety-critical system, but

> **ISTQB Glossary**
>
> **metric:** A measurement scale and the method used for measurement.
>
> **measurement scale:** A scale that constrains the type of data analysis that can be performed on it.
>
> **measurement:** The process of assigning a number or category to an entity to describe an attribute of that entity.
>
> **measure:** The number or category assigned to an attribute of an entity by making a measurement.

if integrated into an emergency dispatch or military system, it becomes part of a safety-critical system.

Formal quality risk management is essential in these situations. Fortunately, a number of such techniques exist, such as failure mode and effect analysis; failure mode, effect, and criticality analysis; hazard analysis; and software common cause failure analysis.

1.4 Metrics and Measurement

Learning objectives
Recall of content only

Throughout this book, we use metrics and measurement to establish expectations and guide testing by those expectations. You can and should apply metrics and measurements throughout the software development lifecycle. This is because well-established metrics and measures, aligned with project goals and objectives, will enable test analysts to track and report test and quality results to management in a consistent and coherent way.

A lack of metrics and measurements leads to purely subjective assessments of quality and testing. This results in disputes over the meaning of test results toward the end of the lifecycle. It also results in a lack of clearly perceived and communicated value, effectiveness, and efficiency for testing.

Not only must we have metrics and measurements, but also we need baselines. What is a "good" result for a given metric? An acceptable result? An unacceptable result? Without defined baselines, successful testing is usually impossible. In fact, when we perform assessments for our clients, we more often than not find ill-defined metrics of test team effectiveness and efficiency, with no baselines and thus bad and unrealistic expectations (which of course aren't met).

There's just about no end to what can be subjected to a metric and tracked through measurement. Consider the following:

- Planned schedule and coverage
- Requirements and their schedule, resource, and task implications for testing
- Workload and resource usage
- Milestones and scope of testing
- Planned and actual costs
- Risks, both quality and project risks
- Defects, including total found, total fixed, current backlog, average closure periods, and configuration, subsystem, priority, or severity distribution

During test planning, we establish expectations, which I mentioned as the baselines previously. As part of test control, we can measure actual outcomes and trends against these expectations. As part of test reporting, we can consistently explain to management various important aspects of the process, product, and project, using objective, agreed-upon metrics with realistic, achievable targets.

When thinking about a testing metrics and measurement program, there are three main areas to consider: definition, tracking, and reporting. Let's start with definition.

In a successful testing metrics program, you define a useful, pertinent, and concise set of quality and test metrics for a project. You avoid too large a set of metrics, as this will prove difficult and perhaps expensive to measure while often confusing rather than enlightening the viewers and stakeholders.

You also want to ensure uniform, agreed-upon interpretations of these metrics to minimize disputes and divergent opinions about the meaning of certain measures of outcomes, analyses, and trends. There's no point in having a metrics program if everyone has an utterly divergent opinion about what particular measures mean.

Finally, define metrics in terms of objectives and goals for a process or task, for components or systems, and for individuals or teams.

Victor Basili's well-known *Goal Question Metric* technique is one way to evolve meaningful metrics. Using this technique, we proceed from the goals of the effort—in this case, testing—to the questions we would have to answer to know if we were meeting those goals—to, ultimately, the specific metrics.

For example, one typical goal of testing is to build confidence. One natural question that arises in this regard is, "How much of the system has been tested?". Metrics for coverage include percentage requirements covered by tests, percentage of branches and statements covered by tests, percentage of interfaces covered by tests, percentage of risks covered by tests, and so forth.

Let's move on to tracking.

Because tracking is a recurring activity in a metrics program, the use of automated tool support can reduce the time required to capture, track, analyze, report, and measure the metrics.

Be sure to apply objective and subjective analyses for specific metrics over time, especially when trends emerge that could allow for multiple interpretations of meaning. Try to avoid jumping to conclusions, or delivering metrics that encourage others to do so.

Be aware of and manage the tendency for people's interests to affect the interpretation they place on a particular metric or measure. Everyone likes to think they are objective—and, of course, right as well as fair!—but usually people's interests affect their conclusions.

Finally, let's look at reporting.

Most importantly, reporting of metrics and measures should enlighten management and other stakeholders, not confuse or misdirect them. In part, this is achieved through smart definition of metrics and careful tracking, but it is possible to take perfectly clear and meaningful metrics and confuse people with them through bad presentation. Edward Tufte's series of books, starting with *The Graphical Display of Quantitative Information*, is a treasure trove of ideas about how to develop good charts and graphs for reporting purposes.[1]

---

1. The three books of Tufte's that I have read and can strongly recommend on this topic are *The Graphical Display of Quantitative Information*, *Visual Explanations*, and *Envisioning Information*.

> **ISTQB Glossary**
>
> **ethics:** No definition provided in the ISTQB Glossary.

Good testing reports based on metrics should be easily understood, not overly complex and certainly not ambiguous. The reports should draw the viewer's attention toward what matters most, not toward trivialities. In that way, good testing reports based on metrics and measures will help management guide the project to success.

Not all types of graphical displays of metrics are equal—or equally useful. A snapshot of data at a moment in time, as shown in a table, might be the right way to present some information, such as the coverage planned and achieved against certain critical quality risk areas. A graph of a trend over time might be a useful way to present other information, such as the total number of defects reported and the total number of defects resolved since the start of testing. An analysis of causes or relationships might be a useful way to present still other information, such as a scatter plot showing the correlation (or lack thereof) between years of tester experience and percentage of bug reports rejected.

1.5   Ethics

Learning objectives
Recall of content only

Many professions have ethical standards. In the context of professionalism, ethics are "rules of conduct recognized in respect to a particular class of human actions or a particular group, culture, etc."[2]

Because, as a test analyst, you'll often have access to confidential and privileged information, ethical guidelines can help you to use that information appropriately. In addition, you should use ethical guidelines to choose the best possible behaviors and outcomes for a given situation, given your constraints. Note that "Best possible" means for everyone, not just the tester.

---

2. Definition from dictionary.com.

Let me give you an example of ethics in action. I am president of three related international software testing consultancies, RBCS, RBCS NZ, and PureTesting. I also serve on the International Software Testing Qualifications Board (ISTQB) and American Software Testing Qualifications Board (ASTQB) boards of directors. As such, I might and do have insight into the direction of the ISTQB program that our competitors in the software testing consultancy business don't have.

In some cases, such as helping to develop syllabi, I have to make those business interests clear to people, but I am allowed to help do so. I helped write both the Foundation and Advanced syllabi.

In other cases, such as developing exam questions, I agreed, along with my colleagues on the ASTQB, that I should not participate. Direct access to the exam questions would make it all too likely that, consciously or unconsciously, I would warp our training materials to "teach the exam."

As you advance in your career as a tester, more and more opportunities to show your ethical nature—or to be betrayed by a lack of it—will come your way. It's never too early to inculcate a strong sense of ethics.

The ISTQB Advanced Syllabus makes it clear that the ISTQB expects certificate-holders to adhere to the following code of ethics.

PUBLIC—Certified software testers shall act consistently with the public interest. For example, if you are working on a safety-critical system and are asked to quietly cancel some defect reports, that's an ethical problem.

CLIENT AND EMPLOYER—Certified software testers shall act in a manner that is in the best interests of their client and employer and consistent with the public interest. For example, if you know that your employer's major project is in trouble and you short-sell the stock and then leak information about the project problems to the Internet, that's a real ethical lapse—and probably a criminal one, too.

PRODUCT—Certified software testers shall ensure that the deliverables they provide (on the products and systems they test) meet the highest professional standards possible. For example, if you are working as a consultant and you leave out important details from a test plan so that the client has to hire you on the next project, that's an ethical lapse.

JUDGMENT—Certified software testers shall maintain integrity and independence in their professional judgment. For example, if a project manager asks you not to report defects in certain areas due to potential business sponsor reactions, that's a blow to your independence and an ethical failure on your part if you comply.

MANAGEMENT—Certified software test managers and leaders shall subscribe to and promote an ethical approach to the management of software testing. For example, favoring one tester over another because you would like to establish a romantic relationship with the favored tester's sister is a serious lapse of managerial ethics.

PROFESSION—Certified software testers shall advance the integrity and reputation of the profession consistent with the public interest. For example, if you have a chance to explain to your child's classmates or your spouse's colleagues what you do, be proud of it and explain the ways software testing benefits society.

COLLEAGUES—Certified software testers shall be fair to and supportive of their colleagues and promote cooperation with software developers. For example, it is unethical to manipulate test results to arrange the firing of a programmer who you detest.

SELF—Certified software testers shall participate in lifelong learning regarding the practice of their profession and shall promote an ethical approach to the practice of the profession. For example, attending courses, reading books, and speaking at conferences about what you do help to advance you—and the profession. This is called doing well while doing good, and fortunately, it is very ethical!

1.6 Sample Exam Questions

To end each chapter, you can try one or more sample exam questions to reinforce your knowledge and understanding of the material and to prepare for the ISTQB Advanced Level Test Analyst exam.

1. You are working as a test analyst at a bank. At the bank, test analysts work closely with users during user acceptance test. The bank has bought two financial applications as commercial off-the-shelf (COTS) software from large software vendors. Previous history with these vendors has shown that they deliver quality applications that work on their own, but this is the first time the bank will attempt to integrate applications from these two vendors. Which of the following test levels would you expect to be involved in? [Note: There might be more than one right answer.]

    A Component test

    B Component integration test

    C System integration test

    D Acceptance test

2. Which of the following is necessarily true of safety critical systems?

    A They are composed of multiple COTS applications.

    B They are complex systems of systems.

    C They are systems upon which lives depend.

    D They are military or intelligence systems.

2 Testing Processes

Put the lime in the coconut and drink 'em both together,
Put the lime in the coconut, and you'll feel better...

From the lyrics of "Coconut," by Harry Nilsson

The second chapter of the Advanced syllabus is concerned with the process of testing and the activities that occur within that process. It establishes a framework for all the subsequent material in the syllabus and allows you to visualize organizing principles for the rest of the concepts. There are seven sections:

1. Introduction
2. Test Process Models
3. Test Planning and Control
4. Test Analysis and Design
5. Test Implementation and Execution
6. Evaluating Exit Criteria and Reporting
7. Test Closure Activities

Let's look at each section and how it relates to test analysis.

2.1 Introduction

Learning objectives
Recall of content only

The ISTQB Foundation syllabus describes the ISTQB fundamental test process. It provides a generic, customizable test process, shown in figure 2-1. That process consists of the following activities:

- Planning and control
- Analysis and design
- Implementation and execution
- Evaluating exit criteria and reporting
- Test closure activities

For test analysts, we can focus on the middle three activities.

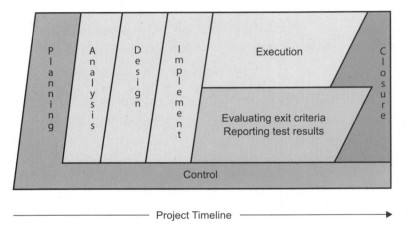

Figure 2–1   *ISTQB Fundamental test process*

2.2   **Test Process Models**

Learning objectives
Recall of content only

The concepts in this section apply primarily for test managers. There are no learning objectives defined for test analysts in this section. In the course of studying for the exam, read this section in chapter 2 of the Advanced syllabus for general recall and familiarity only.

2.3   Test Planning and Control

Learning objectives
Recall of content only

The concepts in this section apply primarily for test managers. There are no learning objectives defined for test analysts in this section. In the course of studying for the exam, read this section in chapter 2 of the Advanced syllabus for general recall and familiarity only.

2.4   Test Analysis and Design

Learning objectives

(K2) Explain the causes of functional testing taking place in specific stages of an application's life cycle.

(K2) Give examples of the criteria that influence the structure and level of test condition development.

(K2) Describe how test analysis and design are static testing techniques that can be used to discover defects.

(K2) Explain by giving examples the concept of test oracles and how a test oracle can be used in test specifications.

During the test planning activities in the test process, test leads and test managers work with project stakeholders to identify test objectives. The Institute of Electrical Electronics Engineers provides the IEEE 829 template—which was introduced at the Foundation Level and which we'll review later in this book—the lead or manager can document these in the section "Features to be Tested."

The test objectives are a major deliverable for test analysts because without them we wouldn't know what to test. During test analysis and design activities, we use these test objectives as our guide to carry out two main subactivities:

- Identify and refine the test conditions for each test objective
- Create test cases that exercise the identified test conditions

> **ISTQB Glossary**
>
> **test planning:** The activity of establishing or updating a test plan.
>
> test plan: A document describing the scope, approach, resources, and schedule of intended test activities. It identifies, among other test items, the features to be tested, the testing tasks, who will do each task, the degree of tester independence, the test environment, the test design techniques, the entry and exit criteria to be used and the rationale for their choice, and any risks requiring contingency planning. It is a record of the test planning process.
>
> **test case:** A set of input values, execution preconditions, expected results, and execution postconditions developed for a particular objective or test condition such as to exercise a particular program path or to verify compliance with a specific requirement.
>
> **test condition:** An item or event of a component or system that could be verified by one or more test cases, e.g., a function, transaction, feature, quality attribute, or structural element.

However, test objectives are not enough by themselves. We not only need to know what to test, but in what order and how much. Because of time constraints, the desire to test the most important areas first, and the need to expend our test effort in the most effective and efficient manner possible, we need to prioritize the test conditions.

When following a risk-based testing strategy—which we'll discuss in detail in chapter 3—the test conditions are quality risk items identified during quality risk analysis. The assignment of priority for each test condition usually involves determining the likelihood and impact associated with each quality risk item; i.e., we assess the level of risk for each risk item. The priority determines the allocation of test effort (throughout the test process) and the order of design, implementation, and execution of the related tests.

Throughout the process, the specific test conditions and their associated priorities can change as the needs—and our understanding of the needs—of the project and project stakeholders evolve.

This prioritization, use of prioritization, and reprioritization occurs regularly in the test process. It starts during risk analysis and test planning, of

> **ISTQB Glossary**
>
> **exit criteria:** The set of generic and specific conditions, agreed upon with the stakeholders, for permitting a process to be officially completed. The purpose of exit criteria is to prevent a task from being considered completed when there are still outstanding parts of the task that have not been finished. Exit criteria are used to report against and to plan when to stop testing.
>
> **test execution:** The process of running a test on the component or system under test, producing actual result.

course. It continues throughout the process, from analysis and design to implementation and execution. It influences evaluation of exit criteria and reporting of test results.

2.4.1 Functional Test Objectives

Before we get deeper into this process, let's look more closely at functional test objectives.

First, it's important to remember that functional test objectives can apply to any test level and exist throughout the lifecycle. Too often, test teams do not address major functional test objectives until the very end of the project, resulting in much gnashing of teeth and wailing when they find show-stopping failures.

Consider a video game as an example. For a video game, most users would consider the ability to save and reload games a key function, so testing of this feature is a key test objective.

To be smart about this testing, various members of the project team should test this ability at the unit, integration, system, and acceptance levels. Finding a save/reload failure during system test might affect the schedule, and that's not good for a consumer product like a game.

Furthermore, why wait until test execution starts at any level, early or late? Instead, start with reviews of requirements specifications, design specifications, and code to assess this function as well.

To identify test conditions, we can perform analysis of the test basis, the test objectives, the quality risks, and so forth using any and all information inputs and sources we have available. For analytical risk-based testing strategies, I'll cover exactly how this works in chapter 3.

If you're not using analytical risk-based testing, then you'll need to select the specific inputs and techniques according to the test strategy or strategies you are following. Those strategies, inputs, and techniques should align with the test plan or plans, of course, as well as with any broader test policies or test handbooks.

Now, in this book, we're concerned primarily with the test analyst role, so we are focused on functional tests. However, let me mention that this analysis work can identify functional and non functional test conditions. We should consider the level and structure of the test conditions for use in addressing functional and non functional characteristics of the test items.

There are two important choices when identifying and documenting test conditions:

■ The level of detail we need to describe the test conditions in the documentation

■ The structure of the documentation for the test conditions

There are a number of common ways to determine the level of detail and structure of the test conditions.

One is to work in parallel with the test basis documents. For example, if you have a marketing requirements document and a system requirements document in your organization, the former is usually high level and the latter is low level. So, you can use the marketing requirements document to generate the high-level test conditions and then use the system requirements document to elaborate one or more low-level test conditions underneath each high-level test condition.

Another approach is often used with quality risk analysis (sometimes called product risk analysis). In this approach, we can outline the key features and quality characteristics at a high level. We can then identify one or more detailed quality risk items for each feature or characteristics. These quality risk items are thus the test conditions.

Another approach, if you have only detailed requirements, is to go directly to the low-level requirements. In this case, traceability from the detailed test conditions to the requirements (which impose the structure) is needed for management reporting and to document what the test is to establish.

Yet another approach is to identify high-level test conditions only, sometimes without any formal test bases. For example, in exploratory testing some advocate the documentation of test conditions in the form of test charters. At that point, there is little to no additional detail created for the unscripted or barely scripted tests.

Again, it's important to remember that the chosen level of detail and the structure must align with the test strategy or strategies, and those strategies should align with the test plan or plans, of course, as well as with any broader test policies or test handbooks.

Also, remember that it's easy to capture traceability information while you're deriving test conditions from test basis documents like requirements, designs, use cases, user manuals, and so forth. It's much harder to re-create that information later by inspection of test cases.

Let's look at an example of applying a risk-based testing strategy to this step of identifying test conditions.

Suppose you are working on an online banking system project. During a risk analysis session, system response time, a key aspect of system performance, is identified as a high-risk area for the online banking system. Several different failures are possible, each with its own likelihood and impact.

So, discussions with the stakeholders lead us to elaborate the system performance risk area, identifying three specific quality risk items:

- Slow response time during login
- Slow response time during queries
- Slow response time during a transfer transaction

At this point, the level of detail is specific enough that the risk analysis team can assign specific likelihood and impact ratings for each risk item.

Now that we have test conditions, the next step is usually to elaborate those into test cases. I say "usually" because some test strategies, like the reactive ones discussed in the Foundation syllabus and in this book in chapter 4, don't always use written test cases. For the moment, let's assume that we want to specify test cases that are repeatable, verifiable, and traceable back to requirements, quality risk, or whatever else our tests are based on.

ISTQB Glossary

test design: The process of transforming general testing objectives into tangible test conditions and test cases.

test design specification: A document specifying the test conditions (coverage items) for a test item, specifying the detailed test approach, and identifying the associated high-level test cases.

high-level test case: A test case without concrete (implementation-level) values for input data and expected results. Logical operators are used; instances of the actual values are not yet defined and/or available.

low-level test case: A test case with concrete (implementation-level) values for input data and expected results. Logical operators from high-level test cases are replaced by actual values that correspond to the objectives of the logical operators.

If we are going to create test cases, then, for a given test condition—or two or more related test conditions—we can apply various test design techniques to create test cases. These techniques are covered in chapter 4. Keep in mind that you can and should blend techniques in a single test case.

I mentioned traceability to the requirements, quality risks, and other test bases. We can capture that directly, by relating the test case to the test basis element or elements that gave rise to the test conditions from which we created the test case. Alternatively, we can relate the test case to the test conditions, which are in turn related to the test basis elements.

As with test conditions, we'll need to select a level of detail and structure for our test cases. It's important to remember that the chosen level of detail and the structure must align with the test strategy or strategies. Those strategies should align with the test plan or plans, of course, as well as with any broader test policies or test handbooks.

So, can we say anything else about the test design process? Well, the specific process of test design depends on the technique. However, it typically involves defining the following:

> **ISTQB Glossary**
>
> **test implementation:** The process of developing and prioritizing test procedures, creating test data and, optionally, preparing test harnesses and writing automated test scripts.

- Preconditions
- Test environment requirements
- Test inputs and other test data requirements
- Expected results
- Post conditions

Defining the expected result of a test can be tricky, especially as expected results are not only screen outputs, but also data and environmental post conditions. Solving this problem requires that we have what's called a test oracle, which we'll look at in a moment.

First, though, let me point out the mention of test environment requirements earlier. This is an area of fuzziness in the ISTQB fundamental test process. Where is the line between test design and test implementation, exactly?

The Advanced syllabus says, "[D]uring test design the required detailed test infrastructure requirements may be defined, although in practice these may not be finalized until test implementation." Okay, but maybe we're doing some implementation as part of the design? Can't the two overlap? To me, trying to draw sharp distinctions results in many questions along the lines of, "How many angels can dance on the head of a pin?"

Whatever we call defining test environments and infrastructures—design, implementation, environment setup, or some other name—it is vital to remember that testing involves more than just the test objects and the testware. There is a test environment, and this isn't just hardware. It includes rooms, equipment, personnel, software, tools, peripherals, communications equipment, user authorizations, and all other items required to run the tests.

2.4.2   Test Oracles

Okay, I said I'd cover this issue of test oracles, so let's look at what they are and what oracle-related problems face the test analyst.

A test oracle is a source we use to determine the expected results of a test. We can compare these expected results with the actual results when we run a test. Sometimes the oracle is the existing system. Sometimes it's a user manual. Sometimes it's an individual's specialized knowledge. We should never use the code itself as an oracle, even for structural testing, because that's simply testing that the compiler, operating system, and hardware work.

So, what is the oracle problem? Well, if you haven't experienced this first-hand, ask yourself how, in general, we know what "correct results" are for a test? The difficulty of knowing is the oracle problem.

If you've just entered the workforce from the ivory towers of academia, you might have learned about perfect software engineering projects. You might have heard stories about detailed, clear, and consistent test bases like requirements and design specifications that define all expected results. Those stories were myths, if you heard them.

In the real world, on real projects, test basis documents like requirements are vague. Two documents, such as a marketing requirements document and a system requirements document, will often contradict each other. These documents have gaps, omitting any discussion of important characteristics of the product—especially non functional characteristics, and especially usability and user interface characteristics.

Sometimes these documents are missing entirely. Sometimes they exist but are so superficial as to be useless. One of my clients showed me a handwritten scrawl on a letter-size piece of paper, complete with crude illustrations, which was all he received by way of requirements on a project that involved 100 or so person-months of effort.

When test basis documents are delivered, they are often delivered late, often too late to wait for them to be done before we begin test design (at least if we want to finish test design before we start test execution).

Even with the best intentions on the part of business analysts, sales and marketing staff, and users, test basis documents won't be perfect. Real-world applications are complex and not entirely amenable to complete, unambiguous specification.

So, we have to augment the written test basis documents we receive with tester expertise or access to expertise, along with judgment and professional pessimism. Using all available oracles—written and mental, provided and derived—the tester can define expected results before and during test execution.

Because I've been talking a lot about requirements, you might assume that the oracle problem applies only to high-level test levels like system test and acceptance test. Nope. The oracle problem—and its solutions—apply to all test levels. The test bases will vary from one level to another, though. Higher test levels like user acceptance test and system test rely more on requirements specification, use cases, and defined business processes. Lower test levels like component test and integration test rely more on low-level design specification.

While this is a hassle, remember that you must solve the oracle problem in your testing. If you run tests with no way to evaluate the results, you are wasting your time. You will provide low, zero, or negative value to the team. Such testing generates false positives and false negatives. It distracts the team with spurious results of all kinds. It creates false confidence in the system.

By the way, as for my sarcastic aside about the "ivory tower of academia" a moment ago, let me mention that, when I studied computer science at UCLA quite a few years ago, my software engineering professors told me about this problem right from the start. I guess I couldn't say I wasn't warned!

Let's look at an example of a test oracle, from the real world.

I worked on a project to develop a banking application to replace a legacy system. There were two test oracles. One was the requirements specification, such as it was. The other was the legacy system. We faced two challenges.

For one thing, the requirements were vague. The original concept of the project, from the vendor's side, was "Give the customer whatever the customer wants," which they then realized was a good way to go bankrupt given the indecisive and conflicting ideas about what the system should do amongst the customer's users. The requirements were the outcome of a belated effort to put more structure around the project.

For another thing, sometimes the new system differed from the legacy system in minor ways. I remember one infamous situation. There was a single bug report that we opened, then deferred, then reopened, then deferred again, at least four or five times. It described situations where the monthly payment varied by $0.01.

The absence of any reliable, authoritative, consistent set of oracles lead to a lot of "bug report ping-pong." We also had bug report prioritization issues as people argued over whether some problems were problems at all. We had high rates of false positives and negatives. The entire team—including the test team—was frustrated. So, you can see that the oracle problem is not some abstract concept; it has real-world consequences.

2.4.3   Standards

At this point, let's review some standards from the Foundation that will be useful in test analysis and design.

First, let's look at two documentation templates you can use to capture information as you analyze and design your tests, assuming you intend to document what you are doing, which is usually true. The first is the IEEE 829 test design specification.

The test design specification describes a collection of test cases and the test conditions they cover at a high level. This template includes the following sections:

- Test design specification identifier (following whatever standard your company uses for document identification)
- Features to be tested (in this test suite)
- Approach refinements (specific techniques, tools, etc.)
- Test identification (tracing to test cases in suites)
- Feature pass/fail criteria (e.g., how we intend to determine whether a feature works, such as via a test oracle, a test basis document, or a legacy system)

The collection of test cases outlined in the test design specification is often called a test suite.

The sequencing of test suites and cases within suites is often driven by risk and business priority. Of course, project constraints, resources, and progress must affect the sequencing of test suites.

Next comes the IEEE 829 test case specification. A test case specification describes the details of a test case. This template includes the following sections:

- Test case specification identifier
- Test items (what is to be delivered and tested)
- Input specifications (user inputs, files, etc.)

- Output specifications (expected results, including screens, files, timing, etc.)
- Environmental needs (hardware, software, people, props, and so forth)
- Special procedural requirements (operator intervention, permissions, etc.)
- Intercase dependencies (if needed to set up preconditions)

While this template defines a standard for contents, the question of what a test case is is certainly an open one. In practice, test cases vary significantly in effort, duration, and number of test conditions covered.

We'll return to the IEEE 829 standard again in the next section. However, let me also review another related topic from the Foundation syllabus, on the matter of documentation.

In the real world, the extent of test documentation varies considerably. It would be hard to list all the different reasons for this variance, but they include the following:

- Risks to the project created by documenting or not documenting.
- How much value, if any, the test documentation creates—and is meant to create.
- Any standards that are or should be followed.
- The software development lifecycle model used. Advocates of agile approaches try to minimize documentation by ensuring close and frequent team communication.
- The extent to which we must provide traceability from the test basis to the test cases.

The key idea here is to remember that you should keep an open mind and a clear head when deciding how much to document.

Now, because I mentioned that we would focus on functional characteristics during the test analyst course, let's review the ISO 9126 standard.

The ISO 9126 quality standard for software defines six software quality characteristics: functionality, reliability, usability, efficiency, maintainability, and portability. Each characteristic has three or more sub characteristics, as shown in figure 2-2.

Tests that address functionality and its sub characteristics are functional tests. Those are the focus of this book, though the scope of testing will

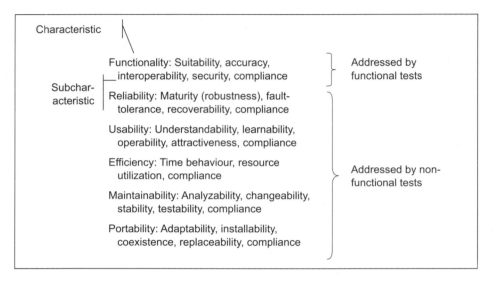

Figure 2–2 *ISO 9126 quality standard*

determine which of the specific sub characteristics apply for a given functional test effort.

Tests that address the other five characteristics and their sub characteristics are non functional tests. Those are covered more extensively in another volume in this series on technical test analysis. Finally, keep in mind that, when you're testing hardware/software systems, additional quality characteristics can and will apply.

2.4.4 Static Tests

Now, let's review three important ideas from the Foundation syllabus. One is the value of static testing early in the lifecycle to catch defects when they are cheap and easy to fix. The next is the preventive role testing can play when involved early in the lifecycle. The last is that testing should be involved early in the project. These three ideas are related because test analysis and design is a form of static testing, it is synergistic with other forms of static testing, and we can exploit that synergy only if we are involved at the right time.

Notice that, depending on when the test analysis and design work is done, you could possibly define test conditions and test cases in parallel with reviews and static analyses of the test basis. In fact, you could prepare for a requirements review meeting by doing test analysis and design on the requirements. Test analysis and design can serve as a structured, failure-focused static test of a requirements specification generating useful inputs to a requirements review meeting.

Of course, we should also take advantage of the ideas of static testing and, the early involvement if we can, to have test and non test stakeholders participate in reviews of various test work products, including risk analyses, test designs, test cases, and test plans. We should also use appropriate static analysis techniques on these work products.

Let's look at an example of how test analysis can serve as a static test. Suppose you are following an analytical risk-based testing strategy. If so, then, in addition to quality risk items—which are the test conditions—a typical quality risk analysis session can provide other useful deliverables.

I refer to these additional useful deliverables as by-products, along the lines of industrial by-products, in that they are generated by the way as you create the target work product, which in this case is a quality risk analysis document. These by-products are generated when you and the other participants in the quality risk analysis process notice aspects of the project you haven't considered before.

These by-products include the following:

- Project risks—things that could happen and endanger the success of the project
- Identification of defects in the requirements specification, design specification, or other documents used as inputs into the quality risk analysis
- A list of implementation assumptions and simplifications, which can improve the design as well as set up checkpoints you can use to ensure your risk analysis is aligned with actual implementation later

By directing these by-products to the appropriate members of the project team, you can prevent defects from escaping to later stages of the software lifecycle. That's always a good thing.

> **ISTQB Glossary**
>
> **test procedure:** A document specifying a sequence of actions for the execution of a test. Also known as test script or manual test script.
>
> **test script:** Commonly used to refer to a test procedure specification, especially an automated one.

2.4.5   Metrics

To close this section, let's look at metrics and measurements for test analysis and design. To measure completeness of this portion of the test process, we can measure the following:

- Percentage of requirements or quality (product) risks covered by test conditions
- Percentage of test conditions covered by test cases
- Number of defects found during test analysis and design

We can track test analysis and design tasks against a work breakdown structure, which is useful in determining whether we are proceeding according to the estimate and schedule.

2.5   Test Implementation and Execution

Learning objectives

(K2) Describe the pre-conditions for test execution, including: testware, test environment, configuration management, and, defect management.

Test implementation includes all the remaining tasks necessary to enable test case execution to begin. At this point, remember, we have done our analysis and design work, so what remains?

For one thing, if we intend to use explicitly specified test procedures—rather than relying on the tester's knowledge of the system—we'll need to organize the test cases into test procedures (or test scripts). When I say, "organize the test cases," I mean, at the very least, document the steps to carry out the test. How much detail do we put in these procedures? Well, the same considerations that lead to more (or less) detail at the test condition and test case level would apply here. For example, if a regulatory standard like the United States Federal Aviation Administration's DO-178B applies, that's going to require a high level of detail.

Because testing frequently requires test data for both inputs and the test environment itself, we need to make sure that data is available now. In addition, we must set up the test environments. Are both the test data and the test environments in a state such that we can use them for testing now? If not, we must resolve that problem before test execution starts. In some cases test data requires the use of data generation tools or production data. Ensuring proper test environment configuration can require the use of configuration management tools.

With the test procedures in hand, we need to put together a test execution schedule. Who is to run the tests? In what order should they run them? What environments are needed for what tests? We need to answer these questions.

Finally, because we're about to start test execution, we need to check whether all explicit and implicit entry criteria are met. If not, we need to work with project stakeholders to make sure they are met before the scheduled test execution start date.

Now, keep in mind that you should prioritize and schedule the test procedures to ensure that you achieve the objectives in the test strategy in the most efficient way. For example, in risk-based testing, we usually try to run tests in risk priority order. Of course, real-world constraints like availability of test configurations can change that order. Efficiency considerations like the amount of data or environment restoration that must happen after a test is over can change that order too.

Let's look more closely at two key areas, readiness of test procedures and readiness of test environments.

2.5.1   Test Procedure Readiness

Are the test procedures ready to run? Let's examine some of the issues we need to address before we know the answer.

As mentioned earlier, we must have established clear sequencing for the test procedures. This includes identifying who is to run the test procedure, when, in what test environment, with what data.

We have to evaluate constraints that might require tests to run in a particular order. Suppose we have a sequence of test procedures that together make up an end-to-end workflow? There are probably business rules that govern the order in which those test procedures must run.

So, based on all the practical considerations as well as the theoretical ideal of test procedure order—from most important to least important—we need to finalize the order of the test procedures. That includes confirming that order with the test team and other stakeholders. In the process of confirming the order of test procedures, you might find that the order you think you should follow is in fact impossible or perhaps unacceptably less efficient than some other possible sequencing.

We also might have to take steps to enable test automation. Of course, I say, "might have to take steps" rather than "must take steps" because not all test efforts involve automation. If some tests are automated, we'll have to determine how those fit into the test sequence. It's real easy for automated tests, if run in the same environment as manual tests, to damage or corrupt test data, sometimes in a way that causes both the manual and automated tests to generate huge numbers of false positives and false negatives. Guess what? That means you get to run the tests all over again. We don't want that!

Now, the Advanced syllabus says that we will create the test harness and test scripts during test implementation. Well, that's theoretically true, but as a practical matter you really need the test harness ready weeks, if not months, before you start to use it to automate test scripts.

We definitely need to know all the test procedure dependencies. If we find that there are reasons why—due to these dependencies—we can't run the test procedures in the sequence we established earlier, we have two choices: One, we can change the sequence to fit the various obstacles we have discovered, or, two, we can remove the obstacles.

Let's look more closely at two very common categories of test procedure dependencies—and thus obstacles.

The first is the test environment. You need to know what is required for each test procedure. Now, check to see if that environment will be available during the time you have that test procedure scheduled to run. Notice that "available" means not only is the test environment configured, but also no other test procedure—or any other test activity for that matter—that would interfere with the test procedure under consideration is scheduled to use that test environment during the same period of time.

The interference question is usually where the obstacles emerge. However, for complex and evolving test environments, the mere configuration of the test environment can become a problem. I worked on a project a while back that was so complex I had to construct a special database to track, report, and manage the relationships between test procedures and the test environments they required.

The second category of test procedure dependencies is the test data. You need to know what data each test procedure requires. Now, similar to the process before, check to see if that data will be available during the time you have that test procedure scheduled to run. As before, "available" means not only is the test data created, but also no other test procedure—or any other test activity for that matter—that would interfere with the viability and accessibility of the data is scheduled to use that test data during the same period of time.

With test data, interference is again often a large issue. I had a client who tried to run manual tests during the day and automated tests overnight. This resulted in lots of problems until a process was evolved to properly restore the data at the handover points between manual testing and automated testing (at the end of the day) and between automated testing and manual testing (at the start of the day).

2.5.2   Test Environment Readiness

Are the test environments ready to use? Let's examine some of the issues we need to address before we know the answer.

First, let's make clear the importance of a properly configured test environment. If we run the test procedures perfectly but use a misconfigured test environment, we obtain useless test results. Specifically, we get many false positives. A false positive in software testing is analogous to one in medicine—a test that should have passed instead fails, leading to wasted time analyzing "defects" that turn out to be test environment problems. Often the false positives are so large in number that we also get false negatives, which is where a test that should have failed instead passes, often in this case because we didn't see it hiding among the false positives. The overall outcome is very low defect detection effectiveness; very high field or production failure rates; very high defect report rejection rates; a lot of wasted time for testers, managers, and developers; and a severe loss of credibility for the test team. Need I say more about how bad this is?

So, we have to ensure properly configured test environments. Now, in the ISTQB fundamental test process, implementation is the point where this happens. As with automation, though, I feel this is probably too late, at least if we think of implementation as an activity that starts after analysis and design. If, instead, we think of implementation of the test environment as a subset of the overall implementation activity, and one that can start as soon as the test plan is done, then we are in better shape.

What is a properly configured test environment and what does it do for us?

For one thing, a properly configured test environment enables finding defects under the test conditions we intend to run. For example, if we want to test for performance, it allows us to find unexpected bottlenecks that would slow down the system.

For another thing, a properly configured test environment operates normally when failures are not occurring. In other words, it doesn't generate many false positives.

Additionally, at higher levels of testing such as system test and system integration test, a properly configured test environment replicates the production or end-user environment. Many defects, especially non functional defects like performance and reliability problems, are hard if not impossible to find in scaled-down environments.

There are some other things we need for a properly configured test environment. We'll need someone to set up and support the environment. For complex environments, this is usually someone outside the test team. We also need to make sure that someone—perhaps a tester, perhaps someone else—has loaded the testware, test support tools, and associated processes on the test environment.

Test support tools include, at the least, configuration management, incident management, test logging, and test management. Also at the very least you'll need procedures to gather data for exit criteria evaluation and test results reporting. Ideally, your test management system will handle some of that for you.

> **ISTQB Glossary**
>
> **test log:** A chronological record of relevant details about the execution of tests.
>
> test logging: The process of recording information about tests executed into a test log.

2.5.3   Blended Test Strategies

It is often a good idea to use a blend of test strategies, leading to balanced test approach, throughout testing, including during test implementation. For example, when my associates and I run test projects, we typically blend analytical risk-based test strategies with dynamic test strategies. We reserve some percentage (often 10 to 20 percent) of the test execution effort for testing that does not follow predetermined scripts.

Analytical strategies follow the ISTQB fundamental test process nicely, with work products produced along the way. However, the risk with blended strategies is that the reactive portion can get out of control. Testing without scripts should not be ad hoc or aimless. Such tests are unpredictable in duration and coverage.

Some techniques like session-based test management, which we'll look at later, can help deal with that inherent control problem in reactive strategies. In addition, to structure reactive test strategies, we can use experience-based test techniques such as attacks, error guessing, and exploratory testing. We'll discuss these topics further in chapter 4.

The common trait of a reactive test strategy is that we—for the most part—react to the actual system presented to us. This means that test analysis, test design, and test implementation occur primarily during test execution. In other words, reactive test strategies allow—indeed, require—that the results of each test influence the analysis, design, and implementation of the subsequent tests.

As discussed in the Foundation syllabus, these reactive strategies are lightweight in terms of total effort both before and during test execution. Experience-based test techniques are often effective at finding bugs, sometimes 5 or 10 times more so than scripted techniques. However, being experience based, naturally enough, they require expert testers. As I mentioned earlier, reactive test strategies result in test execution periods that are sometimes unpredictable in duration. Their lightweight nature means they don't provide much coverage information and are difficult to repeat for regression testing. Some claim that tools can address this coverage and repeatability problem, but I've never seen that work in actual practice.

That said, when reactive test strategies are blended with analytical test strategies, they tend to balance each other's weak spots. An analogy for this is blended scotch whiskey. Blended scotch whiskey consists of malt whiskey—either a single malt or more frequently a blend of various malt whiskeys—further blended with grain alcohol (basically, vodka). It's hard to imagine two liquors more different than vodka and single malt scotch, but together they produce a liquor that many people find much easier to drink and enjoy than the more assertive, sometimes almost medicinal single malts.

2.5.4   Starting Test Execution

We've now come to the point where we're ready to start test execution. To do so, we need the delivery of the test object or objects and the satisfaction (or waiver) of entry criteria.

Of course, this presumes that the entry criteria alone are enough to ensure that the various necessary implementation tasks discussed earlier in this section are complete. If not, then we have to go back and check those issues of test data, test environments, test dependencies, and so forth.

Now, during test execution, people will run the manual test cases via the test procedures. To execute a test procedure to completion, we would expect that at least two things had happened. First, we covered all of the test conditions or quality risk items traceable to the test procedure. Second, we carried out all of the steps of the test procedure.

You might ask, "How could I carry out the test procedure without covering all the risks or conditions?" In some cases, the test procedure is written at a high level. In that case, you would need to understand what the test was about and augment the written test procedure with on-the-fly details that ensure you cover the right areas.

You might also ask, "How could I cover all the risks and conditions without carrying out the entire test procedure?" Some steps of a test procedure are there more to enable testing than to cover conditions or risk. For example, some steps set up data or other preconditions, some steps capture logging information, and some steps restore the system to a known good state at the end.

A third kind of activity can apply during manual test execution. We can incorporate some degree of exploratory testing into the procedures. One way to accomplish this to leave the procedures somewhat vague and to tell the tester to select their favorite way of carrying out a certain task. Another way is to tell the testers, as I often do, that a test script is a road map to interesting places and, when they get somewhere interesting, they should stop and look around. This has the effect of giving them permission to transcend, to go beyond, the scripts. I've found it very effective.

Finally, during execution, tools will run automated tests. These tools follow the defined scripts without deviation. That can seem like an unalloyed "good thing" at first. However, if we did not design the scripts properly, that can mean that the script get out of sync with the system under test and generate a bunch of false positives. If you read the volume on technical test analysis, I'll talk more about that problem—and how to solve it.

2.5.5 Running a Single Test Procedure

Let's zoom in on the act of a tester running a single test procedure. After the logistical issues of initial setup are handled, the tester starts running the specific steps of the test. These yield actual results.

Now we have come to the heart of test execution. We compare actual results with expected results. This is indeed the moment when testing either adds value or removes value from the project. Everything up to this point—all of the work designing and implementing our tests—was about getting us to this point. Everything after this point is about using the value this comparison has delivered. Because this is so critical, so central to good testing, attention and focus on your part is essential at this moment.

So, what if we notice a mismatch between the expected results and the actual results? The ISTQB glossary refers to each difference between the expected results and the actual results as an anomaly. There can be multiple differences, and thus multiple anomalies, in a mismatch. When we observe an anomaly, we have an incident.

Some incidents are failures. A failure occurs when the system misbehaves due to one or more defects. This is the ideal situation when an incident has occurred. If we are looking at a failure, a symptom of a true defect, we should start to gather data to help the developer resolve the defect. We'll talk more about incident reporting and management in detail in chapter 7.

Some incidents are not failures but rather are false positives. False positives occur when the expected and actual results don't match due to bad test specifications, invalid test data, incorrectly configured test environments, a simple mistake on the part of the person running the test, and so forth.

If we can catch a false positive right away, the moment it happens, the damage is limited. The tester should fix the test, which might involve some configuration management work if the tests are checked into a repository. The tester should then rerun the test. Thus, the damage done was limited to the tester's wasted time along with the possible impact of that lost time on the schedule plus the time needed to fix the test plus the time needed to rerun the test.

All of those activities, all of that lost time, and the impact on the schedule would have happened even if the tester had simply assumed the failure was valid and reported it as such. It just would have happened later, after an additional loss of time on the part of managers, other testers, developers, and so forth.

Here's a cautionary note on these false positives too. Just because a test has never yielded a false positive before, in all the times it has been run before, doesn't mean you're not looking at one this time. Changes in the test basis, the proper expected results, the test object, and so forth can obsolete or invalidate a test specification.

2.5.6 Logging Test Results

Most testers like to run tests—at least the first few times they run them—but sometimes they don't always like to log results. "Paperwork!" they snort. "Bureaucracy and red tape!" they protest.

If you are one of those testers, get over it. I said previously that all the planning, analysis, design, and implementation was about getting to the point of running a test procedure and comparing actual and expected results. I then said that everything after that point is about using the value the comparison delivered. Well, you can't use the value if you don't capture it, and the test logs are about capturing the value.

So, remember that, as testers run tests, testers log results. Failure to log results means either doing the test over (most likely) or losing the value of running the tests. When you do the test over, that is pure waste, a loss of your time running the test. Because test execution is usually on the critical path for project completion, that waste puts the planned project end date at risk. People don't like that much.

A side note here, before we move on: I mentioned reactive test strategies and the problems they have with coverage earlier. Note that, with adequate logging, while you can't ascertain reactive test coverage in advance, at least you can capture it afterwards. So, again, log your results, both for scripted and unscripted tests.

During test execution, there are many moving parts. The test cases might be changing. The test object and each constituent test item are often changing. The test environment might be changing. The test basis might be changing. So, logging should identify the versions tested.

The military strategist Clausewitz referred famously to the "fog of war." What he meant was not a literal fog—though black-powder cannons and fire-arms of his day created plenty of that!—but rather a metaphorical fog whereby no one observing a battle, be they an infantryman or a general, could truly grasp the whole picture.

Clausewitz would recognize his famous fog if he were to come back to life and work as a tester. Test execution periods tend to have a lot of fog. Good test logs are the fog-cutter. Test logs should provide a detailed, rich chronology of test execution.

To do so, test logs need to be test-by-test and event-by-event. Each test, uniquely identified, should have status information logged against it as it goes through the test execution period. This information should support not only understanding the overall test status but also the overall test coverage.

You should also log events that occur during test execution and affect the test execution process, whether directly or indirectly. We should document anything that delays, interrupts, or blocks testing.

Test analysts are not always also test managers, but they should work closely with the test managers. Test managers need logging information for test control, test progress reporting, and test process improvement. Test analysts need

> **ISTQB Glossary**
>
> **test control:** A test management task that deals with developing and applying a set of corrective actions to get a test project on track when monitoring shows a deviation from what was planned.

logging information too, along with the test managers, for measurement of exit criteria, which we'll cover in the next section.

Finally, let me point out that the extent, type, and details of test logs will vary based on the test level, the test strategy, the test tools, and various standards and regulations. Automated component testing results in the automated test gathering logging information. Manual acceptance testing usually involves the test manager compiling the test logs or at least collating the information coming from the testers. If we're testing regulated, safety-critical systems like pharmaceutical systems, we might have to log certain information for audit purposes.

2.5.7   Use of Amateur Testers

Amateur testers. This phrase is rather provocative, so let me explain what I mean. A person who primarily works as a tester to earn her living is a professional tester. Anyone else engaged in testing is an amateur tester.

I am a professional tester now, and have been since 1987. Before that, I was a professional programmer. I still write programs from time to time, but I'm now an amateur programmer. I make many typical amateur-programmer mistakes when I do it. Before I was a professional tester, I unit-tested my code as a programmer. I made many typical amateur-tester mistakes when I did that. Because one of the companies I worked for as a programmer relied entirely on programmer unit testing, that sometimes resulted in embarrassing outcomes for our customers—and for me.

There's nothing wrong with involving amateur testers. Sometimes, we want to use amateur testers such as users or customers during test execution. It's important to understand what we're trying to accomplish with this and why it will (or won't) work. For example, often the objective is to build user confidence in the system, but that can backfire! Suppose we involve them too early, when the system is still full of bugs. Oops!

2.5.8 Standards

Let's look at some standards that relate to implementation and execution as well as to other parts of the test process.

Let's start with the IEEE 829 standard. Most of this material about IEEE 829 should be a review of the Foundation syllabus for you, but it might be a while since you've looked at it.

The first IEEE 829 template, which we would use during test implementation, is the IEEE 829 test procedure specification. A test procedure specification describes how to run one or more test cases. This template includes the following sections:

- Test procedure specification identifier
- Purpose (e.g., which tests are run)
- Special requirements (skills, permissions, environment, etc.)
- Procedure steps (log, set up, start, proceed [the steps themselves], measure results, shut down/suspend, restart [if needed], stop, wrap up/tear down, contingencies)

While the IEEE 829 standard distinguishes between test procedures and test cases, in practice test procedures are often embedded in test cases.

A test procedure is sometimes referred to as a test script. A test script can be manual or automated.

The IEEE 829 standard for test documentation also includes ideas on what to include in a test log. According to the standard, a test log should record the relevant details about test execution. This template includes the following sections:

- Test log identifier.
- Description of the testing, including the items under test (with version numbers), the test environments being used, and the like.
- Activity and event entries. These should be test-by-test *and* event-by-event. Events include things like test environments becoming unavailable, people being out sick, and so forth. You should capture information on the test execution process; the results of the tests; environmental changes or issues;

bugs, incidents, or anomalies observed; the testers involved; any suspension or blockage of testing; changes to the plan and the impact of change; and so forth.

The British Standards Institute produces the BS 7925/2 standard. It has two main sections, test design techniques, and test measurement techniques.

For test design, it reviews a wide range of techniques, including black-box, white-box, and others. It covers the following black-box techniques that were also covered in the Foundation syllabus:

- Equivalence partitioning
- Boundary value analysis
- State transition testing

It also covers a black-box technique called cause-effect graphing, which is a graphical version of a decision table, and a black-box technique called syntax testing.

It covers the following white-box techniques that were also covered in the Foundation syllabus:

- Statement testing
- Branch and decision testing

It also covers some additional white-box techniques that were covered only briefly or not at all in the Foundation syllabus:

- Data flow testing
- Branch condition testing
- Branch condition combination testing
- Modified condition decision testing
- Linear Code Sequence and Jump (LCSAJ) testing

Rounding out the list are two sections, "Random Testing" and "Other Testing Techniques." Random testing was not covered in the Foundation syllabus—and won't be covered in this book, though I will address it in the volume on technical test analysis. The section on other testing techniques doesn't provide any examples but merely talks about rules on how to select them.

You might be thinking, "Hey, wait a minute, that was too fast. Which of those do I need to know for the Advanced Level Test Analyst exam?" The answer is in two parts. First, any test design technique that was on the Foundation syllabus, you had better know it. It's fair for the Advanced Level Test Analyst exam. Second, we'll cover the new test design techniques that might be on the Advanced Level Test Analyst exam in detail in chapter 4.

BS 7925/2 provides one or more coverage metrics for each of the test measurement techniques. The choice of organization is curious indeed because there is no clear reason why the coverage metrics weren't covered at the same time as the design techniques.

However, from the point of view of the ISTQB fundamental test process, perhaps it is easier that way. For example, our entry criteria might require some particular level of test coverage, as it would if we were testing safety-critical avionics software subject to the United States Federal Aviation Administration's standard DO-178B. (I'll cover that standard in a moment.) So, during test design, we would employ the test design techniques. During test implementation, we would use the test measurement techniques to ensure adequate coverage.

In addition to these two major sections, this document also includes two annexes. Annex B brings the dry material in the first two major sections to life by showing an example of applying them to realistic situations. Annex A covers process considerations, which is perhaps closest to our area of interest here. It discusses the application of the standard to a test project, following a test process given in the document. To map that process to the ISTQB fundamental test process, we can say the following:

- Test analysis and design along with test implementation in the ISTQB process is equivalent to test specification in the BS 7925/2 process.
- BS 7925/2 test execution, logically enough, corresponds to test execution in the ISTQB process. Note, though, that the ISTQB process includes that as part of a larger activity, test implementation and execution. Note also that the ISTQB process includes test logging as part of test execution, while BS 7925/2 has a separate test recording process.
- Finally, BS 7925/2 has checking for test completion as the final step in its process. That corresponds roughly to the ISTQB's evaluating test criteria and reporting.

The United States Federal Aviation Administration provides a standard called DO-178B for avionics systems. In Europe, it's called ED-12B. The standard

Table 2–1 *FAA DO 178B mandated coverage*

Criticality	Potential Failure Impact	Required Coverage
Level A: Catastrophic	Software failure can result in a catastrophic failure of the system.	Modified Condition/ Decision, Decision, and Statement
Level B: Hazardous/ Severe	Software failure can result in a hazardous or severe/major failure of the system.	Decision and Statement
Level C: Major	Software failure can result in a major failure of the system.	Statement
Level D: Minor	Software failure can result in a minor failure of the system.	None
Level E: No effect	Software failure cannot have an effect on the system.	None

assigns a criticality level, based on the potential impact of a failure. Based on the criticality level, a certain level of white-box test coverage is required, as shown in table 2-1.

Let me explain table 2-1 a bit more thoroughly:

Criticality level A, or Catastrophic, applies when a software failure can result in a catastrophic failure of the system. For software with such criticality, the standard requires Modified Condition/ Decision, Decision, and Statement coverage.

Criticality level B, or Hazardous and Severe, applies when a software failure can result in a hazardous, severe, or major failure of the system. For software with such criticality, the standard requires Decision and Statement coverage.

Criticality level C, or Major, applies when a software failure can result in a major failure of the system. For software with such criticality, the standard requires only Statement coverage.

Criticality level D, or Minor, applies when a software failure can only result in a minor failure of the system. For software with such criticality, the standard does not require any level of coverage.

Finally, criticality level E, or No Effect, applies when a software failure cannot have an effect on the system. For software with such criticality, the standard does not require any level of coverage.

This makes a certain amount of sense. You should be more concerned about software that affects flight safety, such as rudder and aileron control modules, than you are about software that doesn't, such as video entertainment systems. However, there is a risk of using a one-dimensional white-box measuring stick to determine how much confidence we should have in a system. Coverage metrics are a measure of confidence, it's true, but we should use multiple coverage metrics, both white-box and black-box.

By the way, if you found this a bit confusing, note that all of the white-box coverage metrics I mentioned were discussed in the Foundation syllabus, in chapter 4. If you don't remember what they mean, you should go back and review the material in that chapter on white-box coverage metrics.

2.5.9   Metrics

Finally, what metrics and measurements can we use for the test implementation and execution of the ISTQB fundamental test process? Different people use different metrics, of course.

Typical metrics during test implementation are the percentage of test environments configured, the percentage of test data records loaded, and the percentage of test cases automated.

During test execution, typical metrics look at the percentage of test conditions covered, test cases executed, and so forth.

We can track test implementation and execution tasks against a work-breakdown-structure, which is useful in determining whether we are proceeding according to the estimate and schedule.

Note that here we are discussing metrics to measure the completeness of these processes; i.e., the progress we have made. You should use a different set of metrics for test reporting.

2.6 Evaluating Exit Criteria and Reporting

Learning objectives

(K3) Determine from a given set of measures if a test completion criterion has been fulfilled.

In one sense, the evaluation of exit criteria and reporting of results is a test management activity. And, in the volume on advanced test management, we'll examine ways to analyze, graph, present, and report test results as part of the test progress monitoring and control activities.

However, in another sense, there is a key piece of this process that belongs to the test analyst. As test analysts, in this book we are more interested with two main areas. First, we need to collect the information necessary to support test management reporting of results. Second, we need to measure progress toward completion, and by extension, we need to detect deviation from the plan. (Of course, if we do detect deviation, it is the test manager's role, as part of the control activities, to get us back on track.)

To measure completeness of the testing with respect to exit criteria, and to generate information needed for reporting, we can measure properties of the test execution process such as the following:

- Number of test conditions, cases, or test procedures planned, executed, passed, and failed
- Total defects, classified by severity, priority, status, or some other factor
- Change requests proposed, accepted, and tested
- Planned versus actual costs, schedule, effort
- Quality risks, both mitigated and residual
- Lost test time due to blocking events
- Confirmation and regression test results

We can track evaluation and reporting milestones and tasks against a work-breakdown-structure, which is useful in determining whether we are proceeding according to the estimate and schedule.

In the remainder of this section, we'll look at examples of test metrics and measures that you can use to evaluate where you stand with respect to exit

Test Suite Summary
Test Pass Two

Suite	Total Cases	Planned Tests Fullfilled				Weighted Failure	Planned Tests Unfullfilled				Earned Value			
		Count	Skip	Pass	Fail		Count	Queued	IP	Block	Plan Hrs	Actual Hrs	%Effort	%Exec
Functionality	14	14	0	4	10	10.6	0	0	0	0	36.0	49.0	163%	100%
Performance	5	4	0	1	3	8.7	1	1	0	0	7.0	11.5	164%	80%
Reliability	2	2	2	0	0	0.0	0	0	0	0	0.0	0.0	0%	0%
Robustness	3	1	0	0	1	0.5	2	2	0	0	12.5	8.0	64%	33%
Installation	4	0	0	0	0	0.0	4	4	0	0	72.0	0.0	0%	0%
Localization	8	1	0	0	1	0.5	7	0	7	0	128.0	22.0	17%	13%
Security	4	2	0	2	0	1.1	2	2	0	0	17.0	8.5	50%	50%
Documentation	3	1	0	0	1	4.0	2	2	0	0	28.0	15.0	54%	33%
Integration	4	4	0	3	1	1.0	0	0	0	0	8.0	12.5	156%	100%
Usability	2	0	0	0	0	0.0	2	0	2	0	16.0	0.0	0%	0%
Exploratory	6	0	0	0		0.0	6	6	0	0	12.0	0.0	0%	0%
Total	55	29	2	10	17	26.4	26	17	9	0	336.5	126.5	38%	51%
Percent	100%	53%	4%	18%	31%	N/A	47%	31%	16%	0%				

Figure 2–3   *Test suite summary worksheet*

criteria. Most of these are drawn from actual case studies, projects where RBCS helped a client with their testing.

2.6.1   Test Suite Summary

Figure 2-3 shows a test suite summary worksheet. Such a worksheet summarizes the test-by-test logging information described in a previous section. As a test analyst, you can use this worksheet to track a number of important properties of the test execution so far:

- Test case progress
- Test case pass/fail rates
- Test suite defect priority/severity (weighted failure)
- Earned value

As such, it's a useful chart for the test analyst to understand the status of the entire test effort.

Down the left side of figure 2-3, you see two columns, the test suite name and the number of test cases it contains. Again, in some test log somewhere, we have detailed information for each test case.

On the middle-left side, you see four columns under the general heading of "Planning Tests Fulfilled." These are the tests for which no more work remains, at least during this pass of testing.

The weighted failure numbers for each test suite, found in the column about in the middle of the table, give a metric of how many bugs the test suite found. Each bug is weighted by priority and severity—only the severity one, priority one bugs count for a full weighted failure point, while lower severity and priority can reduce the weighted failure point count for a bug to as little 0.04. So this is a metric of the technical risk, the likelihood of finding problems, associated with each test suite based on historical finding data.

On the middle-right side, you see four columns under the general heading of "Planning Tests Unfulfilled." These are the tests for which more work remains during this pass of testing. IP, by the way, stands for "in progress."

Finally, on the right side you see four columns under the general heading of "Earned Value." Earned value is a simple project management concept. It says that, in a project, we accomplish tasks by expending resources. So if the percentage of tasks accomplished is about equal to the percentage of resources expended, we're on track. If the percentage of tasks accomplished is greater than the percentage of resources expended, we're on our way to being under budget. If the percentage of tasks accomplished is less than the percentage of resources expended, we're on our way to being over budget.

Similarly, from a schedule point of view, the percentage of tasks accomplished should be approximately equal to the percentage of project time elapsed. As with effort, if the tasks percentage is over the schedule percentage, we're happy. If the tasks percentage is below the schedule percentage, we're sad and worried.

In test execution, we can consider the test case or test procedure to be our basic task. The resources—for manual testing, anyway—are usually the person-hours required to run the tests. That's the way this chart shows earned value, test suite by test suite.

Take a moment to study figure 2-3. Think about how you might be able to use it on your current (or future) projects.

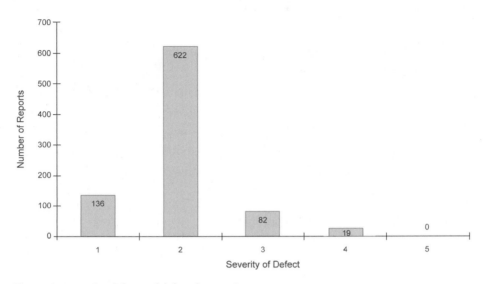

Figure 2–4   *Breakdown of defects by severity*

2.6.2   Defect Breakdown

We can analyze defect (or bug) reports in a number of ways. There's just about no end to the analysis that I have done as a test analyst, test manager, and test consultant. As a test professional, I think of good, proper analysis of bug reports much the same way as a doctor thinks of good, proper analysis of blood samples.

Just one of these many ways to examine bug reports is by looking at the breakdown of the defects by severity, priority, or some combination of the two. If you use a numerical scale for severity and priority, it's easy to multiply them together to get a weighted metric of overall bug importance, as we just saw.

Figure 2-4 shows an example of such a chart. What can we do with it? Well, for one thing, we can compare this chart with previous projects to get a sense of whether we're in better or worse shape. Remember, though, that the distribution will change over the life of the project. Ideally, the chart will start skewed toward high-priority bugs—at least it will if we're doing proper risk-based testing, which we'll discuss in chapter 3.

Figure 2-4 shows lots of severity ones and twos. Usually, severity one is loss of data. Severity two is loss of functionality without a workaround. Either way, bad news.

This chart tells me, as a test professional, to take a random sample of 10 or 20 of these severity one and two reports and see if we have severity inflation going on here. Are our severity classifications accurate? If not, the poor test manager's reporting will be biased and alarmist, which will get the manager in trouble.

As I mentioned previously, though, if I'm doing risk-based testing, this is probably about how this chart should look during the first quarter or so of the project. Find the scary stuff first, I always tell testers. If these severity classifications are right, the test team is doing just that.

2.6.3   Confirmation Test Failure Rate

As test analysts, we can count on finding some bugs. Hopefully many of those bugs will be sent back to us, allegedly fixed. At that point, we confirmation-test the fix. How many of those fixes fail the confirmation test? I know that it can feel like it's quite a few, but is it really? Figure 2-5 shows the answer, graphically, for an actual project.

On this banking project, we can see that quite a few bug fixes failed the confirmation test. We had to reopen fully one in six defect reports at least once. That's a lot of wasted time. It's also a lot of potential schedule delay. Study figure 2-5, thinking about ways you could use this information during test execution.

2.6.4   System Test Exit Review

Finally, let's look at another case study. Figure 2-6 shows an excerpt of the exit criteria for an Internet appliance project that RBCS provided testing for. You'll see that we have graded the criteria as part of a system test exit review.

Each of the three criteria here is graded on a three-point scale:

- Green: Totally fulfilled, with little remaining risk
- Yellow: Not totally fulfilled, but perhaps an acceptable risk
- Red: Not in any sense fulfilled, and poses a substantial risk

Of course, you would want to provide additional information and data for the yellows and the reds.

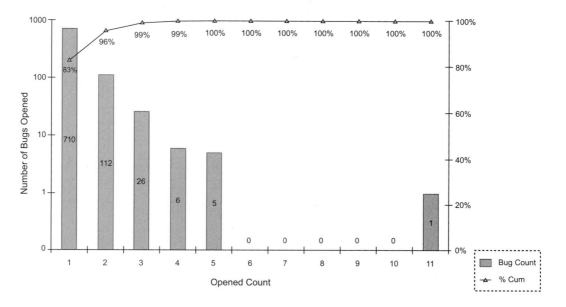

Figure 2–5   *Confirmation test failure analysis*

2.6.5 Standards

Finally, let's look at one more IEEE 829 template, one that applies to this part of the test process. The IEEE 829 standard for test documentation includes a template for test summary reports.

A test summary report describes the results of a given level or phase of testing. The IEEE 829 template includes the following sections:

- Test summary report identifier
- Summary (e.g., what was tested, what the conclusions are, etc.)
- Variances (from plan, cases, procedures)
- Comprehensive assessment
- Summary of results (e.g., final metrics, counts)
- Evaluation (of each test item vis-à-vis pass/fail criteria)
- Summary of activities (resource use, efficiency, etc.)
- Approvals

System Test Exit Review

Per the Test Plan, System Test was planned to end when following criteria were met:

1. All design, implementation, and feature completion, code completion, and unit test completion commitments made in the System Test Entry meeting were either met or slipped to no later than four (4), three (3), and three (3) weeks, respectively, prior to the proposed System Test Exit date.
    STATUS: RED. Audio and demo functionality have entered System Test in the last three weeks. The modems entered System Test in the last three weeks. On the margins of a violation, off-hook detection was changed significantly.

2. No panic, crash, halt, wedge, unexpected process termination, or other stoppage of processing has occurred on any server software or hardware for the previous three (3) weeks.
    STATUS: YELLOW. The servers have not crashed, but we did not complete all the tip-over and fail-over testing we planned, and so we are not satisfied that the servers are stable under peak load or other inclement conditions.

3. Production Devices have been used for all System Test execution for at least three (3) weeks.
    STATUS: GREEN. Except for the modem situation discussed above, the hardware has been stable.

Figure 2–6   *Case study of system test exit review*

The summaries can be delivered during test execution as part of a project status report or meeting. They can also be used at the end of a test level as part of test closure activities.

2.7   Evaluating Exit Criteria and Reporting Exercise

Consider the complete set of actual exit criteria from the Internet appliance project, which is shown in the following subsection. Toward the end of the project, the test team rated each criterion on the following scale:

■   Green: Totally fulfilled, with little remaining risk
■   Yellow: Not totally fulfilled, but perhaps an acceptable risk
■   Red: Not in any sense fulfilled, and poses a substantial risk

> **ISTQB Glossary**
>
> **test closure:** During the test closure phase of a test process, data is collected from completed activities to consolidate experience, testware, facts, and numbers. The test closure phase consists of finalizing and archiving the testware and evaluating the test process, including preparation of a test evaluation report.
>
> **test summary report:** A document summarizing testing activities and results. It also contains an evaluation of the corresponding test items against exit criteria.

You can see the ratings we gave each criterion in the STATUS block below the criterion itself.

We used this evaluation of the criteria as an agenda for a System Test Exit Review meeting. I led the meeting and walked the team through each criterion. As you can imagine, the RED ones required more explanation than the YELLOW and GREEN ones.

While narrative explanation is provided for each evaluation, perhaps more information and data are needed. So, for each criterion, determine what kind of data and other information you would want to collect to support the conclusions shown in the status evaluations for each.

2.7.1 System Test Exit Review

Per the Test Plan, System Test was planned to end when following criteria were met:

1. All design, implementation, and feature completion, code completion, and unit test completion commitments made in the System Test Entry meeting were either met or slipped to no later than four (4), three (3), and three (3) weeks, respectively, prior to the proposed System Test Exit date.
    STATUS: RED. Audio and demo functionality have entered System Test in the last three weeks. The modems entered System Test in the last three weeks. On the margins of a violation, off-hook detection was changed significantly.

2. No panic, crash, halt, wedge, unexpected process termination, or other stoppage of processing has occurred on any server software or hardware for the previous three (3) weeks.
   STATUS: YELLOW. The servers have not crashed, but we did not complete all the tip-over and fail-over testing we planned, and so we are not satisfied that the servers are stable under peak load or other inclement conditions.

3. Production Devices have been used for all System Test execution for at least three (3) weeks.
   STATUS: GREEN. Except for the modem situation discussed above, the hardware has been stable.

4. No client systems have become inoperable due to a failed update for at least three (3) weeks.
   STATUS: YELLOW. No system has become permanently inoperable during update, but we have seen systems crash during update and these systems required a reboot to clear the error.

5. Server processes have been running without installation of bug fixes, manual intervention, or tuning of configuration files for two (2) weeks.
   STATUS: RED. Server configurations have been altered by Change Committee–approved changes multiple times over the last two weeks.

6. The Test Team has executed all the planned tests against the release-candidate hardware and software releases of the Device, Server, and Client.
   STATUS: RED. We had planned to test Procurement and Fulfillment, but disengaged from this effort because the systems were not ready. Also, we have just received the release-candidate build; complete testing would take two weeks. In addition, the servers are undergoing Change Committee–approved changes every few days and a new load balancer has been added to the server farm. These server changes have prevented volume, tip-over, and fail-over testing for the last week and a half. Finally, we have never had a chance to test the server installation and boot processes because we never received documentation on how to perform these tasks.

7. The Test Team has retested all priority one and two bug reports over the life of the project against the release-candidate hardware and software releases of the Device, Server, and Client.
   STATUS: RED. Testing of the release-candidate software and hardware has

been schedule-limited to one week, which does not allow for retesting of all bugs.

8. The Development Teams have resolved all "must-fix" bugs. "Must-fix" will be defined by the Project Management Team.

    STATUS: RED. Referring to the attached open/closed charts and the "Bugs Found Since 11/9" report, we continue to find new bugs in the product, though there is good news in that the find rate for priority one bugs has leveled off. Per the closure period charts, it takes on average about two weeks—three weeks for priority one bugs—to close a problem report. In addition, both open/close charts show a significant quality gap between cumulative open and cumulative closed, and it's hard to believe that taken all together, a quantity of bugs that significant doesn't indicate a pervasive fit-and-finish issue with the product. Finally, note that WebGuide and E-commerce problems are design issues—the selected browser is basically incompatible with much of the Internet—which makes these problems much more worrisome.

9. The Test Team has checked that all issues in the bug tracking system are either closed or deferred and, where appropriate, verified by regression and confirmation testing.

    STATUS: RED. A large quality gap exists and has existed for months. Because of the limited test time against the release-candidate build, the risk of regression is significant.

10. The open/close curve indicates that we have achieved product stability and reliability.

    STATUS: RED. The priority-one curve has stabilized, but not the overall bug-find curve. In addition, the run chart of errors requiring a reboot shows that we are still showing about one crash per eight hours of system operation, which is no more stable than a typical Windows 95/Windows 98 laptop. (One of the ad claims is improved stability over a PC.)

11. The Project Management Team agrees that the product, as defined during the final cycle of System Test, will satisfy the customer's reasonable expectations of quality.

    STATUS: YELLOW. We have not really run enough of the test suite at this time to give a good assessment of overall product quality.

12. The Project Management Team holds a System Test Exit Meeting and agrees that we have completed System Test.
STATUS: In progress.

2.8   Evaluating Exit Criteria and Reporting Exercise Debrief

I have added a section called "ADDITIONAL DATA AND INFORMATION" below each criterion. In that section, you'll find my own solution to this exercise, based both on what kind of additional data and information I actually had during this meeting and what I would have brought if I knew then what I know now.

1. All design, implementation, and feature completion, code completion, and unit test completion commitments made in the System Test Entry meeting were either met or slipped to no later than four (4), three (3), and three (3) weeks, respectively, prior to the proposed System Test Exit date.
STATUS: RED. Audio and demo functionality have entered System Test in the last three weeks. The modems entered System Test in the last three weeks. On the margins of a violation, off-hook detection was changed significantly.
ADDITIONAL DATA AND INFORMATION: The specific commitments made in the System Test Entry meeting. The delivery dates for the audio functionality, the demo functionality, the modem, and the off-hook detection functionality.

2. No panic, crash, halt, wedge, unexpected process termination, or other stoppage of processing has occurred on any server software or hardware for the previous three (3) weeks.
STATUS: YELLOW. The servers have not crashed, but we did not complete all the tip-over and fail-over testing we planned, and so we are not satisfied that the servers are stable under peak load or other inclement conditions.
ADDITIONAL DATA AND INFORMATION: Metrics indicate the percentage completion of tip-over and fail-over tests. Details on which specific quality risks remain uncovered due to the tip-over and fail-over tests not yet run.

3. Production Devices have been used for all System Test execution for at least three (3) weeks.
   STATUS: GREEN. Except for the modem situation discussed above, the hardware has been stable.
   ADDITIONAL DATA AND INFORMATION: None. Good news requires no explanation.

4. No client systems have become inoperable due to a failed update for at least three (3) weeks.
   STATUS: YELLOW. No system has become permanently inoperable during update, but we have seen systems crash during update and these systems required a reboot to clear the error.
   ADDITIONAL DATA AND INFORMATION: Details, from bug reports, on the system crashes described.

5. Server processes have been running without installation of bug fixes, manual intervention, or tuning of configuration files for two (2) weeks.
   STATUS: RED. Server configurations have been altered by Change Committee–approved changes multiple times over the last two weeks.
   ADDITIONAL DATA AND INFORMATION: List of tests that have run in prior to the last change, along with an assessment of the risk posed to each test by the change. (Note: Generating this list and the assessment could be a lot of work unless you have good traceability information.)

6. The Test Team has executed all the planned tests against the release-candidate hardware and software releases of the Device, Server, and Client.
   STATUS: RED. We had planned to test Procurement and Fulfillment, but disengaged from this effort because the systems were not ready. Also, we have just received the release-candidate build; complete testing would take two weeks. In addition, the servers are undergoing Change Committee–approved changes every few days and a new load balancer has been added to the server farm. These server changes have prevented volume, tip-over, and fail-over testing for the last week and a half. Finally, we have never had a chance to test the server installation and boot processes because we never received documentation on how to perform these tasks.
   ADDITIONAL DATA AND INFORMATION: List of Procurement and Fulfillment tests skipped, along with the risks associated with those tests. List of tests that will be skipped due to time compression of the last pass of

testing against the release-candidate, along with the risks associated with those tests. List of changes to the server since the last volume, tip-over, and fail-over tests along with an assessment of reliability risks posed by the change. (Again, this could be a big job.) List of server install and boot process tests skipped, along with the risks associated with those tests.

7. The Test Team has retested all priority one and two bug reports over the life of the project against the release-candidate hardware and software releases of the Device, Server, and Client.

   STATUS: RED. Testing of the release-candidate software and hardware has been schedule-limited to one week, which does not allow for retesting of all bugs.

   ADDITIONAL DATA AND INFORMATION: The list of all the priority one and two bug reports filed during the project, along with an assessment of the risk that those bugs might have re-entered the system in a change-related regression not otherwise caught by testing. (Again, potentially a huge job.)

8. The Development Teams have resolved all "must-fix" bugs. "Must-fix" will be defined by the Project Management Team.

   STATUS: RED. Referring to the attached open/closed charts and the "Bugs Found Since 11/ 9" report, we continue to find new bugs in the product, though there is good news in that the find rate for priority one bugs has leveled off. Per the closure period charts, it takes on average about two weeks—three weeks for priority one bugs—to close a problem report. In addition, both open/close charts show a significant quality gap between cumulative open and cumulative closed, and it's hard to believe that taken all together, a quantity of bugs that significant doesn't indicate a pervasive fit-and-finish issue with the product. Finally, note that Web and E-commerce problems are design issues—the selected browser is basically incompatible with much of the Internet—which makes these problems much more worrisome.

   ADDITIONAL DATA AND INFORMATION: Open/closed charts, list of bugs since November 9, closure period charts, and a list of selected important sites that won't work with the browser. (Note: The two charts mentioned are covered in the Advanced Test Manager course, if you're curious.)

9.   The Test Team has checked that all issues in the bug tracking system are either closed or deferred and, where appropriate, verified by regression and confirmation testing.

STATUS: RED. A large quality gap exists and has existed for months. Because of the limited test time against the release-candidate build, the risk of regression is significant.

ADDITIONAL DATA AND INFORMATION: List of bug reports that are neither closed nor deferred, sorted by priority. Risk of tests that will not be run against the release-candidate software, along with the associated risks for each test.

10. The open/close curve indicates that we have achieved product stability and reliability.

STATUS: RED. The priority-one curve has stabilized, but not the overall bug-find curve. In addition, the run chart of errors requiring a reboot shows that we are still showing about one crash per eight hours of system operation, which is no more stable than a typical Windows 95/Windows 98 laptop. (One of the ad claims is improved stability over a PC.)

ADDITIONAL DATA AND INFORMATION: Open/closed chart (run for priority one defects only and for all defects). Run chart of errors requiring a reboot; i.e., a trend chart that shows how many reboot-requiring crashes occurred each day.

11. The Project Management Team agrees that the product, as defined during the final cycle of System Test, will satisfy the customer's reasonable expectations of quality.

STATUS: YELLOW. We have not really run enough of the test suite at this time to give a good assessment of overall product quality.

ADDITIONAL DATA AND INFORMATION: List of all the tests not yet run against the release-candidate build, along with their associated risks.

12. The Project Management Team holds a System Test Exit Meeting and agrees that we have completed System Test.

STATUS: In progress.

ADDITIONAL DATA AND INFORMATION: None.

2.9 Test Closure Activities

Learning objectives
Recall of content only

The concepts in this section apply primarily for test managers. There are no learning objectives defined for test analysts in this section. In the course of studying for the exam, read this section in chapter 2 of the Advanced syllabus for general recall and familiarity only.

2.10 Sample Exam Questions

To end each chapter, you can try one or more sample exam questions to reinforce your knowledge and understanding of the material and to prepare for the ISTQB Advanced Level Test Analyst exam.

1. Identify all of the following which can be useful as a test oracle the first time a test case is run?

    A Incident report

    B Requirements specification

    C Test summary report

    D Legacy system

2. Assume you are a test analyst working on a banking project to upgrade an existing automated teller machine system to allow customers to obtain cash advances from supported credit cards. During test design, you identify a discrepancy between the list of supported credit cards in the requirements specification and the design specification. This is an example of what?

    A Test design as a static test technique

    B A defect in the requirements specification

    C A defect in the design specification

    D Starting test design too early in the project

3.   Which of the following is *not always* a pre condition for test execution?

   A A properly configured test environment

   B A thoroughly specified test procedure

   C A process for managing identified defects

   D A test oracle

4.   Assume you are a test analyst working on a banking project to upgrade an existing automated teller machine system to allow customers to obtain cash advances from supported credit cards. One of the exit criteria in the test plan requires documentation of successful cash advances of at least 500 euros for all supported credit cards. The correct list of supported credit cards is American Express, Visa, Japan Credit Bank, Eurocard, and MasterCard.

   After test execution, a complete list of cash advance test results shows the following:

   - American Express allowed advances of up to 1,000 euros.
   - Visa allowed advances of up to 500 euros.
   - Eurocard allowed advances of up to 1,000 euros.
   - MasterCard allowed advances of up to 500 euros.

   Which of the following statements is true?

   A The exit criterion fails due to excessive advances for American Express and Eurocard.

   B The exit criterion fails due to a discrepancy between American Express and Eurocard on the one hand and Visa and MasterCard on the other hand.

   C The exit criterion passes because all supported cards allow cash advances of at least the minimum required amount.

   D The exit criterion fails because we cannot document Japan Credit Bank results.

3   Test Management

"If a tree falls in the forest, and we've already sold it, does it have quality?"

The Pointy-Haired Boss of the Dilbert cartoon strip, mutilating the famous Zen koan to respond to Ratbert the Tester's protestations that the test results do not support product release.

The third chapter of the Advanced syllabus is concerned with test management. It discusses test management activities from the start to the end of the test process and introduces the consideration of risk for testing. There are eleven sections:

1. Introduction
2. Test Management Documentation
3. Test Plan Documentation Templates
4. Test Estimation
5. Scheduling and Test Planning
6. Test Progress Monitoring and Control
7. Business Value of Testing
8. Distributed, Outsourced, and Insourced Testing
9. Risk-Based Testing
10. Failure Mode and Effects Analysis
11. Test Management Issues

Let's look at each section and how it relates to test analysis.

> **ISTQB Glossary**
>
> **test management:** The planning, estimating, monitoring, and control of test activities, typically carried out by a test manager.

3.1   Introduction

Learning objectives
Recall of content only

This chapter, as the name indicates, is focused primarily on test management topics. Thus, it is mainly the purview of Advanced Test Manager exam candidates. Because this course is for test analysts, most of our coverage in this chapter is simple recall.

However, there is one key area that, as a test analyst, you need understand very well: risk-based testing. In this chapter, you'll learn how to perform risk analysis, to allocate test effort based on risk, and to sequence tests according to risk. These are the key tasks for a test analyst doing risk-based testing.

This chapter in the Advanced syllabus also covers test documentation templates for test managers. It focuses on the IEEE 829 standard. As a test analyst, you'll need to know that standard as well. If you plan take the Advanced Level Test Analyst exam, remember that all material from the Foundation syllabus, including that related to the use of the IEEE 829 templates and the test management material in chapter 5 of the Foundation syllabus, is examinable.

3.2   Test Management Documentation

Learning objectives
Recall of content only

The concepts in this section apply primarily for test managers. There are no learning objectives defined for test analysts in this section.

> **ISTQB Glossary**
>
> **test policy:** A high-level document describing the principles, approach, and major objectives of the organization regarding testing.
>
> **test strategy:** A high-level description of the test levels to be performed and the testing within those levels for an organization or program (one or more projects).
>
> **test level:** A group of test activities that are organized and managed together. A test level is linked to the responsibilities in a project. Examples of test levels are component test, integration test, system test, and acceptance test.
>
> **level test plan:** A test plan that typically addresses one test level.
>
> **master test plan:** A test plan that typically addresses multiple test levels.
>
> **test plan:** A document describing the scope, approach, resources, and schedule of intended test activities. It identifies, amongst others test items, the features to be tested, the testing tasks, who will do each task, degree of tester independence, the test environment, the test design techniques and entry and exit criteria to be used, and the rationale for their choice, and any risks requiring contingency planning. It is a record of the test planning process.

However, the Foundation syllabus covered test management, including the topic of test management documentation. Anything covered in the Foundation is examinable. In addition, all sections of the Advanced exam are examinable in terms of general recall.

So, if you are studying for the exam, you'll want to read this section in chapter 3 of the Advanced syllabus for general recall and familiarity and review the test management documentation material from the Foundation syllabus.

3.3 Test Plan Documentation Templates

Learning objectives
Recall of content only

The concepts in this section apply primarily for test managers. There are no learning objectives defined for test analysts in this section.

Earlier, in chapter 2, we reviewed portions of the IEEE 829 test documentation standard. Specifically, we looked at the test design specification template, the test case specification template, the test procedure specification template, the test summary report template, and the test log template. However, the Foundation covered the entire IEEE 829 standard, including the test plan template, test item transmittal report template, and the incident report template.

Anything covered in the Foundation syllabus is examinable. All sections of the Advanced syllabus are examinable in terms of general recall. So, if you are studying for the exam, you'll want to read this section in chapter 3 of the Advanced syllabus for general recall and familiarity and review the test management documentation material from the Foundation syllabus.

3.4 Test Estimation

Learning objectives
Recall of content only

The concepts in this section apply primarily for test managers. There are no learning objectives defined for test analysts in this section.

However, chapter 5 of the Foundation syllabus covered test estimation as part of the material on test management. Anything covered in the Foundation syllabus is examinable. All sections of the Advanced syllabus are examinable in terms of general recall. So, if you are studying for the exam, you'll want to read this section in chapter 3 of the Advanced syllabus for general recall and familiarity and review the test estimation material from the Foundation syllabus.

3.5 Scheduling and Test Planning

Learning objectives
Recall of content only

The concepts in this section apply primarily for test managers. There are no learning objectives defined for test analysts in this section. In the course of

> **ISTQB Glossary**
>
> **test estimation:** The calculated approximation of a result (e.g., effort spent, completion date, costs involved, number of test cases, etc.) that is usable even if input data may be incomplete, uncertain, or noisy.
>
> **test schedule:** A list of activities, tasks, or events of the test process identifying their intended start and finish dates and/or times and interdependencies.
>
> **test point analysis (TPA):** A formula-based test estimation method based on function point analysis.
>
> **Wideband Delphi:** An expert-based test estimation technique that aims at making an accurate estimation using the collective wisdom of the team members.

studying for the exam, read this section in chapter 3 of the Advanced syllabus for general recall and familiarity only.

3.6 Test Progress Monitoring and Control

Learning objectives
Recall of content only

The concepts in this section apply primarily for test managers. There are no learning objectives defined for test analysts in this section.

However, chapter 5 of the Foundation syllabus covered test progress monitoring and control as part of the material on test management. Anything covered in the Foundation syllabus is examinable. All sections of the Advanced syllabus are examinable in terms of general recall. So, if you are studying for the exam, you'll want to read this section in chapter 3 of the Advanced syllabus for general recall and familiarity and review the test progress monitoring and control material from the Foundation syllabus.

> **ISTQB Glossary**
>
> **test monitoring:** A test management task that deals with the activities related to periodically checking the status of a test project. Reports are prepared that compare the actuals to that which was planned.

3.7   Business Value of Testing

Learning objectives
Recall of content only

The concepts in this section apply primarily for test managers. There are no learning objectives defined for test analysts in this section. In the course of studying for the exam, read this section in chapter 3 of the Advanced syllabus for general recall and familiarity only.

3.8   Distributed, Outsourced, and Insourced Testing

Learning objectives
Recall of content only

The concepts in this section apply primarily for test managers. There are no learning objectives defined for test analysts in this section. In the course of studying for the exam, read this section in chapter 3 of the Advanced syllabus for general recall and familiarity only.

3.9 Risk-Based Testing

Learning objectives

(K3) Prioritize test case selection, test coverage, and test data based on risk and document this appropriately in a test schedule and test procedure.

(K2) Outline the activities of a risk-based approach for planning and executing domain testing.

Risk is the possibility of a negative or undesirable outcome or event. A specific risk is any problem that may occur that would decrease customer, user, participant, or stakeholder perceptions of product quality or project success.

In testing, we're concerned with two main types of risks. This first type of risk is product or quality risks. When the primary effect of a potential problem is on product quality, such potential problems are called product risks. A synonym for *product risks*, which I use most frequently myself, is *quality risks*. An example of a quality risk is a possible reliability defect that could cause a system to crash during normal operation.

The second type of risk is project or planning risks. When the primary effect of a potential problem is on project success, such potential problems are called a project risk. Some people also refer to project risks as planning risks. An example of a project risk is a possible staffing shortage that could delay completion of a project.

Not all risks are equal in importance. There are a number of ways to classify the level of risk. The simplest is to look at two factors:

- The likelihood of the problem occurring
- The impact of the problem should it occur

Likelihood of a problem arises primarily from technical considerations, such as the programming languages used, the bandwidth of connections, and so forth. The impact of a problem arises from business considerations, such as the financial loss the business will suffer from a problem, the number of users or customers affected by a problem, and so forth.

ISTQB Glossary

risk: A factor that could result in future negative consequences; usually expressed as impact and likelihood.

risk type: A specific category of risk related to the type of testing that can mitigate (control) that category. For example, the risk of user interactions being misunderstood can be mitigated by usability testing.

product risk: A risk directly related to the test object.

project risk: A risk related to management and control of the (test) project, e.g., lack of staffing, strict deadlines, changing requirements, etc.

risk-based testing: An approach to testing to reduce the level of product risks and inform stakeholders on their status, starting in the initial stages of a project. It involves the identification of product risks and their use in guiding the test process.

In risk-based testing, we use the risk items identified during risk analysis together with the level of risk associated with each risk item to guide our testing. In fact, under a true analytical risk-based testing strategy, risk is the primary basis of testing.

Risk can guide testing in various ways, but there are three very common ones:

■ First, during all test activities, test managers and test analysts allocate effort for each quality risk item proportionally to the level of risk. Test analysts select test techniques in a way that matches the rigor and extensiveness of the technique with the level of risk. Test managers and test analysts carry out test activities in reverse risk order, addressing the most important quality risks first and only at the very end spending any time at all on less important ones. Finally, test managers and test analysts work with the project team to ensure that the repair of defects is appropriate to the level of risk.

■ Second, during test planning and test control, test managers provide both mitigation and contingency responses for all significant, identified project risks. The higher the level of risk, the more thoroughly that project risk is managed.

> **ISTQB Glossary**
>
> **test control:** A test management task that deals with developing and applying a set of corrective actions to get a test project on track when monitoring shows a deviation from what was planned.
>
> **risk level:** The importance of a risk as defined by its impact and likelihood. The level of risk can be used to determine the intensity of testing to be performed. A risk level can be expressed either qualitatively (e.g., high, medium, low) or quantitatively.

■ Third, test managers and test analysts report test results and project status in terms of residual risks. For example, which tests have not yet been run or have been skipped? Which tests have been run? Which have passed? Which have failed? Which defects have not yet been fixed or retested? How do the tests and defects relate back to the risks?

When following a true analytical risk-based testing strategy, it's important that risk management not happen only once in a project. The three responses to risk I just covered—along with any others that might be needed—should occur throughout the lifecycle. Specifically, we should try to reduce quality risk by running tests and finding defects and reduce project risks through mitigation and, if necessary, contingency actions. Periodically in the project we should reevaluate risk and risk levels based on new information. This might result in our reprioritizing tests and defects, reallocating test effort, and taking other test control activities.

One metaphor sometimes used to help people understand risk-based testing is that testing is a form of insurance. In your daily life, you buy insurance when you are worried about some potential risk. You don't buy insurance for risks that you are not worried about. So, we should test the areas and test for bugs that are worrisome and ignore the ones that aren't.

One potentially misleading aspect of this metaphor is that insurance professionals and actuaries can use statistically valid data for quantitative risk analysis. Typically, risk-based testing relies on qualitative analyses because we don't have the same kind of data that insurance companies have.

During risk-based testing, you have to remain aware of many possible sources of risks. There are safety risks for some systems. There are business and economic risks for most systems. There are privacy and data security risks for many systems. There are technical, organizational, and political risks, too.

3.9.1   Risk Management

Risk management includes three primary activities:

- Risk identification, figuring out what the different project and quality risks are for the project
- Risk analysis, assessing the level of risk—typically based on likelihood and impact—for each identified risk item
- Risk mitigation, which is really more properly called "risk control" because it consists of mitigation, contingency, transference, and acceptance actions for various risks

In some sense, these activities are sequential, at least in terms of when they start. They are staged such that risk identification starts first. Risk analysis comes next. Risk control starts once risk analysis has determined the level of risk. However, because risk management should be continuous in a project, the reality is that risk identification, risk analysis, and risk control are all recurring activities.

Everyone has their own perspective on how to manage risks on a project, including what the risks are, the level of risk, and the appropriate controls to put in place for risks. So, risk management should include all project stakeholders.

In many cases, though, not all stakeholders can participate or would be willing to do so. In such cases, some stakeholders may act as surrogates for other stakeholders. For example, in mass-market software development, the marketing team might ask a small sample of potential customers to help identify potential defects that would affect their use of the software most heavily. In this case, the sample of potential customers serves as a surrogate for the entire eventual customer base. As another example, business analysts on IT projects can sometimes represent the users rather than involving users in potentially distressing risk analysis sessions where we have conversations about what could go wrong and how bad it would be.

> **ISTQB Glossary**
>
> **risk management:** Systematic application of procedures and practices to the tasks of identifying, analyzing, prioritizing, and controlling risk.
>
> **risk identification:** The process of identifying risks using techniques such as brainstorming, checklists, and failure history.
>
> **risk analysis:** The process of assessing identified risks to estimate their impact and probability of occurrence (likelihood).
>
> **risk mitigation** or risk control: The process through which decisions are reached and protective measures are implemented for reducing risks to, or maintaining risks within, specified levels.

Test analysts bring particular expertise to risk management due to their defect-focused outlook. So they should participate whenever possible. In fact, in many cases, the test manager will lead the quality risk analysis effort, with test analysts providing key support in the process.

With that overview of risk management in place, let's look at the three risk management activities more closely.

3.9.2   Risk Identification

For proper risk-based testing, we need to identify both product and project risks. We can identify both kinds of risks using techniques like these:

- Expert interviews
- Independent assessments
- Use of risk templates
- Project retrospectives
- Risk workshops and brainstorming
- Checklists
- Calling on past experience

Conceivably, you can use a single integrated process to identify both project and product risks. I usually separate them into two separate processes because they have two separate deliverables. I include the project risk identification process in the test planning process. In parallel, the quality risk identification process occurs early in the project.

That said, project risks—and not just for testing but also for the project as a whole—are often identified as by-products of quality risk analysis. In addition, if you use a requirements specification, design specification, use cases, or other documentation as inputs into your quality risk analysis process, you should expect to find defects in those documents as another set of by-products. These are valuable by-products, which you should plan to capture and escalate to the proper person.

Previously, I encouraged you to include representatives of all possible stakeholder groups in the risk management process. For the risk identification activities, the broadest range of stakeholders will yield the most complete, accurate, and precise risk identification. The more stakeholder group representatives you omit from the process, the more you will miss risk items and even whole risk categories.

How far should you take this process? Well, it depends on the technique. In informal techniques that I frequently use, risk identification stops at the risk items. You have to be specific enough about the risk items to allow for analysis and assessment of each risk item to yield an unambiguous likelihood rating and an unambiguous impact rating.

Techniques that are more formal often look "downstream" to identify potential effects of the risk item if it becomes an actual negative outcome. These effects include effects on the system—or the system of systems if applicable—as well as potential users, customers, stakeholders, and even society in general. Failure Mode and Effect Analysis is an example of such a formal risk management technique, and it is commonly used on safety-critical and embedded systems.

Other formal techniques look "upstream" to identify the source of the risk. Hazard Analysis is an example of such a formal risk management technique. I've never used it myself, but I have talked to clients who have used it for safety-critical medical systems.[1]

3.9.3 Risk Analysis or Risk Assessment

The next step in the risk management process is referred to in the Advanced syllabus as risk analysis. I prefer to call it risk assessment, because analysis would

> **ISTQB Glossary**
>
> **Failure Mode and Effect Analysis (FMEA):** A systematic approach to risk identification and analysis in which you identify possible modes of failure and attempting to prevent their occurrence.
>
> Failure Mode, Effect and Criticality Analysis (FMECA): An extension of FMEA, as in addition to the basic FMEA, it includes a criticality analysis, which is used to chart the probability of failure modes against the severity of their consequences. The result highlights failure modes with relatively high probability and severity of consequences, allowing remedial effort to be directed where it will produce the greatest value.

seem to include both identification and assessment of risk to me. Regardless of what we call it, risk analysis or risk assessment involves the study of the identified risks. We typically want to categorize each risk item appropriately and assign each risk item an appropriate level of risk.

We can use ISO 9126 or other quality categories to organize the risk items. In my opinion, usually it doesn't matter so much what category a risk item goes into, as long as we don't forget it. However, in complex projects and for large organizations, the category of risk can determine who has to deal with the risk. A practical implication of categorization like this will make the categorization important.

The other part of risk assessment is determining the level of risk. This often involves likelihood and impact as the two key factors. Likelihood arises from technical considerations, typically, while impact arises from business considerations.

So what technical factors should we consider when assessing likelihood? Here's a list to get you started:

---

1. For more information on risk identification and analysis techniques, you can see either of my two books, *Managing the Testing Process, 2e* (for more both formal and informal techniques) or *Pragmatic Software Testing* (for informal techniques). You can also find alternative views on risk-based testing techniques in Rick Craig's *Systematic Software Testing* and Paul Gerrard's *Risk-based E-business Testing*. If you want to use Failure Mode and Effect Analysis, then I recommend reading D.H. Stamatis's *Failure Mode and Effect Analysis* for a thorough discussion of the technique, followed by *Managing the Testing Process, 2e* for a discussion of how the technique applies to software testing.

- Complexity of technology and teams
- Personnel and training issues
- Intrateam and interteam conflict
- Supplier and vendor contractual problems
- Geographical distribution of the development organization, as with outsourcing
- Legacy or established designs and technologies versus new technologies and designs
- The quality—or lack of quality—in the tools and technology used
- Bad managerial or technical leadership
- Time, resource, and management pressure, especially when financial penalties apply
- Lack of earlier testing and quality assurance tasks in the lifecycle
- High rates of requirements, design, and code changes in the project
- High defect rates
- Complex interfacing and integration issues

What business factors should we consider when assessing impact? Here's a list to get you started:

- The frequency of use of the affected feature
- Potential damage to image
- Loss of customers and business
- Potential financial, ecological, or social losses or liability
- Civil or criminal legal sanctions
- Loss of licenses, permits, and the like
- The lack of reasonable workarounds
- The visibility of failure and the associated negative publicity

When determining the level of risk, we can try to work quantitatively or qualitatively. In quantitative risk analysis, we have numerical ratings for both likelihood and impact. Likelihood is a percentage, and impact is often a monetary quantity. If we multiple the two values together, we can calculate the cost of exposure, which is called—in the insurance business—the expected payout or expected loss.

While perhaps some day in the future of software engineering we can do this routinely, typically we find that we have to determine the level of risk. Why?

Because we don't have statistically valid data on which to perform quantitative quality risk analysis. So we can speak of likelihood being very high, high, medium, low, or very low, but we can't say—at least, not in any meaningful way—whether the likelihood is 90%, 75%, 50%, 25%, or 10%.

This is not to say—by any means—that a qualitative approach should be seen as inferior or useless. In fact, given the data most of us have to work with, use of a quantitative approach is almost certainly inappropriate on most projects. The illusory precision of such techniques misleads the stakeholders about the extent to which you actually understand and can manage risk. What I've found is that if I accept the limits of my data and apply appropriate informal quality risk management approaches, the results are not only perfectly useful, but also indeed essential to a well-managed test process.[2]

Unless your risk analysis is based on extensive and statistically valid risk data, it will reflect perceived likelihood and impact. In other words, personal perceptions and opinions held by the stakeholders will determine the level of risk. Again, there's absolutely nothing wrong with this, and I don't bring this up to condemn the technique at all. The key point is that project managers, programmers, users, business analysts, architects, and testers typically have different perceptions and thus possibly different opinions on the level of risk for each risk item. By including all these perceptions, we distill the collective wisdom of the team.

However, we do have a strong possibility of disagreements between stakeholders. The risk analysis process should include some way of reaching consensus. In the worst case, if we cannot obtain consensus, we should be able to escalate the disagreement to some level of management to resolve. Otherwise, risk levels will be ambiguous and conflicted and thus not useful as a guide for risk mitigation activities—including testing.

3.9.4 Risk Mitigation or Risk Control

Having identified and assessed risks, we now must control them. As I mentioned before, the Advanced syllabus refers to this as risk mitigation, but that's not right. We actually have four main options for risk control:

---

2. I cover informal approaches and primarily qualitative assessments of risk in *Pragmatic Software Testing*, as does Rick Craig in *Systematic Software Testing* and Erik van Veenendaal, ed., in *The Testing Practitioner*.

- Mitigation, where we take preventive measures to reduce the likelihood of the risk occurring and/or the impact of a risk should it occur
- Contingency, where we have a plan or perhaps multiple plans to reduce the impact if a risk should it occur
- Transference, where we get another party to accept the consequences of a risk should it occur
- Finally, ignoring or accepting the risk and its consequences should it occur

For any given risk item, selecting one or more of these options creates its own set of benefits and opportunities as well as costs and, potentially, additional risks associated.

Analytical risk-based testing is focused on creating risk mitigation opportunities for the test team, including for test analysts, especially for quality risks. Risk-based testing mitigates quality risks via testing throughout the entire lifecycle.

Let me mention that, in some cases, there are standards that can apply. We've already looked at one such standard, the United States Federal Aviation Administration's DO-178B. We'll look at another one of those standards shortly.

It's important too that project risks be controlled. For test analysts, we're particularly concerned with test-affecting project risks like the following:

- Test environment and tools readiness
- Test staff availability and qualification
- Low quality of inputs to testing
- Too high change traffic for inputs to testing
- Lack of standards, rules, and techniques for the testing effort

While it's usually the test manager's job to make sure these risks are controlled, the lack of adequate controls in these areas will affect the test analyst.

One idea discussed in the Foundation syllabus, a basic principle of testing, is the principle of early testing and QA. This principle stresses the preventive potential of testing. Preventive testing is part of analytical risk-based testing. We should try to mitigate risk before test execution starts. This can entail early preparation of testware, pretesting test environments, pretesting early versions of the product well before a test level starts, insisting on tougher entry criteria to testing, ensuring requirements for and designing for testability, participating in reviews (including retrospectives for earlier project activities), participating in problem and change management, and monitoring of the project progress and quality.

In preventive testing, we take quality risk control actions throughout the lifecycle. Test analysts should look for opportunities to control risk using various techniques:

- Choosing an appropriate test design technique
- Reviews and inspection
- Reviews of test design
- An appropriate level of independence for the various levels of testing
- The use of the most experienced person on test tasks
- The strategies chosen for confirmation testing (retesting) and regression testing

Preventive test strategies acknowledge that quality risks can and should be mitigated by a broad range of activities, many of them not what we traditionally think of as "testing." For example, if the requirements are not well written, perhaps we should institute reviews to improve their quality rather than relying on tests that we will run after the badly written requirements become a bad design and ultimately bad, buggy code.

Of course, testing is not effective against all kinds of quality risks. In some cases, you can estimate the risk reduction effectiveness of testing in general and for specific test techniques for given risk items. There's not much point in using testing to reduce risk where there is a low level of test effectiveness. For example, code maintainability issues related to poor commenting or use of unstructured programming techniques will not tend to show up—at least, not initially—during testing.

Once we get to test execution, we use test execution to mitigate quality risks. Where testing finds defects, testers reduce risk by providing the awareness of defects and opportunities to deal with them before release. Where testing does not find defects, testing reduces risk by ensuring that under certain conditions the system operates correctly.

I mentioned earlier that we use level of risk to prioritize tests in a risk-based strategy. This can work in a variety of ways, with two extremes, referred to as depth-first and breadth-first. In a *depth-first* approach, all of the highest-risk tests are run before any lower risk tests, and tests are run in strict risk order. In a *breadth-first* approach, we select a sample of tests across all the identified risks using the level of risk to weight the selection while at the same time ensuring coverage of every risk at least once.

As we run tests, we should measure and report our results in terms of residual risk. The higher the test coverage in an area, the lower the residual risk. The fewer bugs we've found in an area, the lower the residual risk.[3] Of course, in doing risk-based testing, if we only test based on our risk analysis, this can leave blind spots, so we need to use testing outside the predefined test procedures to see if we have missed anything.

If, during test execution, we need to reduce the time or effort spent on testing, we can use risk as a guide. If the residual risk is acceptable, we can curtail our tests. Notice that, in general, those tests not yet run are less important than those tests already run. If we do curtail further testing, that property of risk-based test execution serves to transfer the remaining risk onto the users, customers, help desk and technical support personnel, or operational staff.

Suppose we do have time to continue test execution? In this case, we can adjust our risk analysis—and thus our testing—for further test cycles based on what we've learned from our current testing. First, we revise our risk analysis. Then, we reprioritize existing tests and possibly add new tests. What should we look for to decide whether to adjust our risk analysis? We can start with the following main factors:

■ Totally new or very much changed product risks
■ Unstable or defect-prone areas discovered during the testing
■ Risks, especially regression risk, associated with fixed defects
■ Discovery of unexpected bug clusters
■ Discovery of business-critical areas that were missed

So, if you have time for new additional test cycles, consider revising your quality risk analysis first. You should also update the quality risk analysis at each project milestone.

---

3. You can find examples of how to do report test results based on risk in my books *Critical Testing Processes* and in the companion volume to this book, which addresses test management.

	System Function or Feature	Potential Failure Mode(s)-Quality Risk(s)	Potential Effect(s) of Failure	Critical?	Severity	Potential Cause(s) of Failure	Priority	Detection Method(s)	Detection	Risk Pri No	Recommended Action	Who/When?

Failure Mode and Effects Analysis (Quality Risks Analysis) Form--RPN Sorted

Inital FMEA--RPN Sorted

#	System Function or Feature	Potential Failure Mode(s)-Quality Risk(s)	Potential Effect(s) of Failure	Critical?	Severity	Potential Cause(s) of Failure	Priority	Detection Method(s)	Detection	Risk Pri No	Recommended Action	Who/When?
10	Shreds Swap Files	Fails to Shred	Security Breach	Y	1	Program Error	1	Test; Debug Trace; Code Review	1	1	Test; Debug Tracing; Code Review	
11	Shreds Swap Files	Shreds Excessively	Data Loss	Y	1	Program Error	1	Test; Debug Trace; Code Review	1	1	Test; Debug Tracing; Code Review	
12	Compression Compatibility	Damages Data	Data Loss	Y	1	Program Error	1	Test	2	2	Test	
13	Compression Compatibility	Hangs System	Data Loss	Y	1	Program Error	1	Test	2	2	Test	
14	Compression Compatibility	Shreds Improperly	Data Loss	Y	1	Program Error	1	Test	2	2	Test	
15	Internet Files Recognition	Recognizes Incorrectly	Data Loss	Y	1	Program Error	1	Test; Debug Trace; Code Review	2	2	Test; Rules Validation	
16	Network Compatibility	Shreds Network	Data Loss	Y	1	Program Error	1	Test	2	2	Test Selected/Improve Network Coverage	
17	Removes File Name	Damages FS	Data Loss	Y	1	Program Error	1	Test; Debug Trace; Code Review	2	2	Test; Debug Tracing; Code Review	
18	Removes File Name	Fails to Remove	Security Breach	Y	1	Program Error	1	Test; Debug Trace; Code Review	2	2	Test; Debug Tracing; Code Review	

Figure 3–1   *An example of a quality risk analysis document using FMEA*

3.9.5   An Example of Risk Identification and Assessment Results

In figure 3-1, you see an example of a quality risk analysis document. It is a case study from an actual project. This document—and the approach we used—followed the Failure Mode and Effect Analysis approach.

As you can see, we start—at the left side of the table—with a specific function and then identify failure modes and their possible effects. Criticality is determined based on the effects, as is the severity and priority. Possible causes are listed to enable bug prevention work during requirements, design, and implementation.

Next, we look at detection methods—those methods we expect to be applied anyway for this project. The more likely the failure mode is to escape detection, the worse the detection number. We calculate a risk priority number based on the severity, priority, and detection numbers. Smaller numbers are worse. Severity, priority, and detection each range from 1 to 5, so the risk priority number ranges from 1 to 125.

This particular table shows the highest-level risk items only because I sorted it by risk priority number. For these risk items, we would expect a lot of additional detection and other recommended risk control actions. You can see that we have assigned some additional actions at this point but have not yet assigned the owners.

During testing actions associated with a risk item, we would expect that the number of test cases, the amount of test data, and the degree of test coverage would all increase as the risk increases. Notice that we can allow any test procedures that cover a risk item to inherit the level of risk from the risk item. That documents the priority of the test procedure, based on the level of risk.

3.9.6   Risk-Based Testing throughout the Lifecycle

I've mentioned that, properly done, risk-based testing manages risk throughout the lifecycle. Let's look at how that happens, based on my usual approach to a test project.

During test planning, risk management comes first. I perform a quality risk analysis early in the project, ideally once the first draft of a requirements specification is available. From that quality risk analysis, I build an estimate for negotiation with and, I hope, approval by project stakeholders and management.

Once the project stakeholders and management agree on the estimate, I create a plan for the testing. The plan assigns testing effort and sequences tests based on the level of quality risk. It also plans for project risks that could affect testing.

During test control, I will periodically adjust the risk analysis throughout the project. That can lead to adding, increasing, or decreasing test coverage; removing, delaying, or accelerating the priority of tests; and other such activities.

During test analysis and design, I work with the test team to allocate test development and execution effort based on risk. Because I want to report test results in terms of risk, I ensure that we maintain traceability to the quality risks.

During implementation and execution, I sequence the procedures based on the level of risk. I ensure that the test team uses exploratory testing and other reactive techniques to detect unanticipated high-risk areas.

During the evaluation of exit criteria and reporting, I work with my test team to measure test coverage against risk. When reporting test results (and thus release readiness), we talk not only in terms of test cases run and bugs found, but also in terms of residual risk.

3.9.7   Risk-Aware Testing Standards

As we saw in chapter 2, the United States Federal Aviation Administration's DO-178B standard bases the extent of testing—measured in terms of white-box code coverage—on the potential impact of a failure. That makes DO-178B a risk-aware testing standard.

Another interesting example of how risk management, including quality risk management, plays into the engineering of complex and/or safety-critical systems is found in the ISO/IEC standard 61508, which is mentioned in the Advanced syllabus. This standard applies to embedded software that controls systems with safety-related implications, as you can tell from its title, "Functional safety of electrical/electronic/programmable electronic safety-related systems."

The standard is very much focused on risks. Risk analysis is required. It considers two primary factors as determing the level of risk, likelihood, and impact. During a project, we are to reduce the residual level of risk to a tolerable level, specifically through the application of electrical, electronic, or software improvements to the system.

The standard has an inherent philosophy about risk. It acknowledges that we can't attain a level of zero risk—whether for an entire system or even for a single risk item. It says that we have to build quality, especially safety, in from the beginning, not try to add it at the end. Thus we must take defect-preventing actions like requirements, design, and code reviews.

The standard also insists that we know what constitutes tolerable and intolerable risks and that we take steps to reduce intolerable risks. When those steps are testing steps, we must document them, including a software safety validation plan, software test specification, software test results, software safety validation, verification report, and software functional safety report.

The standard addresses the author-bias problem. As discussed in the Foundation Syllabus, this is the problem with self-testing, the fact that you bring the same blind spots and bad assumptions to testing your own work that you brought to creating that work. So the standard calls for tester independence, indeed insisting on it for those performing any safety-related tests. And because testing is most effective when the system is written to be testable, that's also a requirement.

The standard has a concept of a safety integrity level (or SIL), which is based on the likelihood of failure for a particular component or subsystem. The safety integrity level influences a number of risk-related decisions, including the choice of testing and QA techniques.

Some of the techniques are ones we'll cover in this book, such as the various functional and black-box testing design techniques. Many of the techniques are ones that I'll cover in the companion volume for technical test analysts, including probabilistic testing, dynamic analysis, data recording and analysis, performance testing, interface testing, static analysis, and complexity metrics. Additionally, because thorough coverage, including during regression testing, is important in reducing the likelihood of missed bugs, the standard mandates the use of applicable automated test tools.

Again, depending on the safety integrity level, the standard might require various levels of testing. These levels include module testing, integration testing, hardware-software integration testing, safety requirements testing, and system testing.

If a level is required, the standard states that it should be documented and independently verified. In other words, the standard can require auditing or outside reviews of testing activities. In addition, continuing on with that theme of "guarding the guards," the standard also requires reviews for test cases, test procedures, and test results along with verification of data integrity under test conditions.

The standard requires the use of structural test design techniques. Structural coverage requirements are implied, again based on the safety integrity level. (This is similar to DO-178B.) Because the desire is to have high confidence in the safety-critical aspects of the system, the standard requires complete requirements coverage not once, but multiple times, at multiple levels of testing. Again, the level of test coverage required depends on the safety integrity level.

Now, this might seem a bit excessive, especially if you come from a very informal world. However, the next time you step between two pieces of metal that can move—e.g., elevator doors—ask yourself how much risk you want to remain in the software that controls that movement.

3.10 Risk-Based Testing Exercise 1

Read the HELLOCARMS System Requirements Document in Appendix B, a hypothetical project derived from a real project that RBCS helped to test.

If you are working in a classroom, break into groups of three to five. If you are working alone, you'll need to do this yourself. Perform a quality risks analysis for this project. Because this book focuses mainly on domain testing, identify and assess risks for *functional* quality characteristics only. Use the templates shown in figure 3-2 and table 3-1 on the following pages.

To keep the time spent reasonable, I suggest spending 30 to 45 minutes identifying quality risks, then 15 to 30 minutes assessing the level of each risk. If you are working in a classroom, once each group has finished its analysis, discuss the results.

3.11 Risk-Based Testing Exercise Debrief 1

You can see my solution to the exercise starting on the next page, in table 3-2. Immediately after that table are two lists of by-products. One is the list of project risks discovered during the analysis. The other is the list of requirements document defects discovered during the analysis.

As a first pass for this quality risk analysis, I went through each functional requirement and identified one or more risk items for it. I assumed that the priority of the requirement was a good surrogate for the impact of the risk, so I used that. Even using all of these shortcuts, it took me about an hour to get through this.

3.11.1 Project Risk By-Products

In the course of preparing the quality risk analysis document, I observed the following project risk inherent in the requirements.

> *Given the lack of clarity around security requirements (see 010-040-010), there's a strong chance that the necessary infrastructure won't be in place as needed to support this project's schedule.*

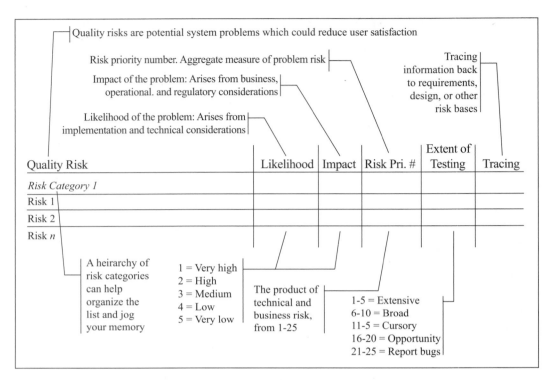

Figure 3–2   *Annotated template for informal quality risk analysis*

3.11.2 Requirements Defect By-Products

In the course of preparing the quality risk analysis document, I observed the following defects in the requirements:

1. For 010-010-150, what are the supported States, Provinces, and Countries?
2. For 010-010-150, the phrase "all support States" should be "all supported States."
3. For 010-020-020, the phrase "dept-to-income" should be "debt-to-income."
4. For some requirements, the ID number is duplicated; e.g., 010-030-140.
5. Not all requirements are prioritized; e.g., 010-030-150.
6. For 010-040-010, what are the agreed-upon security approaches discussed here?
7. There doesn't appear to be any direct mention of regulatory compliance requirements, though certainly many would apply for a bank.

Table 3–1 *Functional quality risk analysis template showing quality risk categories to address*

No.	Quality Risk	Likeli-hood	Impact	Risk Pri. #	Extent of Testing	Tracing
1.1.000	Functionality: Suitability					
1.1.001	[Functional risks related to suitability go in this section.]					
1.2.000	Functionality: Accuracy					
1.2.001	[Functional risks related to accuracy go in this section.]					
1.3.000	Functionality: Interoperability					
1.3.001	[Functional risks related to interoperability go in this section.]					
1.4.000	Functionality: Security					
1.4.001	[Functional risks related to security go in this section.]					
1.5.000	Functionality: Compliance					
1.5.001	[Functional risks related to functional compliance go in this section.]					

Table 3–2 *Functional quality risk analysis for HELLOCARMS*

No.	Quality Risk	Likeli-hood	Impact	Risk Pri. #	Extent of Testing	Tracing
1.1.000	*Functionality: Suitability*					
1.1.001	Reject all applications for home equity loans.	5	1	5	Extensive	010-010-010
1.1.002	Reject all applications for home equity lines of credit.	5	1	5	Extensive	010-010-010
1.1.003	Reject all applications for reverse mortgages.	5	1	5	Extensive	010-010-010
1.1.004	Fail to properly process some home equity applications.	3	1	3	Extensive	010-010-190
1.1.005	Fail to properly process some home equity line of credit applications.	3	2	6	Broad	010-010-200
1.1.006	Fail to properly process some home equity reverse mortgage applications.	3	3	9	Broad	010-010-210
1.1.007	Fail to properly process some combined products (e.g., home equity and credit cards).	3	4	12	Cursory	010-010-220
1.1.008	Fail to properly process some original mortgage applications.	3	5	15	Cursory	010-010-230
1.1.009	Fail to properly process some preapproved applications.	3	4	12	Cursory	010-010-240
1.1.010	Scripts not available for all fields and screens.	4	2	8	Broad	010-010-020
1.1.011	Customer source data not collected.	3	2	6	Broad	010-010-030
1.1.012	Customer source data categories not well defined.	2	2	4	Extensive	010-010-030
1.1.013	Accepts invalid data at input fields.	1	1	1	Extensive	010-010-040
1.1.014	Existing trade lines not displayed and/or processed properly.	3	1	3	Extensive	010-010-050 010-010-100
1.1.015	Trade line payoff details not passed to LoDoPS.	2	1	2	Extensive	010-010-050 010-010-100
1.1.016	Loan to be paid off included in debt-to-income calculations.	4	3	12	Cursory	010-010-110

Table continues

Table 3–2 *Functional quality risk analysis for HELLOCARMS (continued)*

1.1.017	Cannot resume incomplete/interrupted applications.	3	2	6	Broad	010-010-060
1.1.018	Applicant not asked about existing relationship.	5	2	10	Broad	010-010-070
1.1.019	Applicant existing relationship not passed to GLADS.	3	2	6	Board	010-010-070
1.1.020	Loan status information lost after initiation.	3	2	6	Broad	010-010-080
1.1.021	Cannot abort or abandon an application cleanly (i.e., must close browser).	4	3	12	Cursory	010-010-090
1.1.022	Cannot retrieve existing application by customer ID.	4	4	16	Opportunity	010-010-120
1.1.023	Loans over $500,000 not transferred for approval.	4	1	4	Extensive	010-010-130
1.1.024	Loans over $500,000 automatically denied.	3	1	3	Extensive	010-010-130
1.1.025	Property valuation over $1,000,000 not transferred for approval.	4	2	8	Broad	010-010-140
1.1.026	Property valuation over $1,000,000 automatically denied.	3	2	6	Extensive	010-010-140
1.1.027	Inbound telemarketing operations fail in supported region.	1	2	2	Extensive	010-010-150
1.1.028	Outbound telemarketing operations fail in supported region.	1	2	2	Extensive	010-010-150
1.1.029	Branding for brokers and other business partners not supported.	4	2	8	Broad	010-010-160
1.1.030	Untrained users (e.g., end customers) cannot enter applications via Internet.	4	3	12	Cursory	010-010-170
1.1.031	Product operations for retail bank branches not supported.	4	4	16	Opportunity	010-010-180
1.1.032	Flexible pricing schemes not supported.	4	5	20	Opportunity	010-010-250
1.2.000	*Functionality: Accuracy*					
1.2.001	Customer presented with products for which they are ineligible.	3	1	3	Extensive	010-020-010
1.2.002	Customer not presented with products for which they are eligible.	4	1	4	Extensive	010-020-010
1.2.003	Application decisioning inconsistent with Globobank credit policies.	3	1	3	Extensive	010-020-010

Table continues

Table 3–2 Functional quality risk analysis for HELLOCARMS (continued)

No.	Quality Risk	Likeli-hood	Impact	Risk Pri. #	Extent of Testing	Tracing
1.2.004	Risk-based pricing miscalculated based on credit score, loan-to-value, and debt-to-income.	4	1	4	Extensive	010-020-020
1.2.005	New loan payment not included in credit scoring.	3	2	6	Broad	010-020-030
1.2.006	Pricing add-ons not calculated correctly.	3	3	9	Broad	010-020-040
1.2.007	Government retirement income not handled properly.	3	1	3	Extensive	010-020-050
1.2.008	Duration of additional income not captured.	4	3	12	Cursory	010-020-060
1.3.000	*Functionality: Interoperability*					
1.3.001	Can't pull information from GloboRainBQW into HELLOCARMS.	2	2	4	Extensive	010-030-010
1.3.002	HELLOCARMS and Scoring Mainframe reject joint applications.	3	1	3	Extensive	010-030-020
1.3.003	HELLOCARMS and Scoring Mainframe cannot handle/resolve duplication of information on joint applications.	1	2	2	Extensive	010-030-030
1.3.004	HELLOCARMS trade line communication to LoDoPS fails.	3	1	3	Extensive	010-030-040 010-030-070
1.3.005	Loan status information from LoDoPS to HELLOCARMS lost or corrupted.	5	2	10	Broad	010-030-050 010-030-140
1.3.006	HELLOCARMS can't continue if the Scoring Mainframe indicates an undischarged bankruptcy or foreclosure.	4	3	12	Cursory	010-030-060
1.3.007	HELLOCARMS communication of government retirement income to LoDoPS fails.	5	1	5	Extensive	010-030-080
1.3.008	HELLOCARMS application information not passed to Scoring Mainframe properly.	3	1	3	Extensive	010-030-090

Table continues

Table 3–2 Functional quality risk analysis for HELLOCARMS (continued)

1.3.009	HELLOCARMS does not receive information from Scoring Mainframe properly.	3	1	3	Extensive	010-030-100
1.3.010	Decisioning requests not queued for Scoring Mainframe as needed.	4	2	8	Broad	010-030-110
1.3.011	Tentatively approved, customer-accepted loans not passed to LoDoPS.	5	2	10	Broad	010-030-120
1.3.012	Declined applications not passed to LoDoPS.	5	2	10	Broad	010-030-130
1.3.013	Changes made in loan information in LoDoPS not propagated back to HELLOCARMS.	5	2	10	Broad	010-030-140
1.3.014	Computer-telephony integration not supported.	3	5	15	Cursory	010-030-150
1.3.015	Applicant existing relationship not passed to GLADS.	4	3	12	Broad	010-010-070
1.4.000	*Functionality: Security*					
1.4.001	Agreed-upon security requirements not supported.	1	2	2	Extensive	010-040-010
1.4.002	"Created By" and "Last Changed By" audit trail information lost.	3	1	3	Extensive	010-040-020
1.4.003	Outsourced telemarketers see actual credit scores and other privileged information.	3	2	6	Broad	010-040-030
1.4.004	Internet applications insecure against intentional attacks.	1	2	2	Extensive	010-040-040
1.4.005	Internet applications insecure against unintentional attacks.	3	2	6	Broad	010-040-040
1.4.006	Anonymous browsing on Internet not permitted.	2	4	8	Broad	010-040-050
1.4.007	Fraud detection too lenient.	3	1	3	Extensive	010-040-060
1.4.008	Fraud detection too strict.	3	1	3	Extensive	010-040-060
1.5.000	*Functionality: Compliance*					
1.5.001	*[Functional risks related to functional compliance go in this section.]*					

3.12 Risk-Based Testing Exercise 2

Using the quality risks analysis for the HELLOCARMS, outline a set of functional test suites to run for HELLOCARMS system integration testing and system testing. Specifically, the system integration test level should have, as an overall objective, looking for defects in and building confidence around the ability of the HELLOCARMS application to work with the other applications in the datacenter. The system test level should have, as an overall objective, looking for defects in and building confidence around the ability of the HELLOCARMS application to provide the necessary capabilities.

Finally, state general guidelines for sequencing the test cases within each test suite during test execution.

Again, if you are working in a classroom, once each group has finished its work on the test suites and guidelines, discuss the results.

3.13 Risk-Based Testing Exercise Debrief 2

Based on the quality risk analysis I performed, I created the following lists of system integration test suites and system test suites.

System Integration Test Suites
- HELLOCARMS/Scoring Mainframe Interfaces
- HELLOCARMS/LoDoPS Interfaces
- HELLOCARMS/GLADS Interfaces
- HELLOCARMS/GloboRainBQW Interfaces

System Test Suites
- Basic Functionality
- Undesirable Applicants
- End-to-End Transactions
- Error Handling and Recovery
- Security
- Compliance

3.13.1 Test Case Sequencing Guidelines

Because this application exhibits a broad range of functions and must handle many different situations, I decided on a breadth-first set of test sequencing guidelines, shown below the test suite lists. In a breadth-first approach, we select a sample of tests across all the identified risks using the level of risk to weight the selection while at the same time ensuring coverage of every risk at least once.

So, prior to starting test execution, we use traceability information from our quality risk analysis to make the test procedures "inherit" the risk priority number of the high-risk quality risk item to which the test procedure traces. We then break the complete set of test cases into three subsets:

- **High priority:** Consists of a subset of test procedures that account for one-third of the total planned scripted test effort. Fifty percent of the test procedures have a risk priority number from 1 to 5. Thirty-five percent of the test procedures have a risk priority number from 6 to 10. Fifteen percent of the test procedures have a risk priority number from 11 to 15.
- **Medium priority:** Consists of a subset of test procedures that account for one-third of the total planned scripted test effort. Thirty-five percent of the test procedures have a risk priority number from 1 to 5. Fifty percent of the test procedures have a risk priority number from 6 to 10. Fifteen percent of the test procedures have a risk priority number from 11 to 15.
- **Low priority:** Consists of a subset of test procedures that account for one-third of the total planned scripted test effort. Fifteen percent of the test procedures have a risk priority number from 1 to 5. Fifteen percent of the test procedures have a risk priority number from 6 to 10. Seventy percent of the test procedures have a risk priority number from 11 to 15.

We then have a high-priority test period, a medium-priority test period, and a low-priority test period. During each of the three test execution periods, we run the test cases in the subset of tests in strict risk priority order.

This sequencing approach would need to flex based on the test release schedules and size of the overall test set. For example, if the overall test set is scheduled to last six weeks and test releases are scheduled to be received every week, then we have three two-week periods, each of which involves accepting two test releases. If the overall test set is scheduled to last eight weeks, then having four subsets rather than three would make more sense.

You'll notice that this sequencing approach assumes a roughly equal balance between test procedures with risk priority numbers from 1 to 5, from 6 to 10, and from 11 to 15. If that is not that case, the plan would need to be adjusted. However, the basic intent of the plan is achievable regardless of the actual risk priority number mixture of the test procedures.

Above and beyond the planned scripted test effort, there is additional time reserved for unscripted testing of two types:

- **Confirmation testing:** Testing of any defect fixes we receive in planned or unplanned test releases.
- **Reactive testing:** The use of exploratory testing, Whittaker's attacks, bug taxonomies, Hendrickson's bug hunting techniques, and other non systematic test techniques. (These techniques were covered in the Foundation and will be covered in more detail later in this course.) Some reactive testing will address risk items ranked as "opportunity" or below, along with risk items not identified during the risk analysis , to serve as a check-and-balance on the quality risk analysis.

Approximately 60 to 70% of each test period will be spent on scripted testing and about 30 to 40% spent on confirmation testing and reactive testing.

3.14 Failure Mode and Effects Analysis

Learning objectives
Recall of content only

The concepts in this section apply primarily for test managers. There are no learning objectives defined for test analysts in this section. In the course of studying for the exam, read this section in chapter 3 of the Advanced syllabus for general recall and familiarity only.

> **ISTQB Glossary**
>
> **session-based test management:** No definition in the glossary.

3.14.1 Test Management Issues

Learning objectives
Recall of content only

The concepts in this section apply primarily for test managers. There are no learning objectives defined for test analysts in this section. In the course of studying for the exam, read this section in chapter 3 of the Advanced syllabus for general recall and familiarity only.

3.15 Sample Exam Questions

To end each chapter, you can try one or more sample exam questions to reinforce your knowledge and understanding of the material and to prepare for the ISTQB Advanced Level Test Analyst exam.

1. In many of the IEEE 829 templates, a section in one of the documents used early in the project lifecycle is related to a similar section in multiple documents used later in the project lifecycle. For example, an IEEE 829 test plan has a section called "Features to Be Tested," and you would expect to find each of the features listed in this section of the test plan to be listed in one or more of the sections called "Features to Be Tested" in all of the test design specifications. Which of the following statements best expresses another similar relationship in the IEEE 829 templates?

    A Test case specification is to test procedure specification as test plan is to test design specification.

    B Test procedure specification is to test case specification as test plan is to test design specification.

C Test case specification is to test item transmittal report as test plan is to test design specification.

D Test plan is to test item transmittal report as test plan is to test design specification.

2. Assume you are a test analyst working on a banking project to upgrade an existing automated teller machine system to allow customers to obtain cash advances from supported credit cards. The system should allow cash advances of at least 500 euros for all supported credit cards. The correct list of supported credit cards is American Express, Visa, Japan Credit Bank, Eurocard, and MasterCard.

Among the various quality risk items you identify during risk analysis, you have the following, listed in order of perceived level of risk from most risky to least risky:

- Visa or MasterCard unable to obtain any cash advances

- American Express or Eurocard unable to obtain any cash advances

- Japan Credit Bank unable to obtain any cash advances

- Visa or MasterCard cash advances improperly limited

- American Express or Eurocard cash advances improperly limited

- Japan Credit Bank cash advances improperly limited

Assume that, in the following list, each test case requires exactly one hour of test analyst effort to run. Which of the following is a comma-separated, sequenced list of test cases that covers these risks in a way that is appropriate to the level of risk and that minimizes test effort?

A Test minimum American Express and Eurocard advances; test minimum Visa and MasterCard advances; test minimum Japan Credit Bank advances.

B Test minimum and maximum Visa and MasterCard advances; test minimum and maximum American Express and Eurocard advances; test minimum and maximum Japan Credit Bank advances.

C Test minimum Visa and MasterCard advances; test minimum American Express and Eurocard advances; test minimum Japan Credit Bank advances; test maximum Visa and MasterCard advances; test maximum American Express and Eurocard advances; test maximum Japan Credit Bank advances.

D Test maximum American Express and Eurocard advances; test maximum Visa and MasterCard advances; test maximum Japan Credit Bank advances.

3. Assume you have the following three documents or reports available to you at the appropriate point during a project:

I   Checklist of important quality characteristics for your product

II   Historical information from similar past projects on where defects were found and how serious those defects were

III A Pareto analysis of the subsystems where defects have been discovered so far during test execution on this project

Which of the following statements matches each of these items with the risk management activity the item will most benefit?

A I: risk identification; II: risk assessment; III: risk control

B I: risk control; II: risk assessment; III: risk identification

C I: risk identification; II: risk control; III: risk assessment

D I: risk assessment; II: risk control; III: risk identification

4 Test Techniques

"You've got to understand the basics of aerodynamics in a thing like this."

—The Gyro Captain

"Shut up, shut up!"

—"Mad" Max Rockatansky
Max politely declines a just-in-time lesson in aeronautical
engineering principles from the gyrocopter pilot, as scripted
by Terry Hayes and George Miller in "The Road Warrior."

The fourth chapter of the Advanced syllabus is concerned with test techniques. To make the material manageable, it uses a taxonomy—a hierarchical classification scheme—to divide the material into sections and subsections. Conveniently for us, it uses the same taxonomy of test techniques given in the Foundation syllabus, namely specification-based, structure-based, and experience-based, adding additional techniques and further explanation in each category. It also discusses both static and dynamic analysis.[1]

This chapter contains six sections:

1. Introduction
2. Specification-based
3. Structure-based
4. Defect- and Experience-based
5. Static Analysis
6. Dynamic Analysis

Let's look at each section and how it relates to test analysis.

---

1. You might notice a slight change from the organization of the Foundation syllabus here. The Foundation syllabus covers static analysis in the material on static techniques in chapter 3, while to the limited extent that it covers dynamic analysis, the Advanced syllabus does so in the material on tools in chapter 6.

4.1   Introduction

Learning objectives
Recall of content only

In this chapter and the next two chapters, we cover a number of test techniques. Let's start by putting some structure around these techniques, and then I'll tell you which ones are in scope for the test analyst and which are in scope for the technical test analyst.

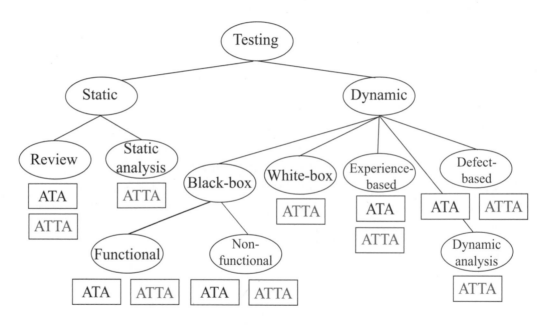

Figure 4–1   *A taxonomy for Advanced syllabus test techniques*

Figure 4-1 shows the highest-level breakdown of testing techniques as the distinction between static and dynamic tests. Static tests, as described in the Foundation syllabus, are those that do not involve running (or executing) the test object itself, while dynamic tests are those that do involve running the test object.

The Advanced syllabus breaks down static tests into reviews and static analysis. Reviews are any method where the human being is the primary defect finder and scrutinizer of the item under test, while static analysis relies on a tool as the primary defect finder and scrutinizer.

The Advanced syllabus divides dynamic tests into five main types:

- **Black-box** (also called specification-based or behavioral): We test based on the way the system is supposed to work. The Advanced syllabus further divides black-box tests into two main subtypes, functional and non functional, following the ISO 9126 standard. The easy way to distinguish between functional and non functional is that functional tests address *what* the system does and non functional tests address *how* the system does what it does.
- **White-box** (also called structural): We test based on the way the system is built.
- **Experience-based**: We test based on our skills and intuition, along with our experience with similar applications or technologies.
- **Dynamic analysis**: We analyze an application while it is running, usually via some kind of instrumentation in the code.
- **Defect-based**: We use our understanding of the type of defect targeted by a test as the basis for test design, with tests derived systematically from what is known about the defect.

There's always a temptation, when presented with a taxonomy like this one, to try to put things into neat, exclusive categories. If you're familiar with biology, you'll remember that every living being, the herpes virus to trees to chimpanzees, has a unique Latin name based on where in the big taxonomy of life it fits. However, when dealing with testing, remember that these techniques are complementary. You should use whichever and as many as are appropriate for any given test activity, whatever level of testing you are doing.

Now, below each bubble in figure 4-1 that shows the lowest-level breakdown of test techniques, you see one or two boxes. Boxes with ATA in them mean that I cover this test technique in this volume for advanced test analysts. Boxes with ATTA in them mean that I cover this test technique in the companion volume for advanced technical test analysts. The fact that I cover most techniques in both volumes does not, however, mean that the coverage is the same.

You should also keep in mind that this assignment of types of techniques into particular roles is based on common usage, which might not correspond to your own organization. You might have the title of test analyst and be responsible for dynamic analysis. You might have the title of technical test analyst and not be responsible for static analysis at all.

Okay, so that gives you an idea of where we're headed, basically for the rest of this book. There are some supporting materials about incident management and test teams and test tools toward the end, but figure 4-1 gives an overview of the heart of this book, probably 75 percent of the material covered. In this chapter, we cover dynamic testing, except for non functional tests, which I cover in the next chapter. The subsequent chapter covers reviews.

You might want to make a copy of figure 4-1 and have it available as you go through this chapter and the next two, as a way of orienting yourself to where we are in the book.

4.2 Specification-Based Techniques

Learning objectives

(K2) List examples of typical defects that can be identified by each specific specification-based technique, provide corresponding coverage criteria .

(K3) Write test cases from given software models, that achieve the given model's coverage, using the following test design techniques: equivalence partitioning; boundary value analysis; decision tables; state transition testing; classification tree method; pairwise testing; and, use cases.

(K4) Analyze a system, or its requirement specification, in order to determine which specification-based techniques to apply for specific objectives, and outline a test specification based on IEEE 829, focusing on functional and domain test cases and test procedures.

Let's start with a broad overview of specification-based tests before we dive into the details of each technique.

In specification-based testing, we are going to derive and select tests by analyzing the test basis. Remember that the test basis is—or, more accurately, the test bases are—the documents that tell us, directly or indirectly, how the component or system under test should and shouldn't behave, what it is required to do, and how it is required to do it. These are the documents we can base the tests on. Hence the name, test basis.

It's probably worth a quick compare-and-contrast with the term *test oracle*, which is similar and related but not the same as the test basis. The test oracle is anything we can use to determine expected results that we can compare with the actual results of the component or system under test. Anything that can serve as a test basis can also be a test oracle, of course. However, an oracle can also be an existing system, either a legacy system being replaced or a competitor's system. An oracle can also be someone's specialized knowledge. An oracle should not be the code, because otherwise we are only testing whether the compiler works.

For structural tests—which are covered in the next section—the internal structure of the system is the test basis but not the test oracle. However, for specification-based tests, we do not consider the internal structure at all—at least theoretically.

Beyond being focused on behavior rather than structure, what's common in specification-based test techniques? Well, for one thing, there is some model, whether formal or informal. The model can be a graph or a table. There is some systematic way to derive or create tests using the model. And, typically, each technique has a set of coverage criteria that tell you, in effect, when the model has run out of interesting and useful test ideas. It's important to remember that fulfilling coverage criteria for a particular test design technique does not mean that your tests are in any way complete or exhaustive. Instead, it means that the model has run out of useful tests to suggest based on that technique.

There is also typically some family of defects that the technique is particularly good at finding. Boris Beizer, in his books on test design, referred to this as the "bug hypothesis." He meant that, if you hypothesize that a particular kind of bug is likely to exist, you could then select the technique based on that

ISTQB Glossary

requirements-based testing: An approach to testing in which test cases are designed based on test objectives and test conditions derived from requirements, e.g., tests that exercise specific functions or probe non functional attributes such as reliability or usability.

specification: A document that specifies, ideally in a complete, precise, and verifiable manner, the requirements, design, behavior, or other characteristics of a component or system and, often, the procedures for determining whether these provisions have been satisfied.

black-box testing: Testing, either functional or non functional, without reference to the internal structure of the component or system.

specification-based technique (or black-box test design technique): Procedure to derive and/or select test cases based on an analysis of the specification, either functional or non functional, of a component or system without reference to its internal structure.

test basis: All documents from which the requirements of a component or system can be inferred. The documentation on which the test cases are based. If a document can be amended only by way of formal amendment procedure, then the test basis is called a frozen test basis.

test oracle: A source to determine expected results to compare with the actual results of the software under test. An oracle may be the existing system (for a benchmark), a user manual, or an individual's specialized knowledge, but it should not be the code.

hypothesis. This provides an interesting linkage with the concept of defect-based testing, which we'll cover in a later section of this chapter.[2]

Often, specification-based tests are requirements-based. Requirements specifications often describe behavior, especially functional behavior. (The tendency for non functional requirements to be underspecified is a whole separate quality-influencing problem that we'll not address at this point but simply

---

2. Boris Beizer's books on this topic would include *Black-Box Testing* (perhaps most pertinent to test analysts), *Software System Testing and Quality Assurance* (good for test analysts, technical test analysts, and test managers), and *Software Test Techniques* (perhaps most pertinent to technical test analysts).

accept as a given.) So, we can use the description of the system behavior in the requirements to create the models. We can then derive tests from the models.

4.2.1 Equivalence Partitioning

We start with the most basic of specification-based test design techniques, equivalence partitioning. Conceptually, equivalence partitioning is about testing various groups that we expect the system to handle the same way and, in dealing with them, exhibit similar behavior.

The underlying model is a graphical or mathematical one that identifies equivalent classes—which are also called equivalent partitions—of inputs, outputs, internal values, time relationships, calculations, or just about anything else of interest. These classes or partitions are called *equivalent* because the system should handle them the same way. We can call some of the classes *valid equivalence classes* because they describe valid situations that the system should handle normally. We can call other classes *invalid equivalence classes* because they describe invalid situations that the system should reject or at least escalate to the user for correction or exception handling.

Once we've identified the equivalent classes, we can derive tests from them. Usually, we are working with more than one set of equivalence classes at one time. For example, each input field on a screen has its own set of valid and invalid equivalence classes. So we can create one set of valid tests by selecting one valid member from each equivalence partition. We continue this process until each valid class for each equivalence partition is represented in at least one valid test.

Next, we can create invalid tests. For each equivalence partition, we select one invalid class for one equivalence partition and a valid class for every other equivalence partition. This rule—don't combine multiple invalids in a single test—prevents us from running into a situation where the presence of one invalid value might mask the incorrect handling of another invalid value. We continue this process until each invalid class for each equivalence partition is represented in at least one invalid test.

Notice the coverage criteria implicit in the discussion above. Every class member, both valid and invalid, is represented in at least one test case.

What is our bug hypothesis with this technique? For the most part, we are looking for a situation where some equivalence class is handled improperly.

> **ISTQB Glossary**
>
> equivalence partition: A portion of an input or output domain for which the behavior of a component or system is assumed to be the same, based on the specification.
>
> **equivalence partitioning:** A black-box test design technique in which test cases are designed to execute representatives from equivalence partitions. In principle, test cases are designed to cover each partition at least once.

That could mean the value is accepted when it should have been rejected or vice versa or that a value is properly accepted or rejected but handled in a way appropriate to another equivalence class, not the class to which it actually belongs.

You might find this concept a bit confusing verbally, so let's try some figures. Figure 4-2 shows a way that we can visualize equivalence partitioning.

As you can see in the top half of figure 4-2, we start with some set of interest. This set of interest can be an input field, an output field, a test precondition or postcondition, a configuration, or just about anything we're interested in testing. The key is that we can apply the operation of equivalence partitioning to split the set into two or more disjoint subsets, where all the members of each subset share some trait in common that was not shared with the members of the other subset. For example, if you have a simple drawing program that can fill figures in with red, green, or blue, you can split the set of fill colors into three disjoint sets: red, green, and blue.

In the bottom half of figure 4-2, we see the selection of test case values from the subsets. The dots in the subsets represent the value we chose from each subset to represent the subset in the test case. This involves selecting at least one member from each subset. Pure equivalence partitioning does not say anything about which member to select. You can select any member of the subset you please. If you're thinking, "Some members are better than others," that's fine; hold that thought for a few minutes and we'll come back to it.

Now, at this point we'll generate the rest of the test case. If the set that we partitioned was an input field, we might refer to the requirements specification to understand how the system should handle each subset. If the set that we

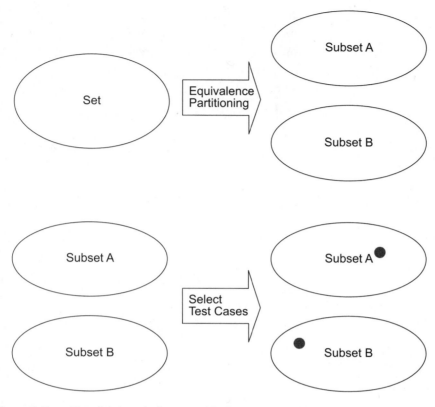

Figure 4–2   *Visualizing equivalence partitioning*

partitioned was an output field, we might refer to the requirements to derive inputs that should cause that output to occur. We might use other test techniques to design the rest of the test cases.

Figure 4-3 shows that we can iteratively apply equivalence partitioning. In this figure, we apply a second round of equivalence partitioning to one of the subsets to generate three smaller subsets. Only at that point do we select four members—one from subset B and one each from subset A1, A2, and A3—for test cases. Note that we don't have to select a member from subset A, because each of the members from subsets A1, A2, and A3 are also members of subset A.

4.2.2   Avoiding Equivalence Partitioning Errors

While this technique is fairly straightforward, people do make some common errors when applying it. Let's look at these errors so you can avoid them.

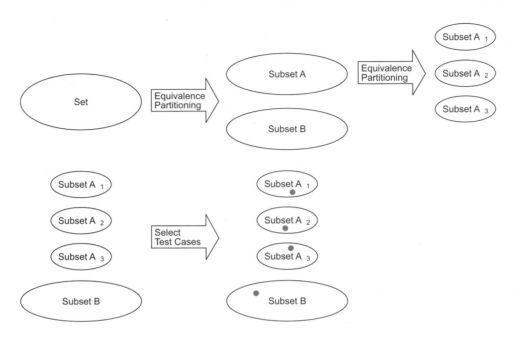

Figure 4–3   *Subpartitioning*

First, as shown in the top half of figure 4-4, the subsets must be *disjoint*. That is, no two of the subsets can have one or more members in common. The whole point of equivalence partitioning is to test whether a system handles different situations differently (and properly, of course). If it's ambiguous as to which handling is proper, then how do we define a test case around this? "Try it out and see what happens?" Not much of a test!

Second, as shown in the bottom half of figure 4-4, none of the subsets may be *empty*. That is, if the equivalence partitioning operation produces a subset with no members, that's hardly very useful for testing. We can't select a member of that subset because it has no members.

Third, while not shown graphically—in part because I couldn't figure out a clear way to draw the picture—note that the equivalence partitioning process does not subtract; it divides. What I mean by this is that, in terms of mathematical set theory, the union of the subsets produced by equivalence partitioning must be the same as the original set that was equivalence partitioned. In other words, equivalence partitioning does not generate "spare" subsets that are somehow disposed of in the process—at least, not if we do it properly.

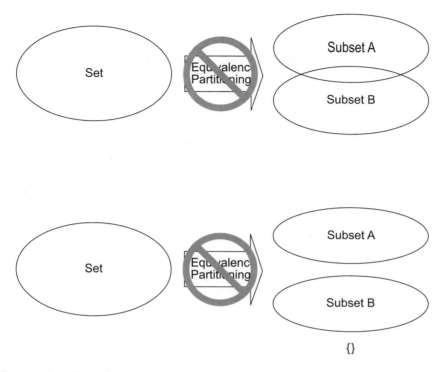

Figure 4–4   *Equivalence partitioning errors*

Notice that this is important because, if it's not true, then we stand the chance of failing to test some important subset of inputs, outputs, configurations, or some other factor of interest that somehow was dropped in the test design process.

4.2.3   Composing Test Cases with Equivalence Partitioning

When we compose test cases in situations where we've performed equivalence partitioning on more than one set, we select from each subset, as shown in figure 4-5. Here, we start with set X and set Y. We partition set X into two subsets, X1 and X2. We partition set Y into three subsets, Y1, Y2, and Y3. We select test case values from each of the five subsets, X1, X2, Y1, Y2, and Y3. We then compose three test cases, because we can combine the values from the X subsets with values from the Y subsets (assuming the values are independent and all valid).

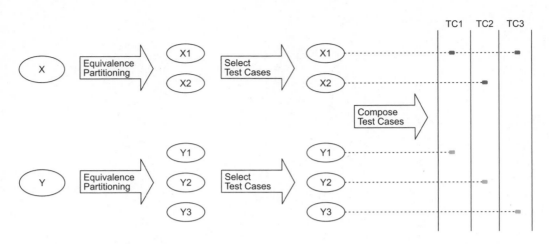

Figure 4–5   *Composing test cases with valid values*

For example, imagine you are testing a browser-based application. You are interested in two browsers: Internet Explorer and Firefox. You are interested in three connection types: dial-up, DSL, and cable modem. Because the browser and the connection types are independent, we can create three test cases. In each of the test cases, one of the connection types and one of the browser types will be represented. One of the browser types will be represented twice.

Regarding figure 4-4, I made a brief comment that we can combine values across the equivalence partitions when the values are independent and all valid. Of course, that's not always the case.

In some cases, values are not independent in that the selection of one value from one subset constrains the choice in another subset. For example, imagine if you're trying to test combinations of applications and operating systems. You can't test an application running on an operating system if there is no version of that application available for that operating system.

In some cases, values are not valid. For example, in figure 4-5, imagine that we are testing a project management application, something like Microsoft Project. Suppose that set X is the type of event we're dealing with; it can be either a task (X1) or a milestone (X2). Suppose that set Y is the start date of the event, which can be in the past (Y1), today (Y2), or in the future (Y3). Suppose that set Z is the end date of the event, which can be either on or after the start date (Z1) or before the start date (Z2). Of course, Z2 is invalid because no event can have a negative duration.

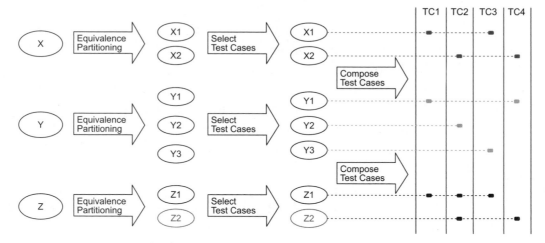

Figure 4–6   *Composing tests with invalid values*

So, we test combinations of tasks and milestones with past, present, and future start dates and valid end dates in test cases TC1, TC2, and TC3. In TC4, we check that illegal end dates are correctly rejected. We try to enter a task with a start date in the past and an end date prior to the start date. If we wanted to sub-partition the invalid situation, we could add two more test cases. One would test a start date in the present and an end date prior to the start date. The other would test a start date in the future and an end date prior to the start date.

In this particular example, we had a single subset for just one of the sets that was invalid. The more general case is that many—perhaps all—of the subsets will have invalid subsets. Imagine testing an e-commerce application. On the checkout screens of the typical e-commerce application, there are multiple required fields, and usually there is at least one way for such a field to be invalid. When there are multiple invalid values, we have to select one invalid value per test case—at least to start with. That way, we can check that any given invalid value is correctly rejected or in some way handled by the system.

Now, I said one invalid value per test case to start with. If, after testing the invalid values separately, you want to test combinations of invalids, by all means, do so—if the risk is sufficient to justify it. Any time you start down the trail of combinatorial testing, you are taking a chance that you'll spend a lot of time testing things that aren't terribly important.

Here's a simple example of equivalence partitioning on a single value, in this case, system configuration. On the Internet appliance project I've mentioned before, there were four possible configurations for the appliances. They could be configured for kids, teens, adults, or seniors. This configuration value was stored in a database on the Internet service provider's server, and, when an Internet appliance connected to the Internet, this configuration value became a property of its connection.

Based on this configuration value, there were two key areas of difference in the expected behavior. For one thing, for the kids and teens systems, there was a filtering function enabled. This determined the allowed and disallowed websites the system could surf to. The setting was most strict for kids and somewhat less strict for teens. Adults and seniors, of course, were to have no filtering at all and should be able to surf anywhere.

For another thing, each of the four configurations had a default set of e-commerce sites they could visit called the mall. These sites were selected by the marketing team and were meant to be age appropriate.

Of course, these were the expected differences. We were also aware of the fact that there could be weird unexpected differences that could arise because that's the nature of some types of bugs. For example, performance was supposed to be the same, but it's possible that performance problems with the filtering software could introduce perceptible response-time issues with the kids and teens systems. We had to watch for those kinds of misbehaviors.

So, to test for the unexpected differences, we simply had at least one of each configuration in the test lab at all times and spread the non configuration-specific tests more or less randomly across the different configurations. (More on testing combinations of configurations in a subsequent part of this section.) To test expected differences related to filtering and e-commerce, we made sure these configuration-specific tests were run on the correct configuration. The challenge here was that, while the expected results were concrete for the mall—the marketing people gave us four sets of specific sites, one for each configuration—the expected results for the filtering were not concrete but rather logical. This lead to an enormous number of very disturbing defect reports during test execution, as we found creative ways to sneak around the filters and access age-inappropriate materials on kids and teens configurations.

4.2.4 Equivalence Partitioning Exercise

A screen prototype for one screen of the HELLOCARMS system is shown in figure 4-7. This screen asks for three pieces of information:

- The product being applied for, which is one of the following:
  - Home equity loan
  - Home equity line of credit
  - Reverse mortgage
- Whether someone has an existing Globobank checking account, which is either Yes or No.
- Whether someone has an existing Globobank savings account, which is either Yes or No.

If the user indicates an existing Globobank account, then the user must enter the corresponding account number. This number is validated against the bank's central database upon entry. If the user indicates no such account, the user must leave the corresponding account number field blank.

If the fields are valid, including the account number fields, then the screen will be accepted. If one or more fields are invalid, an error message is displayed.

The exercise consists of two parts:

1. Show the equivalence partitions for each of the three pieces of information, indicating valid and invalid members.
2. Create test cases to cover these partitions, keeping in mind the rules about combinations of valid and invalid members.

The answers to the two parts are shown on the next pages. You should review the answer to the first part (and, if necessary, revise your answer to the second part) before reviewing the answer to the second part.

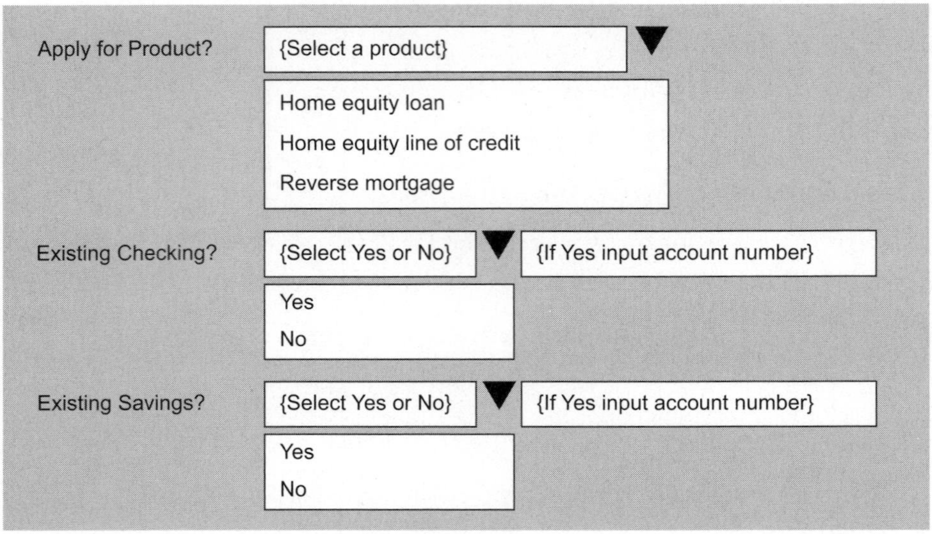

Figure 4–7   *HELLOCARMS system product screen prototype*

4.2.5   Equivalence Partitioning Exercise Debrief

First, let's take a look at the equivalence partitions.

For the application-product field, the equivalence partitions are as follows:

#	Partition
1	Home equity loan
2	Home equity line of credit
3	Reverse mortgage

Note that the screen prototype shows this information as selected from a pull-down list, so there is no possibility of entering an invalid product here.

For each of two existing-account entries, the situation is best modeled as a single input field, which consists of two subfields. The first subfield is the Yes/No field. This subfield determines the rule for checking the second subfield, which is the account number. If the first subfield is Yes, the second subfield must be a valid account number. If the first subfield is No, the second subfield must be blank.

So, the existing checking account information partitions are as follows:

#	Partition
1	Yes-Valid
2	Yes-Invalid
3	No-Blank
4	No-Nonblank

And here are the existing savings account information partitions:

#	Partition
1	Yes-Valid
2	Yes-Invalid
3	No-Blank
4	No-Nonblank

Note that, for both of these, partitions 2 and 4 are invalid partitions, while partitions 1 and 3 are valid partitions.

Now, let's create tests from these equivalence partitions. As we do so, I'm going to capture traceability information from the test case number back to the partitions. Once I have a trace from each partition to a test case, I'm done—provided that I'm careful to follow the rules about combining valid and invalid partitions!

Inputs	1	2	3	4	5	6	7
Product	HEL	LOC	RM	HEL	LOC	RM	HEL
Existing Checking?	Yes	No	No	Yes	No	No	No
Checking Account	Valid	Blank	Blank	Invalid	Nonblank	Blank	Blank
Existing Savings?	No	Yes	No	No	No	Yes	No
Savings Account	Blank	Valid	Blank	Blank	Blank	Invalid	Nonblank
Outputs							
Accept?	Yes	Yes	Yes	No	No	No	No
Error?	No	No	No	Yes	Yes	Yes	Yes

Product:

#	Partition	Test Case
1	Home equity loan (HEL)	1
2	Home equity line of credit (LOC)	2
3	Reverse mortgage (RM)	3

Checking:

#	Partition	Test Case
1	Yes-Valid	1
2	Yes-Invalid	4
3	No-Blank	2
4	No-Nonblank	5

Savings:

#	Partition	Test Case
1	Yes-Valid	2
2	Yes-Invalid	6
3	No-Blank	1
4	No-Nonblank	7

You should notice that these test cases do not cover all interesting possible combinations of factors here. For example, we don't test to make sure that the system properly handles a situation where a person has a valid savings account and a valid checking account. That could be an interesting test because the accounts might have been established at different times and might have information that now conflicts in some way; e.g., in some countries it is still relatively common for a woman to take her husband's last name upon marriage. We also don't test the combination of invalid accounts, or the combination of account numbers that are valid alone but not valid together; e.g., the two accounts belong to entirely different people.

We'll discuss techniques for testing combinations of conditions in subsequent portions of this section.

4.2.6   Boundary Value Analysis

Let's refine our equivalence partitioning test design technique with the next technique, boundary value analysis. Conceptually, boundary value analysis is about testing the edges of equivalence classes. In other words, instead of selecting one member of the class, we select the largest and smallest members of the class and test them.

The underlying model is again either a graphical or mathematical one that identifies two boundary values at the boundary between one equivalence class and another. (In some techniques, the model identifies three boundary values, which I'll address later.) Now, whether such a boundary exists for subsets where we've performed equivalence partitioning is another question, which I'll get to in just a moment. Right now, notice that, assuming the boundary does exist, the boundary values are just special members of the equivalence classes that happen to be right next to each other and right next to the point where the expected behavior of the system changes. If the boundary values are members of a valid equivalence class, they are valid, of course, and if they're members of an invalid equivalence class, they are invalid.

Deriving tests with boundary values as the equivalence class members is much the same as deriving tests equivalence classes when boundary values are not considered. We test valid boundary values together and then combine one invalid boundary value with other valid boundary values.

We have to represent each boundary value in a test case, analogous to the equivalence partitioning situation. In other words, the coverage criterion is that every boundary value, both valid and invalid, must be represented in at least one test.

The main difference is that there are at least two boundary values in each equivalence class. So we'll have more test cases, about twice as many.

Hmm, okay, more test cases. Well, that's not something we like unless there's a good reason for them. What is the point of these extra test cases? That is revealed by the bug hypothesis for boundary value analysis. Because we are testing equivalence class members—every boundary value is an equivalence class member—we are testing for situations where some equivalence class is handled improperly. Again, improper hanlding could mean acceptance of values that should be rejected. Improper handling could mean rejection of values that should be accepted. Improper handling could mean proper acceptance or

> **ISTQB Glossary**
>
> **boundary value analysis:** A black-box test design technique in which test cases are designed based on boundary values.
>
> boundary value: An input value or output value that is on the edge of an equivalence partition or at the smallest incremental distance on either side of an edge, such as, for example the minimum or maximum value of a range.

rejection, but improper handling subsequently, as if the value given were in another equivalence class, not the class to which it actually belongs. However, by testing boundary values, we also test whether the boundary between equivalence classes is defined in the right place.

Do all equivalence classes have boundary values? No, definitely not. Boundary value analysis is an extension of equivalence partitioning that applies only when the members of an equivalence class are ordered.

So, what does that mean? Well, an ordered set is one where we can say that one member is greater than or less than some other member if those two members are not the same. We have to be able to say this meaningfully too. Just because some item is right above or below some other item on a pull-down menu does not mean that, within the program, the two items have a greater-than/less-than relationship.

4.2.7 Examples of Equivalence Partitioning and Boundary Values

Let's look at examples where a test analyst can (and can't) use boundary value analysis on equivalence classes.

In figure 4-8, you can see the Insert menu that you can pull down from the PowerPoint menu bar at the top of the screen. This is a typical pull-down menu.

For a situation like this, each selection is its own equivalence class. Yes, there is a first item and a last item on the menu, but the ordering of the set is arbitrary and has no meaning below the user interface. Inside the software, it's very unlikely that there is any "greater-than/less-than" relationship between the items on this menu. So we can use equivalence partitioning (and we must test each selection on the menu) but not boundary values.

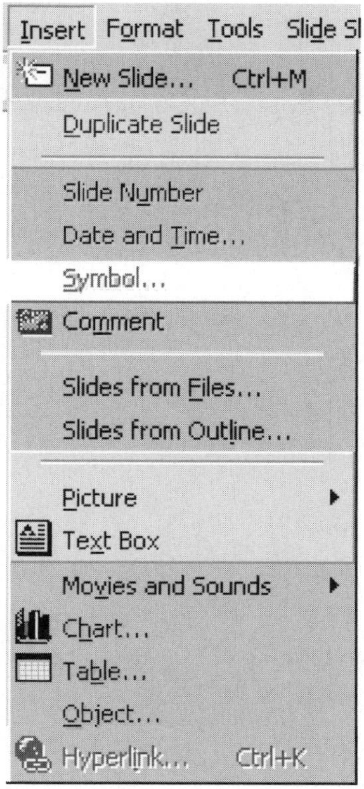

Figure 4–8   *Pull-down menus*

Notice that there is apparently no "invalid" selection possible here, as the only selections we can't choose are grayed out. Does that always work? Well, no. It's up to you to test that those things that should be grayed out are, those that shouldn't be "grayed out" aren't, and that those that are grayed out are indeed inaccessible.

So, for this menu, as shown in figure 4-9, we will partition each menu selection into its own subset. Note that some are invalid selections.

For each valid menu selection, we'll need further equivalence partitioning and in most cases boundary value analysis. For example, we might want to try inserting slides from a file that contains only one slide as well as a file that contain the maximum number of slides (whatever that is). We will also want to try

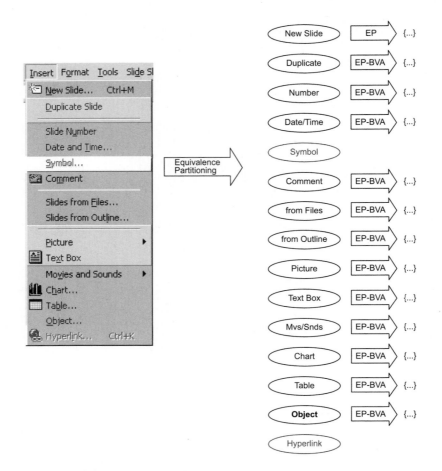

Figure 4–9   *Pull-down menu example*

inserting a file that contains zero slides (if that's possible) and a file that contains one more than the maximum number of slides.

Not all pull-down menus are unordered sets. Some are menus that are sitting "on top of" an integer field. Integers are an ordered set. For example, consider Microsoft Word font sizes. In this situation, the menu shown in figure 4-10 is one way to enter data; direct, manual entry is another.

So we can use equivalence partitioning on ways to enter the font size:

■ Select from menu
■ Enter the value in the field

Figure 4–10   *Integer fields*

You might be saying, "Hey, these aren't disjoint sets, though, because I can select and then enter and enter and then select." You'd be right in that, but at any moment in time, you're doing one or the other (if you're setting font sizes). Later, when we look at state transition testing, we'll examine a technique that allows us to deal with this situation.

Now, we can use boundary value analysis on each of the two ways to enter font sizes. Font size is an integer value in Word, and integer values are ordered sets. We can select the largest and smallest menu font. We can also test the largest and smallest entered font.

What are these largest and smallest font values? Well, ideally we would have a requirements specification that would tell us. Barring that, though, we can try some experimentation, as I did here. You can see that the smallest font size is 1 point and the largest 1638. Is that okay? Well, who knows? And all I know now is that these are the largest and smallest font sizes for the Arial font. It's possible that the font selection could influence the largest and smallest allowed font size.

Must I try to figure out the limits for each font? What a testing nightmare that would be! So it would be good to get clarification on these values before we start testing.

Finally, notice that invalid values are not possible on the menu, but they are possible when entered. Also, the question of what the largest and smallest values are doesn't arise with the menu, either. From a testability point of view, it is much better to require the user to select from a menu rather than allowing them to directly enter data into or directly edit fields.

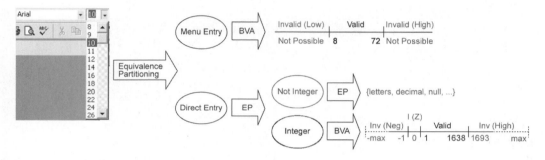

Figure 4–11   *Integer example*

In figure 4-11, you can see the application of equivalence partitioning and boundary value analysis on the font size field, all the way down to the generation of test inputs.

Using these techniques, we can generate the following test input values:

■ From the menu, we would want to test 8 and 72. Any value lower or higher is impossible, at least from the menu.

■ From direct entry into the field, we can start with the invalid equivalence partition of non integers. We could enter the letter *a*, the number 6.5, a null value (i.e., no entry at all), a slash character, a minus sign, and a plus sign. We could continue the generation of invalid values here to almost infinite length, but at some point, it gets silly.

■ For the equivalence partition of integers, we can enter −1, 0, 1, 1638 (the largest legal font size according to the message shown here), 1639 (the smallest illegal-too-large font size), some big positive number, and some big negative number. What is big in this situation? Well, one natural thing to try is to use the Notepad feature or some other simple text editor to generate a string of 10 9s, then copy and paste that into the field. If that works, copy and paste to generate 20 9s. Then 40. Then 100. Again, at some point this gets silly.

The answer to the question, "How deep should I go with these invalid inputs?" is, of course, a matter of risk. Overflowing buffers with invalid inputs is a well-known security attack. If your application has to deal with secure, private data—customer account data, for example—then running a whole array of carefully designed buffer overflow tests against every input field in your system makes sense. However, spending hours pumping invalid strings of various types into the font size input field in Word does not make sense. Be smart. Be risk based in your testing-depth decisions.

As you'll recall, the IEEE 829 test case specification template requires that a test case consist of both an input and an output. So we expect the system to reject the invalid inputs with a helpful error message. For the valid inputs, we expect the system to change the font size on the selected text.

Integers are about the simplest ordered sets we deal with as testers. We also sometimes have to test floating point numbers. Floating point numbers are also called *real numbers* or *decimal numbers*. Floating point numbers, like integers, are also ordered sets. However, while integers do not have decimal points, floating point numbers do.

This immediately brings up the important testing question, How many decimal points? That is a question of the particular field's precision. This is sometimes referred to as *epsilon* or the *smallest recognizable difference*.

There are two reasons that this question of precision is an important testing question. First, we can't figure out what the boundary values are without knowing the answer to this question. Second, problems with precision, and particularly ambiguity about it, are fertile ground for bugs.

Most software, by virtue of the programming language used, has a basic floating point data type built in. One problem with that is that the precision of this data type can vary from one machine to another. Another potential testing challenge is that the range of the floating point data type—i.e., its maximum and minimum values—can vary too.

Without getting too technical about the issue, another problem arises from the way that floating point data types are stored. The precision is not given in terms of digits before and after the decimal point, as you might expect. The precision is given in terms of total number of significant digits. There can be a very large number of zeros between the significant digits and the decimal point. For example, 999,999 trillion trillion is a very large number, but perhaps only the first six digits—the 999,999 part—will be stored as significant digits. This means that, with very large positive and negative numbers and very small positive and negative numbers—i.e., numbers very close to zero—we an have some interesting rounding errors that arise, especially in calculations.

I spent an entire quarter at UCLA when getting my computer science degree studying numerical analysis. Lots of time is spent on issues like this in the field of computing, and the careless programmer can easily make many mistakes.

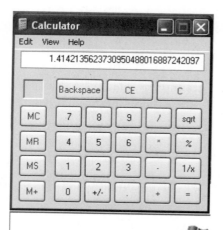

Figure 4–12   *Floating point (decimal) numbers*

In figure 4-12, you can see the Microsoft Calculator applet. The main input field is, by default, a floating point field. Rather than rely on the internal representation of floating points, Microsoft provides a feature called Extended Precision. As shown here, this provides us with at least 32 decimal digits of precision. Furthermore, rational numbers—those numbers that can be written as fractions like ½ or ⅜—are stored as fractions to further promote accuracy of calculations. Of course, irrational numbers like pi and other such constants with unlimited digits after the decimal point will be inaccurate in any system like this with a fixed number of digits of accuracy.

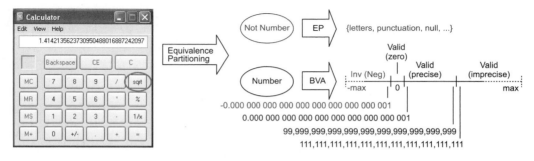

Figure 4–13   *Floating point example*

In figure 4-13, you can see the application of equivalence partitioning and boundary value analysis on the calculator input field for the square root function, all the way down to the generation of test inputs. The square root function accepts any floating point number greater than or equal to zero as an input and returns a number that, if multiplied by itself, yields the original number.

Using the boundary value analysis and equivalence partitioning techniques, we can come up with the following test values.

As with integers, we can test nonnumeric inputs like *a*, ampersand, null (if that's possible), and so forth. There's no limit to the effort you could expend subpartitioning this equivalence class, so remember to use risk as your guide.

We can apply four equivalence classes to the numeric, floating point inputs. There are three valid classes:

Price	Shares	Amount Comm/Fee		Clr	Share Bal
9.81	4.778	46	87	R	1,197 35
9.77	5.072	49	55	R	1,202 42
9.74	5.331	51	92	R	1,207 75
9.74	5.331	51	92	R	1,213 08
9.82	4.652	45	68	R	1,217 74

Market Value: 18,958.56   **Ending Share Bal:**   2,004.076

Figure 4–14   *Quicken investment account screen*

1. Zero, which is both the upper and lower boundary value of its own equivalence class.
2. Valid with 32 or fewer digits, and thus represented precisely. We have a small number close to zero, but not quite zero, and a number with 30 9s as the boundary values.
3. Valid with 33 or more digits, and thus represented imprecisely. It takes some effort to create these values because you have to enter the largest possible values and then multiply them together to create even larger values. I spent a few minutes doing this and could not find the point at which the calculator overflowed. I did find that the calculator would eventually take so long to complete a calculation that it would come back to me and ask permission to continue! It would be best, again, to have this in a requirements specification somewhere.

There is one invalid class, the negative numbers. That starts with the negative number closest to zero. It continues up to the maximum negative number, which again might take some time to find without a requirements specification.

Here's an investment account screen from Quicken, the financial application (figure 4-14). Testing of financial operations involves floating point numbers, so all of the issues just discussed apply. However, notice that the question of precision has serious real-world implications. People tend to be very sensitive to rounding errors that involve things like money, investment account balances, and the like. Furthermore, there are regulations and contracts that often apply along with any specified requirements. So testing financial applications involves a great deal of care when these kinds of issues are involved.

Let's take a closer look. In figure 4-15 you can see the application of equivalence partitioning and boundary value analysis to the input of a stock purchase transaction in Quicken. In Quicken, when you enter a stock purchase transaction, after entering the stock, you input the number of shares, the price per share, and the commission, if any. Quicken calculates the amount of the transaction.

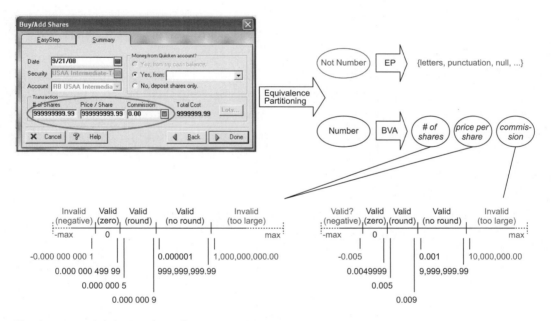

Figure 4-15   *Quicken stock purchase transaction*

First, for each of the three fields—number of shares, price per share, and commission—we can say that any nonnumeric input is invalid. So that's common across all three.

For the numeric inputs, the price per share and the number of shares are handled the same. The number must be zero or greater. Notice the interesting rounding that happens because we can enter numbers that aren't zero but are rounded down to zero. For the number to be greater than zero, we have to enter at least .0000005, which is rounded up to .000001.

For the commission, something similar happens, but the rounding is to cents, which—pardon the pun—makes sense. One thing that didn't make much sense to me as I created figure 4-15 was the fact that a negative commission is allowed. I guess sometimes that happens, but I've never been so lucky!

As figure 4-15 is an information-dense figure, you might take a moment to study the various values identified for testing here.

Notice that you could apply the same approach to the Total Cost field. However, this is an output field, so you'd have to create inputs that would cause the output to be populated appropriately. You can see from figure 4-15 that there is clearly a problem here!

Presumably, you would use these various test values to populate some set of test cases that involved entering stock purchase transactions. We'll look more at where those test cases would come from when we talk about use cases.

Date fields (like those shown in figure 4-16) and time fields are ordered sets, so both equivalence partitioning and boundary value analysis apply. They are more complex than integers and floating point numbers, though, becauses dates and times are fields that consist of two or more subfields. In the case of dates, one or two subfields determine the valid range of another subfield. In the case of times, the format of the field determines validity of one of the subfields.

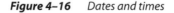

Figure 4–16   *Dates and times*

Now, there's mixed news for test analysts here. Most applications use standard libraries to validate date and time inputs, and we won't need to test that so much. However, applications often accept as inputs two or more dates or times that have a relationship between them, like arrival and departure dates on airline flights. So most test analysts will focus on testing relationships between dates, and this can be quite complicated.

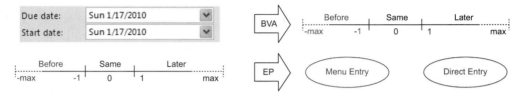

Figure 4–17   *Date and time example*

In figure 4-17, you can see the application of boundary value analysis and then equivalence partitioning to the relationship between the Start Date and Due Date fields of the task dialog box in Outlook. We can generate the test values and also decide on the means of entering them.

First, boundary value analysis allows us to generate the test values for the relationship between the due date and the start date. These include having the due date be the same day as the start date, which is valid. We can also have the due date be later than the start date, which is also valid. This can range from one day later up to some maximum number of days. Again, a requirements specification would help to determine what that maximum is.

For invalid inputs, note that we could try to enter a due day that is before the start date. That is definitely invalid. It could be one day before, up to some maximum number of days.

Now, we can use equivalence partitioning on the ways in which the dates are entered. This does matter in terms of when the validation happens, so we would want to test it multiple ways. Pulling down a menu and selecting a date from it triggers immediate validation, while manually entering the date means the validation doesn't happen until you try to save the task.

Many inputs occur in free-form, editable fields, submitting character strings of various lengths and contents. The rules for validating these fields depend on what the field is. The boundary values and equivalence partitions that can exist arise not from the nature of the data itself—as was the case with integers, floating point numbers, and so forth—but rather from rules imposed on the data by the application. So, in some cases there are boundary values for strings—especially in terms of length—while in other cases there aren't.

Figure 4–18   *RBCS' website e-commerce payment processing screen*

As with dates, it's also quite possible for related fields to be individually valid but not valid together. You can see the payment processing screen from the RBCS website in figure 4-18. Each of the six fields can be correct yet the entire set of information not correspond to a real credit card. In figure 4-19, you can see the application of equivalence partitioning and boundary value analysis to the credit card type and the card number.

Using these techniques, we see that each card type is its own equivalence class. That's necessary because the specific leading digits and the number of digits will vary depending on the card type. For each card type, we want to try the usual nonnumeric inputs we've discussed for other fields. For numeric inputs, we can use boundary value analysis on the length to determine validity. There are four equivalence classes:

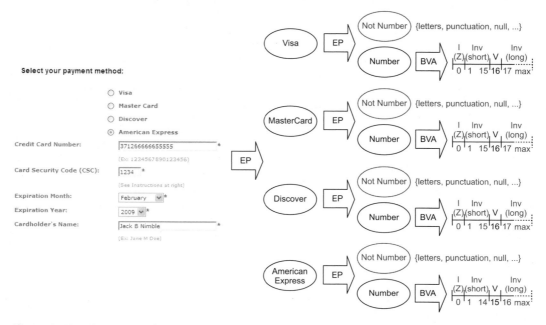

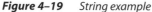

Figure 4–19   *String example*

1. The number has zero length, it is null, which is invalid. Okay, we already
    caught that one with the nonnumerics, but that's not a problem. Better that
    our techniques generate the same interesting test values twice than not at
    all. Just remember that when this happens you don't actually have to test it
    twice!

2. The number is too short, which is invalid. We want to test with 1 digit and
    15 for most cards, though we want to test with 14 for American Express
    because it has a 15-digit card number.

3. The number is the proper length, which makes it valid—at least from an
    input-field perspective. We'll address the question of whether the card
    number is actually valid in relationship to the other fields in a minute.

4. The number is too long, which is invalid. We want to test with 17 digits for
    most cards, though we want to test with 16 for American Express because it
    has a 15-digit card number. We also need to try some sort of maximum
    entry.

All of this hacking away at the credit card input field might strike you as absurd and overdone. However, from a security point of view, this screen is one you'll want to test heavily, right? Risk justifies extensive testing of these types of fields on such a screen.

I didn't have space to show the application of this approach to the card security code, expiration month and year, or cardholder name. The card security code would look much like the equivalence partitioning for the card number, including the different number of digits for the American Express card compared to all the others.

The month and year is easy, because the RBCS website designers had the brains to restrict these two fields to pull-down menu selection only. That aids testability, because it's not possible to enter "Februly" as the month or "20ZB" as the expiry year.

The cardholder name is a bit tricky because here we'd need to know what the maximum and minimum lengths are for this field. Also, are there any rules about the characters allowed in this field? Again, a requirements specification would be useful for this.

Of course, this covers only validation of the individual fields. Once the fields are individually validated, the payment method information has to be sent to the credit card processing company for validation. We could handle that with equivalence partitioning, but there is actually a whole set of conditions that determine this processing:

- Does the named person hold the credit card entered, and is the other information correct?
- Is the credit card still active or has it been cancelled?
- Is the person within or over their limit?
- Is the transaction coming from a normal or a suspicious location?

We'll look at a technique that helps us test situations where conditions combine to determine outcomes when we cover decision tables in a subsequent section.

4.2.8   How Many Boundary Values Are There?

Let's wind down our discussion of boundary value analysis by mentioning a somewhat obscure point that can nevertheless arise if you do some reading about testing. This is the question of how many boundary values exist at a boundary.

In the material so far, I've shown just two boundary values per boundary. The boundary lies between the largest member of one equivalence class and the smallest member of the equivalence class above it. In other words, the boundary itself doesn't correspond to any member of any class.

However, some authors say there are three boundary values. Boris Beizer is probably the most notable. Why would there be three?

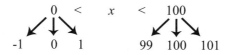

The user must order a quantity
greater than 0 and less than 100...

Mathematical inequality model (v1)

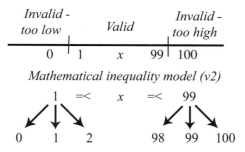

Graphical ("number line") model

Mathematical inequality model (v2)

Figure 4–20   *Two boundary values or three?*

The difference arises from the use of a mathematical analysis rather than the graphical one that I've used. You can see that the two mathematical inequalities shown in figure 4-20 describe the same situation as the graphical model. Applying Beizer's rule, you select the value itself as the middle boundary value, then

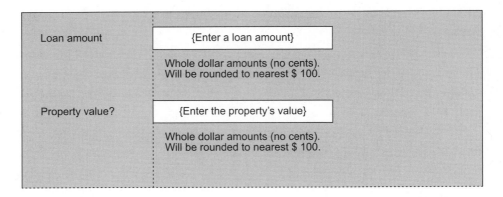

Figure 4–21   *HELLOCARMS system amount screen prototype*

you add the smallest possible amount to that value and subtract the smallest possible amount from that value generate the two other boundary values. Remember, with integers as in this example, the smallest possible amount is one, while for floating points we have to consider that pesky issue of precision.

As you can see from this example in figure 4-20, the mathematical boundary values will always include the graphical boundary values. To me, the three-value approach is wasteful of effort. We have enough to do already without creating more test values to cover, especially when those don't address any risks that haven't already been covered by other test values.

4.2.9 Boundary Value Exercise

A screen prototype for one screen of the HELLOCARMS system is shown in figure 4-21. This screen asks for two pieces of information:

■ Loan amount
■ Property value

For both fields, the system allows entry of whole dollar amounts only (no cents), and it rounds to the nearest $100.

Assume the following rules apply to loans:

- The minimum loan amount is $5,000.
- The maximum loan amount is $1,000,000.
- The minimum property value is $25,000.
- The maximum property value is $5,000,000.

Refer also to requirements specification elements 010-010-130 and 010-010-140 in the section "Functional System Requirements" in the HELLOCARMS system requirements document in Appendix B.

If the fields are valid, then the screen will be accepted. Either the Telephone Banker will continue with the application or the application will be transferred to a Senior Telephone Bank for further handling. If one or both fields are invalid, an error message is displayed.

The exercise consists of two parts:

1. Show the equivalence partitions and boundary values for each of the two fields, indicating valid and invalid members and the boundaries for those partitions.
2. Create test cases to cover these partitions and boundary values, keeping in mind the rules about combinations of valid and invalid members.

The answers to the two parts are shown on the next pages. You should review the answer to the first part (and, if necessary, revise your answer to the second part) before reviewing the answer to the second part.

4.2.10 Boundary Value Exercise Debrief

First, let's look at the equivalence partitions and boundary values, which are shown in figure 4-22.

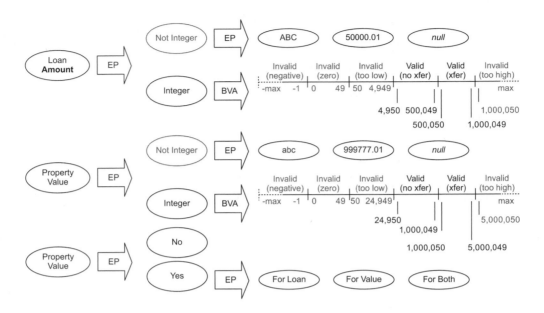

Figure 4–22   *Equivalence partitions and boundary values for amount, value, and transfer*

So, for the loan amount we can show the boundary values and equivalence partitions as follows:

#	Partition	Boundary Value
1	Letter: ABC	–
2	Decimal: 50,000.01	–
3	Null	–
4	Invalid (negative)	–max
5	Invalid (negative)	–1
6	Invalid (zero)	0
7	Invalid (zero)	49
8	Invalid (too low)	50
9	Invalid (too low)	4,949
10	Valid (no transfer)	4,950
11	Valid (no transfer)	500,049
12	Valid (transfer)	500,050
13	Valid (transfer)	1,000,049
14	Invalid (too high)	1,000,050
15	Invalid (too high)	max

For the property value, we can show the boundary values and equivalence partitions as they are shown here:

#	Partition	Boundary Value
1	Letter: abc	–
2	Decimal: 999,777.01	–
3	Null	–
4	Invalid (negative)	–max
5	Invalid (negative)	–1
6	Invalid (zero)	0
7	Invalid (zero)	49
8	Invalid (too low)	50
9	Invalid (too low)	24,949
10	Valid (no transfer)	24,950
11	Valid (no transfer)	1,000,049
12	Valid (transfer)	1,000,050
13	Valid (transfer)	5,000,049
14	Invalid (too high)	5,000,050
15	Invalid (too high)	max

For the transfer decision, we can show the equivalence partitions for the loan amount as follows:

#	Partition
1	No
2	Yes, for the loan amount
3	Yes, for the property value
4	Yes, for both

Now, let's create tests from these equivalence partitions and boundary values. I'll capture traceability information from the test case number back to the partitions or boundary values, and, as before, once I have a trace from each partition to a test case, I'm done—as long as I didn't combine invalids!

Inputs	1	2	3	4	5	6
Loan amount	4,950	500,050	500,049	1,000,049	ABC	50,000.01
Property value	24,950	1,000,049	1,000,050	5,000,049	100,000	200,000
Outputs						
Accept?	Y	Y	Y	Y	N	N
Transfer?	N	Y (loan)	Y (prop)	Y (both)	–	–

Inputs	7	8	9	10	11	12
Loan amount	null	100,000	200,000	300,000	–max	–1
Property value	300,000	abc	999,777.01	null	400,000	500,000
Outputs						
Accept?	N	N	N	N	N	N
Transfer?	–	–	–	–	–	–

Inputs	13	14	15	16	17	18
Loan amount	0	49	50	4,949	1,000,050	max
Property value	600,000	700,000	800,000	900,000	1,000,000	1,100,000
Outputs						
Accept?	N	N	N	N	N	N
Transfer?	–	–	–	–	–	–

Inputs	19	20	21	22	23	24
Loan amount	400,000	500,000	600,000	700,000	800,000	900,000
Property value	–max	–1	0	49	50	24,949
Outputs						
Accept?	N	N	N	N	N	N
Transfer?	–	–	–	–	–	–

Inputs	25	26	27	28	29	30
Loan amount	1,000,000	555,555				
Property value	5,000,050	max				
Outputs						
Accept?	N	N				
Transfer?	–	–				

Loan amount:

#	Partition	Boundary Value	Test Case
1	Letter: ABC	–	5
2	Decimal: 50,000.01	–	6
3	Null	–	7
4	Invalid (negative)	–max	11
5	Invalid (negative)	–1	12
6	Invalid (zero)	0	13
7	Invalid (zero)	49	14
8	Invalid (too low)	50	15
9	Invalid (too low)	4,949	16
10	Valid (no transfer)	4,950	1
11	Valid (no transfer)	500,049	3
12	Valid (transfer)	500,050	2
13	Valid (transfer)	1,000,049	4
14	Invalid (too high)	1,000,050	17
15	Invalid (too high)	max	18

Property value:

#	Partition	Boundary Value	Test Case
1	Letter: abc	–	8
2	Decimal: 999,777.01	–	9
3	Null	–	10
4	Invalid (negative)	–max	19
5	Invalid (negative)	–1	20
6	Invalid (zero)	0	21
7	Invalid (zero)	49	22
8	Invalid (too low)	50	23
9	Invalid (too low)	24,949	24
10	Valid (no transfer)	24,950	1
11	Valid (no transfer)	1,000,049	2
12	Valid (transfer)	1,000,050	3
13	Valid (transfer)	5,000,049	4
14	Invalid (too high)	5,000,050	25
15	Invalid (too high)	max	26

Transfer decision:

#	Partition	Test Case
1	No	1
2	Yes, for the loan amount	2
3	Yes, for the property value	3
4	Yes, for both	4

Notice that's there's another interesting combination related to the transfer decision that we covered in our tests. This was when the values were rejected as inputs, in which case we should not even be able to leave the screen, not to mention transfer the application. We did test with both loan amounts and property values that would have triggered a transfer had the other value been valid. I could have shown that as a third set of equivalence classes for the transfer decision.

> **ISTQB Glossary**
>
> cause-effect graph: A graphical representation of inputs and/or stimuli (causes) with their associated outputs (effects), which can be used to design test cases.
>
> **cause-effect graphing:** A black-box test design technique in which test cases are designed from cause-effect graphs.

4.2.11 Decision Tables

Equivalence partitioning and boundary value analysis are very useful techniques. They are especially useful, as we saw in the earlier parts of this section, when testing input field validation at the user interface. However, lots of testing that we do as test analysts involves testing the business logic that sits underneath the user interface. We can use boundary values and equivalence partitioning on business logic too, but three additional techniques, decision tables, use cases, and state-based testing, will often prove to be handier and more powerful. Let's start with decision tables. Conceptually, decision tables express the rules that govern handling of transactional situations. By their simple, concise structure, decision tables make it easy for us to design tests for those rules, usually at least one test per rule.

When I said "transactional situations," what I meant was those situations where the conditions—inputs, preconditions, etc.—that exist at a given moment in time for a single transaction are sufficient by themselves to determine the actions the system should take. If the conditions are not sufficient, but we must also refer to what conditions have existed in the past, then we'll want to use state-based testing, which we'll cover in a moment.

The underlying model is either a table—most typically—or a Boolean graph—less typically. Either way, the model connects combinations of conditions with the action or actions that should occur when each particular combination of conditions arises.

If the graph is used, this technique is also referred to as a cause-effect graph because that is the formal name of the graph. However, it's important to keep in mind that any given decision table can be converted into a cause-effect graph, and any given cause-effect graph can be converted into a decision table. So, which one you choose to use is up to you. I prefer decision tables, and they are more commonly used, so I'll focus on that here. However, I'll show you how the conversion can be done.

To create test cases from a decision table or a cause-effect graph, we are going to design test inputs that fulfill the conditions given. The test outputs will correspond to the action or actions given for that combination of conditions. During test execution, we check that the actual actions taken correspond to the expected actions.

We create enough test cases that every combination of conditions is covered by at least one test case. Oftentimes, we relax that coverage criterion to say that we must cover those combinations of conditions that can determine the action or actions. If that's a little confusing—which it might be, depending on how you prepared for the Foundation exam, as this isn't always explained properly in books and classes—the distinction I'm drawing will become clear to you when we talk about collapsed decision tables.

With a decision table, the coverage criterion boils down to an easy-to-remember rule of at least one test per column in the table. For cause-effect graphs, you have to generate a so-called "truth table" that contains all possible combinations of conditions and ensure that you have one test per row in the truth table.

So, what is our bug hypothesis with decision tables? What kind of bugs are we looking for? There are two. First, under some combination of conditions, the wrong action might occur. In other words, there is some action that the system is not to take under this combination of conditions, yet it does. Second, under some combination of conditions, the system might not take the right action. In other words, there is some action that the system is to take under this combination of conditions, yet it does not.

Earlier, we looked at the e-commerce section of the RBCS website, www.rbcs-us.com. Specifically, we worked through a complicated example of validating payment information, specifically credit card type, card number, card security code, expiration month, expiration year, and cardholder name. The objective was to apply boundary value analysis and equivalence partitioning to test the ability of the application to verify the payment information, as much as possible, before sending it to the server.

So, once that information goes to the credit card processing company for validation, how can we test that? Again, we could handle that with equivalence partitioning, but there are actually a whole set of conditions that determine this processing:

- Does the named person hold the credit card entered, and is the other information correct?
- Is the credit card still active or has it been cancelled?
- Is the person within or over their limit?
- Is the transaction coming from a normal or a suspicious location?

Conditions	1	2	3	4	5	6	7	8	9	10	11	12	13	14	15	16
Real account?	Y	Y	Y	Y	Y	Y	Y	Y	N	N	N	N	N	N	N	N
Active account?	Y	Y	Y	Y	N	N	N	N	Y	Y	Y	Y	N	N	N	N
Within limit?	Y	Y	N	N	Y	Y	N	N	Y	Y	N	N	Y	Y	N	N
Location okay?	Y	N	Y	N	Y	N	Y	N	Y	N	Y	N	Y	N	Y	N
Actions									?							
Approve?	Y	N	N	N	N	N	N	N	N	N	N	N	N	N	N	N
Call cardholder?	N	Y	Y	Y	N	Y	Y	Y	N	N	N	N	N	N	N	N
Call vendor?	N	N	N	N	Y	Y	Y	Y	Y	Y	Y	Y	Y	Y	Y	Y

Figure 4–23   *Decision table example (full)*

The decision table in figure 4-23 shows how these four conditions interact to determine which of the following three actions will occur:

- Should we approve the transaction?
- Should we call the cardholder (e.g., to warn them about a purchase from a strange place)?
- Should we call the vendor (e.g., to ask them to seize the cancelled card)?

Take a minute to study the table to see how this works. The conditions are listed at the top left of the table, and the actions at the bottom left. Each column to the right of this leftmost column contains a business rule. Each rules says, in essence, "Under this particular combination of conditions (shown at the top of the rule), carry out this particular combination of actions (shown at the bottom of the rule)."

Notice that the number of columns—i.e., the number of business rules—is equal to 2 (two) raised to the power of the number of conditions. In other words, 2 times 2 times 2 times 2, which is 16. When the conditions are strictly Boolean—true or false—and we're dealing with a full decision table (not a collapsed one), that will always be the case.

Did you notice how I populated the conditions? The topmost condition changes most slowly. Half of the columns are Yes, then half No. The condition under the topmost changes more quickly than the topmost but more slowly than all the others. The pattern is quarter Yes, then quarter No, then quarter Yes, then quarter No. Finally, for the bottommost condition, the alternation is Yes, No, Yes, No, Yes, etc. This pattern makes it easy to ensure you don't miss anything. If you start with the topmost condition, set the left half of the rule columns to Yes and the right half of the rule columns to No, then following the pattern I showed, you get to the bottom and the Yes, No, Yes, No, Yes, etc., pattern doesn't hold, you did something wrong.

Deriving test cases from this example is easy: Each column of the table produces a test case. When the time comes to run the tests, we'll create the conditions that are each test's inputs. We'll replace the "yes/no" conditions with actual input values for credit card number, security code, expiration date, and cardholder name, either during test design or perhaps even at test execution time. We'll verify the actions that are the test's expected results.

In some cases, we might generate more than one test case per column. I'll cover this possibility more later as we enlist our previous test techniques, equivalence partitioning and boundary value analysis, to extend decision table testing.

ISTQB Glossary

decision table testing: A black-box test design technique in which test cases are designed to execute the combinations of inputs and/or stimuli (causes) shown in a decision table.

4.2.12 Collapsing Columns in the Table

Notice that, in this case, some of the test cases don't make much sense. For example, how can the account not be real but yet active? How can the account not be real but within limit? This kind of situation is a hint that maybe we don't need all the columns in our decision table.

We can sometimes collapse the decision table, combining columns, to achieve a more concise—and in some cases sensible—decision table. In any situation where the value of one or more particular conditions can't affect the actions for two or more combinations of conditions, we can collapse the decision table.

This involves combining two or more columns where, as I said, one or more of the conditions don't affect the actions. As a hint, combinable columns are often *but not always* next to each other. You can at least start by looking at columns next to each other.

To combine two or more columns, look for two or more columns that result in the same combination of actions. Note that the actions must be the same for all of the actions in the table, not just some of them. In these columns, some of the conditions will be the same, and some will be different. The ones that are different obviously don't affect the outcome. We can replace the conditions that are different in those columns with dash. The dash usually means I don't care, it doesn't matter, or it can't happen given the other conditions.

Now, repeat this process until the only further columns that share the same combination of actions for all the actions in the table are ones where you would be combining a dash with a Yes or No value and thus wiping out an important distinction for cause of action. What I mean by this will be clear in the example I present in a moment, if it's not clear already.

Another word of caution at this point: Be careful when dealing with a table where more than one rule can apply at one single point in time. These tables have nonexclusive rules. We'll discuss that further later in this section.

Conditions	1	2	3	5	6	7	9
Real account?	Y	Y	Y	Y	Y	Y	N
Active account?	Y	Y	Y	N	N	N	–
Within limit?	Y	Y	N	Y	Y	N	–
Location okay?	Y	N	–	Y	N	–	–
Actions							
Approve?	Y	N	N	N	N	N	N
Call cardholder?	N	Y	Y	N	Y	Y	N
Call vendor?	N	N	N	Y	Y	Y	Y

Figure 4–24   *Decision table example (collapsed)*

Figure 4-24 shows the same decision table as before but collapsed to eliminate extraneous columns. Most notably, you can see that what were columns 9 through 16 in the original decision table collapsed into a single column.

I've kept the original column numbers for ease of comparison. Again, take a minute to study the table to see how I did this. Look carefully at columns 1, 2, and 3. Notice that we can't collapse 2 and 3 because that would result in "dash" for both "within limit" and "location okay." If you study this table or the full one, you can see that one of these conditions must *not* be true for the cardholder to receive a call. The collapse of rule 4 into rule 3 says that, if the card is over limit, the cardholder will be called regardless of location. The same logic applies to the collapse of rule 8 into rule 7.

Notice that the format is unchanged. The conditions are listed at the top left of the table and the actions at the bottom left. Each column to the right of this leftmost column contains a business rule. Each rules says, "Under this particular combination of conditions (shown at the top of the rule, some of which might not be applicable), carry out this particular combination of actions (shown at the bottom of the rule, all of which are fully specified)."

Notice that the number of columns is no longer equal to 2 raised to the power of the number of conditions. This makes sense, because otherwise no collapsing would have occurred. If you are concerned that you might miss something important, you can always start with the full decision table. A full table, because of the way you generate it, is guaranteed to have all the combinations of conditions. You can mathematically check if it does. Then, carefully collapse the table to reduce the number of test cases you create.

Also, notice that, when you collapse the table, that pleasant pattern of Yes and No columns present in the full table goes away. This is yet another reason to be very careful when collapsing the columns, because you can't count on the pattern or the mathematical formula to check your work.[3]

4.2.13 Cause-Effect Graphs

When you're collapsing a decision table, a cause-effect graph can be helpful to make sure you don't accidentally collapse columns you shouldn't. Some people like to use them for test design directly, but, as I mentioned earlier, I'm not too fond of trying to do that.

The process for creating a cause-effect graph from a decision table or decision table from a cause-effect graph is shown in figure 4-25. Let's start with the left-hand side.

To create a cause-effect graph from a decision table, first list all the conditions on the left of a blank page. Next, list all the actions on the right of a blank page. Obviously, if there are a lot of conditions and actions, this will be a big page of paper, but then your decision table would be big too.

Now, read the table to identify how combinations of conditions cause each action. Connect one or more conditions with each action using Boolean operators, which I'll show in figure 4-26. Repeat this process for all actions in the decision table.

---

3. You can find a discussion of decision tables, both full and collapsed, in both my book *Pragmatic Software Testing* and Lee Copeland's book *The Practitioner's Guide to Software Test Design*.

Table to graph	Graph to table
– List all the conditions on left of the blank page	– List all the conditions on the top left of decision table
– List all the actions on right of a blank page	– List all the actions on the bottom left of decision table
– Read the table to identify how combinations of conditions cause an action	– Generate all possible combinations of conditions
– Connect one or more conditions with each action using Boolean operators	– Determine actions taken/not taken for each combination using graph
– Repeat for all actions	– Collapse when complete if desired

Figure 4–25   *Converting to/from a cause-effect graph*

If you happen to be given a cause-effect graph and want to create a decision table, first list all the conditions on the top left of a "blank" decision table. Next, list all the actions on the bottom left of the decision table, under the conditions. Following the pattern shown earlier, generate all possible combinations of conditions. Now, referring to the cause-effect graph, determine the actions taken and not taken for each combination of conditions. Once the actions section is fully populated, you can collapse the table if you'd like.

In figure 4-26, you see the cause-effect graph that corresponds to the example decision tables we've looked at so far. You might ask, "Which one, the full or collapsed?" Both. The full and the collapsed are logically equivalent unless there's something wrong with the collapsed version.

At the bottom left of this figure, you see the legend that tells you how to read the operations. Let's go clockwise from the top left of the legend.

We have simple causality: If A is true, B will occur, or in other words, A causes B.

We have negation: When A is not true, B will occur, or not A causes B.

We have AND operation: When A1 and A2 are both true, B will occur, or A1 and A2 causes B.

We have OR operation: When A1 or A2 is true, B will occur, or A1 or A2 causes B.

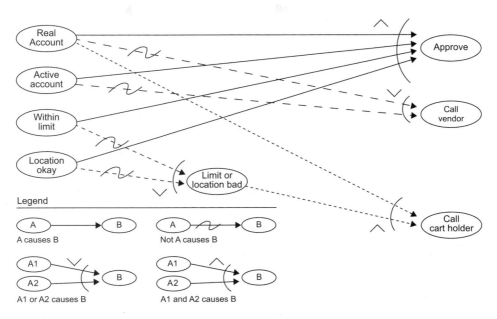

Figure 4–26   *Cause-effect graph example*

Let's look at the connection between conditions and actions. The solid causality lines, together with an AND operator, show that all four conditions must be met for the transaction to be approved.

The dashed causality lines, together with negation operators and an OR operator, show that, if the account is not real or the account is not active, we will call the vendor.

The dotted causality lines are a bit more complicated. First, we combine the "within limit" and "location okay" conditions, with negation operators and an OR operator, to create an intermediate condition of "Limit or location bad." Now, we combine that with the "real account" condition to say that if we have an over-limit or bad location situation, and the account is real, we will call the cardholder.

4.2.14 Combining Decision Table Testing with Other Techniques

Let's address an issue I brought up earlier, the possibility of multiple test cases per column in the decision table via the combination of equivalence partitioning with the decision table technique. Let's refer back to our example decision table shown in figure 4-23, specifically column 9.

We can apply equivalence partitioning to the question, "How many interesting—from a test point of view—ways are there to have an account not be real?" As you can see from figure 4-27, this could happen six potentially interesting ways:

- Card number and cardholder mismatch
- Card number and expiry mismatch
- Card number and CSC mismatch
- Two of the above mismatches (three possibilities)
- All three mismatches

So, there could be seven tests for that column.

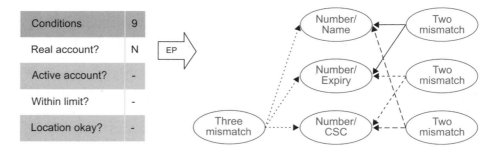

Figure 4–27   *Equivalence partitions and decision tables*

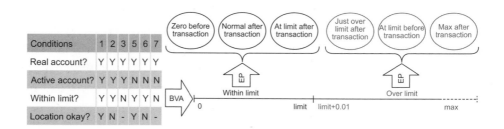

Figure 4–28   *Boundary values and decision tables*

How about boundary value analysis? Yes, that too can be applied to decision tables to find new and interesting tests. For example, how many interesting test values are there that relate to the credit limit?

As you can see from figure 4-28, equivalence partitioning and boundary value analysis show us six interesting possibilities:

- The account starts at zero balance.
- The account would be at a normal balance after transaction.
- The account would be exactly at the limit after the transaction.
- The account would be exactly over the limit after the transaction.
- The account was at exactly the limit before the transaction (which would ensure going over if the transaction concluded).
- The account would be at the maximum overdraft value after the transaction (which might not be possible).

Combining this with the decision table, we can see that would end up again with more "over limit" tests than we have columns—one more, to be exact—so we would increase the number of tests just slightly. In other words, there would be four within-limit tests and three over-limit tests. That's true unless you wanted to make sure that each within-limit equivalence class was represented in an approved transaction, in which case column 1 would go from one test to three.

4.2.15 Nonexclusive Rules in Decision Tables

Let's finish our discussion about decision tables by looking at the issue of non-exclusive rules I mentioned earlier.

Sometimes more than one rule can apply to a transaction. In figure 4-29, you see a table that shows the calculation of credit card fees. There are three conditions, and notice that zero, one, two, or all three of those conditions could be met in a given month. How does this situation affect testing? It complicates the testing a bit, but we can use a methodical approach and risk-based testing to avoid the major pitfalls.

Conditions	1	2	3
Foreign exchange?	Y	–	–
Balance forward?	–	Y	–
Late payment?	–	–	Y
Actions			
Exchange fee?	Y	–	–
Charge interest?	–	Y	–
Charge late fee?	–	–	Y

Figure 4–29   *Nonexclusive rules example*

To start with, test the decision table like a normal one, one rule at a time, making sure that no conditions not related to the rule you are testing are met. This allows you to test rules in isolation—just as you are forced to do in situations where the rules are exclusive.

Next, consider testing combinations of rules. Notice I said "consider," not "test all possible combinations of rules." You'll want to avoid combinatorial explosions, which is what happens when testers start to test combinations of factors without consideration of the value of those tests. Now, in this case, there are only 8 possible combinations—3 factors, 2 options for each factor, 2 times 2 times 2 is 8. However, if you have 6 factors with 5 options each, you now have 15,625 combinations.

One way to avoid combinatorial explosions is to identify the possible combinations and then use risk to weight those combinations. Try to get to the important combinations and don't worry about the rest.

Another way to avoid combinatorial explosions is to use techniques like classification trees and pairwise testing, which we'll cover later in this section.[4]

---

4. I cover the topic of decision tables with nonexclusive rules extensively in *Pragmatic Software Testing*.

4.2.16 **Decision Table Exercise**

During development, the HELLOCARMS project team adds a feature to the HELLOCARDS system. This feature allows the system to sell a life insurance policy to cover the amount of a home equity loan so that, should the borrower die, the policy will pay off the loan. The premium is calculated annually, at the beginning of each annual policy period and based on the loan balance at that time. The base annual premium will be $1 for $10,000 in loan balance. The insurance policy is not available for lines of credit or for reverse mortgages.

The system will increase the base premium by a certain percentage based on some basic physical and health questions that the Telephone Banker will ask during the interview.

A "Yes" answer to any of the following questions will trigger a 50 percent increase to the base premium:

1. Have you smoked cigarettes in the past 12 months?
2. Have you ever been diagnosed with cancer, diabetes, high cholesterol, high blood pressure, a heart disorder, or stroke?
3. Within the last 5 years, have you been hospitalized for more than 72 hours except for childbirth or broken bones?
4. Within the last 5 years, have you been completely disabled from work for a week or longer due to a single illness or injury?

The Telephone Banker will also ask about age, weight, and height. (Applicants cannot be under 18.) The weight and height are combined to calculate the body mass index (BMI). Based on that information, the Telephone Banker will apply table 4-1 to decide whether to increase the rate or even decline to issue the policy, based on possible weight-related illnesses in the person's future.

Table 4–1 *BMI/age policy increase*

Age	Body Mass Index (BMI)			
	<17	**34–36**	37–39	>39
18-39	Decline	75%	100%	Decline
40-59	Decline	50%	75%	Decline
>59	Decline	25%	50%	Decline

The increases are cumulative. For example, if the person has normal weight, smokes cigarettes, and has high blood pressure, the annual rate is increased from $1 per $10,000 to $2.25 per $10,000. If the person is a 45-year-old male diabetic with a body mass index of 39, the annual rate is increased from $1 per $10,000 to $2.625 per $10,000.

The exercise consists of four steps:

1. Create a decision table that shows the effect of the four health questions and the body mass index.
2. Translate the decision table into a cause-effect graph.
3. Show the boundary values for body mass index and age.
4. Create test cases to cover the decision table and the boundary values, keeping in mind the rules about testing nonexclusive rules.

The answers to the four parts are shown on the next pages. You should review the answer to each part (and, if necessary, revise your answer to the next parts before reviewing the answer to the next part.

Note: If you prefer, you can reverse the order of steps 1 and 2.

4.2.17 Decision Table Exercise Debrief

First, I created the decision table from the four health questions and the BMI/age table. The answer is shown in table 4-2. Note that the increases are shown in percentages.

Table 4–2 *Decision table for life insurance rate increases*

Conditions	1	2	3	4	5	6	7	8	9	10	11	12
Smoked?	Y	–	–	–	–	–	–	–	–	–	–	–
Diagnosed?	–	Y	–	–	–	–	–	–	–	–	–	–
Hospitalized?	–	–	Y	–	–	–	–	–	–	–	–	–
Disabled?	–	–	–	Y	–	–	–	–	–	–	–	–
BMI	–	–	–	–	34–36	34–36	34–36	37–39	37–39	37–39	<17	>39
Age	–	–	–	–	18–39	40–59	>59	18–39	40–59	>59	–	–
Actions												
Increase	50	50	50	50	75	50	25	100	75	50	–	–
Decline	–	–	–	–	–	–	–	–	–	–	Y	Y

It's important to notice that rules 1 through 4 are nonexclusive, though rules 5 through 12 are exclusive.

In addition, there is an implicit rule that the age must be greater than 17 or the applicant will be denied not only insurance, but the loan itself. I could have put that here in the decision table, but my focus is primarily on testing business functionality, not input validation. I'll cover those tests with boundary values.

Next, I created the cause-effect graph, shown in figure 4-30.

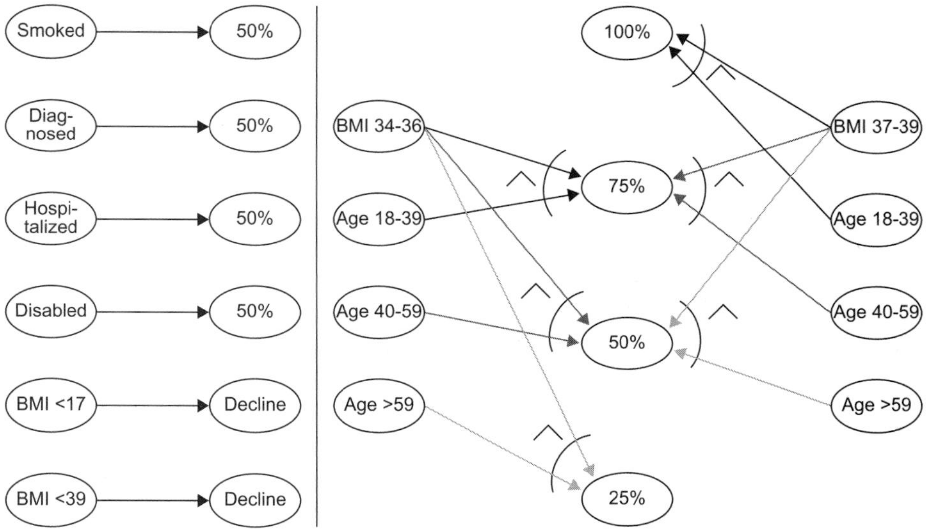

Figure 4–30   *Life insurance cause-effect graph*

Note on the left side of the graph that each nonexclusive rule is shown on its own, not as combining with an OR operator on the 50% action. Why? Because if I had shown it as combining with an OR operator, then the cumulative increase would not occur. I've also shown the two BMI conditions that can result in a decline action here.

Now, let's look at the boundary values for body mass index and age, shown in figure 4-31.

Three important testing notes relate to the body mass index. First, the body mass index is not entered directly but rather by entering height and weight. Depending on the range and precision of these two fields, there could be dozens

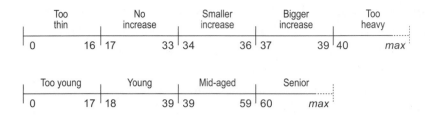

Figure 4–31   *BMI and age boundary values*

of ways to enter a given body mass index. Second, the maximum body mass index is achieved by entering the smallest possible height and the largest possible weight. Third, we would need to separately understand the boundary values for these two fields and make sure those were tested properly.

An important testing note relates to the age. You can see that I omitted equivalence classes related to invalid ages, such as negative ages and non integer input for ages. Again, my idea is that we would need to separately test the input field validation. Here, my focus is on testing business logic.

Finally, for both fields, I omit any attempt to figure out the maximums. Either someone will give me a requirements specification that tells me that during test design, or I'll try to ascertain it empirically during test execution.

So, for the BMI, we can show the boundary values and equivalence partitions as follows:

#	Partition	Boundary Value
1	Too thin	0
2	Too thin	16
3	No increase	17
4	No increase	33
5	Smaller increase	34
6	Smaller increase	36
7	Bigger increase	37
8	Bigger increase	39
9	Too heavy	40
10	Too heavy	max

So, for the age, we can show the boundary values and equivalence partitions as shown here:

#	Partition	Boundary Value
1	Too young	0
2	Too young	17
3	Young	18
4	Young	39
5	Mid-aged	40
6	Mid-aged	59
7	Senior	60
8	Senior	max

Finally, here are the test cases. They are much like the decision table, but note that I have shown the rate (in dollars per $10,000 of loan balance) rather than the percentage increase.

	Test case											
Conditions	1	2	3	4	5	6	7	8	9	10	11	12
Smoked?	Y	N	N	N	N	N	N	N	N	N	N	N
Diagnosed?	N	Y	N	N	N	N	N	N	N	N	N	N
Hospitalized?	N	N	Y	N	N	N	N	N	N	N	N	N
Disabled?	N	N	N	Y	N	N	N	N	N	N	N	N
BMI	N	N	N	N	34	36	35	34	36	35	37	39
Age	N	N	N	N	18	39	40	59	60	max	20	30
Actions												
Rate	1.5	1.5	1.5	1.5	1.75	1.75	1.5	1.5	1.25	1.25	2	2
Decline	N	N	N	N	N	N	N	N	N	N	N	N

	Test case											
Conditions	13	14	15	16	17	18	19	20	21	22	23	24
Smoked?	N	N	N	N	N	N	N	N	N	N	N	N
Diagnosed?	N	N	N	N	N	N	N	N	N	N	N	N
Hospitalized?	N	N	N	N	N	N	N	N	N	N	N	N
Disabled?	N	N	N	N	N	N	N	N	N	N	N	N
BMI	38	37	39	38	16	40	0	max	17	33	20	30
Age	45	55	65	75	35	50	25	70	37	47	0	17
Actions												
Rate	1.75	1.75	1.50	1.50	N/A	N/A	N/A	N/A	1	1	N/A	N/A
Decline	N	N	N	N	Y	Y	Y	Y	N	N	Y	Y

	Test case											
Conditions	25	26	27	28	29	30	31	32	33	34	35	36
Smoked?	Y	N	N	N	Y							
Diagnosed?	N	Y	N	N	Y							
Hospitalized?	N	N	Y	N	Y							
Disabled?	N	N	N	Y	Y							
BMI	35	36	34	38	37							
Age	20	50	70	30	35							
Actions												
Rate	2.625	2.25	1.875	3	10.125							
Decline	N	N	N	N	N							

Notice my approach to testing the nonexclusive rules. First, I tested every rule, exclusive and nonexclusive, in isolation. Then, I tested the remaining untested boundary values. Next, I tested combinations of only one nonexclusive rule with one exclusive rule, making sure each nonexclusive rule had been tested once in combination (but not all the exclusive rules were tested in combination). Finally, I tested a combination of all four nonexclusive rules with one exclusive rule. I did not use combinations with the "decline" rules because presumably there's no way to check if the increase was correctly calculated.

You might also have noticed that I managed to sneak in covering the minimum and maximum increases. However, I probably didn't cover every possible increase. Because I didn't test every possible pair, every possible triple, or every possible quadruple combination of rules, I certainly didn't test every way an increase could be calculated by that table. I'll spend more time on that topic in the section on classification trees and pairwise testing.

For the decision table and the boundary values, I've captured test coverage in the following tables, to make sure I missed nothing. The following shows decision table coverage, using three coverage metrics.

Conditions	1	2	3	4	5	6	7	8	9	10	11	12
Smoked?	Y	–	–	–	–	–	–	–	–	–	–	–
Diagnosed?	–	Y	–	–	–	–	–	–	–	–	–	–
Hospitalized?	–	–	Y	–	–	–	–	–	–	–	–	–
Disabled?	–	–	–	Y	–	–	–	–	–	–	–	–
BMI	–	–	–	–	34–36	34–36	34–36	37–39	37–39	37–39	<17	>39
Age	–	–	–	–	18–39	40–59	>59	18–39	40–59	>59	–	–
Actions												
Increase	50	50	50	50	75	50	25	100	75	50	–	–
Decline	–	–	–	–	–	–	–	–	–	–	Y	Y
Single Rule Coverage												
Test case(s)	1	2	3	4	5, 6	7, 8	9, 10	11, 12	13, 14	15, 16	17,19	18,20
Pairs of Rules Coverage												
Test case(s)	25	26	27	28	25	26	27	28				
Maximum Combination of Rules Coverage												
Test case(s)	29	29	29	29				29				

The following shows BMI coverage:

#	Partition	Boundary Value	Test Case
1	Too thin	0	19
2	Too thin	16	17
3	No increase	17	21
4	No increase	33	22
5	Smaller increase	34	5
6	Smaller increase	36	6
7	Bigger increase	37	11
8	Bigger increase	39	12
9	Too heavy	40	18
10	Too heavy	max	20

The following shows age coverage:

#	Partition	Boundary Value	Test Case
1	Too young	0	23
2	Too young	17	24
3	Young	18	5
4	Young	39	6
5	Mid-aged	39	7
6	Mid-aged	59	8
7	Senior	60	9
8	Senior	max	10

4.2.18 Use Cases

Okay, we just covered decision tables as a powerful technique for testing the business logic of a system. I mentioned that we would look at two other techniques, use cases and state-based testing, for that same purpose. Let's move on to use cases in this subsection.

Conceptually, use case testing is a way to ensure that we have tested typical and exceptional workflows and scenarios for the system, from the point of view

> **ISTQB Glossary**
>
> **use case testing:** A black-box test design technique in which test cases are designed to execute user scenarios.
>
> use case: A sequence of transactions in a dialogue between a user and the system with a tangible result.

of the various actors who directly interact with the system and from the point of view of the various stakeholders who indirectly interact with the system. If we (as test analysts) receive use cases from business analysts or system designers, then these can serve as convenient frameworks for creating test cases.

Remember that with decision tables we were focused on transactional situations, where the conditions—inputs, preconditions, and so forth—that exist at a given moment in time for a single transaction are sufficient by themselves to determine the actions the system should take. Use cases aren't quite as rigid on this point, but generally, the assumption is that the typical workflows are independent of each other. An exceptional workflow occurs when a typical workflow can't occur, but usually we have independency from one workflow to the next. This is ensured—at least for formal use cases—by clearly defined preconditions and postconditions, which guarantee that certain things are true at the beginning and end of the workflow. This acts to insulate one workflow from the next. Again, if we have heavy interaction of past events and conditions with the way current events and conditions should be handled, we'll want to use state-based testing.

The model is less formal than what we've seen with equivalence partitions, boundary values, and decision tables. Indeed, the concept of a "use case" itself can vary considerably in formality and presentation. The basic idea is that we have some numbered (or at least sequential) list of steps that describes how an actor interacts with the system. The steps can be shown in text or as part of a flowchart.

The use case should also show the results obtained at the end of that sequence of steps. The results obtained should benefit some party, either the actor interacting directly with the system or some other stakeholder who indirectly receives the value of the results.

At the very least, the set of steps should show a typical workflow, the normal processing. This normal processing is sometimes called the primary scenario, the normal course, the basic course, the main course, the normal flow, or the happy path. However, because things are not always happy, the set of steps should also show abnormal processing, sometimes called exceptions, exceptional processing, or alternative courses.

Approaches to documenting use cases that are more formal cover not only typical and exceptional workflows, but also explicit identification of the actor, the preconditions, the postconditions, the priority, the frequency of use, special requirements, assumptions, and potentially more. The formal approach might also entail the creation of a use case diagram that shows all the actors, all the use cases, and the relationship between the actors and the use cases.

Now, an assumption that I'm making here—in fact, it's an assumption implicitly embedded within the ISTQB syllabi—is that you are going to receive use cases, not create them. If you look at both the Advanced and Foundation syllabi, they talk about use cases as something that test analysts receive, upon which they base their tests. So rather than try to cover the entire gamut of use case variation that might exist in the wild and wooly world of software development, I'm going to talk about using basic, informal use cases for test design and about using more formalized use cases for test design and leave out too much discussion about variations.

Assuming we receive a use case, how do we derive tests? Well, at the very least, we should create a test for every workflow, including both the typical and exceptional workflows. If the exceptional workflows were omitted, then you'll need to figure those out, possibly from requirements or some other source. Failing to test exceptions is a common testing mistake when using informal use cases.

Creating tests can involve applying equivalence partitioning and boundary value analysis along the way. In fact, if you find a situation where combinations of conditions determine actions, then you might have found an embedded, implied decision table. Covering the partitions, boundaries, and business rules you discover in the use case might result in 2, 5, 10, 20, or more test cases per workflow, when you're all done.

Remember that I said that a use case has a tangible result. Part of evaluating the results of the test is verifying that result. That's above and beyond verifying proper screens, messages, input validation, and the like as you proceed through the workflow.

Note the coverage criterion implied: at least one test per workflow, including both typical and exceptional workflows. That's not a formal criterion, but it's a good one to remember as a rule of thumb.

What is our underlying bug hypothesis? Remember in decision tables we were looking for combinations of conditions that result in the wrong action occurring or the right action not occurring. With use cases, we're a bit more coarse-grained. Here, we are looking for a situation where the system interacts improperly with the user or delivers an improper result.

E-commerce purchase: Normal workflow

1. Customer places one or more Items in shopping cart
2. Customer selects checkout
3. System gathers address, payment, and shipping information from Customer
4. System displays all information for User confirmation
5. User confirms order to System for delivery

Exceptions
- Customer attempts to checkout with empty shopping cart; System gives error message
- Customer provides invalid address, paymeny, or shipping information; System gives error messages as appropriate
- Customer abandons transaction before or during checkout; System logs Customer out after 10 minutes of inactivity

---

Figure 4–32   *Informal use case example*

In figure 4-32, we see an example of an informal use case describing purchases from an e-commerce site, like the rbcs-us.com example shown for decision tables.

At the top, we have the website purchase normal workflow. This is the happy path.

1. Customer places one or more Items in shopping cart.
2. Customer selects checkout.
3. System gathers address, payment, and shipping information from Customer.
4. System displays all information for User confirmation.
5. User confirms order to System for delivery.

Note that the final result is that the order is in the system for delivery. Presumably another use case having to do with order fulfillment will describe how this order ends up arriving at the customer's home or place of business.

We also see some exception workflows defined.

- For one thing, the Customer might attempt to check out with an empty shopping cart. In that case, the System gives an error message.
- For another thing, the Customer might provide an invalid address, payment, or shipping information. On each screen—if we're following the typical e-commerce flow—the System gives error messages as appropriate and blocks any further processing until the errors are resolved.
- Finally, the Customer might abandon the transaction before or during checkout. To handle this, the System logs the Customer out after 10 minutes of inactivity.

Now, let's look at deriving tests for this use case. In figure 4-33, you see the body of the test procedure to cover the typical workflow. (For brevity's sake, I've left off the typical header and footer information found on a test procedure.)

As you can see, each step in the workflow has mapped into a step in the test procedure. You can also see that I did some equivalence partitioning and boundary value analysis on the number of items, the payment type, and the delivery address. Because all of these selections are valid, I've combined them. Note the space-saving approach of describing how to repeat the core steps of the test procedure with variations, rather than a complete restatement of the test procedure, at the bottom.

#	Test Step	Expected Result
1	Place 1 item in cart	Item in cart
2	Click checkout	Checkout screen
3	Input valid US address, valid payment using American Express, and valid shipping method information	Each screen displays correctly and valid inputs are accepted
4	Verify order information	Shown as entered
5	Confirm order	Order in system
6	Repeat steps 1-5, but place 2 items in cart, and pay with Visa, and ship international	As shown in 1-5
7	Repeat steps 1-5, but place the maximum number of items in cart and pay with Mastercard	As shown in 1-5
8	Repeat steps 1-5, but pay with Discover	As shown in 1-5

Figure 4–33   *Deriving tests example (typical)*

#	Test Step	Expected Result
1	Do not place any items in cart	Cart empty
2	Click checkout	Error message
3	Place item in cart, click checkout, enter invalid address, then invalid payment, then invalid shipping information	Error messages, can't proceed to next screen until resolved
4	Verify order information	Shown as entered
5	Confirm order	Order in system
6	Repeat steps 1-3, but stop activity and abandon transaction after placing item in cart	User logged out exactly 10 minutes after last activity
7	Repeat steps 1-3, but stop activity and abandon transaction on each screen	As shown in 6
8	Repeat steps 1-4; do not confirm order	As shown in 6

Figure 4–34   *Deriving tests example (exception)*

> **ISTQB Glossary**
>
> high-level (or logical) test case: A test case without concrete (implementation level) values for input data and expected results. Logical operators are used; instances of the actual values are not yet defined and/or available.
>
> low-level (or concrete) test case: A test case with concrete (implementation level) values for input data and expected results. Logical operators from high-level test cases are replaced by actual values that correspond to the objectives of the logical operators.

In figure 4-34, you see the body of the test procedure to cover the exception flows. You can see that I use equivalence partitioning on the points at which the customer could abandon a transaction.

This is a good point at which to bring up an important distinction, that between logical and concrete test cases. For the ISTQB exam, you'll want to make sure you know the glossary definitions for these terms. For our purposes here, we can say that a logical or high-level test case describes the test conditions and results. A concrete or low-level test case gives the input data to create the test conditions and the output data observed in the results.

As you just saw in figure 4-33 and figure 4-34, you can easily translate a use case into one or more logical test cases. However, translation of the logical test case into concrete test cases can require additional documentation. For example, what was the maximum number of items we could put in the shopping cart? We would need some further information, ideally a requirements specification, to know that. What items *can* we put in shopping cart? Some description of the store inventory is needed.

Is it cheating to define logical test cases rather than concrete ones? No, absolutely not. However, notice that, at some point, a test case must become concrete. You have to enter specific inputs. You have to verify specific outputs. This translation from logical test case to concrete test case is considered an implementation activity in the ISTQB fundamental test process. If you choose to leave implementation for the testers to handle during test execution, that's fine, but you'll need to make sure that adequate information is at hand during test execution to do so. Otherwise, you risk delays.

So, what's different or additional in a formal use case? Usually, a formal use case contains more information than an informal one. Here, you can see some of the typical elements of a formal use case:

- ID—some use case identifier number
- Name—a short name, like E-commerce Purchase
- Actor—the actor, such as Customer
- Description—a short description of the use case
- Priority—the priority, from an implementation point of view
- Frequency of use—how often this will occur
- Preconditions—what must be true to start the use case normally
- Typical workflow—often like the informal use case, but sometimes broken into two columns, one for the actor actions and one for the system response
- Exception workflows—one for each exception, often also with actor action and system response columns
- Postconditions—what should be true about the state of the system after the use case completes normally

Notice that you can use some of this information as a test analyst. Some, like the priority and frequency of use, you might not use, except during the risk analysis process. Also, notice that the breakdown on the workflows, especially the exception workflows, is finer-grained, so your test traceability can be finer-grained too.

Figure 4-35 shows the header information on a formal version of the informal use case we saw earlier. Notice that some of the steps of the informal use case became preconditions. This means that the shopping portion of the use case would become its own use case, allowing this use case to focus entirely on the purchase aspects of the e-commerce site. Notice also that we didn't know about that "logged in" requirement before. That's important information for our testing.

Figure 4-36 shows the main body of the formal use case, the normal workflow and the three exceptions. Notice the normal workflow is a bit shorter now because some of its steps became preconditions. Also, each exception is its own row in the table. Finally, notice that the postcondition is true only if the normal workflow ultimately completed.

ID	02.001
Name	E-commerce Purchase
Actor	Customer
Description	Allow customer to complete a transaction by purchasing the item(s) in her shopping cart
Priority	Very high
Frequency of use	25% of customers, up to 1,000 customers per day
Preconditions	1. One or more items in shopping cart 2. Customer is logged in 3. Customer has clicked on checkout

Figure 4–35   *Formal use case example (Part 1)*

Typical workflow	1. System gathers address, payment, and shipping information from Customer 2. System displays all information for User confirmation 3. User confirms order to System for delivery
Exception 1	Customer attempts to checkout with empty shopping cart System gives error message
Exception 2	Customer provides invalid address, payment, or shipping information System gives error messages as appropriate
Exception 3	Customer abandons transaction before or during checkout System logs Customer our after 10 minutes of inactivity
Postconditions	Order is active in system

Figure 4–36   *Formal use case example (part 2)*

4.2.19 Use Case Exercise

Refer to section 001 of the HELLOCARMS system requirements document. Assume that the life insurance discussed in the previous exercise is offered during step 5 of that use case.

The exercise consists of two steps:

1. Translate the informal use case given in section 001 into a slightly more formal version that shows the Actor, the Preconditions, the Exception Workflows, and the Postconditions. Include the insurance offering.
2. Create logical test cases in a test procedure to cover the use case, applying equivalence partitioning and boundary value analysis as appropriate.

The answers to the two parts are shown on the next pages. You should review the answer to the first part (and, if necessary, revise your answer to the second part) before reviewing the answer to the second part.

4.2.20 Use Case Exercise Debrief

For ease of reference, here is the informal use case from section 001 again.

The following informal use case applies for typical transactions in the HELLO-CARMS System:

1. A Globobank Telephone Banker in a Globobank Call Center receives a phone call from a Customer.
2. The Telephone Banker interviews the Customer, entering information into the HELLOCARMS System through a Web browser interface on their Desktop. If the Customer is requesting a large loan or borrowing against a high-value property, the Telephone Banker escalates the application to a Senior Telephone Banker who decides whether to proceed with the application.
3. Once the Telephone Banker has gathered the information from the Customer, the HELLOCARMS System determines the creditworthiness of the Customer using the Scoring Mainframe.
4. Based on all of the Customer information, the HELLOCARMS System displays various Home Equity Products (if any) that the Telephone Banker can offer to the customer.

5. If the Customer chooses one of these Products, the Telephone Banker will conditionally confirm the Product.

6. The interview ends. The Telephone Banker directs the HELLOCARMS System to transmit the loan information to the Loan Document Printing System (LoDoPS) in the Los Angeles Datacenter for origination.

7. The HELLOCARMS system receives an update from the LoDoPS System when the following events occur:

   a. LoDoPS system sends documents to customer.

   b. Globobank Loan Servicing Center receives signed documents from customer.

   c. Globobank Loan Servicing Center sends check or other materials as appropriate to the Customer's product selection.

Notice that step 7 actually belongs in another use case, because, at the end of step 6, a tangible, useful result has been produced, namely the submitted application.

So, I've moved steps 1 through 6 into a semiformal use case, shown in table 4-3. I've added the life insurance offering in step 5.

Table 4–3 *Semiformal HELLOCARMS use case*

Actor	Telephone Banker
Preconditions	The Globobank Telephone Banker is logged into HELLOCARMS system.
Normal Workflow	1 The Telephone Banker receives a phone call from a Customer. 2 The Telephone Banker interviews the Customer, entering information into the HELLOCARMS System through a Web browser interface on their Desktop. 3 Once the Telephone Banker has gathered the information from the Customer, the HELLOCARMS System determines the creditworthiness of the Customer using the Scoring Mainframe. 4 Based on all of the Customer information, the HELLOCARMS System displays various Home Equity Products that the Telephone Banker can offer to the customer. 5 If the Customer chooses one of these Products, the Telephone Banker will conditionally confirm the Product. 6 The interview ends. The Telephone Banker directs the HELLOCARMS System to transmit the loan information to the Loan Document Printing System (LoDoPS) in the Los Angeles Datacenter for origination.

Table continues

Table 4–3 *Semiformal HELLOCARMS use case (continued)*

Exception Workflow 1	During step 2 of the normal workflow, if the Customer is requesting a large loan or borrowing against a high-value property, the Telephone Banker escalates the application to a Senior Telephone Banker who decides whether to proceed with the application. If the decision is to proceed, then the Telephone Banker completes the remainder of step 2 and proceeds normally. If the decision is not to proceed, the Telephone Banker informs the Customer that the application is declined and the interview ends.
Exception Workflow 2	During step 4 of the normal workflow, if the System does not display any Home Equity Products as available, the Telephone Banker informs the Customer that the application is declined and the interview ends.

Exception Workflow 3	During step 5 of the normal workflow, if the Product chosen by the Customer was a Home Equity Loan, the Telephone Banker offers the Customer the option of applying for life insurance to cover the loan. If the Customer wants to apply, the following steps occur:
	1 The Telephone Banker interviews the Customer, entering health information into the HELLOCARMS System through a Web browser interface on their Desktop.
	2 The HELLOCARMS System processes the information as described in the previous exercise. One of two outcomes will occur:
	   a The HELLOCARMS System declines to offer insurance based on the health information given. The Telephone Banker informs the Customer that the insurance application was denied. This exception workflow is over and processing returns to step 5.
	   b The HELLOCARMS System offers insurance at a rate based on the loan size and the health information given. The Telephone Banker informs the Customer of the offer.
	3 The Customer makes one of two decisions:
	   a Accept the offer. The Telephone Banker makes the life insurance purchase part of the overall application. This exception workflow is over and processing returns to step 5.
	   b Reject the offer. The Telephone Banker excludes the life insurance purchase from the overall application. This exception workflow is over and processing returns to step 5.

Exception Workflow 4	During any of steps 1 through 5 of the normal workflow, if the Customer chooses to end the interview without continuing the process or selecting a product, the application is cancelled and the interview ends.

Table continues

Table 4–3 *Semiformal HELLOCARMS use case (continued)*

Exception Workflow 5	If no Telephone Banker is logged into the system (e.g., because the system is down) and step 1 of the normal workflow begins, the following steps occur:
	1 The Telephone Banker continues to take the information manually. At the end of the interview, the Telephone Banker informs the Customer that a Telephone Banker will call back shortly with the decision on the application.
	2 Once a Telephone Banker is logged into the system, the application information is entered into HELLOCARMS and normal processing resumes at step 2.
	3 The Telephone Banker calls the Customer once one of the following outcomes has occurred:
	   a Step 5 of normal processing is reached. Processing continues at step 5.
	   b At step 2 of normal processing, exception workflow 1 was triggered. Processing continues at step 2.
	   c At step 4 of normal processing, exception workflow 2 was triggered. No processing remains to be done.

Postconditions	Loan application is in LoDoPS system for origination.

Now I'll create logical test cases in a test procedure to cover this use case. I'm going to following the pattern I used in the course, where I broke the test procedure into a normal workflow procedure (see table 4-2) and an exception procedure for each exception workflow (see table 4-3, table 4-4, table 4-5, table 4-6, and table 4-7).

Table 4–4 *Normal workflow test procedure*

#	Test Step	Expected Results
1	Enter a Home Equity Loan application for a creditworthy customer into the HELLOCARMS System.	Validate screens and messages.
2	Submit the Customer information for processing of the creditworthiness via the Scoring Mainframe.	Verify communication with Scoring Mainframe.
3	Check the various Home Equity Products that can be offered.	Verify appropriate products offered. Validate screen and messages.
4	Choose the Home Equity Loan.	Validate screens and messages.
5	Direct the HELLOCARMS System to transmit the loan information to the Loan Document Printing System (LoDoPS).	Verify communication with LoDoPS.
6	Repeat steps 1–5, but select a home equity line of credit in step 4.	As shown in steps 1–5.
7	Repeat steps 1–5, but select a reverse mortgage in step 4.	As shown in steps 1–5.

Table 4–5 *Exception 1 workflow test procedure*

#	Test Step	Expected Results
1	Enter a Home Equity Loan application for a creditworthy customer into the HELLOCARMS System.	Validate screens and messages.
2	When entering the loan amount, enter a requested loan amount that exceeds the maximum.	Verify escalation screens.
3	Enter the "Proceed" authorization code.	Verify processing resumes at step 2 of the normal workflow.
4	Complete the normal workflow.	Verify loan is properly submitted to LoDoPS.
5	Repeat steps 1–2, but enter a property value that exceeds the maximum, and in step 3 enter the "Decline" authorization code.	Verify that the Decline script shows and that this application is terminated.
6	Repeat steps 1–4, but enter a property value and a loan amount that both exceed the maximum.	As shown in steps 1–4.

Table 4–6 *Exception 2 workflow test procedure*

#	Test Step	Expected Results
1	Enter a Home Equity Loan application for a non-creditworthy customer into the HELLOCARMS System.	Validate screens and messages.
2	Submit the Customer information for processing of the creditworthiness via the Scoring Mainframe.	Verify communication with Scoring Mainframe.
3	Check the various Home Equity Products that can be offered.	Verify no products offered. Validate screen and messages. Verify that the Decline script shows and that this application is terminated.

Table 4–7 *Exception 3 workflow test procedure*

#	Test Step	Expected Results
1	Enter a Home Equity Loan application for a creditworthy and insurance-qualified customer into the HELLOCARMS System.	Validate screens and messages.
2	Submit the Customer information for processing of the creditworthiness via the Scoring Mainframe.	Verify communication with Scoring Mainframe.
3	Check the various Home Equity Products that can be offered. Select the Home Equity Loan. Indicate Customer wants to apply for insurance.	Verify appropriate products offered. Validate screen and messages.
4	Enter Customer health information.	Validate screens and messages.
5	Check insurance offer, accept the offer, and complete the application, including sending to LoDoPS.	Verify amount of offer. Verify that life insurance application is included in LoDoPS information.
6	Repeat steps 1–5, but decline the offer.	As shown in steps 1–5, but verify that life insurance application is not included in LoDoPS information.
7	Repeat steps 1–5, but use a non insurance-qualified customer.	As shown in steps 1–5, but verify that no life insurance is offered and that no life insurance application is included in LoDoPS information.

Table 4–8 *Exception 4 workflow test procedure*

#	Test Step	Expected Results
1	Enter a Home Equity Loan application for a creditworthy customer into the HELLOCARMS System.	Validate screens and messages.
2	Submit the Customer information for processing of the creditworthiness via the Scoring Mainframe.	Verify communication with Scoring Mainframe.
3	Check the various Home Equity Products that can be offered.	Verify appropriate products offered. Validate screen and messages.
4	Indicate that the Customer cancelled the application.	Validate the screen that displays. Verify that the application is cancelled.
5	Repeat steps 1–2, but cancel on the penultimate screen.	As shown in step 4.
6	Repeat step 5, canceling on each of the possible screens including the first screen.	As shown in steps 1–5.
7	Repeat steps 1–5, but select a home equity line of credit in step 4.	As shown in steps 1–5.

Table 4–9 *Exception 5 workflow test procedure*

#	Test Step	Expected Results
1	Activate the Manual Application Entry mode. Enter a Home Equity Loan application for a normal loan amount and property value and a creditworthy Customer into the HELLOCARMS System.	Validate screens and messages. Verify directive to call Customer at step 5 of the normal workflow. Verify normal processing and submission from that point.
2	Repeat step 1, but using a high-loan-amount application. Enter the "Proceed" authorization code when requested.	Validate screens and messages. Verify directive to call Customer at step 2 of the normal workflow. Verify normal processing and submission from that point.
3	Repeat step 1, but using a non creditworthy Customer.	Validate screens and messages. Verify directive to call Customer at step 4 of the normal workflow. Verify that application is declined.

Notice that I equivalence partitioned the Customer as follows:

- Creditworthy
- Not creditworthy

You might also have decided to use boundary value analysis here, based on credit scores, to test Customers who were just barely creditworthy and those who were almost creditworthy.

I equivalence partitioned the Products as follows:

- Home equity loan
- Home equity line of credit
- Reverse mortgage

Again, you might have decided to use boundary value analysis to apply for the largest and smallest possible product in each category.

I equivalence partitioned the Senior Telephone Banker decline as follows:

- Property value too high
- Loan too high

I would also want to test the boundary values and equivalence partitions previously identified for this situation in the second exercise for this section.

4.2.21　State-Based Testing and State Transition Diagrams

I said that after our discussion of equivalence partitioning and boundary value analysis, we would cover three techniques that would prove useful for testing business logic, often more useful than equivalence partitioning and boundary value analysis. We covered decision tables, which are best in transactional testing situations. We covered use cases, where preconditions and postconditions help to insulate one workflow from the previous workflow and the next workflow.

Now we move on to state-based testing. State-based testing is ideal when we have sequences of events that occur and conditions that apply to those events and the proper handling of a particular event/condition situation depends on the events and conditions that have occurred in the past. In some cases, the sequences of events can be potentially infinite, which of course exceeds our testing capabilities, but we want to have a test design technique that allows us to handle arbitrarily long sequences of events.

The underlying model is a state transition diagram or table. The diagram or table connects beginning states, events, and conditions with resulting states and actions.

In other words, some status quo prevailed and the system was in a current state. Then some event occurs, some event that the system must handle. The handling of that event might be influenced by one or more conditions. The event/condition combination triggers a state transition, either from the current state to a new state or from the current state back to the current state again. In the course of the transition, the system takes one or more actions.

Given this model, we generate tests that traverse the states and transitions. The inputs trigger events and create conditions, while the expected results of the test are the new states and actions taken by the system.

Various coverage criteria apply for state-based testing. The weakest criterion requires that the tests visit every state and traverse every transition. We can apply this criterion to state transition diagrams. A higher coverage criterion is that at least one test cover every row in a state transition table. Achieving

> **ISTQB Glossary**
>
> **state transition testing:** A black-box test design technique in which test cases are designed to execute valid and invalid state transitions.

"every-row" coverage will achieve "every state and transition" coverage, which is why I said it was a high coverage criterion.

Another potentially higher coverage criterion requires that at least one test cover each transition sequence of N or less length. The N can be 1, 2, 3, 4, or higher. This is called alternatively *Chow's switch coverage*—after Professor Chow, who developed it—or *N-1 switch coverage*, after the level given to the degree of coverage. If you cover all transitions of length one, then N-1 switch coverage means 0-switch coverage. Notice that this is the same as the lowest level of coverage discussed. If you cover all transitions of length one and two, then N-1 switch coverage means 1-switch coverage. This is a higher level of coverage than the lowest level, of course.

Now, 1-switch coverage is not necessarily a higher level of coverage than "every-row" coverage. This is because the state transition table forces testing of state and event/condition combinations that do not occur in the state-transition diagram. The so-called "switches" in N-1 switch coverage are derived from the state transition diagram, not the state transition table.

You might find all this a bit confusing if you're fuzzy on the test design material covered at the Foundation level. This is a common problem for those who took "brain cram" courses to prepare for the Foundation exam. Don't worry, though, it will be clear to you shortly.

So, what is the bug hypothesis in state-based testing? We're looking for situations where the wrong action or the wrong new state occurs in response to a particular event under a given set of conditions based on the history of event/condition combinations so far.

Figure 4-37 shows the state transition diagram for shopping and buying items online from an e-commerce application. It shows the interaction of the system with a customer from the customer's point of view. Let's walk through it, and I'll point out the key elements of state transition diagrams in general and the features of this one in particular.

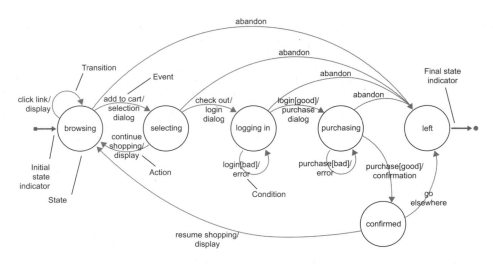

Figure 4–37   *State transition diagram example*

First, notice that we have at the leftmost side a small dot-and-arrow element labeled "initial state indicator." This notation shows that, from the customer's point of view, the transaction starts when they start browsing the website. We can click on links and browse the catalog of items, remaining in a browsing state. Notice the looping arrow above the browsing state. The nodes or bubbles represent states, as shown by the label below the browsing state. The arrows represent transitions, as shown by the label above the looping arrow.

Next we see that we can enter a "selecting" state by adding an item to the shopping cart. "Add to cart" is the event, as shown by the label above. The system will display a "selection dialog" where we ask the customer to tell us how many of the item they want, along with any other information we need to add the item to the cart. Once that's done, the customer can tell the system they want to continue shopping, in which case the system displays the home screen again and the customer is back in a browsing state. From a notation point of view, notice that the actions taken by the system are shown under the event and after the slash symbol, on the transition arrow, as shown by the label below.

Alternatively, the customer can choose to check out. At this point, they enter a logging-in state. They enter login information. A condition applies to that login information: either it was good or it was bad. If it was bad, the system displays an error and the customer remains in the logging-in state. If it was good, the system displays the first screen in the purchasing dialog. Notice that the "bad" and "good" shown in brackets are, notationally, conditions.

While in the purchasing state, the system will display screens and the customer will enter payment information. That information either is good or bad—conditions again—which determines whether we can complete and confirm the transaction. Once the transaction is confirmed, the customer can either resume shopping or go somewhere else.

Notice also that the user can always abandon the transaction and go elsewhere.

When we talk about state-based testing during our training courses, people often ask, "How do I distinguish a state, an event, and an action?" The main distinctions are as follows:

- A state persists until something happens—something external to the thing itself, usually—to trigger a transition. A state can persist for an indefinite period.
- An event occurs, either instantly or in a limited, finite period. It is the something that happened—the external occurrence—that triggered the transition.
- An action is the response the system has during the transition. An action, like an event, is either instantaneous or requires a limited, finite period.

That said, it is sometimes possible to draw the same situation differently, especially when a single state or action can be split into a sequence of finer-grained states, events, and actions. We'll see an example of that in a moment, splitting the purchase state into substates.

Finally, notice that, at the outset, I said that I drew figure 4-37 from the customer's point of view. Notice that if I drew this from the system's point of view, it would look different. Maintaining a consistent point of view is critical when drawing these charts; otherwise, nonsensical things will happen.

State-based testing uses a formal model, so we can have a formal procedure for deriving tests from them. The following list shows a procedure that will work to derive tests that achieve state/transition cover (i.e., 0 switch cover).

1. Adopt a rule for where a test procedure or test step must start and where it may or must end. An example is to say that a test step must start in an initial state and may only end in a final state. The reason for the "may" or "must" wording on the ending part is because, in situations where the initial and final states are the same, you might want to allow sequences of states and transitions that pass through the initial state more than once.

2. From an allowed test starting state, define a sequence of event/condition combinations that leads to an allowed test ending state. For each transition that will occur, capture the expected action that the system should take. This is the expect result.

3. As you visit each state and traverse each transition, mark it as covered. The easiest way to do this is to print the state transition diagram and then use a marker to highlight each node and arrow as you cover it.

4. Repeat steps 2 and 3 until all states have been visited and all transitions traversed—in other words, every node and arrow has been marked with the marker.

This procedure will generate logical test cases. To create concrete test cases, you would have to generate the actual input values and the actual output values. For this course, I intend to generate logical tests to illustrate the techniques, but remember, as I mentioned before, at some point before execution the implementation of concrete test cases must occur.

Let's apply this process to the example e-commerce application we've just looked at, as shown in figure 4-38, where the dashed lines indicate states and transitions that were covered. Here, we see two things:

■ First, we have the rule that says that a test must start in the initial state and must end in the final state.

■ Next, we generate the first test step (browsing, click link, display, add to cart, selection dialog, continue shopping, display, add to cart, selection dialog, checkout, login dialog, login[bad], error, login[good], purchase dialog, purchase[bad], error, purchase[good], confirmation, resume shopping, display, abandon, left).

At this point, we check completeness of coverage, which we've been keeping track of on our state transition diagram.

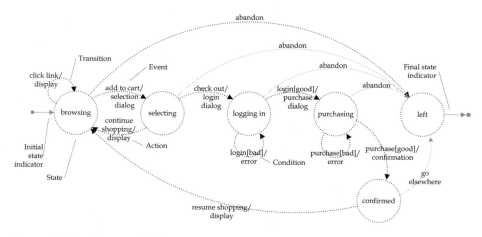

Figure 4–38   *Coverage check 1*

As you can see, we covered all of the states and most transitions, but not all of the transitions. We need to create some more tests.

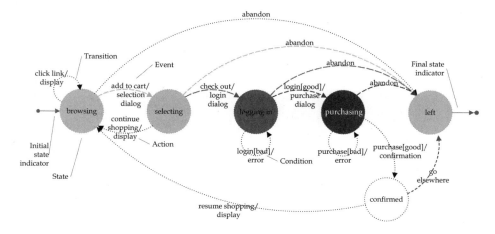

Figure 4–39   *Coverage check completed*

Figure 4-39 shows the test coverage achieved by the following additional test steps, which covers the state transition diagram:

1. (browsing, click link, display, add to cart, selection dialog, continue shopping, display, add to cart, selection dialog, checkout, login dialog, login[bad], error, login[good], purchase dialog, purchase[bad], error, purchase[good], confirmation, resume shopping, display, abandon, left)
2. (browsing, add to cart, selection dialog, abandon, <no action>, left)
3. (browsing, add to cart, selection dialog, checkout, login dialog, abandon, <no action>, left)
4. (browsing, add to cart, selection dialog, checkout, login dialog, login[good], purchase dialog, abandon, <no action>, left)
5. (browsing, add to cart, selection dialog, continue shopping, display, add to cart, selection dialog, checkout, login dialog, login[good], purchase dialog, purchase[good], confirmation, go elsewhere, <no action>, left)

Again, figure 4-39 shows the coverage tracing for the states and transitions. You're not done generating tests until every state and every transition has been highlighted, as shown here.

4.2.22 Superstates and Substates

In some cases, it makes sense to unfold a single state into a superstate consisting of two or more substates. In figure 4-40, you see that I've taken the purchasing state from the e-commerce example and expanded it into three substates.

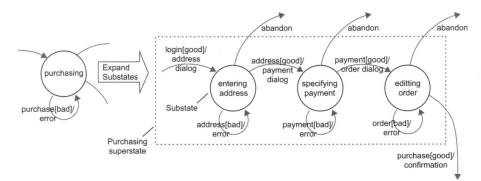

Figure 4–40   *Superstates and substates*

The rule for basic coverage is simple. Cover all transitions into the superstate, all transitions out of the superstate, all substates, and all transitions within the superstate.

Notice that, in our example, this would increase the number of tests because we now have three "abandon" transitions to the "left" state out of the purchasing superstate rather than just one transition from the purchasing state. This would also add a finer-grained element to our tests—i.e., more events and actions—as well as making sure we tested at least three different types of bad purchasing entries.

4.2.23 State Transition Tables

State transition tables are useful because they force us—and the business analysts and the system designers—to consider combinations of states with event/condition combinations that they might have forgotten.

To construct a state transition table, you first list all the states from the state transition diagram. Next, you list all the event/condition combinations shown on the state transition diagram. Then you create a table that has a row for each state with every event/condition combination. Each row has four fields:

- Current state
- Event/condition
- Action
- New state

For those rows where the state transition diagram specifies the action and new state for the given combination of current state and event/condition, we can populate those two fields from the state transition diagram. However, for the other rows in the table, we have found undefined situations.

We can now go to the business analysts, system designers, and other such people and ask, "So, what exactly should happen in each of these situations?"

You might hear them say, "Oh, that can never happen!" As a test analyst, you know what that means. Your job now is to figure out how to make it happen.

You might hear them say, "Oh, well, I'd never thought of that." That probably means you just prevented a bug from ever happening, if you are doing test design during system design.

		Current State	Event/cond	Action	New State
		Browsing	Click link	Display	Browsing
	Click link	Browsing	Add to cart	Selection dia	Selecting
	Add to cart	Browsing	Continue shopping	Undefined	Undefined
	Continue shopping	Browsing	Check out	Undefined	Undefined
Browsing	Check out	Browsing	Login[bad]	Undefined	Undefined
Selecting	Login[bad]	Browsing	Login[good]	Undefined	Undefined
Logging	Login[good]	Browsing	Purchase[bad]	Undefined	Undefined
Purchasing	× Purchase[bad]	= Browsing	Purchase[good]	Undefined	Undefined
Confirmed	Purchase[good]	Browsing	Abandon	<no action>	Left
Left	Abandon	Browsing	Resume shopping	Undefined	Undefined
	Resume shopping	Browsing	Go elsewhere	Undefined	Undefined
	Go elsewhere	Selecting	Click link	Undefined	Undefined

(Fifty-three rows, generated in the pattern shown above, not shown)

		Left	Go elsewhere	Undefined	Undefined

Figure 4–41   *State transition table example*

Figure 4-41 shows an excerpt of the table we would create for the e-commerce example we've been looking at so far. We have six states:

- Browsing
- Selecting
- Logging in
- Purchasing
- Confirmed
- Left

We have 11 event/condition combinations:

- Click link
- Add to cart
- Continue shopping
- Check out
- Login[bad]
- Login[good]
- Purchase[bad]

- Purchase[good]
- Abandon
- Resume shopping
- Go elsewhere

That means our complete state transition table would have 66 rows, one for each possible pairing of a specific state with a specific event/condition combination.

To derive a set of tests that covers the state transition table, we can follow the procedure shown in the following steps. Notice that we build on an existing set of tests created from the state transition diagram to achieve state/transition or 0-switch coverage:

1. Start with a set of tests (including the starting and stopping state rule), derived from a state transition diagram, that achieves state/transition covered.
2. Construct the state transition table and confirm that the tests cover all the defined rows. If they do not, then you didn't generate the existing set of tests properly, or you didn't generate the table properly, or the state transition diagram is screwed up. Do not proceed until you have identified and resolved the problem, including re-creating the state transition table or the set of tests if necessary.
3. Select a test that visits a state for which one or more undefined rows exists in the table. Modify that test to attempt to introduce the undefined event/condition combination for that state. Notice that the action in this case is undefined.
4. As you modify the tests, mark the row as covered. The easiest way to do this is to take a printed version of the table and use a marker to highlight each row as covered.
5. Repeat steps 3 and 4 until all rows have been covered.

Again, this procedure will generate logical test cases.

- Existing test

    - (browsing, add to cart, selection dialog, checkout, login dialog, login[good], purchase dialog, abandon, <no action>, left)

- Modified tests (to cover undefined browsing event/conditions only)

    - (browsing, *attempt*: continue shopping, *action undefined*, add to cart, selection dialog, checkout, login dialog, login[good], purchase dialog, abandon, <no action>, left)

    - (browsing, *attempt*: check out, *action undefined*, add to cart, selection dialog, checkout, login dialog, login[good], purchase dialog, abandon, <no action>, left)

        There are six other modified tests for browsing, not shown …

- Don't try to cover undefined event/conditions combinations for more than one state in any test, because you don't know whether the system will remain testable!

- Best case scenario is that the undefined event/condition combination is ignored or rejected with an intelligent error message, and processing continues normally from there

Figure 4–42 *Deriving tests example*

Figure 4-42 shows an example of deriving table-based tests, building on the e-commerce example already shown. At the top, you can see that I've selected an existing test from the larger set of tests derived before:

(browsing, add to cart, selection dialog, checkout, login dialog, login[good], purchase dialog, abandon, <no action>, left)

Now, from here I started to create modified tests to cover undefined browsing event/conditions, and those undefined conditions only.

One test is (browsing, *attempt*: continue shopping, *action undefined*, add to cart, selection dialog, checkout, login dialog, login[good], purchase dialog, abandon, <no action>, left).

Another test is (browsing, *attempt*: check out, *action undefined*, add to cart, selection dialog, checkout, login dialog, login[good], purchase dialog, abandon, <no action>, left).

There are six other modified tests for browsing, which I've not shown. As you can see, it's a mechanical process to generate these tests. As long as you are careful to keep track of which rows you've covered—using the marker trick I mentioned earlier, for example—it's almost impossible to forget a test.

Now, you'll notice that I only included one undefined event/condition combination in each test step. Why? This is a variant of the equivalence partitioning rule that we should not create invalid test cases that combine multiple invalids. In this case, each row corresponds to an invalid. If we try to cover two rows in a single test step, we can't be sure that the system will remain testable after the first invalid.

Notice that I indicated that the action is undefined. What is the ideal system behavior under these conditions? Well, the best-case scenario is that the undefined event/condition combination is ignored or—better yet—rejected with an intelligent error message. At that point, processing continues normally from there. In the absence of any meaningful input from business analysts, the requirements specification, system designers, or any other authority, I would take the position that any other outcome is a bug, including some inscrutable error message like, "What just happened can't happen." (No, I'm not making that up. An RBCS course attendee once told me she had seen exactly that message when inputting an unexpected value.)

4.2.24 Switch Coverage

Figure 4-43 shows how we can generate sequences of transitions using the concept of switch coverage. I'm going to illustrate this concept with the e-commerce example we've used so far.

At the top of figure 4-43, you see the same state transition as before, except I have replaced the state labels with letters and the transition labels with numbers. Now, a state/transition pair can be specified as a letter followed by a number. Notice that I'm not bothering to list, in the table below, a letter after the number because it's unambiguous from the diagram what state we'll be in after the given transition. There is only one arrow labeled with a given number that leads out of a state labeled with a given letter, and that arrow lands on exactly one state.

The table contains two types of columns. The first is the state/transition pairs that we must cover to achieve 0-switch coverage. Study this for a moment, and assure yourself that, by designing tests that cover each state/transition pair in the 0-switch columns, you'll achieve state/transition coverage as discussed previously.

Constructing the 0-switch columns is easy. The first row consists of the first state, with a column for each transition leaving that state. There are at most

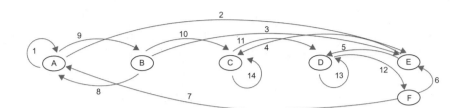

0-switch			1-switch								
A1	A2	A9	A1A1	A1A2	A1A9				A9B10	A9B8	A9B3
B10	B8	B3	B10C14	B10C11	B10C4	B8A1	B8A2	B8A9			
C14	C11	C4	C14C14	C14C11	C14C4	C11D13	C11D12	C11D5			
D13	D12	D5	D13D13	D13D12	D13D5	D12F6	D12F7				
F6	F7					F7A1	F7A2	F7A9			

Figure 4–43   *N-1 switch coverage example*

three transitions from the A state. Repeat that process for each state for which there is an outbound transition. Notice that the E state doesn't have a row, because E is a final state and there's not outbound transition. Notice also that, for this example, there are at most three transitions from any given state.

The 1-switch columns are a little trickier to construct, but there's a regularity here that makes it mechanical if you are meticulous. Notice, again, that after each transition occurs in the 0-switch situation, we are left in a state, which is implicit in the 0-switch cells. As mentioned earlier, there are at most three transitions from any given state. That means that, for this example, each 0-switch cell can expand to at most three 1-switch cells.

So, we can take each 0-switch cell for the A row and copy it into three cells in the 1-switch columns, for nine cells for the A row. Now we ask ourselves, for each triple of cells in the A row of the 1-switch columns, what implicit state did we end up in? We can then refer to the appropriate 0-switch cells to populate the remainder of the 1-switch cell.

Notice that the blank cells in the 1-switch columns indicate situations where we entered a state in the first transition from which there was no outbound transition. In this example, that is the state labeled "E" in figure 4-43, which was labeled "Left" on the full-sized diagram.

So, given a set of state/transition sequences like those shown—whether 0-switch, 1-switch, 2-switch, or even higher—how do we derive test cases to cover those sequences and achieve the desired level of coverage? Again, I'm going to build on an existing set of tests created from the state transition diagram to achieve state/transition or 0-switch coverage.

1. Start with a set of tests (including the starting and stopping state rule), derived from a state transition diagram, that achieves state/transition coverage.
2. Construct the switch table using the technique shown previously. Once you have, confirm that the tests cover all of the cells in the 0-switch columns. If they do not, then you didn't generate the existing set of tests properly, or you didn't generate the switch table properly, or the state transition diagram is screwed up. Do not proceed until you have identified and resolved the problem, including re-creating the switch table or the set of tests, if necessary. Once you have that done, check for higher-order switches already covered by the tests.
3. Now, using 0-switch sequences as needed, construct a test that reaches a state from which an uncovered higher-order switch sequence originates. Include that switch sequence in the test. Check to see what state this left you in. Ideally, another uncovered higher-order switch sequence originates from this state, but if not, see if you can use 0-switch sequences to reach such a state. You're crawling around in the state transition diagram looking for ways to cover higher-order sequence. Repeat this for the current test until the test must terminate.
4. As you construct tests, mark the switch sequences as covered once you include them in a test. The easiest way to do this is to take a printed version of the switch table and use a marker to highlight each cell as covered.
5. Repeat steps 3 and 4 until all switch sequences have been covered.

Again, this procedure will generate logical test cases.

In figure 4-43, we see the application of the derivation technique covered previously to the e-commerce example we've used. After finishing the second step, that of assessing coverage already attained via 0-switch coverage, we can see that most of the table is already shaded. Those are the blue-shaded cells, which are covered by the five existing state/transition cover tests.

Now, we generate five new tests to achieve 1-switch coverage. Those are shown in figure 4-44. The red-shaded cells are covered by five new 1-switch cover tests:

- (A1A1A2)
- (A9B8A1A9B8A2)
- (A9B10C14C14C4)
- (A9B10C11D13D13D5)
- (A9B10C11D12F7A1A9B10C11D12F7A9)

Let me mention something about this algorithm for deriving higher-order switch coverage tests, as well as the one given previously for row-coverage tests. Both build on an existing set of tests that achieve state/transition coverage. That is efficient from a test design point of view. It's also conservative from a test execution point of view because we cover the less challenging stuff first, then move on to the more difficult tests.

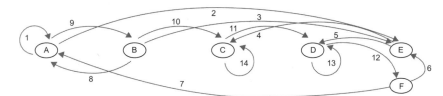

0-switch			1-switch								
A1	A2	A9	A1A1	A1A2	A1A9				A9B10	A9B8	A9B3
B10	B8	B3	B10C14	B10C11	B10C4	B8A1	B8A2	B8A9			
C14	C11	C4	C14C14	C14C11	C14C4	C11D13	C11D12	C11D5			
D13	D12	D5	D13D13	D13D12	D13D5	D12F6	D12F7				
F6	F7					F7A1	F7A2	F7A9			

Figure 4–44   *Deriving tests example*

However, it is quite possible that, starting from scratch, a smaller set of tests could be built, both for the row coverage situation and for the 1-switch coverage situation. If the most important thing is to create the minimum number of tests, then you should look for ways to reduce the tests created, or modify the derivation procedures given here to start from scratch rather than to build on an existing set of 0-switch tests.

4.2.25 State Testing with Other Techniques

Let's finish our discussion on state-based testing by looking at a couple of interesting questions. First, how might equivalence partitioning and boundary value analysis combine with state-based testing? The answer is, quite well.

From the e-commerce example, suppose that the minimum purchase is $10 and the maximum is $10,000. In that case, we can perform boundary value analysis as shown in figure 4-40, performed on the purchase[good] and purchase[bad] event/condition combinations. By covering not only transitions, rows, or transitions sequence, but also boundary values, this forces us to try different purchase amounts.

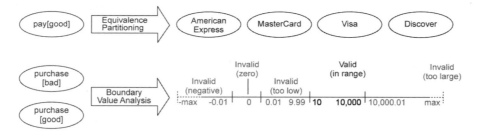

Figure 4–45   *Equivalence partitions and boundary values*

We can also apply equivalence partitioning to the pay[good] event/condition combination. For example, suppose we accept four different types of credit cards. By covering not only transitions, rows, or transition sequences, but also equivalence partitions, this forces us to try different payment types.

Now, to come full circle on a question I brought up at the start of the discussion on these three business-logic test techniques, when do we use decision tables and when do we use state diagrams?

This can be, in some cases, a matter of taste. The decision table is easy to use and compact. If we're not too worried about the higher-order coverage, or the effect of states on the tests, we can model many state-influenced situations as decision tables, using conditions to model states. However, if the decision table's conditions section starts to become very long, you're probably stretching the technique. Also, keep in mind that test coverage is usually more thorough using state-based techniques. In most cases, one technique or the other will clearly fit better. If you are at a loss, try both and see which feels most appropriate.

4.2.26 State Testing Exercise

This exercise consists of four parts:

1. Using the semiformal use case you developed in the previous exercise, translate that use case into a state transition diagram, shown from the point of view of the Telephone Banker.
2. Generate test cases to cover the states and transitions (0-switch coverage).
3. Generate a state transition table from the state transition diagram, and create additional error-handling test cases using the state transition table.
4. Generate a switch table to the 1-switch level, and create additional test cases to achieve 1-switch coverage.

The answers to the four parts are shown on the next pages. You should review the answer to each part (and, if necessary, revise your answer to the part that follows) before reviewing the answer to the following part.

4.2.27 State Testing Exercise Debrief

Figure 4-46 shows the state transition diagram I generated based on the semiformal use case shown in table 4-3.

Let's adopt a rule that says that any test must start in the initial waiting state and may only end in the waiting state or the shift over state. To achieve state and transition coverage, the following tests will suffice:

1. (waiting, phone call, loan screens, exceed[value], escalate, approved, resume, system loan offer, offer screen, offer insurance, insurance screens, cust ins accept, add to package, cust loan accept, send to LoDoPS, waiting)
2. (waiting, phone call, loan screens, exceed[loan], escalate, approved, resume, system loan offer, offer screen, offer insurance, insurance screens, cust ins reject, archive, cust loan accept, send to LoDoPS, waiting)
3. (waiting, phone call, loan screens, system loan offer, offer screen, offer insurance, insurance screens, system ins reject, archive, cust loan reject, archive, waiting)
4. (waiting, phone call, loan screens, exceed[loan], escalate, system loan decline, archive, waiting)

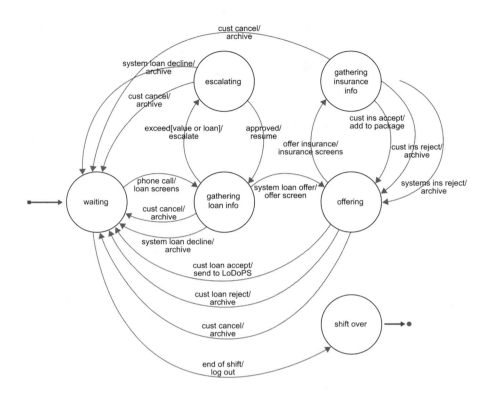

Figure 4–46   *HELLOCARMS state transition diagram*

5. (waiting, phone call, loan screens, system loan decline, archive, waiting)
6. (waiting, phone call, loan screens, cust cancel, archive, waiting)
7. (waiting, phone call, loan screens, exceed[loan], escalate, cust cancel, archive, waiting)
8. (waiting, phone call, loan screens, system loan offer, offer screen, cust cancel, archive, waiting)
9. (waiting, phone call, loan screens, system loan offer, offer screen, offer insurance, insurance screens, cust cancel, archive, waiting)
10. (waiting, end of shift, log out, shift over)

Notice that I didn't do an explicit boundary value or equivalence partitioning testing of, say, the loan amount or the property value, though I certainly could have.

Next, let's generate the state transition table. Notice that there are six distinct states:

1. waiting
2. gathering loan info
3. escalating
4. offering
5. gathering insurance info
6. shift over

There are 13 distinct event/condition combinations:

1. phone call
2. exceed[value or loan]
3. approved
4. system loan decline
5. system loan offer
6. offer insurance
7. cust ins accept
8. cust ins reject
9. system ins reject
10. cust loan accept
11. cust loan reject
12. cust cancel
13. end of shift

Therefore, there are 78 rows in the state transition table, shown in table 4-10.

Table 4–10 *HELLOCARMS state transition table*

#	Current State	Event/Condition	Action	New State
	waiting	phone call	loan screens	gathering loan info
		exceed[value or loan]	undefined	undefined
		approved	undefined	undefined
		system loan decline	undefined	undefined
		system loan offer	undefined	undefined
		offer insurance	undefined	undefined
		cust ins accept	undefined	undefined
		cust ins reject	undefined	undefined
		system ins reject	undefined	undefined
		cust loan accept	undefined	undefined
		cust loan reject	undefined	undefined
		cust cancel	undefined	undefined
		end of shift	undefined	undefined
	gathering loan info	phone call	undefined	undefined
		exceed[value or loan]	escalate	escalating
		approved	undefined	undefined
		system loan decline	archive	waiting
		system loan offer	offer screen	offering
		offer insurance	undefined	undefined
		cust ins accept	undefined	undefined
		cust ins reject	undefined	undefined
		system ins reject	undefined	undefined
		cust loan accept	undefined	undefined
		cust loan reject	undefined	undefined
		cust cancel	archive	waiting
		end of shift	undefined	undefined

Table continues

Table 4–10 *HELLOCARMS state transition table (continued)*

#	Current State	Event/Condition	Action	New State
	escalating	phone call	undefined	undefined
		exceed[value or loan]	undefined	undefined
		approved	resume	gathering loan info
		system loan decline	archive	waiting
		system loan offer	undefined	undefined
		offer insurance	undefined	undefined
		cust ins accept	undefined	undefined
		cust ins reject	undefined	undefined
		system ins reject	undefined	undefined
		cust loan accept	undefined	undefined
		cust loan reject	undefined	undefined
		cust cancel	archive	waiting
		end of shift	undefined	undefined
	offering	phone call	undefined	undefined
		exceed[value or loan]	undefined	undefined
		approved	undefined	undefined
		system loan decline	undefined	undefined
		system loan offer	undefined	undefined
		offer insurance	insurance screens	gather insurance info
		cust ins accept	undefined	undefined
		cust ins reject	undefined	undefined
		system ins reject	undefined	undefined
		cust loan accept	send to LoDoPS	Waiting
		cust loan reject	archive	waiting
		cust cancel	archive	waiting
		end of shift	undefined	undefined

Table continues

Table 4–10 *HELLOCARMS state transition table (continued)*

#	Current State	Event/Condition	Action	New State
	gathering insurance info	phone call	undefined	undefined
		exceed[value or loan]	undefined	undefined
		approved	undefined	undefined
		system loan decline	undefined	undefined
		system loan offer	undefined	undefined
		offer insurance	undefined	undefined
		cust ins accept	add to package	offering
		cust ins reject	archive	offering
		system ins reject	archive	offering
		cust loan accept	undefined	undefined
		cust loan reject	undefined	undefined
		cust cancel	archive	waiting
		end of shift	undefined	undefined
	shift over	phone call	undefined	undefined
		exceed[value or loan]	undefined	undefined
		approved	undefined	undefined
		system loan decline	undefined	undefined
		system loan offer	undefined	undefined
		offer insurance	undefined	undefined
		cust ins accept	undefined	undefined
		cust ins reject	undefined	undefined
		system ins reject	undefined	undefined
		cust loan accept	undefined	undefined
		cust loan reject	undefined	undefined
		cust cancel	undefined	undefined
		end of shift	undefined	undefined

To achieve row coverage, I add the following tests:

11. (waiting, *attempt*: exceed[value or loan], *action undefined*, end of shift, log out, shift over)

12. (waiting, *attempt*: approved, *action undefined*, end of shift, log out, shift over)

13. (waiting, *attempt*: system loan decline, *action undefined*, end of shift, log out, shift over)

14. (waiting, *attempt*: system loan offer, *action undefined*, end of shift, log out, shift over)

15. (waiting, *attempt*: offer insurance, *action undefined*, end of shift, log out, shift over)

16. (waiting, *attempt*: cust ins accept, *action undefined*, end of shift, log out, shift over)

17. (waiting, *attempt*: cust ins reject, *action undefined*, end of shift, log out, shift over)

18. (waiting, *attempt*: system ins reject, *action undefined*, end of shift, log out, shift over)

19. (waiting, *attempt*: cust loan accept, *action undefined*, end of shift, log out, shift over)

20. (waiting, *attempt*: cust loan reject, *action undefined*, end of shift, log out, shift over)

21. (waiting, *attempt*: cust cancel, *action undefined*, end of shift, log out, shift over)

22. (waiting, *attempt*: end of shift, *action undefined*, end of shift, log out, shift over)

23. (waiting, phone call, loan screens, *attempt*: phone call, *action undefined*, cust cancel, archive, end of shift, log out, shift over)

24. (waiting, phone call, loan screens, *attempt*: exceed[value or loan], *action undefined*, cust cancel, archive, end of shift, log out, shift over)

25. (waiting, phone call, loan screens, *attempt*: approved, *action undefined*, cust cancel, archive, end of shift, log out, shift over)

26. (waiting, phone call, loan screens, *attempt*: offer insurance, *action undefined*, cust cancel, archive, end of shift, log out, shift over)

27. (waiting, phone call, loan screens, *attempt*: cust ins accept, *action undefined*, cust cancel, archive, end of shift, log out, shift over)

28. (waiting, phone call, loan screens, *attempt*: cust ins reject, *action undefined*, cust cancel, archive, end of shift, log out, shift over)

29. (waiting, phone call, loan screens, *attempt*: system ins reject, *action undefined*, cust cancel, archive, end of shift, log out, shift over)

30. (waiting, phone call, loan screens, *attempt*: cust loan accept, *action undefined*, cust cancel, archive, end of shift, log out, shift over)

31. (waiting, phone call, loan screens, *attempt*: cust loan reject, *action undefined*, cust cancel, archive, end of shift, log out, shift over)

32. (waiting, phone call, loan screens, *attempt*: end of shift, *action undefined*, cust cancel, archive, end of shift, log out, shift over)

33. (waiting, phone call, loan screens, exceed[loan], escalate, *attempt*: phone call, *action undefined*, cust cancel, archive, end of shift, log out, shift over)

34. (waiting, phone call, loan screens, exceed[value], escalate, *attempt*: exceed[value], *action undefined*, cust cancel, archive, end of shift, log out, shift over)

35. (waiting, phone call, loan screens, exceed[value], escalate, *attempt*: system loan offer, *action undefined*, cust cancel, archive, end of shift, log out, shift over)

36. (waiting, phone call, loan screens, exceed[value], escalate, *attempt*: offer insurance, *action undefined*, cust cancel, archive, end of shift, log out, shift over)

37. (waiting, phone call, loan screens, exceed[value], escalate, *attempt*: cust ins accept, *action undefined*, cust cancel, archive, end of shift, log out, shift over)

38. (waiting, phone call, loan screens, exceed[value], escalate, *attempt*: cust ins reject, *action undefined*, cust cancel, archive, end of shift, log out, shift over) (waiting, phone call, loan screens, exceed[value], escalate, *attempt*: system ins reject, *action undefined*, cust cancel, archive, end of shift, log out, shift over)

39. (waiting, phone call, loan screens, exceed[value], escalate, *attempt*: cust loan accept, *action undefined*, cust cancel, archive, end of shift, log out, shift over)

40. (waiting, phone call, loan screens, exceed[value], escalate, *attempt*: cust loan reject, *action undefined*, cust cancel, archive, end of shift, log out, shift over)

41. (waiting, phone call, loan screens, exceed[value], escalate, *attempt*: end of shift, *action undefined*, cust cancel, archive, end of shift, log out, shift over)

42. (waiting, phone call, loan screens, system loan offer, offer screen, *attempt*: phone call, *action undefined*, cust cancel, archive, end of shift, log out, shift over)

43. (waiting, phone call, loan screens, system loan offer, offer screen, *attempt*: exceed[loan], *action undefined*, cust cancel, archive, end of shift, log out, shift over)

44. (waiting, phone call, loan screens, system loan offer, offer screen, *attempt*: approved, *action undefined*, cust cancel, archive, end of shift, log out, shift over)

45. (waiting, phone call, loan screens, system loan offer, offer screen, *attempt*: system loan decline, *action undefined*, cust cancel, archive, end of shift, log out, shift over)

46. (waiting, phone call, loan screens, system loan offer, offer screen, *attempt*: system loan offer, *action undefined*, cust cancel, archive, end of shift, log out, shift over)

47. (waiting, phone call, loan screens, system loan offer, offer screen, *attempt*: cust ins accept, *action undefined*, cust cancel, archive, end of shift, log out, shift over)

48. (waiting, phone call, loan screens, system loan offer, offer screen, *attempt*: cust ins reject, *action undefined*, cust cancel, archive, end of shift, log out, shift over)

49. (waiting, phone call, loan screens, system loan offer, offer screen, *attempt*: system ins reject, *action undefined*, cust cancel, archive, end of shift, log out, shift over)

50. (waiting, phone call, loan screens, system loan offer, offer screen, *attempt*: end of shift, *action undefined*, cust cancel, archive, end of shift, log out, shift over)

51. (waiting, phone call, loan screens, system loan offer, offer screen, offer insurance, insurance screens, *attempt*: phone call, *action undefined*, cust cancel, archive, end of shift, log out, shift over)

52. (waiting, phone call, loan screens, system loan offer, offer screen, offer insurance, insurance screens, *attempt*: exceed[loan], *action undefined*, cust cancel, archive, end of shift, log out, shift over)

53. (waiting, phone call, loan screens, system loan offer, offer screen, offer insurance, insurance screens, *attempt*: approved, *action undefined*, cust cancel, archive, end of shift, log out, shift over)

54. (waiting, phone call, loan screens, system loan offer, offer screen, offer insurance, insurance screens, *attempt*: system loan decline, *action undefined*, cust cancel, archive, end of shift, log out, shift over)

55. (waiting, phone call, loan screens, system loan offer, offer screen, offer insurance, insurance screens, *attempt*: system loan offer, *action undefined*, cust cancel, archive, end of shift, log out, shift over)

56. (waiting, phone call, loan screens, system loan offer, offer screen, offer insurance, insurance screens, *attempt*: offer insurance, *action undefined*, cust cancel, archive, end of shift, log out, shift over)

57. (waiting, phone call, loan screens, system loan offer, offer screen, offer insurance, insurance screens, *attempt*: cust loan accept, *action undefined*, cust cancel, archive, end of shift, log out, shift over)

58. (waiting, phone call, loan screens, system loan offer, offer screen, offer insurance, insurance screens, *attempt*: cust loan reject, *action undefined*, cust cancel, archive, end of shift, log out, shift over)

59. (waiting, phone call, loan screens, system loan offer, offer screen, offer insurance, insurance screens, *attempt*: end of shift, *action undefined*, cust cancel, archive, end of shift, log out, shift over)

60. (waiting, end of shift, log out, *attempt*: phone call, *action undefined*, shift over)

61. (waiting, end of shift, log out, *attempt*: exceed[value], *action undefined*, shift over)

62. (waiting, end of shift, log out, *attempt*: approved, *action undefined*, shift over)

63. (waiting, end of shift, log out, *attempt*: system loan decline, *action undefined*, shift over)

64. (waiting, end of shift, log out, *attempt*: system loan offer, *action undefined*, shift over)

65. (waiting, end of shift, log out, *attempt*: offer insurance, *action undefined*, shift over)

66. (waiting, end of shift, log out, *attempt*: cust ins accept, *action undefined*, shift over)

67. (waiting, end of shift, log out, *attempt*: cust ins reject, *action undefined*, shift over)

68. (waiting, end of shift, log out, *attempt*: system ins reject, *action undefined*, shift over)

69. (waiting, end of shift, log out, *attempt*: cust loan accept, *action undefined*, shift over)

70. (waiting, end of shift, log out, *attempt*: cust loan reject, *action undefined*, shift over)

71. (waiting, end of shift, log out, *attempt*: cust cancel, *action undefined*, shift over)

72. (waiting, end of shift, log out, *attempt*: end of shift, *action undefined*, shift over)

Note that forcing an "end of shift, log out, shift over" sequence at the end of each test reduces the likelihood that the any error condition created during the test could interfere with subsequent results.

As discussed in the course, these tests are conservative in that each undefined event is tried on its own. During test execution, if testers find that the system ignores undefined events robustly, these tests could be incorporated into other tests and the number of tests reduced.

Now, to generate the switch table to the 1-switch level, I first simplified the state transition diagram with the letter-and-number nomenclature shown in the course. This version is shown in figure 4-47.

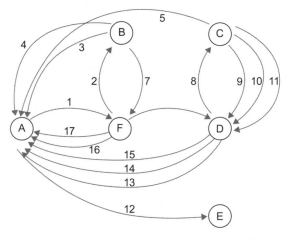

Figure 4–47   *HELLOCARMS state transition diagram for 1-switch table*

From the diagram, I can generate the 1-switch table shown in table 4-11. Notice that I have used patterns in the diagram to generate the table. For example, the maximum number of outbound transitions for any state in the diagram is four, so I use four columns on both the 0-switch and 1-switch columns. I started with six 1-switch rows per 0-switch row, because there are six states, though I was able to delete most of those rows as I went along. This leads to a sparse table, but who cares as long as it makes generating this beast easier.

Table 4–11 HELLOCARMS switch table

0-switch				1-switch			
A1	A12			A1F2	A1F6	A1F16	A1F17
B3	B4	B7		B3A1	B3A12		
				B4A1	B4A12		
				B7F2	B7F6	B7F16	B7F17
C5	C9	C10	C11	C5A1	C5A12		
				C9D8	C9D13	C9D14	C9D15
				C10D8	C10D13	C10D14	C10D15
				C11D8	C11D13	C11D14	C11D15
D8	D13	D14	D15	D8C5	D8C9	D8C10	D8C11
				D13A1	D13A12		
				D14A1	D14A12		
				D15A1	D15A12		
F2	F6	F16	F17	F2B3	F2B4	F2B7	
				F6D8	F6D13	F6D14	F6D15
				F16A1	F16A12		
				F17A1	F17A12		

Now, having generated the table, I can check to see what's already covered by the existing tests. Notice that the row-coverage-generated tests don't count, because you don't want to assume that anything that happens after the invalid event is typical.

Here are the existing tests, rewritten using the letter-number nomenclature to make the coverage check easier.

1. (A1 F2 B7 F6 D8 C9 D15)
2. (A1 F2 B7 F6 D8 C10 D15)
3. (A1 F6 D8 C11 D14)
4. (A1 F2 B4)
5. (A1 F16)
6. (A1 F17)
7. (A1 F2 B3)
8. (A1 F6 D13)
9. (A1 F6 D8 C5)
10. (A12)

The coverage analysis is shown in table 4-12.

Table 4–12 *HELLOCARMS switch table with 0-switch coverage*

0-switch				1-switch			
A1	A12			A1F2	A1F6	A1F16	A1F17
B3	B4	B7		B3A1	B3A12		
				B4A1	B4A12		
				B7F2	B7F6	B7F16	B7F17
C5	C9	C10	C11	C5A1	C5A12		
				C9D8	C9D13	C9D14	C9D15
				C10D8	C10D13	C10D14	C10D15
				C11D8	C11D13	C11D14	C11D15
D8	D13	D14	D15	D8C5	D8C9	D8C10	D8C11
				D13A1	D13A12		
				D14A1	D14A12		
				D15A1	D15A12		
F2	F6	F16	F17	F2B3	F2B4	F2B7	
				F6D8	F6D13	F6D14	F6D15
				F16A1	F16A12		
				F17A1	F17A12		

Now I generate additional tests to achieve 1-switch coverage. To keep this simple, I've used the letter-number nomenclature, though eventually I'd need to translate back into the logical test case style of a full sequence of events and actions, with starting and ending state.

74. (A1 F2 B3 A1 F16 A1 F2 B3 A12)
75. (A1 F2 B4 A1 F2 B4 A12)
76. (A1 F2 B7 F2 B7 F16 A12)

77. (A1 F2 B7 F2 B7 F17 A12)
78. (A1 F17 A1 F6 D14)
79. (A1 F6 D14)
80. (A1 F6 D8 C5 A1 F6 D8 C5 A12)
81. (A1 F6 D8 C9 D8 C9 D13 A12)
82. (A1 F6 D8 C10 D8 C9 D14 A1 F6 D15 A1 F6 D14 A12)
83. (A1 F6 D8 C10 D8 C10 D14)
84. (A1 F6 D8 C10 D13 A1 F17)
85. (A1 F6 D8 C10 D15 A12)
86. (A1 F6 D8 C11 D8 C11 D14)

Notice that much of the testing involves creating tests that go back into a waiting state and then start a new application without logging out. If I were really focused on test execution efficiency, I could compress some of these tests into the initial test set just by requiring that the first 10 tests be run sequentially with no logout between them.

Notice that the 1-switch tests cover two flows that might be impossible:

- Escalating the application more than once for Senior Telephone Banker approval
- Offering insurance more than once during the same application

You would need to check with the business analysts and system designers to see if the system should allow this.

Table 4–13 *HELLOCARMS switch table with 0-switch and 1-switch coverage*

0-switch				1-switch			
A1	A12			A1F2	A1F6	A1F16	A1F17
B3	B4	B7		B3A1	B3A12		
				B4A1	B4A12		
				B7F2	B7B6	B7F16	B7F17
C5	C9	C10	C11	C5A1	C5A12		
				C9D8	C9D13	C9D14	C9D15
				C10D8	C10D13	C10D14	C10D15
				C11D8	C11D13	C11D14	C11D15
D8	D13	D14	D15	D8C5	D8C9	D8C10	D8C11
				D13A1	D13A12		
				D14A1	D14A12		
				D15A1	D15A12		
F2	F6	F16	F17	F2B3	F2B4	F2B7	
				F6D8	F6D13	F6D14	F6D15
				F16A1	F16A12		
				F17A1	F17A12		

4.2.28 Pairwise Testing

For the last three techniques we've discussed—decision tables, use cases, and state-based testing—there has been a discernible, analyzable way in which factors interact. For decision tables and their graphical cousins cause-effect graphs, we see the interaction between conditions and system actions. For use cases, we see how certain conditions are handled normally while others result in exception handling. For state-based tests, events and conditions act on the system, based on its state, resulting in actions and state transitions.

What about situations where the interaction of the factors cannot be so easily determined, or even where there is supposed to be no interaction? For example, if you are testing compatibility of a browser-based application with the various browser types and versions, connection speeds, operating system types and versions and patch levels, and virus and spyware scanning programs, you have four main factors, each with close to a dozen or so options. Your application *should* run properly, regardless of the configuration, but will it? The only way to know for sure is to test all the possible configurations, but that's impossible here. If you have four factors, each with a dozen options, you have 12 times 12 times 12 times 12—or 20,736—distinct configurations.

Pairwise testing is a technique we can use to try to control this combinatorial explosion when we have unconstrained options. Conceptually, in pairwise testing we make sure that each option is represented in at least one test configuration, that each possible pair of options is represented in at least one test configuration, and that each option and pair of options is represented about equally as a percentage of the total configurations. Not all possible higher-order combinations, such as triples, quadruples, quintuples, and so forth, will be covered.

What I meant a moment ago by "unconstrained options" was that, for the most part, the options are independent of each other. Any options for any factor can coexist with any other option for any other factor. Configuration testing is a classic example of that. We have different software versions that should all cohabit and interact appropriately on a computer. Any situation where they don't get along is a bug.

Okay, so what's our model for pairwise testing? There are two basic models. One is called an orthogonal array. The other is called an all-pairs table. Both are tables. The tables, read row-wise, will tell you which particular options to include in a given test configuration. The tables are created either directly (in the case of the all-pairs table) or by mapping the test problem to be solved onto an existing table (in the case of the orthogonal array). By their nature, the tables are guaranteed to contain all existing options for every factor at least once, *and* every pair of options across all pairs of factors.

Our coverage criterion for these tables is obvious, given that statement: We need to have each row represented in at least one test. By doing so, we will have tested every option for every factor at least once and every pair of options across all pairs of factors at least once.

The bug hypothesis is that this level of coverage will suffice. In other words, if there are going to be problems with options, most of those problems will arise either from a single instance of an option or from a given pair of options. The problems that are specific to triples, quadruples, and so forth—the higher-order combinational problems—are less likely.

> **ISTQB Glossary**
>
> orthogonal array: A two-dimensional array constructed with special mathematical properties such that choosing any two columns in the array provides every pair combination of each number in the array.
>
> orthogonal array testing: A systematic way of testing all-pair combinations of variables using orthogonal arrays. It significantly reduces the number of all combinations of variables to test all pair combinations.
>
> **pairwise testing:** A black-box test design technique in which test cases are designed to execute all possible discrete combinations of each pair of input parameters.

There are two basic approaches to pairwise testing, as I mentioned a moment ago. The first is to use orthogonal arrays. There are plenty of these available on the Internet and in various textbooks. For example, there is a library of orthogonal arrays at www.research.att.com/~njas/oadir. Because this comes from AT&T, for use in testing phone systems, it has a certain level of credibility. Alternatively, you can use a tool to build an all-pairs tables. Again, an Internet search will reveal a fair number of these. A clearinghouse for pairwise testing tools, both freeware and commercial, is found at www.pairwise.org.

There is a subtle difference between orthogonal arrays and all-pairs tables. The number of rows will often differ, as will the number of times each pair of options is represented. For compatibility testing, this is usually not important.

In this book, I'm going to demonstrate the use of orthogonal arrays. If you decide to use a tool, you'll follow the directions that come with it.

	Factor	
Test	**1**	**2**
1	0	0
2	0	1
3	1	0
4	1	1

Figure 4–48   *A simple orthogonal array*

Figure 4-48 shows the simplest possible orthogonal array. There are two factors, factor 1 and factor 2. Each factor has two options, zero and one. As you can see, each option for each factor is represented in the orthogonal array. Further, each pair of options across the two factors is represented in one (and only one) row.

Okay, this not a surprise. There are two options, and there are four rows. Surprise, surprise, two times two is four. So far, nothing very interesting has happened with orthogonal arrays.

Test	Factor		
	1	2	3
1	0	0	0
2	0	1	1
3	1	0	1
4	1	1	0

Figure 4–49   A larger orthogonal array

Figure 4-49 is where the interesting things start to happen. We have a slightly larger orthogonal array. There are three factors. There are two options for each factor. But there are still only four rows.

How did that happen? Are we missing pairs? Nope, we're not. Notice that there are four pairs for each pair of factors, as before. So, let's enumerate them:

■ For the first pair of factors, factor 1 and factor 2, we have 00, 01, 10, 11, in rows 1, 2, 3, and 4.

■ For the second pair of factors, factor 1 and factor 3, we have 00, 01, 11, and 10, in rows 1, 2, 3, and 4. All four pairs, just occurring in a different row.

■ For the third pair of factors, factor 2 and factor 3, we have 00, 11, 01, and 10, in rows 1, 2, 3, and 4. All four pairs, again, just occurring in a different row than the previous pairs of factors.

Now, if we wanted all the triples, we would have to have eight rows. However, in pairwise testing, we've explicitly renounced any intention of achieving that level of coverage. We're going to assume that testing every option for every factor, and every pair of options for every pair of factors, will suffice.

Now, the orthogonal array we just looked at isn't very interesting for testing. We can only deal with situations with three factors, which might suffice in some cases, but more importantly, we can only deal with two options per factor. How can we select an orthogonal array that will fit the testing problem we have?

There are three rules to selecting an orthogonal array:

- First, there must be at least as many columns as factors. Now, it's often the case that you'll find an array with too many columns. No problem. If there are too many columns, you can drop the extra columns.
- Second, there must be at least enough numbers in the columns to hold the options for each factor. In the previous examples, there were only two numbers, 0 and 1. If you have three options for a factor, you would have to have at least three numbers, 0, 1, and 2. Again, you'll often find an array with too many numbers. Not a problem. Spare numbers that don't map to any option can be replaced by any valid option for that factor, this being referred to as "tester's choice" and usually shown with a tilde (~).
- Third, there must be at least as many rows as the product of the two largest numbers of options. For example, if one factor has 4 options and another has 3 and yet another has 2, then you need to have at least 4 times 3, or 12 rows. Again, you'll often find an array with too many rows. Here we have something of a problem. If there are too many rows, you cannot drop them if interesting pairs exist in the row. So you'll have to scrutinize rows, two at a time, to see if you can combine them using the "tester's choice" options.

Having selected an orthogonal array, you then map your testing problem onto it following a six-step process. This process is entirely mechanical and very easy to do in Excel or Word. You simply import the text file orthogonal array that you downloaded into Excel or Word and follow these five steps:

1. First, drop any extra columns that you might have.
2. Second, map factors to the columns by adding column headings.
3. Third, select one column at a time and map the options for that factor onto the numbers. In other words, replace each instance of 0 with the first option for that factor, each instance of 1 with the second option for that factor, and

so forth. Using Word's or Excel's search and replace options makes this easy. If you finish this process and there are still numbers in the column, replace those numbers with tildes to indicate "tester's choice".

Now, you can stop here, but often at this point you'll have more rows than you need. If it takes an hour or more to test each configuration and you aren't looking for ways to fill spare time during test execution, you should continue with step 4.

4. In step 4, drop any extra rows with no interesting single options or pairs of options. In other words, any row that consists of all tildes can be deleted. Any pair of rows where one row has tildes and another row has options and vice versa, and where any option specified in each row is the same, you can merge the two rows.

5. At this point, you can run the fifth step now or during test execution. For any spare cells—the ones that still have tildes—you can specify options that will make for easier tests, or to cover popular configurations, or whatever else you like. As I said, it's tester's choice.

By the way, during the mapping process, you'll find out quickly if you made a mistake in your selection of an orthogonal array. One warning sign will be that the mapping process will fail because of insufficient columns or options. Another, somewhat subtler, is that you'll have a large number of rows with all or mostly tildes.

Okay, enough discussion about this process; let's see an example. Let's return to the example of testing the www.rbcs-us.com website. In particular, let's assume we want to do compatibility testing during the functional tests by ensuring that proper combinations of configurations are used. There are four factors we are interested in, each having two, three, or four options:

- ▪ The first factor is connection speed. We have two options: dial-up and broadband.
- ▪ The second factor is the operating system. We have four options: Mac, Linux, Windows XP, and Windows Vista.

■ The third factor is the security settings. We have four options: native operating system security only, Symantec's product, Trend Micro's product, and McAfee's product.

■ The fourth factor is the browser. We have three options: Firefox, Internet Explorer, and Opera.

So, we need an array with four columns, one for each factor. Now, if we could find one, we could use an array with two numbers in one column, three in another column, and four in the other two columns. However, arrays are usually symmetrical in the numbers they have in each column, so we'll probably end up with four numbers per column. Because the two factors with the largest number of options, security setting and operating system, each have four options, we need 16 rows.

In figure 4-50, you see the selection and mapping of the orthogonal array. In the middle of the figure, you see the text file array from the AT&T site. Saving this file to the hard disk, importing it into Excel, adding the column headings, and doing a search-and-replace on each column took less than five minutes. So the mapping is done. Because this array is a perfect fit, we can skip step 4, the compression of rows.

Spend a few moments now verifying all the pairs of options across all the pairs of factors. There are six pairs of factors:

1. Connection speed with operating system
2. Connection speed with security setting
3. Connection speed with browser
4. Operating system with security settings
5. Operating system with browser
6. Security settings with browser

During testing, we just have to make sure that we have at least one test configuration during at least one test that corresponds to a row in this array.[5]

---

5. For a further discussion on pairwise testing, especially the origin and theory behind orthogonal arrays, see Lee Copeland's book *The Practitioner's Guide to Software Test Design*.

00000
01111
02222
03333
10123
11032
12301
13210
20231
21320
22013
23102
30312
31203
32130
33021

Test	Factor			
	Speed	OS	Security	Browser
1	DU	Mac	OS	Firefox
2	DU	Linux	Symantec	IE
3	DU	XP	Trend	Opera
4	DU	Vista	McAfee	~
5	BB	Mac	Symantec	Opera
6	BB	Linux	OS	~
7	BB	XP	McAfee	Firefox
8	BB	Vista	Trend	IE
9	~	Mac	Trend	~
10	~	Linux	McAfee	Opera
11	~	XP	OS	IE
12	~	Vista	Symantec	Firefox
13	~	Mac	McAfee	IE
14	~	Linux	Trend	Firefox
15	~	XP	Symantec	~
16	~	Vista	OS	Opera

Figure 4–50   *Select and map example*

4.2.29 Pairwise Testing Exercise

Assume that you are planning compatibility testing of the HELLOCARMS system for eventual Internet use. Globobank intends to support PCs running the following:

■ Operating systems: Windows XP, Windows Vista, or Mac
■ Browsers: Internet Explorer (but on Windows PCs only), Firefox, or Opera

Globobank intends to support connection speeds of both dial-up and broadband.

Figure 4-51, figure 4-52, and figure 4-53 show orthogonal arrays you might use.

The exercise consists of three parts:

1. Select the appropriate array.
2. Map the factors (OS, browser, and connection speed) and the options within each factor into the array.
3. Handle rows with spare cells and pairs that represent impossible configuration combinations.

The answers to the three parts are shown on the next pages. You should review the answer to the each part (and if necessary, revise your answer to the part that follows) before reviewing the answer to the following part.

	Factors		
Test	**1**	**2**	**3**
1	0	0	0
2	0	1	1
3	1	0	1
4	1	1	0

Figure 4–51   *Orthogonal array 1*

	Factors			
Test	**1**	**2**	**3**	**4**
1	0	0	0	0
2	0	1	1	2
3	0	2	2	1
4	1	0	1	1
5	1	1	2	0
6	1	2	0	2
7	2	0	2	2
8	2	1	0	1
9	2	2	1	0

Figure 4–52   *Orthogonal array 2*

Test	Factors 1	2	3	4	5
1	0	0	0	0	0
2	0	1	1	1	1
3	0	2	2	2	2
4	0	3	3	3	3
5	1	0	1	2	3
6	1	1	0	3	2
7	1	2	3	0	1
8	1	3	2	1	0
9	2	0	2	3	1
10	2	1	3	2	0
11	2	2	0	1	3
12	2	3	1	0	2
13	3	0	3	1	2
14	3	1	2	0	3
15	3	2	1	3	0
16	3	3	0	2	1

Figure 4–53   *Orthogonal array 3*

4.2.30 Pairwise Testing Exercise Debrief

First, we select an appropriate orthogonal array. There are three factors and a maximum of three options per factor. So we need an array with three columns, three numbers per column, and nine rows; that is the array shown figure 4-52.

Now we map the factors and options onto the array, which gives us the result shown in table 4-14.

Table 4–14 *Mapped HELLOCARMS orthogonal array*

Test	Factor		
	OS	Browser	Speed
1	XP	IE	Dialup
2	XP	Firefox	Broadband
3	XP	Opera	~
4	Vista	IE	Broadband
5	Vista	Firefox	~
6	Vista	Opera	Dialup
7	Mac	IE	~
8	Mac	Firefox	Dialup
9	Mac	Opera	Broadband

But we have a problem with table 4-14. The requirements said that we would support Internet Explorer only on Windows systems. Test seven has a combination of Mac with Internet Explorer. Of course, we are guaranteed that this situation would arise because we are guaranteed that all pairs of options across all pairs of factors will occur at least once in the table.

Fortunately, due to the "tester's choice" mapping, the solution is trivia. There are no pairs in that row other than the invalid pair of Mac OS with Internet Explorer browser. So in this case, we can delete the row, obtaining the final test configuration set shown in table 4-15.

Table 4–15 *Final HELLOCARMS test configuration*

Test	Factor		
	OS	Browser	Speed
1	XP	IE	Dialup
2	XP	Firefox	Broadband
3	XP	Opera	~
4	Vista	IE	Broadband
5	Vista	Firefox	~
6	Vista	Opera	Dialup
7	Mac	Firefox	Dialup
8	Mac	Opera	Broadband

At this point, there are four points I should make before we wind down this discussion of pairwise techniques.

First, notice that I don't call table 4-15 an orthogonal array. It isn't because it no longer has the properties of an orthogonal array after I deleted row seven.

Second, if you did the search-and-replace portion of the mapping differently, you might have found that the row with the invalid Mac/Internet Explorer pair had two other pairs in it. In that case, you have to capture those pairs in other rows—using tester's choice or adding a row—before you can delete the row with the invalid pair.

That brings us to the third point: Be very, very cautious about deleting and merging rows. The pairs arise from interactions between pairs of columns.

Make sure there are no unique pairs—i.e., pairs of options not covered in some other row—present in a row before you delete it. If you are going to merge two rows, make sure that any specified options—i.e., options that are not tester's choice—in one row either correspond to a tester's choice option in the other row or that the specified options are the same in both rows.

Finally, all pairs tables can be smaller, so it's worth having a freeware tool handy. However, in many cases, the mapping to an orthogonal array is so quick and easy, and results in so few extra rows, that you might tend to use that technique more.

4.2.31 Classification Trees

The pairwise technique is handy, and compatibility testing of the kind we looked at in the previous part arises frequently in testing. However, sometimes factors are constrained in that certain options for one factor won't coexist with certain options for another factor. Other times, we want to test certain factors or certain combinations of factors more heavily than others. If we are looking at configuration options for a program, for example, some of those options probably do interact.

Conceptually, classification trees are a way to test constrained combinations of factors. They also allow us to test some factors more heavily than others.

The underlying model is a graphical representation of the factors and the options for each factor, usually prepared using equivalence partitioning. There are also rules for factor and option combination, including the level of combinations to achieve across certain factors (e.g., all triples for three factors, but only pairs for the other factors).

Given the model, you can then derive the tests, usually shown as a table of option combinations across the factors. As a practical matter, you will need a tool to do this. As with orthogonal arrays and all pairs tables, the coverage criterion is that you have to have every row represented in a least one test.

Again, as with pairwise testing, the bug hypothesis is that this level of coverage will suffice. The difference is that we can have varying levels of coverage depending on the factors. We are going to hypothesize a higher likelihood of combined option misbehaviors for certain factors or a higher level of risk based on business need. We can have factors combined in all pairs, all triples, all

> **ISTQB Glossary**
>
> **classification tree:** A tree showing equivalence partitions hierarchically ordered, which is used to design test cases in the classification tree method.
>
> **classification tree method:** A black-box test design technique in which test cases, described by means of a classification tree, are designed to execute combinations of representatives of input and/or output domains.

quadruples, or even higher-order combinations. Of course, the more higher-order combinations we have, the bigger the table and the more the tests.

Suppose that we are testing the Microsoft Word font menu, shown in figure 4-54. In particular, we are interested in the following factors and options because we worry that they might interact improperly:

- Style: regular, italic, bold, bold italic
- Size: smallest (8), typical (12), largest (72)
- Strikethrough: no, yes, double
- Height: normal, subscript, superscript
- Caps: normal, small caps, all caps

So, we will use the classification tree technique to generate tests to check for interactions.

To use this technique, a tool is necessary. Fortunately, at this time, there is a free tool available at the following URL:

www.systematic-testing.com/download/cte_download.php.

The website says it is "temporarily" free, but it seems to have been available free for a couple of years now. Once you have the tool downloaded and installed, spend a few minutes reading the manual so you can understand how to use it.

For each testing problem to which you want to apply this technique, you start by identifying some aspect of interest. This is some collection of things you think might interact in some interesting way, so you want to test combinations.

Now, you identify the classifications within that area of interest. These are what I referred to as "factors" in my discussion about pairwise testing. These

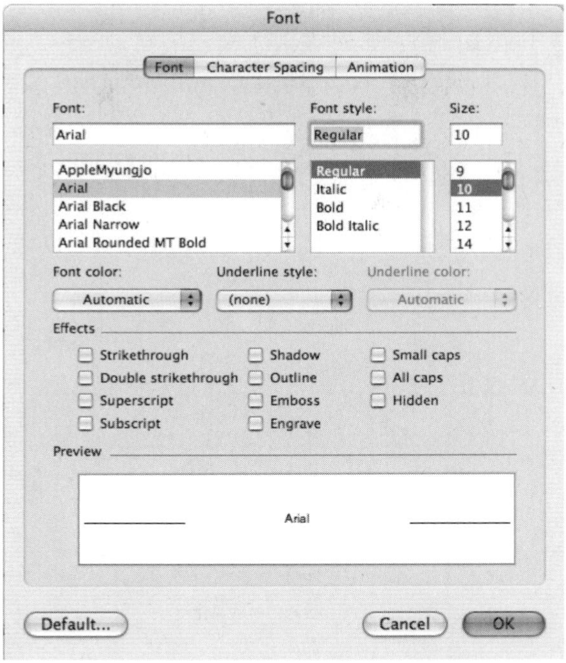

Figure 4–54   *A situation where classification trees might help*

are the things you think might interact. In some cases, you'll identify subclassifications for one or more classifications. Once you are done with that, you use standard equivalence partitioning and boundary value analysis to identify classes for each classification. These correspond to the "options" in my discussion about pairwise testing.

Now you define the rules for combining the classifications. Do you want pairs of all factors? Triples of some factors? Are there exclusions, i.e., classes that can't combine? Once you have that done, you generate the test cases (using the tool). It will create a table, much like the orthogonal array.

Figure 4-55 shows the classification tree that I drew using the CTE XL tool to address font property interaction problems. You can see that font is the root of the tree. We have size, style, strikethrough, height, and caps as the classifications. Each classification has three or more classes.

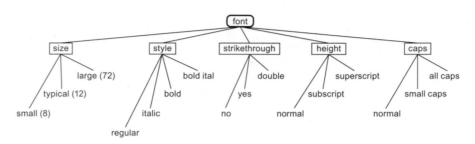

Figure 4–55   *Font classification tree example*

Figure 4-56 shows the table produced when I generated tests for all pairs. There are 14 rows in the table. The first row says we should test a small (8 point) font with regular style, double strikethrough, subscript height, and all caps.

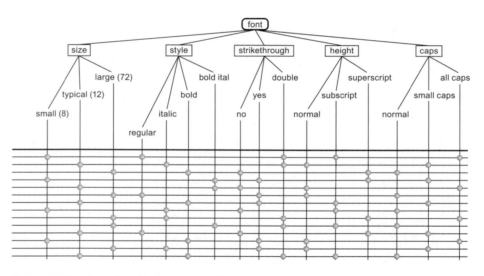

Figure 4–56   *Font classification pairs table*

At this point, we haven't really done anything we couldn't have done with pairwise testing. However, in figure 4-57, you'll see something we couldn't have done with pairwise testing techniques. Here we see the table and tree that result when I tell the tool to generate triples of sizes, height, and caps as well as all pairs across all factors. There are now 30 tests. Study the figure to see some of the combinations covered in the table.[6]

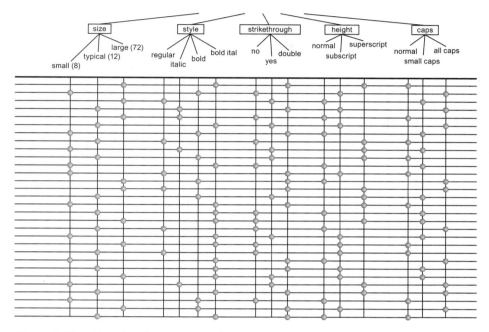

Figure 4–57   *Font classification tree triples*

4.2.32 Classification Trees Exercise

In this exercise, you'll build on your solution to the decision table exercise.

The exercise consists of four parts:

1. Create a classification tree for the decision table, showing classifications and classes.
2. Use the tool to generate all pairs for age and body mass index only.
3. Use the tool to generate all pairs possible.
4. Use the tool to generate all triples possible.

---

6. For more information on classification trees, in addition to what's included with the CTE XL tool, you can find the initial paper that introduced the concept, Matthias Grochtmann's "Test case design using Classification Trees" (which is usually easy to find with an Internet search), or you can read the section on data combination testing in Koomen, et al.'s *TMap Next*.

As usual, check your answer for each part before proceeding to the next part.

Note: You will need to download and install a classification tree tool. As I was writing this book, a freeware version is available at www.systematic-testing.com/download/cte_download.php.

4.2.33 Classification Trees Exercise Debrief

Figure 4-58 shows the classification tree I came up with. Your tree might look a little different, but only in terms of formatting. If you don't have a root node with six classifications on it, with Boolean classes for four of the classifications and the ranges shown for the BMI and age classifications, you made some mistake.

One thing you might have done is to include the ranges of BMI and age as subclassifications with boundary values as classes underneath them if you want to force testing of boundary values. However, notice that you can accomplish this by mapping boundary values onto the table, and you typically will have at least two representatives of each option when you're doing pairwise combinations.

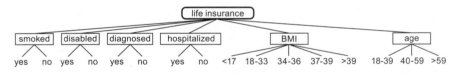

Figure 4–58   *Classification tree for HELLOCARMS life insurance*

Now, figure 4-59 shows the classification tree and table that includes all pairs of BMI and age options.

Changing the rule to require all pairs across all factors, I generate the tests shown in figure 4-60. Notice that this figure also shows the tests generated for pairs of age and BMI, to allow you to compare them.

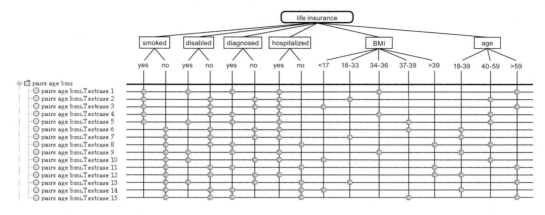

Figure 4–59 *HELLOCARMS classification tree tests (pairs of BMI and age)*

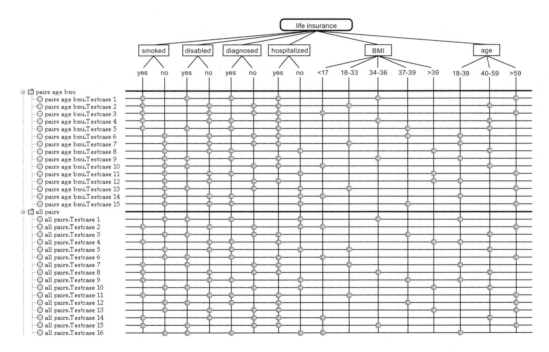

Figure 4–60 *HELLOCARMS classification tree tests (all pairs)*

Finally, changing the rule to require all triples across all factors, I generate the tests shown in figure 4-61. Notice that this figure also shows the tests generated for pairs of age and BMI and for all pairs, to allow you to compare them.

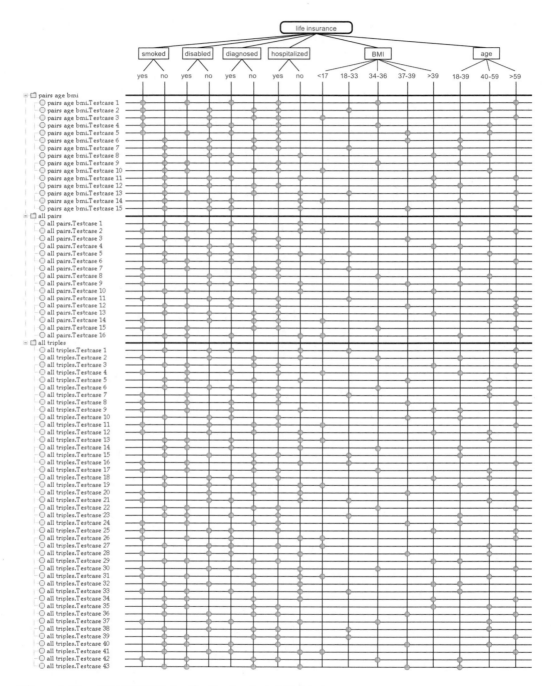

Figure 4–61   *HELLOCARMS classification tree tests (all triples)*

4.2.34 Deriving Tests from the Test Basis

Let's wind down this section by making sure that you understand how to connect the test design techniques we discussed with the test basis. Specification-based tests derive from the test basis, often a requirements specification. This is particularly true at the higher levels of testing like system test, system integration test, and acceptable test. Because requirements specifications focus mostly on behavior, the primary test design techniques are the behavioral (or black-box) techniques we've covered in this section.

Now, seldom do developers, designers, and business analysts give you the models that we described. For example, if you do get a decision table or a use case embedded in the requirements, great, use it. However, you might have to figure out how to create the model yourself. So, to apply the techniques from this section, here's a simple three-step process:

1. Analyze requirements specifications.
2. Create the model or models corresponding to the test design technique or techniques that you think will apply best.
3. Derive tests from models as described in this section.

Let's look at an example. Here are two requirements from the Internet appliance project:

- Support popular email attachments: TXT, JPEG, GIF, AU, WAV, and URL
- If unsupported attachment is received, send automated reply to sender indicating which attachments are okay to send

By discussions with marketing people and designers, we discovered that the maximum attachment size was 1 MB.

Figure 4-62 shows the application of equivalence partitioning and boundary value analysis to those two requirements. Notice that, for the supported partition, we are going to test six supported file types, with five tests per type based on the boundary value analysis. For the unsupported partition, we are going to test four unsupported (but typical) file types. We will also test six examples of correct extensions but corrupted contents. Table 4-16 shows the tests derived from this analysis. Study them to satisfy yourself that all the equivalence class and boundary values were covered.

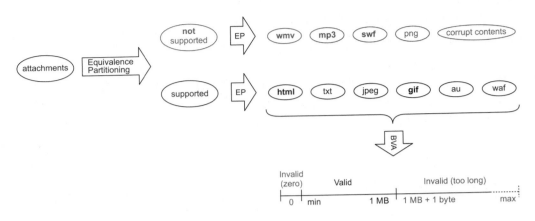

Figure 4–62   *Requirements EP and BVA example*

Table 4–16 *EV and BVA tests example*

#	Test Procedure Step	Expected Result
1.	Send email with minimum length html attachment.	Confirm correct receipt on Internet appliance.
2.	Repeat step 1 with 1 MB html.	Confirm correct receipt.
3.	Repeat steps 1 and 2 for txt, jpeg, gif, au, and wav files.	Confirm correct receipt.
4.	Send 0 length attachment with .html filename extension.	Confirm error message on Internet appliance.
5.	Repeat step 5 for txt, jpeg, gif, au, and wav files.	Confirm error message on Internet appliance.
6.	Repeat steps 4 and 5 with attachments of exactly 1 MB + 1 byte length.	Confirm error message to sender (bounce message).
7.	Repeat step 6 with attachments of maximum outbound send length (usually around 10 MB).	Confirm error message to sender (bounce message). Confirm NO corruption of user's inbox.
8.	Send a wmv file of legal size.	Confirm error message to sender (bounce message).
9.	Repeat step 8 for mp3, swf, and png files.	Confirm error message to sender (bounce message).
10.	Send an html file of legal size but with corrupted contents.	Confirm error message on Internet appliance.
11.	Repeat step 10 for txt, jpeg, gif, au, and wav files.	Confirm error message on Internet appliance.

4.2.35 Deriving Tests from the Test Basis Exercise

Refer to the HELLOCARMS system requirements document. Consider requirement element 010-020-040.

The exercise consists of two parts:

1. Select appropriate techniques for test design.
2. Apply those techniques to generate tests, achieving the coverage criteria for the techniques.

As always, check your work on the first part before proceeding to the second part.

The solutions are shown on the next pages.

4.2.36 Deriving Tests from the Test Basis Exercise Debrief

First, remember from an earlier exercise in this section, we tested escalation of calls and rejection of invalid property values. In that exercise, the following rules applied to loans:

■   The minimum property value is $25,000.
■   The maximum property value is $5,000,000.

We don't need to repeat those tests, but certainly this is interesting input for the fee calculation.

I selected three techniques. First, I use a simple decision table on the fee percentage selection as shown in table 4-17.

Table 4–17   *HELLOCARMS property type fee*

Conditions	1	2	3	4	5
Property Type	one-family	rental	commercial	condo/coop	undeveloped
Actions					
Fee Percentage	0	1.5	2.5	3.5	4.5

Next, for the rental and condominium and cooperatives, I apply equivalence partitioning as shown in table 4-18.

Table 4–18 *Property type equivalence partitions*

#	Partition	Subpartition (if any)
1	One-family	–
2	Rental	Duplex
3	Rental	Apartment
4	Rental	Vacation
5	Commercial	–
6	Condo/coop	Condo
7	Condo/coop	Coop
8	Undeveloped	–

I apply boundary value analysis to each of the fee calculations, including where there is no fee, as shown in table 4-19. You might argue that just calculating a zero fee, a minimum fee, and a maximum fee is enough, but I would say that this is a high-risk calculation that needs extensive testing.

Table 4–19 *Property fee boundary values*

#	Partition	Boundary Value
1	0	0
2	0	0
3	1.5	375
4	1.5	75,000
5	2.5	625
6	2.5	125,000
7	3.5	875
8	3.5	175,000
9	4.5	1125
10	4.5	225,000

Based on these three techniques, I generated the test cases shown in table 4-20.

Table 4–20 *Property type and fee test cases*

Conditions	Test case										
	1	2	3	4	5	6	7	8	9	10	11
Type	1fam	1fam	Rent	Rent	Rent	Com	Com	CC	CC	Und	Und
Subtype	–	–	Dup	Apt	Vaca	–	–	Condo	Coop	–	–
Value	25K	5M	25K	5M	1M	25K	5M	25K	5M	25K	5M
Actions											
Fee %	0	0	1.5	1.5	1.5	2.5	2.5	3.5	3.5	4.5	4.5
Fee Amount	0	0	375	75K	15K	625	125K	875	175K	1,125	225K

Notice that I've only done coverage analysis for the equivalent partitions and boundary values in table 4-21 and table 4-22, because each column in the decision table had at least one partition and at least two boundary values associated with it. Therefore, if I cover the partitions and boundary values, I'm guaranteed to cover the decision table.

Table 4–21 *Equivalence partition coverage*

#	Partition	Subpartition (if any)	Test Case
1	One-family	–	1, 2
2	Rental	Duplex	3
3	Rental	Apartment	4
4	Rental	Vacation	5
5	Commercial	–	6, 7
6	Condo/coop	Condo	8
7	Condo/coop	Coop	9
8	Undeveloped	–	10, 11

Table 4–22 *Boundary value coverage*

#	Partition	Boundary Value	Test Case
1	0	0	1
2	0	0	2
3	1.5	375	3
4	1.5	75,000	4
5	2.5	625	6
6	2.5	125,000	7
7	3.5	875	8
8	3.5	175,000	9
9	4.5	1,125	10
10	4.5	225,000	11

4.3   Structure-Based Techniques

Learning objectives
Recall of content only

The concepts in this section apply primarily for technical test analysts. There are no learning objectives defined for test analysts in this section. In the course of studying for the exam, read this section in chapter 4 of the Advanced syllabus for general recall and familiarity only.

ISTQB Glossary

branch testing: A white-box test design technique in which test cases are designed to execute branches.

condition testing: A white-box test design technique in which test cases are designed to execute condition outcomes.

condition outcome: The evaluation of a condition to True or False.

condition determination testing (or **multiple condition testing):** A white-box test design technique in which test cases are designed to execute single condition outcomes that independently affect a decision outcome.

control flow: A sequence of events (paths) in the execution through a component or system.

control flow analysis: A form of static analysis based on a representation of sequences of events (paths) in the execution through a component or system.

D-D path: *No definition in ISTQB glossary.*

data flow analysis: A form of static analysis based on the definition and usage of variables.

decision testing: A white-box test design technique in which test cases are designed to execute decision outcomes.

LCSAJ: A Linear Code Sequence and Jump, consisting of the following three items (conventionally identified by line numbers in a source code listing): the start of the linear sequence of executable statements, the end of the linear sequence, and the target line to which control flow is transferred at the end of the linear sequence.

path testing: A white-box test design technique in which test cases are designed to execute paths.

path: A sequence of events, e.g., executable statements, of a component or system from an entry point to an exit point.

statement testing: A white-box test design technique in which test cases are designed to execute statements.

structure-based technique (or white-box test design technique**):** Procedure to derive and/or select test cases based on an analysis of the internal structure of a component or system.

4.3.1 Defect- and Experience-based Techniques

Learning objectives

(K2) Describe the principles and reasons for defect-based techniques and differentiate its use from specification- and structure-based techniques.

(K2) Using examples, explain defect taxonomies and their use.

(K2) Understand the principles and reasons for using experienced-based techniques and when to use them.

(K3) Specify, execute, and report tests using exploratory testing .

(K2) Classify defects that can be identified by the different types of software fault attacks according to the defects they target .

(K4) Analyze a system in order to determine which specification-based, defect-based, or experienced-based techniques to apply for specific goals.

Now we're going to move from systematic techniques for test design into less-structured but nonetheless useful techniques. We start with defect-based and defect-taxonomy-based techniques.

Conceptually, we are doing defect-based testing anytime the type of the defect sought is the basis for the test. Usually, the underlying model is some list of detects seen in the past. If this list is organized as a hierarchical taxonomy, then the testing is defect-taxonomy based. To derive tests from the defect list or the defect taxonomy, we create tests designed to reveal the presence of the defects in the list.

Now for defect-based tests, we tend to be more relaxed about the concept of coverage. The general criterion is that we will create a test for each defect type, but it is often the case that the question of whether to create a test at all is risk weighted. In other words, if the likelihood or impact of the defect doesn't justify the effort, don't do it. However, if the likelihood or impact of the defect were high, then you would create not just one test, but perhaps many. This should be starting to sound familiar to you, yes?

The underlying bug hypothesis is that programmers tend to repeatedly make the same mistakes. In other words, a team of programmers will introduce roughly the same types of bugs in roughly the same proportion from one project to the next. This allows us to allocate test design and execution effort based on the likelihood and impact of the bugs.

4.3.2 Defect Taxonomies

Figure 4-63 shows an example of a defect taxonomy. There are eight main categories along with five "bookkeeper" categories that are useful when classifying bugs in a bug tracking system. Let's go through these in detail.[7]

In the category of Functional defects, there are three subcategories:

- **Specification**: The functional specification—perhaps in the requirements document or in some other document—is wrong.
- **Function**: The specification is right, but the implementation of it is wrong.
- **Test**: Upon close research, we found a problem in test data, test designs, test specifications, or somewhere else.

In the category of System defects, there are five subcategories:

- **Internal Interface**: An internal system communication failed. In other words, there was an integration problem of some sort internal to the test object.

---

7. This taxonomy occurs in my book, *Managing the Testing Process*, but I derived it from Boris Beizer's taxonomy in *Software Testing Techniques*.

• Functional	• Data
- Specification	- Type
- Function	- Structure
- Test	- Initial Value
• System	- Other
- Internal Interfaces	• Code
- Hardware Devices	• Documentation
- Operating System	• Standards
- Software Architecture	• Other
- Resource Management	• Duplicate
• Process	• Not a Problem
- Arithmetik	• Bad Unit
- Initialization	• Root cause needed
- Control or Sequence	• Unknown
- Static Logic	
- Other	

Figure 4–63   *Root-cause-focus taxonomies*

■ **Hardware Devices**: The hardware that is part of the system or which hosts the system failed.

■ **Operating System**: The operating system—which presumably is external to the test object—failed.

■ **Software Architecture**: Some fundamental design assumption proved invalid, such as an assumption that data could be moved from one table to another or across some network in some constant period.

■ **Resource Management**: The design assumptions were okay, but some implementation of the assumption was wrong. For example, the design of the data tables introduces delays.

In the category of Process defects, there are five subcategories:

■ **Arithmetic**: The software does math wrong. This doesn't mean just basic math. It can also include sophisticated accounting or numerical analysis functions, including problems that occur due to rounding and precision issues.

- **Initialization**: An operation fails on its first use, when there is no data in a list, and so forth.

- **Control or Sequence**: An action occurs at the wrong time or for the wrong reason, like, say, seeing screens or fields in the wrong order.

- **Static Logic**: Boundaries are misdefined, equivalence classes don't include the right members and exclude the wrong members, and so forth.

- **Other**: A control-flow or processing error that doesn't fit in the preceding categories has occurred.

In the category of Data defects, there are four subcategories:

- **Type**: The wrong data type—whether a built-in or user-defined data type—was used.

- **Structure**: A complex data structure or type is invalid or inappropriately used.

- **Initial Value**: A data element's initialized value is incorrect, like a list of quantities to purchase that defaults to zero rather than one.

- **Other**: A data-related error occurs that doesn't fit in the preceding buckets.

The category of Code applies to some simple typo, misspelling, stylistic error, or other coding error that results in a failure. Theoretically, these shouldn't get past a compiler, but in these days of scripting on browsers, this stuff does happen.

The category of Documentation applies to situations where the documentation says the system does X on condition Y, but the system does Z—a valid and correct action—instead.

The category of Standards applies to situations where the system fails to meet industry, governmental, or vendor standards or regulations; fails to follow coding or user interface standards; or fails to adhere to naming conventions; and so forth.

The Other category applies when the root cause is known but fits none of the preceding categories, which should be rare if this is a useful taxonomy.

The five housekeeping categories are as follows:

- **Duplicate:** You find that two bug reports describe the same bug.

- **Not a problem:** The behavior noted is correct. The report arose from a misunderstanding on the part of the tester about correct behavior. This situation is different than a test failure because this occurs during test execution and is an issue of interpretation of an actual result.

- **Bad Unit:** The bug is a real problem, but it arises from a random hardware failure that is unlikely in the *production environment*.

- **Root cause needed:** Applies when the bug is confirmed as closed by test but no one in development has supplied a root cause.

- **Unknown:** No one knows what is broken. Ideally, this applies to a small number of reports, generally when an intermittent bug doesn't appear for quite awhile, leading to a conclusion that some other change fixed the bug as a side effect.

Notice that this taxonomy is focused on root causes, at least in the sense of what ultimately proved to be wrong in the code that caused the failure.

You could also have a "process root cause" taxonomy that showed at which phase in the development process that bug was introduced. Notice that we could probably not use such a taxonomy to design tests. Even the root-cause-focused taxonomy can be a bit hard to use for purposes of test design.

Figure 4-64 shows an example of a bug taxonomy—a rather coarse-grained one—gathered from the Internet appliance case study we've looked at a few times in this book. This taxonomy is focused on symptoms. Notice that this makes it easier to think about the tests we might design. However, its coarse-grained nature means that we'll need to have additional information—lists of desired functional areas, usability and user interface standards and requirements, reliability specifications, and the like—to use this to design tests. I've also showed the percentage of bugs we actually found in each category during system test.

Description	Count	%
Failed functionality	425	46%
Missing functionality	179	19%
Poor usability	106	11%
Build failed	62	7%
Bad system design/architecture	51	5%
Reliability problem	49	5%
Data loss	18	2%
Slow performance	16	2%
Code obsolete	16	2%
Deviation from specification	8	1%
Bad user documentation	2	0%
Total	**932**	**100%**

Figure 4–64 *Symptom-focused taxonomies*

4.3.3 Error Guessing

Error guessing is a term introduced by Glenford Myers.[8] Conceptually, error guessing involves the tester taking guesses about a mistake that a programmer might make and then developing tests for it. Notice that this is what might be a called a "gray-box" test because it requires the tester to have some idea about typical programming mistakes, how those mistakes become bugs, how those bugs manifest themselves as failures, and how we can force failures to happen.

Now, if error guessing follows an organized hierarchical taxonomy, like defect-taxonomy-based tests, then the taxonomy is the model. The taxonomy also provides the coverage criterion, if it is used, because we again test to the extent appropriate for the various elements of the taxonomy. Usually, error guessing follows mostly from tester inspiration.

As you can tell so far, the derivation of tests is based on the tester's intuition and knowledge about how errors (the programmer's or designer's mistake)

---

8. You can find this technique and others we have discussed in this book in the first book on software testing, *The Art of Software Testing.*

> **ISTQB Glossary**
>
> **error guessing:** A test design technique where the experience of the tester is used to anticipate what defects might be present in the component or system under test as a result of errors made and to design tests specifically to expose them.

become defects that manifest themselves as failures if you poke and prod the system in the right way. Error guessing tests can be part of an analytical, predesigned, scripted test procedure. However, they often aren't but are added to the scripts (ideally) or used instead of scripts (less ideal) at execution time.

The underlying bug hypothesis is very similar to that of defect-taxonomy-based tests. Here, though, we not only count on the programmer to make the same mistakes, but we also count on the tester to have seen bugs like the ones in this system before and to remember how to find them.

At this point, you're probably thinking back to our earlier discussion about quality risk analysis. Some of these concepts sound very familiar, don't they? Certainly, error guessing is something that we do *during* quality risk analysis. It's an important part of determining the likelihood. Perhaps we as test analysts don't do it, but rather we rely on the developers to do it for us. Or maybe we participate with them. Depends on our experience, which is why error guessing is an experience-based test technique.

Maybe a bug taxonomy is a form of risk analysis? It has elements of a quality risk analysis in that it has a list of potential failures and frequency ratings. However, it doesn't always include impact.

Even if a bug taxonomy does include impact ratings for potential bugs, it's still not quite right. Remember that, the way I described it, a quality risk analysis is organized around quality risk categories or quality characteristics. A bug taxonomy is organized around categories of failures or root causes rather than quality risk categories or quality.

4.3.4 Checklist Testing

With checklist testing, we now get into an area that is often very much like quality risk analysis in its structure. Conceptually, the tester takes a high-level list of items to be noted, checked, or remembered. What is important for the system to do? What is important for it not to do?

The checklist is the model for testing, and the checklist is usually organized around a theme. The theme can be quality characteristics, user interface standards, key operations, or any other theme you would like to pick. To derive tests from a checklist, either during test execution time or during test design, you create one to evaluate the system per the test objectives of the checklist.

Now, we can specify a coverage criterion, which is that there be at least one test per checklist item. However, the checklist items are often very high level. By very high level, I don't mean high-level test case. You might remember we looked at those when we talked about use case testing. A high-level or logical test case gives rules about how to generate the specific inputs and expected results, but it doesn't necessarily give the exact values, as a low-level or concrete test case would.

A test checklist is even higher level than that. It will give you a list of areas to test, characteristics to evaluate, general rules for determining test pass or failure, and the like. So you can develop and execute one set of tests while another competent tester might cover the same checklist differently. Notice that this is not true for many of the specification-based techniques we covered, where there was one right answer.

The underlying bug hypothesis in checklist testing is that bugs in the areas of the checklist are likely, important, or both. Notice again that much of this harkens back to risk-based testing. But in some cases, the checklist is predetermined rather than developed by an analysis of the system. As such, checklist testing is often the dominant technique when the testing follows a methodical test strategy. When testing follows an analytical test strategy, the list of test conditions is not a static checklist but rather is generated at the beginning of the project and periodically refreshed during the project, through some sort of analysis, such as quality risk analysis.

Figure 4-65 shows an example of a checklist for usability of a system. Let's go through the checklist to see what it is telling us about system usability.[9]

Simple and natural dialog means that the exact right content and amount of information is provided to the user when needed and where needed (screenwise).

---

9. I've adapted this checklist from Jakob Nielsen's book *Usability Engineering*.

- Simple and natural dialog
- Speak the user's language
- Minimize user memory load
- Consistency
- Feedback
- Clearly marked exits
- Shortcuts
- Good error messages
- Prevent errors
- Help and documentation

Figure 4–65   *Usability heuristics*

The graphics and colors on the screen should reinforce and direct user attention toward—not conflict with or distract the user from—the message. The amount of information should be what is needed, and no more, and certainly not extraneous details that don't matter.

Speaking the user's language means not talking down to the user, but also not using terms, jargon, and acronyms that the user won't understand.

Minimizing user memory load means not forcing the user to keep too many details in their head from one screen to the next, giving useful prompts and visual cues about what to do next or how to get help, and so forth.

Consistency means that screens look and feel the same, hot keys remain constant, color schemes are similar (e.g., red means bad, green means good, throughout), and so forth.

Providing feedback means keeping the user informed about what is happening, especially when there is processing time going by or when something has failed.

Clearly marked exits mean that it's obvious how to get out of the screen, mode, or dialog you're in and back to a place you were before—including out of the system.

Shortcuts allow experts to bypass the handholding the new users need.

Good error messages are intuitive and helpful. They don't use codes, they are precise about the problem, and they are polite and soothing.

Preventing errors means that we minimize opportunities for users to make mistakes. This, of course, improves testability because it reduces the number of invalid test cases we have to try.

And, even though it's used less often than most support people would like, we should provide help and documentation.

Okay, so how do we use this for testing? Well, imagine going through the screens on the system, methodically checking off each of these main areas on each screen and for each transition between screens. If you see problems, you report a bug against this heuristic for the screen or screen transition where you saw the problem. Notice the subjectivity involved in the evaluation of test pass or fail results.

4.3.5 Exploratory Testing

Exploratory testing, like checklist testing, often follows some basic guidelines, like a checklist, and often relies on tester judgment and experience to evaluate the test results. However, exploratory testing is inherently more reactive, more dynamic, in that most of the action with exploratory testing has to happen during test execution.

Conceptually, exploratory testing is happening when a tester is simultaneously learning the system, designing tests, and executing tests. The results of one test largely determine what we test next.

Now, that is not to say that this is random or driven entirely by impulse or instinct. Notice that we could use Nielsen's list of usability heuristics not only as a preplanned checklist but also as a heuristic to guide us to important or problematic software areas. The best kinds of exploratory testing usually do have some type of model, either written or mental. According to this model, we derive tests by thinking how best to explore some area of testing interest. In some cases, to keep focus and provide some amount of structure, the test areas to be covered are constrained by a test charter.

As with checklist testing, we can specify a coverage criterion, which is that there be at least one test per charter (if we have them). However, the charters, like checklist items, are often very high level.

ISTQB Glossary

exploratory testing: An informal test design technique where the tester actively controls the design of the tests as those tests are performed and uses information gained while testing to design new and better tests.

test charter: A statement of test objectives, and possibly test ideas about how to test. Test charters are used in exploratory testing. *[Note: This statement is actually incorrect. Not all exploratory testing uses test charters, and test charters can be used in any dynamic testing strategy.]*

The underlying bug hypothesis is that the system will reveal buggy areas during test execution that would be hidden during test basis analysis. In other words, you can only learn so much about how a system behaves and misbehaves by reading about it. This is, of course, true. It also suggests an important point, which is that exploratory testing, and indeed experience-based tests in general, make a good blend with scripted tests because they offset each other's weak spots.

The focus of testing in the ISTQB Foundation and Advanced syllabi is analytical; that is, following an analytical test strategy. Analytical strategies are good at defect prevention, risk mitigation, and structured coverage. Experience-based tests usually follow a dynamic or reactive test strategy. One way that analytical and dynamic strategies differ is in the process of testing.

The exploratory testing process, unlike the ISTQB Fundamental testing process, is very much focused on taking the system as we find it and going from there. Testers simultaneously learn about the product and its defects, plan the testing work to be done (or, if they have charters, adjust the plan), design and execute the tests, and report the results.

Now, when doing exploratory testing, it's important not to degrade into frenzied, aimless keyboard pounding. Good exploratory tests are planned, interactive, and creative. As I mentioned, the test strategy is dynamic, and one manifestation of this is that the tester dynamically adjusts test goals during execution.[10]

---

10. You can find further information on exploratory testing in Erik van Veenendaal's book *The Testing Practitioner.*

4.3.6   Test Charters

Because there is so much activity happening during test execution—activity that, in an analytical strategy, happens before execution—as you can imagine, some trade-offs must occur. One of those is in the extent of documentation of what was tested, how that related to the test basis, and what the results were.

People have long seen the inability to say what was tested during exploratory testing, to a sufficient degree of accuracy, as its Achilles heel. The whole confidence-building objective of testing is undermined if we can't say what we've tested and how much we've tested it as well as what we haven't yet tested. Notice that analytical test strategies do a good job of this, at least when traceability is present.

One way people have come up with to reduce this problem with exploratory testing is to use test charters. A test charter specifies the tasks, objectives, and deliverables, but in very few words. The charters can be developed well in advance—even, in fact, based on analysis of risks as we have done for some clients—or they can be developed just immediately before test execution starts and then continually adjusted based on the test results.

Right before test execution starts for a given period of testing, exploratory testing sessions are planned around the charters. These plans are not formally written following IEEE 829 or anything like that. In fact, they might not be written at all. However, consensus will exist between test analyst and test manager about the following:

- What the test session is to achieve
- Where the test session will focus
- What is in and out of scope for the session
- What resources should be used, including how long it should last

Now, given how lightweight the charters are—as you'll see in a moment—you might expect that the tester would get more information. And indeed, the charters can be augmented with defect taxonomies, checklists, quality risk analyses, requirements specifications, user manuals, and whatever else might be of use. However, these augmentations are to be used as reference during test execution rather than as objects of analysis—i.e., as a test basis—prior to the test execution starting.

Exploratory Testing Session Log

Tester _Name _____   Date _When _____

Time on-task _1:45 _____   Charter completed? _yes_____

Charter
Test the security of the login page, see if it's possible to log in without a password.

Bugs reported
937 – Log in form vulnerable to SQL injection 939 – System identifies a valid username when the password is wrong

Issues that need follow-up
* Lockout feature on three unsuccessful login attempts doesn't seem to work

Figure 4–66   *Test charter example*

Here in figure 4-66 we see an example of how this works. This is an actual exploratory testing session log from a project we did for a client recently. We were in charge of running an acceptance test for the development organization on behalf of the customers. If that sounds like a weird arrangement, by the way, yes, it was.

At the top of the log, we have captured the tester's name and when the test was run. It also includes a log of how much time was spent and whether the tester believes that the charter was completely explored—remember, this is subjective, as with the checklists.

Below the heading information you see the charter. Now, it's not unusual to have a test procedure called "test login security" or even to have a sentence like this in the description of a test procedure or listed as a condition in a test design specification. However, understand that *this is all there is*. There are no further details specified in the test for the tester. You see how we are relying very heavily on the tester's knowledge and experience?

Under the charter section are two sections that indicate results. The first lists the bugs that were found. The numbers correspond to numbers in a bug tracking system. The second lists issues that need follow-up. These can be—as they are here—things that might be bugs but that we didn't have time to finish researching. Or it could indicate situations where testing was incomplete due to blockages. In that case, of course, we'd expect that the charter would not be complete.

4.3.7   Software Attacks

Finally, we come to a technique that you can think of as an interesting synthesis of all the defect- and experience-based techniques we've covered in this section, software attacks. It combines elements of defect taxonomies, checklist-based tests, error guessing, and exploratory tests.

Conceptually, you can think of software attacks as a directed and focused form of testing that attempts to force specific failures to occur. As you can see, this is like a defect taxonomy in that way. However, it's more structured than a defect taxonomy because it is built on a fault model. The fault model talks about how bugs come to be and how and why bugs manifest themselves as failures. We'll look at this question of how bugs come to be in a second when we talk about the bug hypothesis.

This question of manifestation is very important. It's not enough to suspect or believe a bug is there. In dynamic testing, because we aren't looking at the code, we have to look at behaviors.

Now, here comes the similarity with checklists. Based on this fault model, James Whittaker and his students at Florida Tech (from where this idea originated) developed a simple list of attacks that go after these faults. This hierarchical list of attacks—organized around the ways in which bugs come to be—provides ways in which we can force bugs to manifest themselves as failures.[11]

To derive tests, you analyze how each specific attack might apply to the system you're testing. You then design specific tests for each applicable attack. The analysis, design, and assessment of adequate coverage are discretionary and dependent on the skills, intuition, and experience of the tester. The technique provides ideas on when to apply the attack, what bugs make the attack successful, how to determine if the attack has forced a bug into the open as a failure, and how to conduct the attack. However, two reasonable and experienced testers

---

11. This entire approach, including the fault model, is described in detail in James Whittaker's book *How to Break Software*.

ISTQB Glossary

software attacks (or attack): Directed and focused attempt to evaluate the quality, especially reliability, of a test object by attempting to force specific failures to occur.

might apply the same attack differently against the same system and obtain different results.

So, from where does the fault model say bugs come? The underlying bug hypothesis is that bugs arise from interactions between the software and its environment during operation and from the capabilities it possesses. The software's operating environment consists of the human user, the file system, the operating system, and other cohabitating and interoperating software in the same environment. The software's capabilities consist of accepting inputs, producing outputs, storing data, and performing computations.

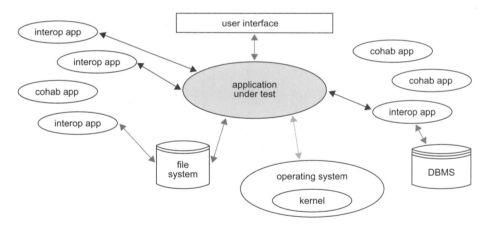

Figure 4–67   *Interfaces to attack*

In figure 4-67, you see a picture of the application under test in its operating environment. The application receives inputs from and sends outputs to its user interface. It interacts in various direct ways with interoperating applications; e.g., through copy-and-paste from one application to another or by sending data to and retrieving data from an application that in turn manages that data with a database management system.

The application also can interact indirectly by sharing data in a file with another application. Yet other applications, with which it does not interact, can potentially affect the application—and vice versa—due to the fact that they cohabit the same system, sharing memory, disk, CPU, and network resources.

The application sends data to and from the file system when it creates, updates, reads, and deletes files. It also relies on the operating system, both its libraries and the kernel, to provide various services and to intermediate interaction with the hardware.

So how can we attack these interfaces? To start with the file system, the technique provides the following attacks:

- Fill the file system to capacity. In fact, you can test while you fill and watch the bugs start to pop up.
- Related to this is the attack of forcing storage to be busy or unavailable. This is particularly true for things that do one thing at a time, like a DVD writer.
- You can damage the storage media, either temporarily or permanently. Dirty or even scratch a CD.
- Use invalid file names, especially special characters in file names.
- Change a file's access permissions, especially while it's being used or between uses.
- And, one of my favorites—for reasons you'll find out in a moment—vary or corrupt file contents.

For interoperating and cohabiting software interfaces, along with the operating system interfaces, the technique suggests the following attacks:

- Force all possible incoming errors from the software/OS interfaces to the application.
- Exhaust resources like memory, CPU, and network resources.
- Corrupt network flows and memory stores.

All of these attacks can involve the use of tools, either homegrown, freeware, or commercial.

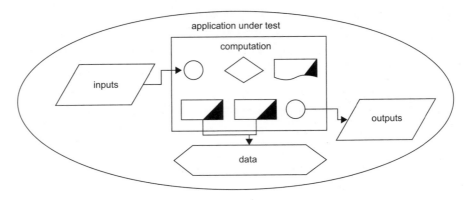

Figure 4–68   *Capabilities to attack*

You'll notice that much of the technique focuses on the file system. I think this is a shame, personally. I would like to see the technique extended to be more useful for system integration testing, particularly for test types like interoperability, end-to-end tests, data quality/data integrity tests with shared databases, and the like. As it is, the technique's interface attacks seem very much focused on PC-based, standalone applications.

In figure 4-68 you see a picture of the application under test in terms of its capabilities. The application accepts inputs. The application performs computations. Data goes into and comes out of data storage (perhaps being persisted to the file system or a database manager in the process, which I've not shown here). The application produces outputs.

So, how can we attack these interfaces? In terms of inputs, we can do the following:

- We can apply various inputs that will force all the error messages to occur. Notice that we'll need a list of error messages from somewhere: user's guide, requirements specification, programmers, wherever.

- We can force the software to use, establish, or revert to default values.

- We can explore the various allowed inputs. You'll notice that equivalence partitioning and boundary value analysis are techniques we can draw upon here.

- We can overflow buffers by putting in really long inputs.

- We can look for inputs that are supposed to interact and test various combinations of their values, perhaps using techniques like equivalence partitioning and decision tables (when we understand and can analyze the interactions) or pairwise testing and classification trees (when we do not understand and cannot analyze the interactions).

- We can repeat the same inputs over and over again.

In terms of outputs, we can do the following:

- We can try to force outputs to be different, including for the same inputs.

- We can try to force invalid outputs to occur.

- We can force properties of outputs to change.

- We can force screen refreshes.

The problem here is that these attacks are mostly focused on stuff we can do, see, or make happen from the user interface. Now that's fertile ground for bugs, but there are certainly other types of inputs, outputs, data, and computations I'm interested in as a tester. Yes, some of that involves access to system interfaces—which is more the province of the technical test analyst—but it's important to keep in mind.

4.3.8   An Example of Effective Attacks

As you might guess, I have to use PowerPoint a lot. It's an occupational hazard. If I sound less than thrilled about this, it's because my experience with Power-Point is that it interoperates poorly with other Office applications and suffers from serious reliability and data integrity problems. In fact, during the time I was creating these materials for the course and this book, I accidentally perpetrated two attacks on PowerPoint that resulted in some serious grief for me.

The first attack occurred when I tried to use some features in Word, Excel, and PowerPoint that share data. Specifically, what I did was to copy tables to and from PowerPoint, Word, and Excel. Now, Word and Excel shared the tables well. However, PowerPoint did not. In fact, I had to resort to things like copy and paste from Notepad (stripping off formatting) and copy and paste column by column.

Now, because I was copying formatted text from Word to PowerPoint, particularly putting that text into text boxes, I found another old nemesis in

PowerPoint, which is that doing that can cause unrecoverable errors in PowerPoint files. All of a sudden, in the middle of your work, you get a message that says your file is screwed up. You have to exit. All data since the last save is lost. And worse yet, sometimes the data that *was* saved is actually the data causing this problem!

To get a better sense of this, you could deliberately run the attack of varying or corrupting file contents. I have a program that will allow me to randomly change as few as one or two *bits* in a file. Now if I use this on a PowerPoint presentation, that will often render the file unreadable, though special recovery software (sold at an extra charge, naturally) can recover all of the text.

However, you don't need to use my special program to corrupt your PowerPoint file. Just assume that you can share data across Office applications and try to do exactly that. Do it long enough and PowerPoint will clobber your file for you.

This situation where PowerPoint creates its own unrecoverable error and file corruption is particularly absurd. You get an error message that says, "PowerPoint has found an error from which it cannot recover" or something like that. I'm sorry, but how can that be? It is its own file! No one else is managing the file. No one else is writing the file. If an application does not understand its own file format and how to get back to a known good state when it damages one of its own files, the application suffers from serious data quality issues.

4.3.9 Other Attacks

So far, I've been describing the specific technique for attacks referenced in the Advanced syllabus, which is Whittaker's technique. However, you should be aware that, if you are testing something other than reliability, interoperability, and functionality of standalone, typically PC-based applications, there are other types of attacks you can and should try.

As another example of software attacks, here is a list of basic security attacks:

- Denial of service, which involves trying to tie up a server with so much traffic that it becomes unavailable.

- Distributed denial of service, which is similar, is using a network of attacking systems to accomplish the denial of service.

- We can try to find a back door—an unsecured port or access point into the system—or we can try to install a back door that provides us with access (which is often accomplished through a Trojan horse like a electronic greeting card, an e-mail attachment, or pornographic websites).

- Sniffing network traffic—watching it as it flows past a port on the system acting as a sniffer—to capture sensitive information like passwords.

- Spoofing traffic, sending out IP packets that appear to come from somewhere else, impersonating another server, and the like.

- Spoofing email, sending out email messages that appear to come from somewhere else, often as a part of a phishing attack.

- Replay attacks, where interactions between some user and a system, or between two systems, are captured and played back later, e.g., to gain access to an account.

- TCP/IP hijacking, where an existing session between a client and a server is taken over, generally after the client has authenticated.

- Weak key detection in encryption systems.

- Password guessing, either by logic or by brute-force password attack using a dictionary of common or known passwords.

- Virus, an infected payload that is attached or embedded in some file, which is then run, causing replication of the virus and perhaps damage to the system that ran the payload.

- Worm, similar to a virus, can penetrate the system under attack itself—generally through some security lapse—and then cause its replication and perhaps damage.

- War-dialing is finding an insecure modem connected to a system, which is rare now, but war-driving is finding unsecured wireless access points, which is amazingly common.

- Finally, social engineering is not an attack on the system, but on a person using the system. It is an attempt to get the user to, say, change their password to something else, to email a file, etc.

Security testing, particularly what's called penetration testing, often follows an attack list like this. The interesting thing about such tests is that, in security testing, as in some user acceptance testing, the tester attempts to emulate the "user"—but in this case, the user is a hacker.[12]

4.3.10 Common Themes

So, what is true about applying these defect- and experience-based techniques?

You probably noticed a distinctly lower level of formality than the specification-based techniques. In addition, the coverage criteria are informal and usually subjective.

Testers must apply knowledge of defects and other experiences to utilize these techniques. Because many of them are defect focused, they are a good way to defect detection.

The extent to which they are dynamic and detection focused rather than analytical and prevention focused varies. They can be quick tests integrated into—or dominating—the test execution period. In these tests, the tester has no formally preplanned activities to perform. They can involve preplanned sessions with charters but no detail beyond that. They can involve the creation of scripted test procedures.

They are useful in almost all projects but are particularly valuable under the following circumstances:

- There are no specifications available.
- There is poor documentation of the system under test.
- You are forced to cope with a situation where insufficient time was allowed for the test process earlier in the lifecycle; specifically, insufficient time to plan, analyze, design, implement.
- Testers have experience with the application domain, with the underlying technology, and, perhaps most importantly, with testing.
- When we can analyze operational failures and incorporate that information into our taxonomies, error guesses, checklists, explorations, and attacks.

I particularly like to use defect- and experience-based techniques in conjunction with behavior-based and structure-based techniques. Each of the techniques covered in the Advanced syllabus—both for test analysts and technical test analysts—has its strengths and weakness. So, using defect- and experienced-based tests fills the gaps in test coverage that result from systematic

---

12. I derived this checklist from Gregory White, et al.'s, book, *Security+ Certification*.

weaknesses in these more-structured techniques. Let's look at an example of mixing these techniques, shown in table 4-23.

Table 4–23 *Selecting and mixing techniques example*

	Scripted Tests	*Chartered Exploratory*
Staff	7 Technicians	3 Engineers + 1 Mgr.
Experience	<10 years total	> 20 years total
Test Documents	Precise scripts	Vague test charts
Test Hrs/Day	42	6
Bugs Found	928 (78%)	261 (22%)
Bug Effectiveness	22	44
Scripts run	850	0
Inputs submitted	~5,000–10,000	~1,000
Results verified	~4,000–8,000	~1,000

In the Internet appliance project, we used a mixture of dynamic, chartered, exploratory testing and analytical, risk-based, scripted testing. The test manager and the three test engineers, who together had over 20 years total experience, did the exploratory testing. Test technicians did the scripted testing. Some of the test technicians had no testing experience and others had just a little.

During test execution, the technicians each spent about six hours per day running test scripts. The rest of the time, three to four hours per day, was spent reading email, attending meetings, updating bug reports, doing confirmation testing, and the like. The engineers and managers, being heavily engaged in other tasks, could only spend one to two hours per day doing exploratory testing. But you can see that, even so, the experienced testers were star bug finders.

However, when we start looking at coverage, we can see the picture change. The technicians ran about 850 test scripts over the three months of system test. That covered a lot of ground, well-documented ground yielding well-documented results that we could show to management. The exploratory testing didn't really leave any clear documentation behind. We weren't using the session-log approach that I showed earlier, in part because we were relying on the technicians to gather the coverage evidence with the scripts.

Now, how about sheer volume of input? I can't say for sure, but I'd estimate that the manual scripted tests resulted in somewhere between 5 and 10 thousand inputs of various kinds—strings, dates, radio buttons, etc.—while the exploratory testing was probably at best a fifth of that. Similarly, scripted tests probably resulted in many more explicit checks of results. Hour for hour the exploratory testing was probably just as effective, but it would have been less effective if we would have had to gather the session logs, as that would have slowed us down.

So, which was better? Ah, it wasn't that kind of experiment. It wasn't an experiment at all; it was a proven way of mixing two strategies, each with different strengths.

The exploratory testing was very effective at finding bugs on an hour-per-hour basis, and we found a number of bugs that wouldn't have been found by the scripts. The reusable test scripts gave us good regression risk mitigation, good risk mitigation, and good confidence building. Overall, a successful blended approach.

4.4 Defect- and Experience-Based Techniques Exercise 1

Consider the following test techniques that we've covered in this course:

- Equivalence partitioning
- Boundary value analysis
- Decision tables
- Use case tests
- State-based tests
- Pairwise tests
- Classification trees
- Defect-taxonomy tests
- Error-guessing tests
- Checklist-based tests
- Exploratory tests
- Software attacks

Without redundancy to previous exercises or examples, identify uses for the techniques on the HELLOCARMS project. List specification element numbers and descriptions of the application as appropriate.

The solutions are shown in the next section.

4.4.1 Defect- and Experience-Based Techniques Exercise Debrief 1

Table 4-24 shows a listing of where I would apply the different techniques covered in this course to the HELLOCARMS project.

Table 4–24 *Applying all the techniques to HELLOCARMS*

Test Technique	Requirements Section or Element/Description
Equivalence partitioning	010-010-040 Armed with the list of the valid inputs for each field, check every input field to ensure they can reject invalid values.
Boundary value analysis	010-010-040 Extend the testing of input validation using boundary value analysis.
Decision tables	010-020-010, 010-020-020, 010-020-030 Develop a decision table based on the credit policies (presumably in another document), then design tests from that decision table.
Use case tests	010-010-050 Develop a use case that describes how the payoff features work, then design tests from that use case.
State-based tests	010-010-060 Develop a state-transition diagram for the application (rather than the Telephone Banker as was done in a previous exercise). Test the application's state-based behaviors, including the ability to interrupt and return to the interview.
Pairwise tests	010-010-220 Test pairwise combinations of existing products from Globobank with potential customers as well as pairwise combinations of products from other banks with Globobank home equity products.
Classification trees	010-030-040 Develop a classification tree for the various attributes of the loan/line-of-credit payoff feature. Design tests to cover that classification tree, emphasizing combinations where various boundaries are reached (e.g., entire loan used to pay off one or more existing loan, just enough loans paid off to allow new loan to be made, etc.).
Defect-taxonomy tests	010-040 Create a defect taxonomy for every security-related failure observed at Globobank for similar applications, augmented by information on security-related failures at other banks for similar applications. Design tests to check for these defects.
Error-guessing tests	Entire system Obtain a list of known and/or past interfacing problems between LoDoPS, GLADS, and other applications that will interoperate with HELLOCARMS. Design tests to provoke those problems where possible.

Table continues

Table 4–24 *Applying all the techniques to HELLOCARMS (continued)*

Test Technique	Requirements Section or Element/Description
Checklist-based tests	010-010-020 Identify every screen, flow between screens, and script. Ensure each was tested.
Exploratory tests	010-010-170 Use a mix of PC configurations, security settings, connection speeds, customer personas, and existing customer relationships to test applications over the Internet.
Software attacks	000 Introduction Use attacks, especially security attacks, on the structure of the system.

4.4.2   Defect- and Experience-Based Techniques Exercise 2

Consider the use of exploratory testing you identified in the previous exercise or some other use of the technique on the HELLOCARMS project.

The exercise consists of four parts:

1. Identify a list of test charters for testing this area.
2. Document your assumption about the testers who will use the charters.
3. Assign a priority to each charter and explain why.
4. Explain how you would report results.

As always, check your work on the preceding part before proceeding to the next part.

The solutions are shown in the next section.

4.4.3   Defect- and Experience-Based Techniques Exercise Debrief 2

In the previous exercise, I selected requirements element 010-010-170, which has to do with allowing applications over the Internet. I wrote that I would "use a mix of PC configurations, security settings, connection speeds, customer personas, and existing customer relationships to test applications over the Internet."

Let's see what that might look like.

First, I would use pairwise techniques to generate a set of target PC configurations, including browser brand and version, operating system, and connection speeds. Because we've already discussed how to do that, I won't rehash it here. I will mention though that I would build these configurations prior to test execution, storing drive images for a quick restore during testing.

Next, I would create a list of customer personas. Personas refer to the habits that a customer exhibits and experience that a customer has.

- **Nervous customer:** Uses back button a lot, revises entries, has long think time
- **Novice Internet user:** Makes a lot of data input mistakes, has long think time
- **Power user:** Types quickly, makes few mistakes, uses copy-and-paste from other PC applications (e.g., account numbers), has very short think time
- **Impatient customer:** Types quickly, makes many mistakes, has very short think time, hits next button multiple times

Now I would create a list of existing customer banking relationship types.

- Limited accounts, none with Globobank
- Limited accounts, some with Globobank
- Limited accounts, all with Globobank
- Extensive accounts, none with Globobank
- Extensive accounts, some with Globobank
- Extensive accounts, all with Globobank

Notice that these two lists allow a lot of tester latitude and discretion. Notice also that, for the existing customer banking relationships, as with the PC configurations, it would again make a lot of sense for the tester to create this customer data before test execution started.

Finally, I would create a list of test charters, as shown in table 4-25.

Table 4–25 *Test charters for HELLOCARMS exploratory testing*

General rules for test charters:
• For each of the following charters, restore your test PC to a previously untested PC configuration prior to starting the charter. Make sure each configuration is tested at least once.
• For each of the following charters, select a persona. Make sure each persona is tested at least once.
• For each of the following charters, select an existing customer banking relationship type. Make sure each customer banking relationship type is tested at least once.
• Allocate 30–45 minutes for each application; thus each charter is 30–120 minutes long.
Charters:
1   Test successful applications with both limited and extensive banking relationships, where customer declines insurance.
2   Test a successful application where customer accepts insurance.
3   Test a successful application where the system declines insurance.
4   Test a successful application where property value escalates application.
5   Test a successful application where loan amount escalates application.
6   Test an unsuccessful application due to credit history.
7   Test an unsuccessful application due to insufficient income.
8   Test an unsuccessful application due to excessive debt.
9   Test an unsuccessful application due to insufficient equity.
10 Test cancellation of an application from all possible screens (120 minutes).
11 Test a fraudulent application, where material information provided by customer does not match decisioning mainframe's data.
12 Test a fraudulent application, where material information provided by customer does not match LoDoPS data.

Yes, these charters might revisit some areas covered by our other, specification-based tests. However, because the testers will be taking side trips that wouldn't be in the scripts, the coverage of the scenarios will be broader.

Now, what is my assumption about the testers who will use these charters? Obviously, they have to be experienced testers because the test specification provided is very limited and provides a lot of discretion. They also have to understand the application well, as I am not giving them any instructions on how to carry out the charters. They also understand PC technology at least well

> **ISTQB Glossary**
>
> **static analysis:** Analysis of software artifacts, e.g., requirements or code, carried out without execution of these software artifacts.

enough to restore a PC configuration from a drive image, though it would be possible to give unambiguous directions to someone on how to do that.

In terms of the priority to each charter, I have listed them in priority order. Notice that I start with the simplest case, a successful application with no insurance, and then add complexity from there. My objective is to use the exploratory tests during the scripted tests in parallel. As the test coverage under the scripts gets greater and greater, so also does the complexity of the exploratory scenarios.

As for results reporting, I would have each charter tracked as a test case in my test management system. For bug reports, though, it would be very important that the tester perform adequate isolation to determine if the configuration, the persona, the banking relationship, or the functionality itself was behind the failure.

4.5 Static Analysis

Learning objectives
Recall of content only

The concepts in this section apply primarily for technical test analysts. There are no learning objectives defined for test analysts in this section. In the course of studying for the exam, read this section in chapter 4 of the Advanced syllabus for general recall and familiarity only.

> **ISTQB Glossary**
>
> **dynamic analysis:** The process of evaluating behavior, e.g., memory performance, CPU usage, of a system or component during execution.
>
> **memory leak:** A defect in a program's dynamic store allocation logic that causes it to fail to reclaim memory after it has finished using it, eventually causing the program to fail due to lack of memory.
>
> **wild pointer:** A pointer that references a location that is out of scope for that pointer or that does not exist.

4.6   Dynamic Analysis

Learning objectives
Recall of content only

The concepts in this section apply primarily for technical test analysts. There are no learning objectives defined for test analysts in this section. In the course of studying for the exam, read this section in chapter 4 of the Advanced syllabus for general recall and familiarity only.

4.7   Sample Exam Questions

To end each chapter, you can try one or more sample exam questions to reinforce your knowledge and understanding of the material and to prepare for the ISTQB Advanced Level Test Analyst exam.

1. Which of the following is a typical defect that equivalence partitioning would identify?

    A Improper handling of sequences of events

    B Improper handling of combinations of conditions

    C Improper handling of large and small values

    D Improper handling of classes of inputs

2. Which of the following is a typical defect that boundary value analysis would identify?

   A Improper handling of sequences of events

   B Improper handling of combinations of conditions

   C Improper handling of large and small values

   D Improper handling of classes of inputs

3. Which of the following is a typical defect that decision table testing would identify?

   A Improper handling of sequences of events

   B Improper handling of combinations of conditions

   C Improper handling of large and small values

   D Improper handling of classes of inputs

4. Which of the following is a typical defect that state-based testing would identify?

   A Improper handling of sequences of events

   B Improper handling of combinations of conditions

   C Improper handling of configuration combinations

   D Improper handling of classes of inputs

5. Which of the following is a typical defect that classification tree testing would identify?

   A Improper handling of sequences of events

   B Improper handling of typical workflows

   C Improper handling of configuration combinations

   D Improper handling of classes of inputs

6. Which of the following is a typical defect that use case would identify?

    A Improper handling of large and small values

    B Improper handling of configuration combinations

    C Improper handling of classes of inputs

    D Improper handling of typical workflows

7. Which of the following is a typical defect that pairwise testing would identify?

    A Improper handling of sequences of events

    B Improper handling of typical workflows

    C Improper handling of configuration combinations

    D Improper handling of classes of inputs

8. Assume you are a test analyst working on a banking project to upgrade an existing automated teller machine system to allow customers to obtain cash advances from supported credit cards. The system should allow cash advances from 20 dollars to 500 dollars, inclusively, for all supported credit cards. The correct list of supported credit cards is American Express, Visa, Japan Credit Bank, Eurocard, and MasterCard.

    Assume that, in the following list of valid test cases, the first item in the parenthesized triple represents the credit card, the second item represents the amount to withdraw, and the third item represents the expected result. Which of the following selections gives a set of test cases that covers the equivalence partitions for credit cards and shows the correct expected result?

    A (American Express, $20, succeed); (Visa, $100, succeed); (Japan Credit Bank, $500, succeed); (Eurocard, $200, succeed); (Master-Card, $400, succeed)

    B (American Express, $20, succeed); (Visa, $600, fail); (Japan Credit Bank, $500, fail); (Eurocard, $200, succeed); (MasterCard, $400, succeed)

   C (American Express, $20, succeed); (Japan Credit Bank, $500, succeed); (Eurocard, $200, succeed); (MasterCard, $400, succeed)

   D (American Express, $20, succeed); (Visa, $600, succeed); (Japan Credit Bank, $500, succeed); (Eurocard, $200, succeed); (Master-Card, $400, succeed)

9. Assume you are a test analyst working on a banking project to upgrade an existing automated teller machine system to allow customers to obtain cash advances from supported credit cards. The system should allow cash advances from 20 dollars to 500 dollars, inclusively, for all supported credit cards. The correct list of supported credit cards is American Express, Visa, Japan Credit Bank, Eurocard, and MasterCard. The user interface starts with a default amount of 100 dollars for advances, and the ATM keypad is used to increase or decrease that amount in 20-dollar increments.

   Assume that, in the following list of test cases, the first item in the parenthesized triple represents the credit card, the second item represents the amount to withdraw, and the third item represents the expected result. Which of the following selections gives a set of test cases that covers the boundary values for cash advances and shows the correct expected result?

   A (American Express, $20, succeed); (Visa, $500, succeed); (Japan Credit Bank, $520, fail); (Eurocard, $0, fail)

   B (American Express, $20, succeed); (Visa, $600, fail); (Japan Credit Bank, $500, fail); (Eurocard, $200, succeed); (MasterCard, $400, succeed)

   C (American Express, $20, succeed); (Japan Credit Bank, $500, succeed); (Eurocard, $520, succeed); (MasterCard, $400, succeed)

   D (American Express, $20, succeed); (Visa, $600, fail); (Japan Credit Bank, $500, succeed); (Eurocard, $200, succeed); (MasterCard, $400, succeed)

10. Assume you are a test analyst working on a banking project to upgrade an existing automated teller machine system to allow customers to obtain cash advances from supported credit cards. The system should

allow cash advances from 20 dollars to 500 dollars, inclusively, for all supported credit cards. The correct list of supported credit cards is American Express, Visa, Japan Credit Bank, Eurocard, and MasterCard. The user interface starts with a default amount of 100 dollars for advances, and the ATM keypad is used to increase or decrease that amount in 20-dollar increments.

Consider the decision table shown in table 4-26 that describes the handling of these transactions.

Table 4–26 *Cash advance decision table*

Conditions	1	2	3	4	5
Supported card	N	Y	Y	Y	Y
User authenticated	-	N	Y	Y	Y
Allowed advance amount	-	-	N	Y	Y
Within available balance	-	-	-	N	Y
Actions					
Reject card	Y	Y	N	N	N
Prompt for new amount	N	N	Y	Y	N
Dispense cash	N	N	N	N	Y

Assume that you want to design a set of test cases where the following coverage is achieved:

■ Decision table coverage
■ Boundary values for allowed and disallowed advance amounts
■ Successful advance for each supported card

Design a set of test cases that achieves this level of coverage with the minimum possible number of test cases. Assume each test case consists of a single combination of conditions to create and a single combination of actions to check. How many test cases do you need?

A 4

B 5

C 6

D 10

11. Assume you are a test analyst working on a project to create a programmable thermostat for home use to control central heating, ventilation, and air conditioning (HVAC) systems. You want to test the ability of the thermostat to properly interact with the central HVAC unit.

    At any given moment, the HVAC unit is in either an *off* state (the initial state) or an *on* state. The thermostat can send the HVAC unit either a *start* event or a *stop* event. If the unit is in an *on* state and it receives a *stop* event, it will always deactivate and display an "idle" message.

    If the unit is in an *off* state and it receives a *start* event, it will activate and display an "active" message if all conditions are normal. However, if the unit is in an *off* state and it receives a *start* event, it might fail to activate under one of three conditions:

    ■ No power to the HVAC unit, the compressor, or other component
    ■ A failure of the HVAC unit, the compressor, or other component
    ■ To prevent damage to the HVAC unit, the compressor, or other component

    If it fails to activate, it displays an error code associated with the condition that caused the failure to activate.

    Analyze these requirements to draw a state transition diagram for this thermostat. Use a separate state transition to show each failure-to-activate event/condition pair.

    Which of the following statements is true?

    A There are two states and three transitions.

    B There are two states and five transitions.

    C There are five states and three transitions.

    D There are five states and two transitions.

12. Continue with the scenario in the previous question. Use the state transition diagram you created to generate tests that achieve state and transition coverage (i.e., 0-switch coverage) subject to the following additional rules for these test cases:

■ A test *must* begin with the HVAC unit in the initial state.

■ A test *must* complete when the HVAC unit returns to the *off* state from the *on* state.

■ All tests *can only* complete with the HVAC unit in the *off* state.

Design the minimum number of test cases possible.

How many test cases did you design?

A 1

B 2

C 4

D 8

13. Assume you are a test analyst working on a project to create a programmable thermostat for home use to control central heating, ventilation, and air conditioning (HVAC) systems. In addition to the normal HVAC control functions, the thermostat also has the ability to download data to a browser-based application that runs on PCs for further analysis.

   You are planning to do some compatibility testing of application and feature. You identify the following factors and, for each factor, the following options:

■ Supported PC/thermostat connections: USB and Bluetooth

■ Supported operating systems: Windows 2000, Windows XP, Windows Vista, Mac X, Linux

■ Supported browsers: Internet Explorer, Firefox, Opera

Assume that you plan to use a classification tree to design the tests. You want to cover all possible pairs of operating systems with PC/thermostat connections because you are concerned about possible data transfer issues, but you only care that every browser be tested at least once. What is the minimum number of configurations you'll need to test?

A 5

B 10

C 15

D 30

14. Continue with the scenario in the previous question.

    Assume instead that you plan to use an orthogonal array to design the tests. You want to cover all possible pairs of options across all three possible pairs of factors.

    What is the minimum number of configurations you'll need to test?

    A 5

    B 10

    C 15

    D 30

15. Continue with the scenario in the previous question.

    Assume that figure 4-69 describes an informal use case for the data transfer feature.

Thermostat data download: Normal workflow

   1.   User connects PC to thermostat using either USB cable or Bluetooth module

   2.   User points browser to analysis site (specified in manual)

   3.   User clicks to Download Thermostat Data button

   4.   Browser displays "Download Complete" message

Exceptions:

- PC-to-thermostat connention fails; browser displays error massage "Could not connect to thermostat" after step 3.

- User cannot connect to analysis site; browser displays appropriate error message depending on the natur of the problem.

- Data download fails before completion; browser displays errormessage "Download failed, please try again" after step 3.

Figure 4–69   *Informal data transfer use case*

Which of the following statements (or some similar statement) would be found in a test procedure designed to cover one of the exception workflows in this use case?

A Click Download Thermostat Data button, wait for the "Download Complete" message, and then proceed to the Analysis workflow to verify the data.

B Click Download Thermostat Data button and immediately disconnect the USB cable or Bluetooth module.

C Click Download Thermostat Data button, wait for the "Download Complete" message, and then disconnect the USB cable or Bluetooth module.

D Click Download Thermostat Data button, wait for the "Download Complete" message, and then close the browser.

16. Which of the following statements captures a key difference between specification-based and defect-based test design techniques?

A Specification-based techniques derive tests from the structure of the system, while defect-based techniques derive tests from what is known about defects.

B Defect-based techniques derive tests from the structure of the system, while specification-based techniques derive tests from the behavior of the system.

C Defect-based techniques derive tests from the structure of the system, while specification-based techniques derive tests from an analysis of the test basis.

D Defect-based techniques derive tests from what is known about defects, while specification-based techniques derive tests from an analysis of the test basis.

17. Which of the following is an example of the use of a defect taxonomy for test design?

    A Using frequency of defect occurrence as an input into quality risk analysis

    B Selecting test inputs that are likely to reveal a failure associated with a particular defect

    C Updating the defect taxonomy after test execution to reflect the latest findings

    D Sending the defect taxonomy, along with frequency of defect occurrence, to development for process improvements

18. Which of the following is an important principle for use of experienced-based test techniques?

    A Tester skill is a critical factor in assignment of test execution tasks.

    B Tester skills are less important than ensuring 100% tester utilization.

    C Testers should always focus on defect-preventing activities.

    D Testers should be evaluated based on the number of defects they find.

19. Assume you are a test analyst working on a project to create a programmable thermostat for home use to control central heating, ventilation, and air conditioning (HVAC) systems. In addition to the normal HVAC control functions, the thermostat also has the ability to download data to a browser-based application that runs on PCs for further analysis.

    Consider the following exploratory test charter:

    Load various thermostat data sets to the application and evaluate the standard reports the application can produce.

Which of the following statements is true and consistent with the approach to exploratory testing described in the Advanced syllabus?

A All actions associated with executing this charter should occur during test execution, after receipt of the initial test object.

B All of the thermostat data sets should be created prior to test execution, while all other actions associated with executing this charter should occur during test execution.

C Most of the thermostat data sets could be created prior to test execution, provided those data sets could be modified during test execution based on test results.

D All data, inputs, and expected results for this test charter should be specified in a concrete test case before the start of test execution.

20. Consider the following software fault attack proposed by Whittaker's technique:

Force all possible incoming errors from the software/OS interfaces to the application.

Which of the following is the kind of failure you are looking for when testing using this attack?

A Application crashes when unsupported characters are pasted into an input field using the Windows Clipboard

B Application splash screen has incorrect spelling of company name

C Application fails to display financial numbers in currency format on reports

D Application miscalculates total monthly balance due on credit cards

21. Assume you are a test analyst working on a banking project to upgrade an existing automated teller machine system to allow customers to obtain cash advances from supported credit cards.

When the user first inserts a valid credit card type, the system considers the user to be in the *unauthenticated* state. Prior to requesting a cash advance, though, the user must enter the *authenticated* state. The user authenticates by entering the proper PIN.

When authenticating the user, the system should allow the user to enter their PIN up to three times before failing the authentication and rejecting the card. On the first and second try, the system should prompt the user to reenter the PIN.

Suppose you are concerned that, depending on the exact number of invalid PINs entered, the system might behave improperly. Which of the following test design techniques is specifically targeted at such failures?

   A Equivalence partitioning extended by boundary value analysis

   B Pairwise testing with orthogonal arrays

   C State-based testing using N-1 switch coverage

   D Classification tree testing using two-factor authentication

22. If we say that a set of tests has achieved 100% structural decision coverage on a particular module in a program, what does that mean?

   A That all bugs present in that module were necessarily revealed by those tests.

   B That every control flow branch had been executed at least once by those tests.

   C That every dataflow in that module was exercised at least once by those tests.

   D That every path through that module was exercised at least once by those tests.

23. Consider the following code fragment:

```
if (a>b) && (b>c)) {

    b = (a+c)/2;

}
```

Assume that, in the following options, each of the three numbers in parentheses represents the inputs for a test case, where the first number is a, the second number b, and the third number c. Which of the following gives a set of test case inputs that achieves decision coverage for this fragment of code in the minimum number of test cases?

A (5, 3, 2)

B (5, 3, 2); (5, 4, 0)

C (5, 4, 0); (4, 5, 0)

D (4, 5, 0); (5, 4, 5)

24. Which of the following is a dynamic analysis technique related to improving application performance?

A Code complexity analysis

B Profiling

C Network packet sniffing

D Spelling and grammar checking

25. Set-use pairs are identified during which of the following static analysis activities?

A Control flow analysis

B Data flow analysis

C Coding standards analysis

D Cyclomatic complexity analysis

5 Tests of Software Characteristics

"[Quality is] fitness for use. Features [that] are decisive as to product performance and as to product satisfaction.... The word 'quality' also refers to freedom from deficiencies...[that] result in complaints, claims, returns, rework and other damage. Those collectively are forms of product dissatisfaction."

Joseph M. Juran, in *Planning for Quality*

The fifth chapter of the Advanced syllabus is concerned with tests of software characteristics. In this chapter, the Advanced syllabus expands on a concept introduced in the Foundation syllabus, that of ISO 9126 software quality characteristics, to explain testing as it relates to these various attributes of functional and non-functional software quality. There are three sections:

1. Introduction
2. Quality Attributes for Domain Testing
3. Quality Attributes for Technical Testing

Let's look at each section and how it relates to test analysis.

5.1 Introduction

Learning objectives
Recall of content only

At the beginning of chapter 4, I introduced a taxonomy—a classification system—for tests. If you recall, I mentioned the distinction between functional and non functional black-box tests, based on the ISO 9126 standard. I then went on in chapter 4 to talk about useful black-box techniques, without returning to this distinction or to the characteristics and subcharacteristics of quality defined in ISO 9126.

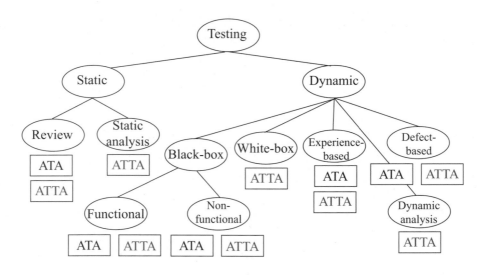

Figure 5–1   *Advanced syllabus testing techniques*

In this chapter, we will return to those topics. Here, we consider how to apply the techniques from chapter 4 to evaluate quality of software applications or systems. While the focus will be different for test analysts in this book than in the companion volume for technical test analysts, the common element is that we need to understand quality characteristics in order to recognize typical risks, develop appropriate testing strategies, and specify effective tests.

5.2   Quality Attributes for Domain Testing

Learning objectives

(K4) Explain by examples which testing techniques listed in chapter 4 are appropriate to test for accuracy, suitability, interoperability, functional security, and accessibility characteristics.

(K3) Outline, design, specify, and execute usability tests using appropriate techniques and covering given test objectives and defects to be targeted.

Functional testing focuses on what the system does rather than how it does it. Non functional testing is focused on how the system does what it does. Both functional and non functional testing are black-box tests, being focused on behavior. White-box tests are focused on how the system works internally, i.e., on its structure.

Functional tests can have, as their test basis, the functional requirements. These include the requirements that are written down in a specification document as well as those that are implicit. The domain expertise of the tester can also be part of the test basis.

Functional tests will vary by test level or phase. A functional integration test will focus on the functionality of a collection of interfacing modules, usually in terms of the partial or complete user workflows, use cases, operations, or feature these modules provide. A functional system test will focus on the functionality of the application as a whole, complete user workflows, use cases, operations, and features. A functional system integration test will focus on end-to-end functionality that spans the entire set of integrated systems.

The test analyst can employ various test techniques during functional testing at any level. All of the techniques discussed in chapter 4 will be useful at some point or another.

We should keep in mind that the test analyst is a role, not a title, job description, or position. In other words, some people play the role of test analyst exclusively, but others play that role as part of another job. So, when dedicated, professional testers do functional testing, they are test analysts both in position and in role. However, when domain experts do the analysis, design, implementation, or execution of functional tests, they are working as test analysts. When developers do the analysis, design, implementation, or execution of functional tests, they are working as test analysts.

> **ISTQB Glossary**
>
> **accuracy testing:** Not defined in the ISTQB glossary.
>
> accuracy: The capability of the software product to provide the right or agreed results or effects with the needed degree of precision.

For test analysts, in the ISTQB Advanced syllabus we consider functional testing as concerned with the following quality attributes:

- Accuracy
- Suitability
- Interoperability
- Functional security
- Accessibility
- Usability

Let's look more closely at each of these areas in the rest of this section.

5.2.1 Functional Accuracy

Functional accuracy testing is concerned with adherence to specified or implied functional requirements. In other words, does the system give the right answer and produce the right effects? The accuracy, in this case, also refers to the right degree of precision in the results.

Functional accuracy testing can include tests of computational accuracy. Indeed, for any application used for math, statistics, accounting, science, engineering, or other similar math-intensive functionality, testing of computation accuracy is critical. Functional accuracy testing can require the use of many of the test techniques in chapter 4.

Let's look at an example. We'll revisit the test designs we did for Quicken's stock buy/add screen, specifically the number of shares, the price per share, and commission fields, shown in figure 5-2. We applied equivalence partitioning and boundary value analysis to these fields and identified 13 specific input values for each field.

In this case, we would also want to add testing of the total cost field. This is a calculated output field. It is calculated by using the three input fields. As we

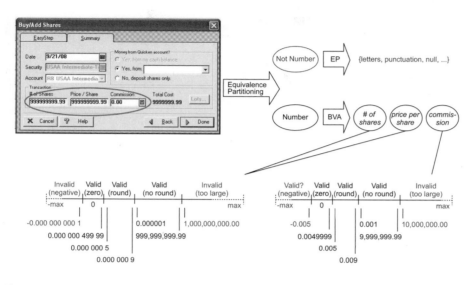

Figure 5–2   *Accuracy testing example*

can see in figure 5-2, there is something not right with the calculation. The combination of maximum number of shares and price per share is not giving us the right result in the total cost field. Or perhaps the number is right, internally, but it's overflowing the display space. Either way, I'd report this as a bug.

5.2.2 Functional Suitability

Functional suitability testing is focused on the appropriateness of a set of functions relative to its intended, specific tasks. In other words, given the problem we need to solve, can the system solve it?

Notice that there is an element of validation to this focus. We are intent on demonstrating the value of the system in some specific situation. As explained in the Foundation syllabus, the shorthand way to think about validation is, "Are we building the right system?" This is in contrast to verification, which is about following the right process, having traceability of functions to requirements, and so forth. The shorthand way to think about verification is, "Are we building the system right?"

Based on what we're trying to accomplish here, it's clear that we need to test in ways that strongly resemble actual workflows. We can employ use cases, test scenarios, and exploratory testing for this. Other techniques tend to be a bit too

> **ISTQB Glossary**
>
> **suitability testing:** No definition in the ISTQB glossary.
>
> suitability: The capability of the software product to provide an appropriate set of functions for specified tasks and user objectives.

fine-grained or distracted by bug hunting to serve the purpose. Indeed, you have to be careful with exploratory testing to make sure that the charters reflect the need to explore real-world usage of the product.

Let's look at an example. We'll revisit the informal e-commerce purchase use case, shown in figure 5-3. Basically, this use case says that we should be able to put items in a shopping cart, initiate a checkout, enter the information the system needs to process the purchase, and confirm the purchase before it's done. The use case also says that the system needs to reject attempts to check out with an empty cart, to reject invalid inputs in the purchase information, and to recognize an abandoned cart when it sees one.

E-commerce purchase: Normal workflow

1. Customer places one or more Items in shopping cart

2. Customer selects checkout

3. System gathers address, payment, and shipping information from Customer

4. System displays all information for User confirmation

5. User confirms order to System for delivery

Exceptions

- Customer attempts to check with empty shopping cart; System gives error message
- Customer provides invalid address, payment, or shipping information; System gives error messages as appropriate
- Customer abandons transaction before or during checkout; System logs Customer out after 10 minutes of inactivity

Figure 5–3   *Suitability testing example: use case*

Table 5–1 *Suitability testing example: tests (typical)*

#	Test Step	Expected Result
1	Place 1 item in cart	Item in cart
2	Click checkout	Checkout screen
3	Input valid U.S. address, valid payment using American Express, and valid shipping method information	Each screen displays correctly and valid inputs are accepted
4	Verify order information	Shown as entered
5	Confirm order	Order in system
6	Repeat steps 1–5, but place 2 items in cart, pay with Visa, and ship international	As shown in 1–5
7	Repeat steps 1–5, but place the maximum number of items in cart and pay with MasterCard	As shown in 1–5
8	Repeat steps 1–5, but pay with Discover	As shown in 1–5

In table 5-1, we test the suitability of the system's functionality to handle the typical workflow. We had an implied requirement to accept all four major credit cards, so we tested those. We also had an implied requirement to support both U.S. and international customers, so we tested those.

In table 5-2, we test the suitability of the system's functionality under exceptional conditions. We check the empty cart. We check the inputs of invalid information on all screens, including the ability of the system to stop us from proceeding unless a form is correctly filled. Finally, we test the abandonment of a cart from all possible screens. We have clear traceability from the tests back to the use cases.

5.2.3   Functional Interoperability

Functional interoperability involves testing correct functionality in all intended environments. Environments refer to hardware, of course, but also software, middleware, connectivity infrastructure, database systems, and operating systems. This would include not only elements of the environment that the system must interoperate directly with, but also those that it interoperates indirectly with or even simply cohabitates with. Cohabitation implies that applications

Table 5-2 *Suitability example: tests (exception)*

#	Test Step	Expected Result
1	Do not place any items in cart	Cart empty
2	Click checkout	Error message
3	Place item in cart, click checkout, enter invalid address, then invalid payment, then invalid shipping information	Error messages, can't proceed to next screen until resolved
4	Verify order information	Shown as entered
5	Confirm order	Order in system
6	Repeat steps 1-3, but stop activity and abandon transaction after placing item in cart	User logged out exactly 10 minutes after last activity
7	Repeats steps 1-3, but stop activity and abandon transaction on each screen	As shown in 6
8	Repeat steps 1-4; do not confirm order	As shown in 6

share network infrastructure, CPU capability, memory space, etc., but do not work together.

As you might imagine, there's a major test configuration element involved with understanding the test environments needed. The environments are then tested with selected major functions. If you suspect that particular functions might interact in particular ways with particular test environments, be sure to test those. If not, then you can test arbitrary combinations of functions with environments.

Interoperability is, of course, about systems interacting with each other. Good interoperability implies ease of integration with other systems with few if any major changes. Design features can raise important considerations for testing software interoperability. Examples include the following:

- The system use of industry-wide data or communications standards, such as XML
- The ability of the system to provide standard, flexible, and robust interfaces

As a test analyst, you can expect to do a lot of interoperability testing when you are developing or integrating commercial off-the-shelf (COTS) software and

> **ISTQB Glossary**
>
> **interoperability testing**: The process of testing to determine the interoperability of a software product.
>
> interoperability: The capability of the software product to interact with one or more specified components or systems.

tools. That's also true if you are developing systems of systems from off-the-shelf or custom-developed applications. Interoperability is important during system integration testing.

For testing of functional interoperability, especially end-to-end functionality, you can employ use cases and test scenarios. To determine the environments, you can use equivalence partitioning when you understand the possible interactions between one or more environments and one or more functions. When interactions are not clear, you can use pairwise testing and classification trees to generate somewhat-more arbitrary configurations.

Let's look at an example. Suppose we combine the use case example—which we just revisited—with the pairwise example shown in chapter 4. We can use the orthogonal array as our environment mix and spread the test cases across it.

Looking at the use cases, we see four typical test cases:

- The first is American Express, to purchase 1 item, for shipping in the U.S. Let's call that test case A.
- The second is Visa, to purchase 2 items, for shipping internationally. Let's call that test case B.
- The third is MasterCard, to purchase as many items as the cart will hold, for shipping in the U.S. Let's call that test case C.
- The fourth is Discover, to purchase one item, for shipping in the U.S. Let's call that test case D.

Here in figure 5-4, you can see the combination of test cases with the environments. To execute the test, you first obtain the correct configuration and then run the test case derived earlier from the use case.

Test	Environment				Test Case
	Speed	OS	Security	Browser	
1	DU	XP	Symantec	Firefox	A
2	DU	Vista	Trend	IE	B
3	DU	Mac	McAfee	Opera	C
4	DU	Linux	OS	~	D
5	BB	XP	Trend	Opera	D
6	BB	Vista	Symantec	~	C
7	BB	Mac	OS	Firefox	B
8	BB	Linux	McAfee	IE	A
9	~	XP	McAfee	~	B
10	~	Vista	OS	Opera	A
11	~	Mac	Symantec	IE	D
12	~	Linux	Trend	Firefox	C
13	~	XP	OS	IE	C
14	~	Vista	McAfee	Firefox	D
15	~	Mac	Trend	~	A
16	~	Linux	Symantec	Opera	B

Figure 5–4   *Testing interoperability example*

The technique would be similar for the exception tests. Remember that we don't want to mix exception and valid tests, especially here because we're testing for the ability of the e-commerce system to complete an entire function—a purchase—on various supported environment configurations.

5.2.4 Functional Interoperability Exercise

The HELLOCARMS system will interoperate with a number of other systems, as described in the HELLOCARMS system requirements document. In chapter 4, you prepared tests based on typical and exception workflows in a use case.

This exercise consists of three parts:

1. Review the HELLOCARMS system requirements document (through sections 010) to identify the systems with which HELLOCARMS interoperates.
2. Evaluate your use case tests to determine whether you cover all end-to-end communications.

3. If needed, suggest additions to your tests that could ensure complete coverage.

As always, check your work before proceeding to the next part.

The solutions are shown on the next pages.

5.2.5   Functional Interoperability Exercise Debrief

To start with, let me mention that my assumption here is that I am developing tests for use during system integration testing, not component integration testing or system testing. If that's not clear to you, you should go back to the materials in this course and in the Foundation syllabus that relate to test levels.

Table 5-3 shows the interoperation of the HELLOCARMS system with other systems in the system of systems in which it lives.

You might have noticed that I did not bother to list intra-HELLOCARMS communications, such as from the Fairbanks Call Center to the San Marcos Data Center. That's because I'm designing tests for system integration testing, not component integration testing.

At this point, I went back and augmented the previous table. First, I deleted the section column that pointed back to the requirements document. Next, I added two new columns. The first shows whether the communication was covered by the use-case-based tests. The possible answers were Yes for "Yes, definitely covered"; No for "No, definitely not covered"; and Maybe for "Maybe, possibly covered, depends on how the tester runs the test."

The second column, the test case column, gives either the test case that covers the interoperation or the test case that I suggest be augmented to cover the interoperation. The letters are either N for the normal workflow or En for an exception workflow, where the n indicates the number of the exception. You should go back and study my test cases because you'll see that most of the additions or modifications to the test cases would be minor. In many cases, the addition would be checking to see that either the Scoring Mainframe or the LoDoPS sent or received the proper information; e.g., on a declined or cancelled application.

Table 5-4 shows actual, possible, and missing coverage along with suggestions on where to fix the possible or actual gaps in coverage.

Table 5–3 *HELLOCARMS interoperation*

System	Interoperation	Section(s)
GLADS	HELLOCARMS sends existing Globobank customer relationship information.	010-010-070
GloboRainBQW	GloboRainBQW sends leads.	003
GloboRainBQW	HELLOCARMS sends "How Did You Hear About Us" identifier code. GloboRainBQW sends customer information.	010-030-010
Internet	HELLOCARMS sends/receives application information from Internet users. Internet users send/receive application information from HELLOCARMS.	001 003 010-010-170 010-040-040 010-040-050
LoDoPS	HELLOCARMS sends loan and initiates loan origination. LoDoPS sends update (when docs sent). LoDoPS sends update (when docs received). LoDoPS sends update (when materials sent).	001 003 010-030-050 010-030-120 010-030-140
LoDoPS	HELLOCARMS sends loan and initiates loan origination. LoDoPS sends changes to loan information (when required). LoDoPS sends update (when docs sent). LoDoPS sends update (when docs received). LoDoPS sends update (when materials sent).	001 003 010-030-050 010-030-120 010-030-140 010-030-145
LoDoPS	HELLOCARMS sends debts to retire as stipulations.	010-010-050 010-010-100 010-030-040 010-030-070
LoDoPS	HELLOCARMS converts net government retirement fund income(s) to gross income(s) and sends gross income(s).	010-020-050 010-030-080
LoDoPS	HELLOCARMS sends all declined applications.	010-030-130
Scoring Mainframe	HELLOCARMS sends information and requests score (property risk, credit score, loan-to-property-value ratio, and debt-to-income ratio). Scoring Mainframe sends score (property risk, credit score, loan-to-property-value ratio, and debt-to-income ratio) and decision.	001 003 010-020-020 010-030-090 010-030-100
Scoring Mainframe	HELLOCARMS sends joint applicant information and requests scores. Scoring Mainframe sends scores for all applicants.	010-030-020

Table continues

Table 5–3 HELLOCARMS interoperation (continued)

System	Interoperation	Section(s)
Scoring Mainframe	HELLOCARMS directs Scoring Mainframe to remove duplicate credit information from joint applicant credit reports. Scoring Mainframe sends scores with duplicate information removed.	010-030-030
Scoring Mainframe	HELLOCARMS queues application information requests (if the Scoring Mainframe is down).	010-030-110

5.2.6 Functional Security

Functional security testing, also called penetration testing, tests the ability of the software to prevent unauthorized access, whether accidental or deliberate. The access can be access to functions or to data. Given the name, you can expect that these tests focus on the gaps in the system's security abilities.

Penetrations tests should include trying to gain user rights you shouldn't have. It should include trying to gain access to data you shouldn't see. It should include trying to gain privileges you shouldn't have, which could include deleting data (whether you can see it or not).

In a perfect world, security information would be available in specifications. However, it is often not. That said, many security weaknesses are fairly well known—and, sadly, recurring. Many security requirements are also common across systems.

Penetration testing can use more systematic techniques, but in my experience, it relies heavily on techniques like attacks and defect taxonomies. These are usually customized for use in security testing

Let's look at an example. Figure 5-5 shows an excerpt from the security test plan for the Internet appliance project I've mentioned a few times. Please read over this, and then I'll point out some key elements.

Notice that we are specifically looking for weakness here, not necessarily confirming what works. That decision was made based on budget constraints. Notice also that the entire server environment is deemed a fair target for the attacks used to test penetration.

Two expert consultants ran the penetration test. One of them, this plan's author, spent some time working with the rest of the test team to evaluate and enhance existing tests that might be useful for security testing as well.

Table 5–4 *HELLOCARMS interoperation coverage*

System	Interoperation	Cover?	Case
GLADS	HELLOCARMS sends existing Globobank customer relationship information.	No	N
GloboRainBQW	GloboRainBQW sends leads.	No	N
GloboRainBQW	HELLOCARMS sends "How Did You Hear About Us" identifier code. GloboRainBQW sends customer information.	No	N
Internet	HELLOCARMS sends/receives application information from Internet users. Internet users send/receive application information from HELLOCARMS.	No	N
LoDoPS	HELLOCARMS sends loan and initiates loan origination. LoDoPS sends update (when docs sent). LoDoPS sends update (when docs received). LoDoPS sends update (when materials sent).	Maybe	N E1 E2 E3 E4 E5
LoDoPS	HELLOCARMS sends loan and initiates loan origination. LoDoPS sends changes to loan information (when required). LoDoPS sends update (when docs sent). LoDoPS sends update (when docs received). LoDoPS sends update (when materials sent).	No	N
LoDoPS	HELLOCARMS sends debts to retire as stipulations.	No	N
LoDoPS	HELLOCARMS converts net government retirement fund income(s) to gross income(s) and sends gross income(s).	No	N
LoDoPS	HELLOCARMS sends all declined applications.	Maybe	N E1 E2 E4 E5
Scoring Mainframe	HELLOCARMS sends information and requests score (property risk, credit score, loan-to-property-value ratio, and debt-to-income ratio). Scoring Mainframe sends score (property risk, credit score, loan-to-property-value ratio, and debt-to-income ratio) and decision.	Maybe	N E1 E2 E3 E4 E5

Table continues

Table 5–4 *HELLOCARMS interoperation coverage (continued)*

Scoring Mainframe	HELLOCARMS sends joint applicant information and requests scores. Scoring Mainframe sends scores for all applicants.	No	N E1 E2
Scoring Mainframe	HELLOCARMS directs Scoring Mainframe to remove duplicate credit information from joint applicant credit reports. Scoring Mainframe sends scores with duplicate information removed.	No	N E1 E2
Scoring Mainframe	HELLOCARMS queues application information requests (if the Scoring Mainframe is down).	No	N E1 E2

ISTQB Glossary

security testing: Testing to determine the security of the software product.

security: Attributes of software products that bear on its ability to prevent unauthorized access, whether accidental or deliberate, to programs and data.

The intent of this security test effort is to define a baseline of vulnerabilities in the XXX production environment and the clients available on MM/DD/YY. The testing can be described as " a vulnerability baseline test with an intent to exploit or penetrate." All servers considered to be components of the server farm are intended targets, and any networking device under XXX management control or oversight at XXX. Clients available during system test will be tested for vulnerabilities. Hosts or devices beyond those mentioned would not be explicit targets of the testing, but there is a chance there may be unintentional contact with hosts on the periphery of this test. Existing tests that have a security context that overlap with other testing [will be] performed by the [non-security testers]. Tests will be performed from contractor supplied systems loaded with commercially and Internet available tools. No custom tools will be created for this security test in order to simulate the dominant threat under consideration, the lightly to medium skilled attacker. In order to assess the defense in depth or layered security, tests will be performed inside and outside he firewall.

A second effort will be performed to capture encrypted sessions that take place in various data flows of the XXX service. The traffic capture will be performed with a commercial protocol analyzer. This effort is intended to facilitate [later] analysis…

Figure 5–5 *Penetration testing example*

Notice the threat model mentioned, specifically the lightly to medium skilled attacker. Finally, notice that some attempts at checking for capture/playback and man-in-the-middle attacks occur, but that it is a "secondary effort."

> **ISTQB Glossary**
>
> **accessibility testing:** Testing to determine the ease by which users with disabilities can use a component or system.

5.2.7 Accessibility

Accessibility testing tests the ability of those with particular requirements, restrictions, or disabilities to use the system. These often arise from national standards or voluntary guidelines, and sometimes compliance is required by law or by contract. To do accessibility testing, we use typical requirements-based test approaches for the standard or guideline. We might also need to design tests using other systematic techniques.

Figure 5-6 shows an excerpt from U.S. Section 508. This is just one of dozens of similar requirements. Notice that we can use equivalence partitioning to identify and test each assistive technology. The standard would seem to require that we do so. By the way, Section 508 defines an "assistive technology" as "any item, piece of equipment, or system, whether acquired commercially, modified, or customized, that is commonly used to increase, maintain, or improve functional capabilities of individuals with disabilities."

> When electronic forms are used, the form shall allow people using assistive technology to access the information, field elements, and functionality required for completion and submission of the form, including all directions and cues.

Figure 5–6   *Excerpt from Section 508*

Now, you might be tempted to try just a few fields and functions with each assistive technology, but that's a risky idea. Remember, we want to use a risk-based testing approach. If we are mandated by law—or by contract—to provide some capability for every field and function, then what is the impact of not doing so?

> **ISTQB Glossary**
>
> **usability testing:** Testing to determine the extent to which the software product is understood, easy to learn, easy to operate, and attractive to the users under specified conditions.
>
> **usability:** The capability of the software to be understood, learned, used, and attractive to the user when used under specified conditions.

Probably high. So the risk is high enough to justify testing every field and function with each assistive technology.

5.2.8   Usability

Usability testing, naturally enough, focuses on the users. This is why many notable usability experts and usability test experts are psychologists in background rather than technologists or domain experts. Knowledge of sociology and ergonomics is also helpful. Finally, an understanding of national standards related to accessibility can be important for applications subject to such standards.

Users can vary in terms of their skills, abilities, and disabilities. Something an old technology hand such as myself finds easy to understand can be mystifying to my business partner, whose background is in psychology. Being a former UNIX programmer and system administrator, I find command lines, short commands, and Internet infrastructure easy to understand, while my business partner finds even the simpler Windows interfaces hard to understand sometimes.

Children tend to be remarkably clever in using technology. One day, I put an old laptop with a CD-ROM player into my seven-year-old daughter's room. I put some CD-ROMs in there too, including an encyclopedia. Later that night, my wife was spooked to hear a man's voice coming from my daughter's room. It turns out she had figured out how to enable a setting on the encyclopedia that reads the entry aloud.

These kinds of settings and features—text-to-speech and speech-to-text—can be very useful to the disabled, especially those who have limited hand mobility or who are sight impaired. The deaf or those with cognitive disabilities might need different types of assistive technologies.

Ultimately, a usable piece of software is one that is suitable for the users. So usability testing measures whether the users are effective, efficient, and satisfied with the software. Effectiveness implies that the software enables the users to achieve their goals accurately and completely under expected usage conditions. Efficiency implies that the users can achieve these goals in some realistic, reasonable period. Satisfaction, in this context, is really the antonym of frustration. In other words, a satisfied user who has effectively and efficiently reached their goals with the system feels that the software was about as helpful as it could have been.

What attributes lead to a satisfied, effective, efficient user? One is understandability, the simplicity or difficulty of figuring out what the software does and why you might need to use it. Another is learnability, the simplicity or difficulty of figuring out how to make the software do what it does. Yet another is operability, the degree of simplicity or difficulty inherent in carrying out certain distinct tasks within the software's feature set. Finally, there is attractiveness, which is the extent to which the software is visibly pleasing, friendly, and inviting to the user.

If we are performing usability testing, as with most other testing we can have as goals both the detection and removal of defects and the demonstration of conformance or nonconformance to requirements. In usability testing, the detection and removal of defects is sometimes referred to as formative evaluation, while the testing of requirements is sometimes referred to as summative evaluation.

In usability testing, we want to observe the effect of the actual system on real people, actual end users. (This is not to say that testers are not real people, but rather that we are not really the people who use the system.) To do so, we need to observe users interacting with the system under realistic conditions, possibly with video cameras, mock-up offices, and review panels.

Usability testing is sometimes seen as its own level, but it can also be integrated into functional system testing. However, because usability testing has a different focus than standard functional testing, you can improve the consistency of the detection and reporting of usability bugs with usability guidelines. These guidelines should apply in all stages of the lifecycle to encourage developers to build usable products in the first place.

> **ISTQB Glossary**
>
> **heuristic evaluation:** A static usability test technique to determine the compliance of a user interface with recognized usability principles (the so-called "heuristics").

There are three main techniques for usability testing. The first is called inspection, evaluation, or review. This involves considering the specification and designs from a usability point of view. Like all such reviews, it's an effective and efficient way to find bugs sooner rather than later. You can use actual users for this when you have things like screenshots and mock-ups.

A form of review, a heuristic evaluation, provides for a systematic inspection of a user interface design for usability. It allows us to find usability problems in the design, resolve them, and then reevaluate. That process continues until we are happy with the design from a usability point of view. Often, a small set of evaluators is selected to evaluate the interface, including evaluation with respect to known and recognized usability principles.

The second form of usability testing is validation of the actual implementation. This can involve running usability test scenarios. Unlike functional test scenarios, which look at the inputs, outputs, and results, the usability test scenarios look at usability attributes, such as speed of learning or operability. Usability test scenarios will often go beyond a typical functional test scenario in that they include pretest and posttest interviews for the users performing the tests. In the pretest interviews, the testers receive instructions and guidelines for running the sessions. The guidelines include a description of how to run the test, time allowed for tests and even test steps, how to take notes and log results, and the interview and survey methods that will be used.

There also are syntax tests that evaluate the interface, what it allows, and what it disallows. And there are semantic tests that evaluate the meaningfulness of messages and outputs. As you might guess, some of the black-box techniques we've looked at, including use cases, can be helpful here.

A final form of usability tests is a survey or questionnaire. These can be used to gather observations of the users' behavior during interaction with the system in a usability test lab. There are standard and publicly available surveys

ISTQB Glossary

Software Usability Measurement Inventory (SUMI): A questionnaire-based usability test technique to evaluate the usability, e.g., user-satisfaction, of a component or system.

like Software Usability Measurement Inventory (SUMI) and Website Analysis and Measurement Inventory (WAMMI). Using a public standard allows you to benchmark against other organizations and software. Also, SUMI provides usability metrics, which can measure usability for completion or acceptance criteria.

Let's look at an example. In figure 5-7 you see some introductory information from a document that described the usability test scenarios for the Internet appliance project I've referred to from time to time. Notice that we define the goals of the test in the first paragraph.

The next paragraph describes the structure of the test set. It consists of four major scenarios. We have weighting on those, which correspond to how important the test designer feels they are. There are then some simple instructions on how to use the checklist.

Each item in this checklist pertains to a [usability characteristic] or quality of [the system under test] that influences how effective a very novice user will be in unpacking, assembling, powering on, and configuring software on a [it]. This [checklist] is intended to predict an end-user's experience with [the system].

This [checklist] consists of four major sections:
- Packaging and hardware (100 points)
- Software installation and configuration (100 points)
- Internet connention and online registration (50 points)
- Software discovery and usage (50 points)

For each section, complete the checklist by choosing the most appropriate answer to each question. To score the section, add up the points corresponding to the selected answers, and record the scores in the summary table at the end of the section.

Figure 5–7   *Usability testing outline example*

In figure 5-8, you see one of the specified steps of the test scenarios. As you might guess, this is from the packaging and hardware scenario. This step is designed to check whether the user has any practical way to see if everything that is supposed to be in the box actually is. Execution of the tests is simple. Just check off the appropriate boxes, and then add up the score after all the scenarios are done.

(pts)	Is there a complete inventory of parts to enable the customer to determine if anything missing? (e.g., outer box labels, packing slip, or setup "roadmap")
5	☐ The inventory list is complete and includes pictures with enough detail to precisely identify parts
3	☐ The inventory list is complete, but is text only
2	☐ The inventory list is complete
0	☐ No inventory list

Figure 5–8   *Design, specify, and execute example*

5.2.9   Usability Exercise

While at first only Globobank employees will use the HELLOCARMS system, eventually a number of different types of users will do so. It's important that the system be usable by each type of user.

This exercise consists of two parts:

1. Identify at least three user groups that will use the HELLOCARMS system.
2. For each user group, outline the usability tests needed for each of the following attributes: understandability, learnability, operability, and attractiveness.

As always, check your work before proceeding to the next part.
    The solutions are shown on the next pages.

5.2.10 Usability Exercise Debrief

The user groups include the following:

- Telephone Bankers and Senior Telephone Bankers
- Customers (via the Internet)
- Branch bank employees at retail banking centers

There are a few others groups identified in the HELLOCARMS system requirements document as well.

The next part of the exercise involves you giving two or three bullet items of what you would want to test to cover the four subcharacteristics of usability.

First, let's make sure we have the same definitions for each subcharacteristic, from ISO 9126:

- **Understandability:** The capability of the software product to enable the user to understand whether the software is suitable and how it can be used for particular tasks and conditions of use.
- **Learnability:** The capability of the software product to enable the user to learn its application.
- **Operability:** The capability of the software product to enable the user to operate and control it.
- **Attractiveness:** The capability of the software product to be attractive to the user.

Here's what I came up with for each user group:

Telephone Bankers and Senior Telephone Bankers

- For learnability, I would have actual bankers first go through a draft of the user's guide and perhaps user training (though I would hope we wouldn't need training for this application). I would then survey them on whether they found various features learnable. After the actual tests were run (next bullet), I would survey them again on how well the user guide taught them the system.
- For understandability and operability, I would have actual bankers participate in an alpha test (overlapping the system integration test) and would ask them to run use-case-based tests and then survey them on their experience.
- Finally, after the test were over, I would ask the users to review screenshots and rate the color scheme, graphics, and text in terms of attractiveness.

Customers

I would repeat the tests I outlined for Telephone Bankers, but with the change that I would not use training or user's guides in the learnability scenario. Rather, I would integrate that into the use of the product and ask them to use online help as needed to learn the application as they use it. I would then survey them just once, after the tests, to see how they felt about the learnability.

Branch bank employees

I would repeat the tests for the Telephone Banker, but with two changes:

1. There would be no training or user's guides, as I would expect them to be too busy for that.
2. I would run the alpha test once, then wait two weeks, then run it again. I would then survey the bankers on how hard they found it to run the application after not using it for a while.

5.3 Quality Attributes for Technical Testing

Learning objectives

(K2) Explain the reasons for including efficiency, reliability, and technical security tests in a testing strategy and provide examples of defects expected to be found.

(K2) Characterize non functional test types for technical testing by typical defects to be targeted (attacked), its typical application within the application lifecycle, and suitable test techniques for test design.

This section of the syllabus is mostly for technical test analysts. The learning objectives for them are much more in depth for this section. However, as advanced test analysts, we need to understand what is done by our more technical colleagues and why. We should also be aware of the bugs they tend to find with these tests, if for no other reason than to remind ourselves that functional testing alone will not suffice.

To reiterate something I mentioned earlier, functional testing, which we covered in the previous section, focuses on what the system does rather than how it does it. Non functional testing focuses on how the system does what it does. Both functional and non functional testing are black-box tests, being focused on behavior. White-box tests focus on how the system works internally, i.e., on its structure.

Non functional tests can and should be done throughout the lifecycle. They can be especially useful in component test and integration testing. When performance is a high risk—and it often is these days—performance testing should permeate every level of testing, including early levels like component and integration test. Similarly, in many systems resource usage is a major concern, especially in embedded systems, so these tests should start early.

Non functional tests can be a major element during later levels like system test and operational acceptance test. These can cover any of the non functional quality characteristics and subcharacteristics defined in ISO 9126, though we will focus on just a few of them in this course. Unfortunately, some types of non functional tests are very expensive. We often are trying to test specific, customer-like systems in the exact intended combinations of hardware and software, including servers, clients, databases, networks, and other resources. This leads to project constraints due to limits on the available resources, but make sure that due thought is given to the risks entailed before agreeing to that.

Sometimes, non functional testing can continue after the software is in production, though the ownership of these tasks might vary. For example, various service level agreements related to reliability, resource usage, and performance might apply to the software. In that case, monitoring will be needed.

In the rest of this section, let's look at the quality attributes that apply and how a technical test analyst might test them.

5.3.1 Technical Security

The first quality attribute we look at is security. Security is a key risk for many applications and has certainly gotten a lot of attention lately. Security is the first quality attribute for software that seems to have attracted the attention of legislators, as there are more legal guarantees of privacy and security of information—and more legal penalties for software vendors' sloppiness—than for any other quality characteristic I can think of.

Security tests and failures are different from functional tests and failures. For one thing, security tests often try to take advantage of unintended side effects and bad assumptions, which is where many failures live. An example from the syllabus is a media player that correctly plays audio but does so by writing files to unencrypted temporary storage. If you can find the unencrypted files, you can subvert the intellectual property rights of the owner.

Here's another good example: For one client, we did a security test of their services early in the system test period. We found many bugs, which they fixed. Later, right before going into production, we reran the tests. We found that the servers that were in the environment during the first security test were all fine. However, all the new servers had exactly the same problems as the original servers had the first time!

Security vulnerabilities often relate to data access, functional privileges, the ability to insert malicious programs into the system, the ability to deny legitimate users the use of the system, the ability to sniff or capture data that should be secret, the ability to break encrypted traffic such as passwords and credit card information, and the ability to deliver a virus or a worms. The vulnerabilities can exist in the user interface, the file system, the operating system, and external software.

An interesting thing about security as a quality characteristic is that increased quality in security can decrease quality in usability, performance, and functionality. For example, it's nice to give users a helpful hint when they input the wrong value. However, if we're talking about a password field, those helpful hints are helpful to hackers and other disfavored users.

We discussed security attacks briefly in chapter 4, and then in the previous section of this chapter we discussed functional security testing (also called penetration testing). Here are some ideas on how to develop technical security tests.

One is information retrieval. Here, we use good old-fashion research—which is not so old-fashioned in these days of unlimited data on the Internet if you know how to search it properly—to find useful weaknesses. This information can include names of employees, physical addresses of offices or data centers, and, best of all, details regarding the network and communication infrastructure, the IP numbers of ports, the locations of wireless access points, and the types and versions of software, hardware, and operating systems in use. All too many organizations rely on "security by obscurity," and the trouble is that it's harder than ever to obscure anything anymore.

Another is vulnerability scanning. This usually involves the use of some openly available hacker tool like John the Ripper, SATAN, Cain, and Network Stumbler, to name just a few examples. These tools will allow you to find vulnerabilities that are breaches of security or can be used to breach security. There are also various vulnerability checklists available. Vulnerability can be particularly fruitful after information retrieval because you will have a better idea of where to point these tools, and checklists will help you target them. Alternatively, you can use vulnerability with little if any information beyond a company's URL, which is called a "zero knowledge" penetration test.

Following either an information retrieval or vulnerability scan—or both—you can then develop an attack plan. This is an outline of testing actions that you believe will allow you to compromise a particular system's security or a particular organizational security policy. The attacks will need to designate the target interface as well as at least logical test cases to run against it.

5.3.2   Security Attacks

A good source of these logical test cases is security attacks. We saw an example of those earlier in this course, in chapter 4. We also saw functional attacks using Whittaker's "how to break software" model. Whittaker has extended this concept to include security, so let's take a closer look.[1]

To refresh your memory, in figure 5-9, you see a picture of the application under test in its operating environment. The application receives inputs from and sends outputs to its user interface. It interacts in various direct ways with interoperating applications; e.g., through copy-and-paste from one application to another or by sending data to and retrieving data from an application that in turn manages that data with a database management system.

The application also can interact indirectly by sharing data in a file with another application. Yet other applications, with which it does not interact, can potentially affect the application—and vice versa—due to the fact that they cohabit the same system, sharing memory, disk, CPU, and network resources.

The application sends data to and from the file system when it creates, updates, reads, and deletes files. It also relies on the operating system, both its libraries and the kernel, to provide various services and to intermediate interac-

---

1. See James Whittaker's book *How to Break Software Security.*

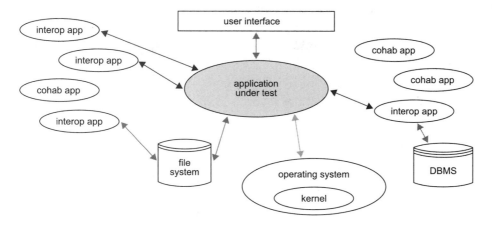

Figure 5–9   *Attacking dependencies and the UI*

tion with the hardware. So based on this picture, we can attack at dependencies and at the user interface.

Dependency attacks would include the following:

- We can block access to libraries (e.g., dynamic link libraries) that the application needs to use or load.

- We can manipulate the Registry, editing various keys in that structure, if we're working on a Windows system. On UNIX and Linux systems, there are often similar information repositories.

- We can force the use of corrupt files, especially if we can figure out just the right way to corrupt them.

- We can edit data and configuration files or replace these files with values that users could not enter through a secured interface. (You'd be surprised how often the front door—the user interface—is locked while the back door—the stored configurations, data, etc.—is wide open.)

- We can try to force low-resource operation, exhausting memory, CPU space, disk space, and the like. As the application gets slowed down, perhaps it will show us something or tell us something it shouldn't.

User interface attacks would include the following:

- We can overflow inputs. The input buffer overflow is the oldest trick in the book at this point, but it still works when done properly. Even if you don't know how to insert malicious code, just showing that the application can be crashed with a long input into a field shows there is a vulnerability.

- We can try the different program switches and configuration options, especially any that relate to privileges or security. (More on that in just a moment.)

- We can also try different character sets, special characters, commands, scripting languages, and database languages. The well-known SQL-injection attack, where a legal SQL database statement is put into a field, causing it to dump out private information, is a variation of this.

In figure 5-10, you see a picture of the application under test in terms of its design and implementation. The application accepts inputs. The application performs computations. Data goes into and comes out of data storage (perhaps being persisted to the file system or a database manager in the process, which I've not shown here). The application produces outputs.

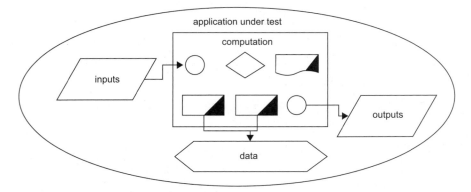

Figure 5–10   *Attacking design and implementation*

So, based on this picture, we can attack at the design and at the implementation. Design attacks would include the following:

- We can try to input common accounts and passwords, including ones that a well-designed, secure program would not even allow.

- We can attack unprotected APIs if we have found them.

- We can try to connect to every port in turn and attack that port.

- We can create loops, especially if the program has a scripting language like TCL, SQL, or the like.

- We can use unusual workflows to try to get something done.

- And, we can force resets of the application.

Implementation attacks would include the following:

- We can manipulate time, moving it unexpectedly forward or (better yet) backward or getting two systems that should share a common time out of sync.

- We can try to duplicate high-privilege files, especially script files or any file that contains an executable type of content, such as database commands.

- We can force all error messages, in the hope that we find a situation that instead results in a security hole.

- And, we can sniff or access temporary files, if we can find them, to see if they store unencrypted data. This includes the swap and temp spaces.

Let's look at an example.

In figure 5-11, you see the security options presented by Adobe's PDF file writing utility. We can set up password-level security, make it compatible with various versions of Adobe PDF readers, and encrypt all, some, or just a little of the document. We can disallow or allow printing and copying contents. We can enable or disable accessibility features like text-to-speech. You might want to spend a moment studying the various options available here and thinking about how to attack them.

Now, you can see that I set up password protection on both opening the document and editing and printing it. The software gets passwords and allows some other options. Unfortunately, when you click OK, the "all bets are off"

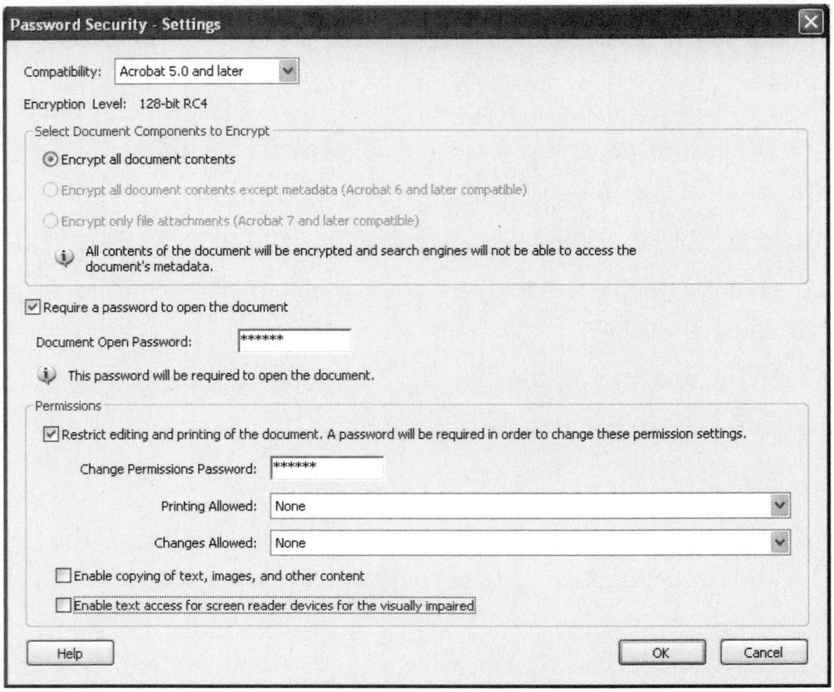

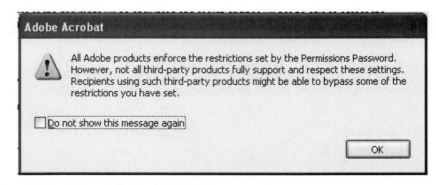

Figure 5–11   *Security setting attack example*

information message shown in figure 5-12 pops up. This kind of thing is a blatant security hole—not only is the security porous, the application will tell you it's porous. It's just a matter of searching the Internet to find tools that will crack Adobe PDF files.

Figure 5–12   *A "how to find security holes" message*

> **ISTQB Glossary**
>
> **reliability growth model:** A model that shows the growth in reliability over time during continuous testing of a component or system as a result of the removal of defects that result in reliability failures.
>
> reliability: The ability of the software product to perform its required functions under stated conditions for a specified period of time or for a specified number of operations.
>
> **reliability testing:** The process of testing to determine the reliability of a software product.

5.3.3   Reliability

Reliability is important for mission-critical, safety-critical, and high-usage systems. We can use reliability testing to reduce the risk of reliability problems. Frequent bugs underlying reliability failures are memory leaks, disk fragmentation and exhaustion, intermittent infrastructure problems, and lower-than-feasible timeout values.

In reliability testing, we monitor software maturity and compare it to desired, statistically valid goals. The system under test can have goals like the mean time between failures (MTBF), the mean time to repair (MTTR), or any other metric that counts the number of failures in terms of some interval or intensity. During reliability testing, as we find bugs that programmers repair, we would expect the reliability to improve. We can use various mathematical models, called reliability growth models or software reliability growth models, to monitor this increase in reliability.

While there are techniques for accelerated reliability testing for hardware—so-called Highly Accelerated Life Tests (or HALT)—software reliability tests usually involve extended duration testing. The tests can be a small set of pre-scripted tests, run repeatedly, which is fine if the workflows are very similar. (For example, you could test an ATM this way.) The tests can be a pool of different tests, selected randomly, which would work if the variation between tests were something that could be predicted or limited. (For example, you could test an e-commerce system this way.) The test can be generated on the fly, using

> **ISTQB Glossary**
>
> **operational profile:** The representation of a distinct set of tasks performed by the component or system, possibly based on user behavior when interacting with the component or system and their probabilities of occurrence. A task is logical rather that physical and can be executed over several machines or be executed in noncontiguous time segments.
>
> **operational acceptance testing:** Operational testing in the acceptance test phase, typically performed in a simulated real-life operational environment by operator and/or administrator focusing on operational aspects, e.g. recoverability, resource-behavior installability, and technical compliance.
>
> operational environment: Hardware and software products installed at users' or customers' sites where the component or system under test will be used. The software may include operating systems, database management systems, and other applications.

some statistical model, which is called stochastic testing. (For example, you could test telephone switches this way, as the variability in called number, call duration, and the like is very large.) The test data can also be randomly generated, sometimes according to a model.

Because this is used for high-risk systems, as you can imagine, a precise, mathematical science has grown up around this topic. These involve the study of patterns of system use, sometimes called *operational profiles*. The reliability growth model and other mathematical elements of reliability testing should be tuned with empirical data. Otherwise, the results are meaningless.

In addition, standard tools and scripting techniques exist. Reliability testing is almost always automated, and I've never seen an example of manual reliability testing that I would consider anything other than an exercise in self-deception at best.

Given a target level of reliability, we can use our reliability tests and metrics as exit criteria. In other words, we continue until we achieve a level of consistent reliability that is sufficient. In some cases, service level agreements and contracts specify what "sufficient" means.

Special reliability test types include robustness and recoverability. Robustness tests involve deliberately subjecting a system to negative, stressful conditions and seeing how it responds. This can include exhausting resources.

Recoverability tests are concerned with the system's ability to recover from some hardware or software failure in its environment. A failover test is a type of recoverability test applied to systems with redundant components to ensure that, should one component fail, redundant component(s) take over. Redundant Array of Independent Disks (RAID) is a system example of this, while disaster recovery testing to hot or warm standby data centers is another. In a failover test, we force the various failures that can occur and then check the ability of the system to recover, ideally silently. The biggest live failover test ever run, that I am aware of, was the failover test that al Qaeda ran on the U.S. financial sector on September 11, 2001. It turned out that the systems recovered well, for the most part, but insufficient backup staff available in the proper locations was a larger problem. As with security, often the human element is overlooked.

Another type of recoverability test is backup/restore. This tests the procedures and equipment used to minimize the effects of a failure. For example, is there a documented, repeatable approach for backing up data and then restoring that data should a loss or corruption of data take place? I heard of one chief information officer (CIO) who was fired for having these procedures but never testing them!

If you need to test backup/restore, make sure you have tests that cover critical paths through the procedures. You should use reviews as well as dynamic tests. You should ideally run these tests in a production-like environment, and, being data-size sensitive, you should use production-size data sets.

During a backup/restore test, you can measure various variables:

- Time taken to perform different types of backup (e.g., full, incremental)
- Time taken to restore data
- Levels of guaranteed data backup (e.g., recovery of all data no more than 24 hours old, recovery of specific transaction data no more than 1 hour old)

Let's look at an example. figure 5-13 shows excerpts from the reliability test plan for a high capacity interactive voice response server, or IVR.

> **ISTQB Glossary**
>
> **recoverability testing:** The process of testing to determine the recoverability of a software product.
>
> recoverability: The capability of the software product to reestablish a specified level of performance and recover the data directly affected in case of failure.

The first paragraph defines something very important, which is what counts as a failure. The key here is that any number of bugs could trigger failures that would not count, unless those failures result in either the operating system or an application crashing, or the need to replace hardware, or the reboot of the server. There are actually a few more paragraphs in the plan discussing this point, as it's important to be unambiguous on the matter.

The second paragraph defines the goal of demonstrating a mean time between failures of at least one year.

The third paragraph describes pass [called here "accept"] criteria for the test. This is one oracle for the test. If, after starting the load generators, the test runs for 114 days with no failures, the test is done and we should accept the

---

Failures [that count against reliability] defined in the Requirements Specification revision 1.7 [as] "… a [failure] such that the IVR system (operating system [or] applications) crashes [or requires] a replacement of some item of hardware [or results in] reboot of the IVR."
These plans are to demonstrate that the [IVR] system MTBF is equal to or greater than 1 year.

Accept criteria (only counting chargeable failures):
1) 114 days with 0 failures; or, 2) 164 days with 1 failure; or, 3) 214 days with 2 failures; or, 4) 265 days with 3 failures; or, 5) 315 days with 4 to 6 failures.

Reject criteria:
1) 17 days with 2 failures; or, 2) 68 days with 3 failures; or, 3) 118 days with 4 failures; or, 4) 168 days with 5 failures; or, 5) 218 days with 6 failures; or, 6) 315 days with 7 failures

Figure 5–13   *Reliability testing example*

MTBF goal as met. If one failure occurs, we have to continue the test for 164 days. If two failures occur, we have to continue the test for 214 days—unless a fail criterion was met first. You can see that as the failures go up, the number of days we'd have to keep running goes up.

The fourth paragraph describes fail [called here "reject"] criteria for the test. This is the other oracle for the test. If, after starting the load generators, the test runs for 17 days and results in two relevant, independent failures, the test is done and we should reject the system as unable to meet the mean time between failures (MTBF) goal. If we see three failures within 68 days, same thing: reject. And so forth.

This being a statistical decision, there is some chance of making the wrong decision. The two wrong decisions are acceptance when you should reject and rejection when you should accept. There's some additional discussion in the plan about how to balance these two decision risks, which are called the consumer's risk and the producer's risk, respectively.

5.3.4 Efficiency Testing

Efficiency is important in a number of situations. Time-critical systems, which include most safety-critical, real-time, and mission-critical systems, must provide their functions in a given amount of time. Even less critical systems like e-commerce and point-of-sales systems must have good time response.

In addition, for some systems, including real-time, consumer-electronics, and embedded systems, resource usage is important. You can't always just add a disk or add memory when resources get tight, as the NASA team managing one of the Mars missions found out when storage space ran out.

Efficiency failures can include slow response times, inadequate throughput, reliability failures under conditions of load, and excessive resource requirements. Efficiency defects are often design flaws, which are very hard to fix during late-stage testing. So, you can and should do efficiency testing at every test level and particularly during design and implantation (via reviews and static analysis).

Let's start with this issue of response time testing, commonly referred to as performance testing. It is seen in various flavors in practice, often called performance (when time response is the issue), load (when response time under different levels of load is the issue), stress (when degradation behavior at or above

> **ISTQB Glossary**
>
> **efficiency testing:** The process of testing to determine the efficiency of a software product.
>
> efficiency: The capability of the software product to provide appropriate performance, relative to the amount of resources used under stated conditions.

maximum load is the issue), and scalability (when the limits of load are the issue).

A classic performance or response-time test looks at the ability of a component or system to respond to user or system inputs within a specified period of time and under various legal conditions. It can also look at the problem slightly differently, by counting the number of functions, records, or transactions completed in a given period, which is often call throughput. The metrics vary according to the objectives of the test.

Load testing involves various mixes and levels of load, usually focused on anticipated and realistic loads. The loads often are designed to look like the transaction requests generated by certain numbers of parallel users. We can then measure response time or throughput. Some people distinguish between multi-user load testing (with realistic numbers of users) and volume load testing (with large numbers of users), but I've not encountered that too often.[2]

Stress testing takes load testing to the extreme and beyond by reaching and then exceeding maximum capacity and volume. The goal here is to ensure that response times, reliability, and functionality degrade slowly and predictably, culminating in some sort of "go away I'm busy" message rather than an application or OS crash, lockup, data corruption, or other antisocial failure mode. A variation of stress testing, called "tip over testing," is designed to find the point where total saturation or failure occurs. The resource that was exhausted at that point is the weak link. Design changes (ideally) or more hardware (if necessary) can often improve stress handling and sometimes response time. Another variation in stress testing, called "bounce" or "spike testing," involves rapidly cycling stress levels up and down.

---

2. See Steve Splaine's book *The Web-Testing Handbook.*

Finally, scalability takes stress testing even further, by finding the bottlenecks and then testing the ability of the system to be enhanced to resolve the problem. In other words, if the plan for handling growth in terms of customers is to add more CPUs to servers, then a scalability test verifies that this will suffice. Having identified the bottlenecks, stress testing can also help establish load monitoring thresholds for production.

Resource utilization tests evaluate the usage of system resources under normal and stress loads. Resources include memory capacity and bandwidth, disk capacity and bandwidth, CPU capacity, and network bandwidth. It's important to focus on the resources of interest, those most limited or most critical, especially on embedded systems.

Like reliability, efficiency tests often involve operational profiles, based on real or predicted usage. These operational profiles are models for how real users will interact with the application. They can vary depending on time of day, day of week, day of month, and week or even day of year. As with reliability testing, if our operational profiles are wrong, our efficiency test results are meaningless—and probably misleading. Also as with reliability testing, the operational profiles are a key input into the creation of test cases for automated tools. Again, manual performance testing is generally misleading, particularly for systems that support large numbers of users or transactions.

5.3.5 Maintainability Testing

Maintainability refers to the ability to update, modify, reuse, and test the system. This is important for most systems because most will be updated, modified, and tested many times during their lifecycle, and often pieces of systems and even whole systems are used in new and different situations.

Maintainability defects include hard-to-understand code, environment dependencies, hidden information and states, and excessive complexity. They can also include "painted myself into a corner" problems when software is released without any practical mechanism for updating it in the field. For example, think of all the problems Microsoft had stabilizing its security-patch process in the mid-2000s.

Maintainability testing should definitely include static analysis and reviews. Many maintainability defects are invisible to dynamic tests but easily found with code analysis tools, design and code walk-throughs, and the like.

> **ISTQB Glossary**
>
> **maintainability testing:** The process of testing to determine the maintainability of a software product.
>
> maintainability: The ease with which a software product can be modified to correct defects, modified to meet new requirements, modified to make future maintenance easier, or adapted to a changed environment.

That is not to say you shouldn't test updates, patches, upgrades, and migration. You definitely should. You should not only test the software pieces of this, but also the procedures and infrastructure involved. For example, verifying that you can patch a system with a 100 MB patch file is all well and good until you find you have forgotten that real users will have to download this patch through a dial-up connection and will need a PhD in computer science to hand-install half of the files!

Sometimes, project or production metrics can point out problems with analyzability, stability, and testability. For example, a large number of regression test failures would indicate stability problems. Long closure periods for bugs might indicate—depending on development team staffing levels—problems with analyzability; i.e., it takes the programmer forever to figure out what the problem is. Long test cycles might indicate—again, depending on test staffing and strategies—problems with testability of the system.

5.3.6   Portability Testing

Finally, portability refers to the ability of the application to install to, use in, and perhaps move to various environments. Of course, the first two are important for all systems. In the case of PC software, given the rapid pace of changes in operating systems, cohabitating and interoperating applications, hardware, bandwidth availability, and the like, being able to move and adapt to new environments is critical too.

A number of types of defects can cause portability problems, but certainly environment dependencies, resource hogging, and nonstandard operating system interactions are high on the list. For example, changing shared Registry

> **ISTQB Glossary**
>
> **portability testing:** The process of testing to determine the portability of a software product.
>
> portability: The ease with which the software product can be transferred from one hardware or software environment to another.

keys during installation or removing shared files during de-installation are classic portability problems.

Fortunately, portability defects are amenable to straightforward test design techniques like pairwise testing, classification trees, equivalence partitioning, decision tables, and state-based testing. Unfortunately, portability defects often require a large number of configurations for testing.

Let's look at some types of portability tests.

The first is installability. Here, we install the software, using its standard installation, update, and patch facilities, on its target environment or environments. Usually, this involves not one test case but a whole suite of tests. We need to check for problems like the following:

- We can't install the software according to the instructions in an installation or user's manual or via an installation wizard. This sounds straightforward, but notice that it includes testing in enough different environments that you can have confidence that it will work in most if not all final environments as well as looking at various installation options like partial, typical, or full installation.
- We observe failures during installation (e.g., failure to load particular DLLs) that are not cleaned up correctly, so they leave the system in an undefined, crashed, or even completely corrupted state. Again it's the variations in possibilities that make this a challenge.
- We find that we can't partially install, can't abort the install, or can't uninstall.
- We find that the installation process or wizard will not shield us from—or perhaps won't even detect—invalid hardware, software, operating systems, or configurations. This is likely to be connected to failures during or after

the installation that leave the system in an undefined, crashed, or even completely corrupted state.

- We find that the installation takes an unbearable amount of time to complete or perhaps never completes.
- We can't downgrade or uninstall after a successful or unsuccessful installation.
- We find that the typical people involved in doing the installation can't figure out how to do it properly, so they are confused, frustrated, and making lots of mistakes (resulting, again, in systems left in an undefined, crashed, or even completely corrupted state). This type of problem is revealed during a usability test of the installation, obviously.

By the way, for each of the types of problems I just mentioned, we have to consider not only installation problems, but also similar problems with updates and patches.

Not only do these tests involve monitoring the install, update, or patch process, but they also require some amount of functionality testing afterwards to detect any problems that might have been silently introduced.

Next comes coexistence testing, which is also called sociability or compatibility testing. Here, we check that one or more systems that work in the same environment do so without conflict. Notice that this is not the same as interoperability because the systems might not be directly interacting. Earlier, I referred to these as "cohabiting" systems, though that phrase is a bit misleading because human cohabitation usually involves a fair amount of direct interaction. We are looking for problems like the following:

- Applications have an adverse impact on each other's functionality when loaded on the same environment, either directly (by crashing each other) or indirectly (by consuming all the resources).
- Applications work fine at first but then are damaged by patches and upgrades to other applications because of undefined dependencies.

It's easy to forget compatibility testing and test applications by themselves. This is often found in siloed organizations where application development takes place separately in different groups. Once everything goes into the data center, though, you are then doing compatibility testing in production, which is not a good idea.

By the way, in the syllabus it mentions that compatibility testing is normally performed when system and user acceptance testing have been successfully completed. This is only a good idea if you don't care about nasty surprises at the end of a project. Seriously, coexistence testing should occur no later than system test.

Next, we have adaptability. Here we check that an application can function correctly in all intended target environments. Confusingly, this is also commonly referred to as compatibility testing. In fact, I hear this type of testing called compatibility testing more frequently than sociability testing or coexistence testing is called that. As you might imagine, when there are lots of options, specifying adaptability or compatibility tests involves pairwise testing, classification trees, and equivalence partitioning. As you might also imagine, you need to install the application on the environment, so this allows testing adaptability and installation at once. Functional tests are then run in the environments that are configured and installed. Usually, a small sample of functions is sufficient to reveal any problems, or at least it is about all that organizations can afford to invest given the potentially enormous size of this task.

There might also be procedure elements of adaptability that need testing. Perhaps data migration is required to move from one environment to another. In that case, we have to test the procedure as well as the adaptability of the software.

Finally, we have replaceability. Here, we check that we can exchange software components within a system for others. This can apply for systems that use commercial off-the-shelf software (COTS) for certain components. For example, we might want to test an application that interfaces with a database management system to ensure that we can choose multiple different database systems.

We can do replaceability testing in system test, but the first and perhaps best opportunity is in functional integration tests. If we include more than one alternative component in the builds, we will test it by default. In addition, we should look at replaceability in design reviews because replaceability as a quality characteristic arises from clearly defined interfaces.

5.4 Sample Exam Questions

To end each chapter, you can try one or more sample exam questions to reinforce your knowledge and understanding of the material and to prepare for the ISTQB Advanced Level Test Analyst exam.

Assume you are a test analyst working on a project to create a programmable thermostat for home use to control central heating, ventilation, and air conditioning (HVAC) systems. In addition to the normal HVAC control functions, the thermostat has the ability to download data to a browser-based application that runs on PCs for further analysis. The application can export that data in the following formats: comma-separated variable (CSV), Excel (XLS), and tab-separated text (TXT). The application can encrypt the data using AES 128-bit, AES 256-bit, and public key encryption.

1. Which of the following tests would address the interoperability of this application?

    A Encrypting data using a public key and checking that the appropriate private key can decrypt it

    B Evaluating the ability of typical users to download and analyze data from this application

    C Logging thermostat operation statistics on a paper log at regular intervals during operation and checking the exported data against the log

    D Exporting data in Excel format and loading it in OpenOffice's spreadsheet application

2. Continue with the scenario in the previous question.

    Which of the following tests would address the functional security of this application?

    A Encrypting data using a public key and checking that the appropriate private key can decrypt it

    B Using a text-to-speech application to read the data from the application's screen

C Logging thermostat operation statistics on a paper log at regular intervals during operation and checking the exported data against the log

D Evaluating the ability of typical users to download and analyze data from this application

3. Continue with the scenario in the previous question.

Which of the following tests would address the accessibility of this application?

A Encrypting data using a public key and checking that the appropriate private key can decrypt it

B Using a text-to-speech application to read the data from the application's screen

C Evaluating the ability of typical users to download and analyze data from this application

D Exporting data in Excel format and loading it in OpenOffice's spreadsheet application

4. Continue with the scenario in the previous question.

Which of the following tests would address the usability of this application?

A Encrypting data using a public key and checking that the appropriate private key can decrypt it

B Using a text-to-speech application to read the data from the application's screen

C Evaluating the ability of typical users to download and analyze data from this application

D Exporting data in Excel format and loading it in OpenOffice's spreadsheet application

5. Which of the following is the best example of a reliability failure for an application?

    A Slow response time

    B Excessive memory consumption

    C Random application termination

    D Failure to encrypt data

6 Reviews

"When I use a word," Humpty Dumpty said, in a rather scornful tone, "it means just what I choose it to mean, neither more nor less."
"The question is," said Alice, "whether you can make words mean so many different things."
"The question is," said Humpty Dumpty, "which is to be master—that's all." Alice was too much puzzled to say anything; so after a minute Humpty Dumpty began again. "They've a temper, some of them—particularly verbs: they're the proudest—adjectives you can do anything with, but not verbs— however, I can manage the whole lot of them! Impenetrability! That's what I say!"
"Would you tell me, please," said Alice, "what that means?"

Alice has a not-so-enlightening requirements clarification
session with Humpty Dumpty, prior to Humpty's
unpleasant lesson about gravity.
From *Through The Looking Glass,* by Lewis Carroll

The sixth chapter of the Advanced syllabus is concerned with reviews. As you will recall from the Foundation syllabus, reviews are a form of static testing where people, rather than tools, analyze the project or one of the project's work products, such as a requirements specification. The primary goal is typically to find defects in that work product before it serves as a basis for further project activity, though other goals can also apply. The Advanced syllabus introduces additional types of reviews and covers strategies for effective and successful reviews. Chapter six of the Advanced syllabus has five sections:

1. Introduction
2. The Principles of Reviews
3. Types of Reviews

4. Introducing Reviews

5. Success Factors for Reviews

Let's look at each section and how it relates to test analysis.

6.1 Introduction

Learning objectives
Recall of content only

Again, think back to the beginning of chapter 4. I introduced a taxonomy for tests, shown in figure 6-1. I mentioned the distinction between static and dynamic tests. Static tests are those tests that do not involve execution of the test object. Dynamic tests do involve execution of the test object. In chapters 4 and 5, we talked about test techniques and quality characteristics, mostly from the point of view of dynamic testing.

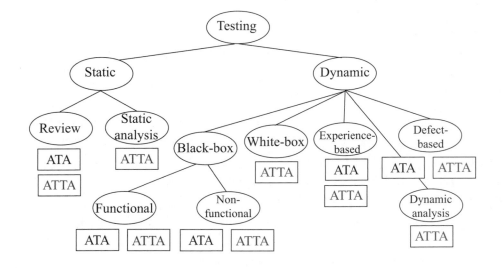

Figure 6–1 *Advanced syllabus testing techniques*

> **ISTQB Glossary**
>
> **review:** An evaluation of a product or project status to ascertain discrepancies from planned results and to recommend improvements. Examples include management review, informal review, technical review, inspection, and walk-through.
>
> **reviewer:** The person involved in the review that identifies and describes anomalies in the product or project under review. Reviewers can be chosen to represent different viewpoints and roles in the review process.

In this chapter, we cover static testing. In fact, we are going to focus on one branch of the static test tree, that of reviews. (Static analysis is something we'll leave for technical test analysts.) Largely, the material in this chapter expands upon what was covered on reviews in the Foundation syllabus.

To have success with reviews, an organization must invest in and ensure good planning, participation, and follow-up. It's more than a room full of people reading a document.

Good testers make excellent reviewers. Good testers have curious minds and a willingness to ask skeptical questions (referred to as professional pessimism in the Foundation). That outlook makes them useful in a review, though they have to remain aware of the need to contribute in a positive way.

This is true not only of testers, but of everyone involved. Being a group activity, all review participants must commit to well-conducted reviews. One negative, confrontational, or belligerent participant can damage the entire process profoundly.

Reviews are easy to do poorly and hard to do well, so many organizations abandon them. However, done properly, reviews have one of the highest payoff rates of any quality-related activity.

Let's review the IEEE 1028 standard for reviews, shown in figure 6-2, which was introduced at the Foundation level. The first section of the standard is an overview. It covers the purpose of the standard, the scope of coverage, and guidelines for conformance with the standard, the organization of the standard, and how to apply the standard in an organization.

1. Overview
   - Purpose, scope, conformance, organisation, application
2. References
3. Definitions
4. Management reviews
   - Responsibilities, inputs/outputs, entry/exit criteria, procedures
5. Technical reviews
   - Responsibilities, inputs/outputs, entry/exit criteria, procedures
6. Inspections
   - Responsibilities, inputs/outputs, entry/exit criteria, procedures, data collection, process improvement
7. Walkthroughs
   - Responsibilities, inputs/outputs, entry/exit criteria, procedures, data collection, process improvement
8. Audits
   - Responsibilities, inputs/outputs, entry/exit criteria, procedures

Figure 6–2   *IEEE 1028 standard for software reviews*

The second section is "References," which, as you might imagine, refers to other documents, standards, and so forth. The third section, "Definitions," defines terms used in the standard.

The fourth section addresses management reviews. Management reviews were out of scope at the Foundation level, you might recall. In this section, the standard talks about who has what responsibilities in a management review, the inputs to and outputs from a management review, the entry criteria to start such a review and the exit criteria to recognize when it's complete, and the procedures a management review should follow.

The fifth section addresses technical reviews. In this section, the standard talks about who has what responsibilities in a technical review, the inputs to and outputs from a technical review, the entry criteria to start such a review and the exit criteria to recognize when it's complete, and the procedures a technical review should follow.

The sixth section addresses inspections. As with the previous two sections, the standard talks about who has what responsibilities in an inspection, the inputs to and outputs from an inspection, the entry criteria to start such a review and the exit criteria to recognize when it's complete, and the procedures an inspection should follow. However, because inspections are more formal than technical reviews, the standard also discusses collecting data from the review process and implementing improvements to the review process.

The seventh section addresses walk-throughs. As with the other sections, the standard talks about who has what responsibilities in a walk-through, the inputs to and outputs from a walk-through, the entry criteria to start such a review and the exit criteria to recognize when it's complete, and the procedures a walk-through should follow. Because the level of formality for walk-throughs is similar to that of inspections, the standard also discusses collecting data from the review process and implementing improvements to the review process.

Finally, the eighth section addresses audits. As with the other sections, the standard talks about who has what responsibilities in an audit, the inputs to and outputs from an audit, the entry criteria to start such a review and the exit criteria to recognize when it's complete, and the procedures an audit should follow.

6.2 The Principles of Reviews

Learning objectives
Recall of content only

Let's look at some review principles that were explained in the Foundation syllabus. First, as mentioned a moment ago, a review is a type of static test. The object being reviewed is not executed or run during the review. Like any test activity, reviews can have various objectives. One common objective is finding defects. Others, typical of all testing, are building confidence that we can proceed with the item under review, reducing risks associated with the item under review, and generating information for management. Unique to reviews is the addition of another common objective, that of ensuring uniform understanding of the document—and its implications for the project—and building consensus around the statements in the document.

Reviews usually precede dynamic tests. Reviews should complement dynamic tests. Because the cost of a defect increases as that defect remains in

ISTQB Glossary

audit: An independent evaluation of software products or processes to ascertain compliance to standards, guidelines, specifications, and/or procedures based on objective criteria, including documents that specify (1) the form or content of the products to be produced, (2) the process by which the products shall be produced, and (3) how compliance to standards or guidelines shall be measured.

inspection: A type of peer review that relies on visual examination of documents to detect defects, e.g., violations of development standards and non-conformance to higher-level documentation. The most formal review technique and therefore always based on a documented procedure.

management review: A systematic evaluation of software acquisition, supply, development, operation, or maintenance process performed by or on behalf of management that monitors progress, determines the status of plans and schedules, confirms requirements and their system allocation, or evaluates the effectiveness of management approaches to achieve fitness for purpose.

technical review: A peer group discussion activity that focuses on achieving consensus on the technical approach to be taken.

walk-through: A step-by-step presentation by the author of a document in order to gather information and to establish a common understanding of its content.

the system, reviews should happen as soon as possible. However, because not all defects are easy to find in reviews, dynamic tests should still occur.

Woody Allen, the New York film director, is reported to have once said that "80 percent of success is showing up." That might be true in the film business, but Woody Allen would not be a useful review participant. Reviews require adequate preparation. If you spend no time preparing for a review, expect to add little value during the review meeting.

In fact, you can easily remove value by asking dumb questions that you could have answered on your own had you read the document thoroughly before showing up. You might think that's a harsh statement, especially in light of the management platitude that "there are no dumb questions." Well, sorry,

there are plenty of dumb questions. Any question that someone asks in a meeting because of their own failure to prepare, resulting in a whole roomful of people having to watch someone else spend their time educating the ill-prepared attendee on something he should have known when he came in the room, qualifies as a dumb question. In fact, to me showing up for a review meeting unprepared qualifies as rude behavior, disrespectful of the time of the others in the room.

Because reviews are so effective when done properly, organizations should review all important documents. That includes test documents. Test plans, test cases, quality risk analyses, bug reports, test status report, you name it. My rule of thumb is, anything that matters is not done until it's been looked at by at least two pairs of eyes. You don't have to review documents that don't matter, but here's a question for you: Why would you be writing a document that didn't matter?

So, what can happen after a review? There are three possible outcomes. The ideal case is that the document is okay as is or with minor changes. Another possibility is that the document requires some changes but not a re-review. The most costly outcome—in terms of both effort and schedule time—is that the document requires extensive changes and a re-review. Now, when that happens, keep in mind that, while this is a costly outcome, it's less costly than simply ignoring the serious problems and then dealing with them during component, integration, system, or—worse yet—acceptance testing.

In an informal review, there are no defined rules, no defined roles, no defined responsibilities, so you can approach these however you please. Of course, keep in mind that Capers Jones has reported that informal reviews typically find only around 20 percent of defects, while very formal reviews like inspections can find up to 85 percent of defects.[20] If something is important, you probably want to have a formal review—unless you think that you and your team are so smart that no one is going to make any mistakes.

During a formal review, there are some essential roles and responsibilities:

- The manager. The manager allocates resources, schedules reviews, and the like. However, they might not be allowed to attend based on the review type.

20.See Capers Jones' book *Software Assessments, Benchmarks, and Best Practices.*

> **ISTQB Glossary**
>
> **informal review:** A review not based on a formal (documented) procedure.
>
> **inspection leader (or moderator):** The leader and main person responsible for an inspection or other review process.

- The moderator or leader: This is the chair of the review meeting.
- The author: This is the person who wrote the item under review. A review meeting, done properly, should not be a sad or humiliating experience for the author.
- The reviewers: These are the people who review the item under review, possibly finding defects in it. Reviewers can play specialized roles, based on their expertise or based on some type of defect they should target.
- The scribe or secretary or recorder: This is the person who writes down the findings.

Now, in some types of reviews, roles can be combined. For example, the author, moderator, and secretary can be the same person. In fact, as test manager, when I've had the test team review my test plans, I've often been the manager, the author, the moderator, and the secretary.

Some additional roles might be involved, depending on the review. We might involve decision makers or project stakeholders. This is especially true if an ancillary or even primary objective of the review is to build consensus or to disseminate information. In some cases, the stakeholders involved can be customer or user representatives. We recently did a review of mock-ups for our new website with our marketing team, our outsource web development team, and our company executives. Because we had hired the web development team, for them we were the customers and, for some features, the users.

Certain very formal review types also use a reader, who is the person responsible for reading, paraphrasing, and explaining the item under review.

You can use more than one review type in an organization. For some documents, time is more important than perfection. For example, on our test teams, we apply the "two pairs of eyes" rule to mean that a tester must read another tester's bug report before it can be filed. However, for more visible documents like test plans, we use a walk-through with the entire test team. For critical documents, you can use more than one review type on a single item. For example, when writing this book, we had an informal review with a core set of RBCS associates and partners followed by a broader, more formal review as the final book came together.

6.3 Types of Reviews

Learning objectives

(K2) Compare review types with each other and show their relative strengths, weaknesses, and fields of use.

The Foundation syllabus discussed four types of reviews:

- At the lowest level of formality (and, usually, defect removal effectiveness), we find the informal review. This can be as simple as two people, the author and a colleague, discussing a design document over the phone.
- Technical reviews are more formalized, but still not highly formal. They are sometimes called peer reviews, which gives a clue about the typical participants.
- Walk-throughs are reviews where the author is the moderator and the item under review itself is the agenda. That is, the author leads the review, and in the review, the reviewers go section by section through the item under review.
- Inspections are the most formalized reviews. The roles are well defined. Managers may not attend. The author may be neither moderator nor secretary. A reader is typically involved.

As you can imagine, as the level of formality goes up, the rate of review—the number of pages per hour—goes down.

You should remember that the IEEE 1028 standard and the Foundation syllabus are discussing idealized situations. In real-world practice, it is quite common to find organizations blending the parts they like from each type and discarding parts they don't like. It's also quite common to hear organizations talking about walk-throughs when the approach they use for the walk-through does not adhere to the IEEE 1028 rules.

While at the Foundation level we ignored management reviews and audits from the IEEE 1028 standard, let's fill that gap here. Let's start with management reviews. Common purposes of management reviews are to monitor progress, assess status, and make decisions about some project, system, ongoing activity, or process. (Of course, in some organizations, management reviews are organized for various political reasons, too, but we can ignore that for the moment.)

Managers involved with the item being reviewed often perform management reviews. Various stakeholders and decision makers can assist them as well. The level of involvement of each of the participants can vary. In some cases, organizations will hire outside consultants to come in and do reviews. For example, a large portion of RBCS's business is doing test process and quality process assessments of various kinds for organizations. These are a hybrid between a management review and an audit, which we'll discuss in a moment. Test managers often drive these test assessments, in which case they are more like a management review. When outside test stakeholders drive these test assessments, they are more like an audit.

Part of a management review is often to assess how a project is doing in terms of plans, estimates, project risk management, and so forth. Another part of a management review is looking at the adequacy of various procedures and controls. Participants must prepare for these reviews, especially those who are going to deliver status information. We've done test assessments for organizations where people had so tenuous a grasp on what was going on in their testing group that our foremost recommendation was, "Get some metrics and tracking mechanisms in place immediately."

Typically, the outcome of a management review includes action items, recommendations, issues to be resolved, and the like. The decisions should be documented and the execution of action items and recommendations checked regularly. Unfortunately, it's not unusual for follow-up to be less than ideal.

Moving on to audits, these can be quite formal, and in some cases, quite adversarial. In an audit, there's a strong chance that the auditors are measuring people against a contract, a standard, an industry best practice, or the like. This can provoke defensiveness. The Advanced syllabus says that audits are least effective at revealing defects, but that really depends on the auditing and audited organization. When we do testing audits for our clients, we are very, very good at finding defects, both project defects and process defects.

One essential element of an audit is the independent evaluation. Like a management review, we can measure a process, a project, an ongoing activity, or a system. However, another essential element of an audit is the idea of being in or out of compliance. Audits can be done by a lead auditor with an auditor team or by a single auditor. The auditors collect evidence through interviews, witnessing, examining documents, analyzing metrics, and so forth. I find that the interviews can be particularly interesting, especially when an audit has become high stakes for some of the participants. Attempts to spin, mislead, misdirect, convince, and stall the auditor occur in such situations.

Like the management review, the outcome of an audit can include action items, recommendations, issues to be resolved, and the like. However, it also includes an assessment of compliance (or noncompliance). This is often measured against a multidimensional scale or checklist, so even if 99 items are in compliance, if 1 is out of compliance, the organization might fail the audit. If noncompliance is the finding, then corrective actions for the item or items that failed would be typical. Again, the decisions should be documented and the execution of action items, recommendations, and corrective actions should be checked regularly, along with periodic reassessment of compliance. In regulated industries or for legally mandated audits, follow-up on audit results are usually excellent, but in nonregulated industries, follow-up is often less than ideal.

In addition to the types of reviews laid out in the IEEE 1028 standard, we can classify reviews in terms of the work products or activities subject to review. A contractual review, naturally enough, corresponds to some sort of project milestone, often one linked to payment or continuation of a contract. It could also be a management review for a safety-critical or safety-related system. The review could involve managers, vendors, customers, and technical staff. When a project is going well, these are routine. When a project starts to go poorly, particularly if there are multiple vendors involved, expect massive amounts of time and energy to be spent by each vendor trying to obscure who is responsible for the problems.

The Foundation syllabus discussed requirements reviews. A requirements review can be informal, it can be a walk-through, it can be a technical review or it can be an inspection. The scope of a requirements review should be whatever it needs to be. If we are building a safety-critical system, a review or part of a review should consider safety. If we are building a high-availability system, a review or part of a review should consider availability and reliability. For all systems, requirements and the requirements reviews should address functional and non functional requirements. We can include in a requirements review acceptance criteria and test conditions.

The Foundation syllabus also discussed design reviews. A design review can range from informal to technical reviews and inspections. Like a requirements review, they can involve technical staff and customers and stakeholders, though you'd expect that as the level of detail becomes more intense, the participants would become more technical. In some organizations, there is a concept of preliminary design review and a critical design review. The preliminary design review is a peer review where technical peers propose the initial approach to deal with technical issues related to system or test designs. The critical design review covers the proposed design solutions, which can include test cases and procedures in some cases.

The operational readiness review, acceptance review, or qualification review is a combination of technical and managerial review. This is sort of a final safety net. We want to review all the data to make a final decision on readiness for production. As important as this is, I have seen situations where the project was so intensive and exhausting that, by the time the operational readiness review—or exit meeting or project launch meeting or whatever it was called—occurred, everyone rubber-stamped a decision to go ahead with production even though there were lots of good reasons to say, "Wait, don't do this." In one case, that decision lead to months of extremely poor system performance in production.

As discussed in the Foundation syllabus, there are six phases for a formal review:

1. Planning, including for each work product to be reviewed and for all reviews to occur on a project
2. Kickoff, again for each work product and for all reviews
3. Individual preparation for each work product; reading the document and noting problems
4. The review meeting itself, for each work product
5. Any rework necessary based on the changes required by the review results

6. Finally, follow-up both for individual work products if needed and for the overall reviews done on the project

Now, remember that good process is important, but the right participants are essential. The participants must match the work product to be reviewed. Inviting the wrong people to reviews guarantees ineffectual reviews, even if you follow the process to the letter.

Capers Jones, in his studies of thousands of projects across hundreds of clients, has found some interesting data on reviews, their applications, and the effectiveness of various types of reviews. Jones mentions that the informal reviews are the least effective, reviews that have some but not all elements of formality are about average, and the most effective are the highly formalized inspections. Of course, to be effective at any level of formality, you have to do the reviews well and you have to have organizational support for the process.[21]

As you can see in table 6-1, both the level of formality and the type of item to which the review is applied has a strong influence on the percentage of defects found and removed. If you think of the reviews as a series of filters, here's a quick mathematical demonstration of how effective reviews can be.

First, imagine that you started with 1,000 defects. You follow worst practices in reviews, but at least you review all types of items. In this case, you would enter testing with about 166 defects. Now, imagine that you started with 1,000 defects again. However, this time you follow best practices (and again you review all types of items). This time, you go into testing with 3 defects.

Table 6–1 *Review types and effectiveness*

	Least	Average	Most
Requirements review	20%	30%	50%
High-level design review	30%	40%	60%
Functional design review	30%	45%	65%
Detailed design review	35%	55%	75%
Code review	35%	60%	85%

---

21. These figures and table 6-1 are derived from Capers Jones, *Software Assessments, Benchmarks, and Best Practices.*

6.4   Introducing Reviews

Learning objectives
Recall of content only

The following steps are useful in successfully introducing reviews:

- Secure management support: Reviews are not expensive from a budget point of view, as test automation is, but they do require a time commitment, especially when time is tight.
- Educate managers: You need to have an honest conversation about the business case for reviews, including the costs, benefits, and potential issues. Avoid exaggerating.
- Put structure in place: Have documented review procedures for the various types of reviews you'll use. Have templates and forms available. Establish an infrastructure such as the reviews metrics database. If you intend to do geographically distributed reviews, make sure you have the tools in place for that.
- Train: Educate the participants on review techniques and procedures.
- Obtain participant support: Make sure that those who will do the reviews and those whose work will be reviewed are comfortable and supportive.
- Do some pilot reviews: Plan to make some mistakes…and learn from them.
- Demonstrate the benefit: You have a defined business case, right? Now show management that you achieved what you promised!
- Apply reviews to all (or at least the most important) documents: Requirements, contracts, project plans, test plans, quality risk analyses, and similar high-visibility documents are obvious targets. However, I have found simply ensuring informal reviews of bug reports to be amazingly valuable.

You won't necessarily need to do every step in every organization, and you don't need to do these steps in perfect, sequential order, but you should think long and hard about why it's okay to skip a step if you think it is.

Your organization will invest time and money in reviews. Managers will expect a return on that investment. To demonstrate a return on the review investment, you can use metrics like the reduced or avoided cost of fixing defects or dealing with failures. What does a defect cost in system test? How about after release? A simple spreadsheet can show the benefits of reviews and evaluate the success of the reviews after their implementation.

Don't forget to measure the return in terms of saved time too. Money is not always the biggest concern for managers. In fact, time to market is usually a bigger issue. So, if you can document that a defect takes 5 hours to resolve when found in a review and 25 hours when found in system test, you have a solid business case for how time investment in reviews during the early stages of a project reduces the likelihood of project delay at the end of the project.

Having established metrics, it's important to continue to monitor them. It's easy for review processes to become ritualistic and stuck, and then the value goes down. If you see the benefit dropping off, ask yourself why? In fact, the benefit should constantly be going up. You should be looking for metrics-based, measurable ways to improve the review processes. Make sure that you—and your managers—see reviews and review process improvement as a long-term investment.

6.5   Success Factors for Reviews

Learning objectives

(K3) Use a review checklist to verify code and architecture from a tester's perspective.

(K3) Use a review checklist to verify requirements and use cases from a tester's perspective.

A number of factors influence the success—or, if absent, the failure—of reviews. The Advanced syllabus classifies those into three groups. Let's start with the technical factors.

Ensure that you are following the defined process correctly. This can be particularly tricky for formal types of reviews like inspection. Now, that doesn't mean you can't tailor these processes, but it's usually a good idea to master them first.

I mentioned this matter of the business case. To support your business case, you have to record the costs of reviews (particularly in terms of effort) and the benefits that the organization obtains. A problem with reviews is that the benefits accrue long after the cost was incurred. That's true for all testing, of course, but it's especially acute for reviews, particularly if you forget to measure the value.

You don't have to wait until a document is done before you start reviewing it. You can and should review early drafts or partial documents when you're dealing with something critical. This can help to identify and prevent patterns of defects before they are built into the whole document.

That said, make sure you have some rules about what it means for something to be ready for review. You can waste people's time by sending them materials that aren't sufficiently mature to be reviewed. You can also waste people's time and frustrate them by sending them stuff to review that's still changing. People who are frustrated because they are wasting their time on some activity tend to find ways to stop wasting their time on that activity, which means that the review process can wither away. So have some entry criteria. These should also include the simple rule that everyone has to show up prepared.

Checklists are helpful for reviews. It's too easy to forget important areas without them. Have some checklists. You can start with checklists from reputable industry experts, but make sure to extend those to be organization specific. They should address common defects based on what you find. Also, have different checklists for different kinds of documents, such as requirements, use cases, and designs. Finally, have different checklists for different review processes.

The appropriate level of formality varies. So be ready to use more than one type of review. Consider your objectives. Is the idea to do a quick document cleanup before sending to a client? To improve some technical design decisions? To educate stakeholders? To generate information for management?

I've mentioned my rule of "two pairs of eyes," and I try hard not to violate that rule. Sometimes, deadlines intervene. However, you should review—or, better yet, inspect—all documents that are vitally important. If a document is involved in making an important decision, such as signing a contract, be sure to inspect the proposal, contract, or high-level requirements specification first. If a major expenditure is being contemplated, have a management review to authorize it.

For large documents, you can use a sampling of a limited subset to estimate the number of defects in the entire document. This can help to determine if a re-review is needed. Keep in mind that this sampling approach won't work for a document cleanup or edit.

Watch out for distractions. It's easy to find a bunch of minor format, spelling, and grammar errors. Focus on finding the most important defects, based on content not format.

Finally, as I mentioned before, continuously improve the review process.

Now, some organizational factors.

Make sure that managers will plan and estimate for adequate time, especially under deadline pressures. It is a false economy to think that if you skip highly efficient bug removal activities early in the process, somehow the schedule end date will be accelerated, but that kind of thinking is rampant in software engineering.

Be careful with the metrics. For one thing, remember that some reviews will find many defects per person-hour invested, while others won't. There are some mathematical models for predicting defect density, which are beyond the scope of this course. Be careful not to use simplistic models. Most importantly, never ever let review defect metrics be used for individual performance evaluations. That introduces a level of defensiveness that will kill the process.

Make sure to allow time for rework of defects. It's a classic testing worst practice to assume that a test activity will conclude without finding any defects.

Make sure that the process involves the right participants. A study by Motorola in the mid-2000s showed that the right participants were the strongest indicator of review success.[22] This includes technical or subject matter expertise, of course. It also includes the issue of balance, making sure the review team has representatives from all key groups. And, it includes understanding the review process, usually through training especially for formal types of reviews. The second-strongest indicator, they found, was having the right number of participants, so make sure to think carefully about who and how many.

If you are in a medium to large organization that is using reviews, have a review forum to allow people to share their experience and ideas. This can be reserved for moderators or leaders.

---

22. Jeff Holmes, "Identifying Code-Inspection Improvements Using Statistical Black Belt Techniques," *Software Quality Professional*, December 2003.

There's no point in having people at a review if they don't contribute. So, ensure that the participants participate. Part of this is ensuring proper preparation. Another part is to draw less-vocal participants into the meeting. Just because someone doesn't have a forceful personality doesn't mean they don't have good ideas.

Again, when dealing with critical documents, apply the strongest, most formal techniques. Remember Jones's figures on review effectiveness. What percentage of defects can you afford to leave in each kind of document?

Make sure to have a process in place for review process improvement. If this isn't supported by metrics, it's likely to point you in the wrong direction. Make sure that the review process improvement process includes a mechanism to recognize and celebrate the improvements gained.

Finally, some people issues.

As with managers, educate all stakeholders and participants to expect defects. Make sure that's not an unpleasant surprise to them. Make sure they have allowed for rework and re-review time. People tend to overbook themselves in today's workplace. If they do so, being confronted with a list of issues to be resolved in their document is likely to be a traumatic experience, as it means overtime.

The review leader is not Torquemada, the Grand Inquisitor of the Spanish Inquisition. The rack, the iron maiden, and waterboarding are not review tools or techniques. Reviews should be a positive experience for authors, where they learn how to do their job better from respected peers. I can still remember review sessions with two or three mentors early in my career that helped me grow significantly. That said, if authors have had bad experiences, be careful with forcing an author to consent to a review. It's best if management handle this.

Given how efficient defect location and removal is during reviews, we should be happy, not unhappy, when we find defects. Make sure people see that as an opportunity to save time and money. Don't look to point fingers or assign blame when defects are found.

Monitor the dialog in the room. We want constructive, helpful, thoughtful, and objective discussion. Make sure that people are thinking about the deeper issues, including how the document under review fits into the broader picture of the project.[23]

6.5.1   Wiegers's Review Checklists

Karl Wiegers has provided a couple of useful checklists, one for reviewing requirements and one for reviewing use cases. I've adapted them both here.[24] As you go through a requirements specification or a use case, you can keep these questions in mind and scrutinize the document accordingly.

Let's go through the requirements checklist first. In the area of document organization and completeness, the checklist asks the following questions:

■   Are internal cross references correct? If we reference another document or a section within this document, is that reference valid? It's a simple mistake to make and very confusing when it is made.

■   Is the level of detail consistent and appropriate? It's very easy for business analysts and marketing people to bounce from laconic to loquacious in their documents.

■   Do the requirements provide an adequate basis for design? This is an especially big problem when non functional requirements are omitted.

■   Is the priority of each requirement included? If not, then making trade-offs and deciding order of implementation will be difficult.

■   Are all external interfaces defined?

■   Is there any missing information? If so, is it clearly marked as TBD "to be determined"?

■   Is the expected behavior documented? Many times, people will say, "Oh, that's obvious." Is it really?

In the area of correctness, the checklist asks the following questions:

■   Do requirements conflict or duplicate? Assessing this means that you have to read the document twice through, usually.

■   Is each requirement clear, concise, and unambiguous?

■   Is each requirement verifiable? Could you design a test to show that this requirement was met or not met? In fact, a good idea with a mature requirements specification is to try to do just that.

---

23. For a discussion of reviews from a formal perspective, see Tom Gilb and Dorothy Graham's book *Software Inspection*.
24. Karl Wiegers, *Software Requirements*.

- Is each requirement in scope? Scope creep is an easy thing to happen on a project, and it will come back to haunt the test team if it does happen, because you'll have more to test than you planned on and less time to test it in that you planned on.
- Is each requirement free from content and grammar errors? It can make it hard to see other more subtle and important mistakes when you're dealing with bad grammar.
- Can the requirements be implemented within constraints? This is a hard one for a tester to answer, but reflect on your experience.
- Are error messages unique and meaningful?

In the area of quality attributes, the checklist asks the following questions:

- Are all performance objectives properly specified?
- Are all security and safety considerations properly specified?
- Are other pertinent quality attribute goals explicitly documented and quantified, with acceptable trade-offs specified?

Really, I would add the entire ISO 9126 list of quality characteristics to the checklist to see if anything is missing. It's just too common to have non-functional requirements left out.

In the area of traceability, the checklist asks the following questions:

- Is each requirement uniquely and correctly identified? You won't be able to trace tests if requirements aren't identified. Also, make sure that the granularity of the requirements is such that it will be possible to have traceability from tests to requirements. In other words, if the requirement covers too much, then you might need 2, 10, 20 tests to test it. What happens when a test fails?
- If you are reviewing a detailed requirement, is each software functional requirement traced to a higher-level requirement?

Finally, the checklist provides some special issues to consider:

- Have we stayed in the proper realm of requirements, not design? In other words, are all requirements actually requirements and not design or implementation solutions?
- Are the time-critical functions identified and their timing criteria specified?

■   Have internationalization issues been adequately addressed?

By following this checklist, you can identify a number of defects in requirements. Of course, when reviewing a requirements specification, if you find something strange, you should not dismiss it from consideration simply because you can't figure out how this relates to Wiegers's checklist. A checklist is a mental aid, not a substitute for thought.

Let's go through the use case checklist now. It asks the following questions about the use case under review:

■   Is the use case a stand-alone, discrete task, or might we have combined two tasks?

■   Is the goal of the use case clear? What are we trying to do here?

■   Is it clear which actor(s) benefit from the use case? What is the benefit?

■   Is the use case written as an abstraction rather than as a specific scenario? In other words, it should be like a logical test case, not a concrete one.

■   Is the use case free of design and implementation details?

■   Are all anticipated exceptions documented? If not, then things could happen that would be undefined, at least in their handling. That's a recipe for unexpected behavior, at least, or program crashes.

■   Is every actor and step in the use case pertinent to the task? Again, might we be mixing tasks in a single use case?

■   Is each workflow defined in the use case feasible? Can this actually happen? Remember to consider the exceptions too.

■   Is each workflow defined in the use case verifiable? Can you test this workflow?

By following this checklist, you can identify a number of defects in a use case, but as before, when reviewing a use case, if you find something wrong, capture it whether or not it relates to Wiegers's checklist.

6.5.2 Deutsch's Review Checklist

You can and should apply reviews to designs, not just requirements and use cases. Let's look at an example of a checklist we can use to review distributed applications. The checklist comes from some work done by L. Peter Deutsch and others at Sun Microsystems in the 1990s. You might remember Sun's early slogan: "The network is the computer." They were in the forefront of distributed application design and development. Deutsch and his colleagues recognized that people designing and developing distributed applications kept making the same mistakes over and over again.

Here's the top-eight list of distributed application design fallacies, assumptions people make that just aren't true:

1. The network is reliable. It will not go down, or will do so only very infrequently.
2. Latency is zero. Information arrives at the receiver at the exact instant it left the sender.
3. Bandwidth is infinite. You can send as much information as you want across the network. Corollaries to this fallacy would be that bandwidth usage doesn't affect latency and that bandwidth usage doesn't affect reliability.
4. The network is secure. No one can hack in, disrupt data flows, steal data, etc.
5. Topology doesn't change. Every computer, once on the network, stays on the network.
6. There is one administrator. All changes made to the network will be made by this one person. Problems can be escalated to this one person. This person is infallible and doesn't make mistakes.
7. Transport cost is zero. So, you can send as much information as you want and no one is paying for it.
8. Finally, the network is homogeneous. It's all the same hardware. It's all the same operating system. It's all the same security software. The configuration of the network infrastructure is all the same.

Even if you are not a very technical person, I expect you can spot one or two of these fallacies in everyday life. For example, think about the huge amount of garbage that gets shoveled across the Internet these days. Transport cost *is* zero apparently, or at least people behave as if it were so.

6.6   Wiegers's Checklist Review Exercise

In this exercise, you apply Wiegers's requirements review checklist and use case review checklist to the HELLOCARMS system requirements document.

This exercise consists of three parts:

1. Prepare: Use Wiegers's checklists to review the HELLOCARMS system requirements document (through section 010 only), documenting the problems you find.
2. Hold a review meeting: If you are using this book to support a class, work in a small group to perform a walk-through, creating a single list of problems.
3. Discuss: After the walk-through, discuss your findings with other groups and the instructor.

The solution to the first part is shown in the next section.

6.7   Wiegers's Checklist Review Exercise Debrief

Senior RBCS Associate Jose Mata reviewed the HELLOCARMS system requirements document using Wiegers's checklist and provided the following feedback.

- Are internal cross references correct? If we reference another document or within this document, is that reference valid?
  - ✓ No. Section 010-010-040 states, "Field validation details are described in a separate document," but that document is not identified anywhere in the requirements document.
- Is the level of detail consistent and appropriate?
  - ✓ No. As an example, see section 010-010-180: "Provide features and screens that support the operations of the Globobank's retail branches." That is too vague to be actionable.
  - ✓ Section 010-010-170 states, "Support the submission of applications via the Internet, which includes the capability of untrained users to properly enter applications." This is a huge, and vague, requirement.

> ✓ Sections 010-010-190 through 010-010-240 start with, "Support the marketing, sales, and processing of…," which is so vague that important functionality can be missed.

■ Do the requirements provide an adequate basis for design?

> ✓ No. Section 010-010-070 states, "Ask each applicant whether there is an existing relationship with Globobank; e.g., any checking or savings accounts," but the list is not complete, and it should be.
>
> ✓ Section 010-010-080 states, "Maintain application status from initiation through to rejection, decline, or acceptance…," but we don't know if these states are a subset or if they are comprehensive.
>
> ✓ Section 010-010-150 states, "Provide inbound and outbound telemarketing support for all States, Provinces, and Countries in which Globobank operates," but the list is not defined.
>
> ✓ Section 010-010-160 states, "Support brokers and other business partners by providing limited partner-specific screens, logos, interfaces, and branding," yet screens, or areas of the interface, are not identified.
>
> ✓ Section 010-010-250 states: "Support flexible pricing schemes including introductory pricing, short-term pricing, and others," but the "and others" needs to be defined.

■ Is the priority of each requirement included?

> ✓ Yes.

■ Are all external interfaces defined?

> ✓ No. We don't know how complete the information is. Data structures are hinted at, but not defined. The implied interfaces are with the following:
>
> - LoDoPS: 010-010-050, 010-010-100, 010-020-050, 010-030-040, 010-030-060, 010-030-070, 010-030-080, 010-030-120, 010-030-103, 010-030-140, 010-030-150
> - GLADS: 010-010-070
> - Scoring Mainframe: 010-020-020, 010-030-020
> - GloboRainBQW: 010-030-010

■ Is there any missing information? If so, is it clearly marked as TBD "to be determined"?

✓ Yes.

■ Is the expected behavior documented?

✓ No. For example, section 010-010-080 states, "Maintain application status from initiation through to rejection…," but how and where the status is maintained is not stated.

■ Is each requirement clear, concise, and unambiguous?

✓ No. For example, section 010-010-070 states, "Ask each applicant whether there is an existing relationship with Globobank," but it is unclear how the applicant is asked.

✓ Sections 010-010-100, 010-030-040, and 010-030-070 state, "Allow user to indicate on a separate screen which, if any, are existing debts that the customer will retire…," but it's not clear what the screen is supposed to be separate from.

✓ Section 010-040-010 states, "Support agreed-upon security requirements (encryption, firewalls, etc.)," which is vague.

✓ Section 010-040-060 states, "Support fraud detection for processing of all financial applications." This is vague, which is especially bad for a priority 1 requirement.

■ Is each requirement verifiable? Could you design a test to show this requirement was met or not met?

✓ No. Section 010-010-150 states, "Provide inbound and outbound telemarketing support for…," which is vague and thus not verifiable.

✓ Sections 010-010-190 through 010-010-240 start with, "Support the marketing, sales, and processing of…" and the marketing part is not verifiable.

✓ Section 010-010-250 states, "Support flexible pricing schemes including introductory pricing, short-term pricing, and others," and the "and others" part is not verifiable.

✓ Section 010-030-150 states, "Support computer-telephony integration to provide customized marketing and sales support for inbound telemarketing campaigns and branded business partners," which is vague and thus not verifiable.

■ Is each requirement in scope?

✓ No. For example, section 010-010-170 states, "Support the submission of applications via the Internet, which includes the capability of untrained users to properly enter applications." This is beyond the scope of section 003, because allowing Internet-based customers is slated for subsequent releases.

✓ Section 010-040-030 states, "Allow outsourced telemarketers to see the credit tier but disallow them from seeing the actual credit score of applicants." This is beyond the scope of section 003.

✓ Section 010-040-050 states, "Allow Internet users to browse potential loans without requiring such users to divulge...." This is beyond the scope of section 003.

■ Is each requirement free from content and grammar errors?

✓ Yes.

■ Can the requirements be implemented within constraints?

✓ Possibly not. Section 010-040-060 states, "Support fraud detection for processing of all financial applications." This might not be able to be implemented. Specific checks would need to be defined.

■ Are all security and safety considerations properly specified?

✓ No. Specific types of users, and their permissions, are not defined. User name and password strength are not addressed. Encryption of specific data is not addressed. Maintenance and purging requirements are not addressed. Server physical security requirements are not addressed.

■ Is each requirement uniquely and correctly identified? Is the granularity of the requirements such that it will be possible to have traceability from tests to requirements?

    ✓ No. For example, sections 010-010-190 through 010-010-240 start with, "Support the marketing, sales, and processing of…." The granularity of these requirements is too large.

    ✓ Section 010-010-250 states, "Support flexible pricing schemes including introductory pricing, short-term pricing, and others." This and several other compound requirements would be clearer if they were separately numbered requirements. It may be somewhat repetitious, but the requirements would be clearer and there would be more balance in scoping development and test efforts.

■ Have we stayed in the proper realm of requirements and not design? In other words, are all requirements actually requirements and not design or implementation solutions?

    ✓ No. Sections 010-010-100, 010-030-040, and 010-030-070 state, "Allow user to indicate on a separate screen which, if any, are existing debts that the customer will retire…." Specifying a separate screen appears to be a design detail.

6.8 Deutsch Checklist Review Exercise

As you can see the diagram at the beginning of the HELLOCARMS system requirements document, the HELLOCARMS system is distributed. In fact, it's highly distributed, as multiple network links must work for the application to function.

In this exercise, you apply Deutsch's distributed application design review checklist to the HELLOCARMS system requirements document.

This exercise consists of three parts:

1. Prepare: Based on Deutsch's checklist, review the HELLOCARMS system requirements document (through section 010 only), identifying potential design issues.

2. Review meeting: Assuming you are working through this class with others, work in a small group to perform a walk-through, creating a single list of problems.

3. Discuss: After the walk-through, discuss your findings with other groups and the instructor.

The solution to the first part is shown on the next page.

6.9   Deutsch Checklist Review Exercise Debrief

Senior RBCS Associate Jose Mata reviewed the HELLOCARMS system requirements document using Deutsch's checklist, and provided the following feedback.

■ The network is reliable. It will not go down, or it will do so only very infrequently.

  ✓ HELLOCARMS design in figure 1 of appendix B does not include any redundancy as in failover servers, backup switches, alternate networking paths. Contingencies for how the system will not lose information when communication is lost are not defined.

■ Latency is zero. Information arrives at the receiver at the exact instant it left the sender.

  ✓ Efficiency is not part of requirements 010.

■ Bandwidth is infinite. You can send as much information as you want across the network.

  ✓ Efficiency is not part of requirements 010.

■ The network is secure. No one can hack in, disrupt data flows, steal data, etc.

  ✓ Section 010-040-010 doesn't include enough detail to lend confidence.

■ Topology doesn't change. Every computer, once on the network, stays on the network.

  ✓ Fault tolerance and recoverability are in section 020 and are TBD. The part regarding application is covered in section 010-010-060.

■   There is one administrator. All changes made to the network will be made by this one person. Problems can be escalated to this one person. This person is infallible and doesn't make mistakes.

   ✓   Specific types of users, and their permissions, are not defined.

■   Transport cost is zero. So, you can send as much information as you want and no one is paying for it.

   ✓   There are no size limitations in section 010-010-160, "Support brokers and other business partners by providing limited partner-specific screens, logos, interfaces, and branding." Some graphics can be large, if left undefined.

■   The network is homogeneous. It's all the same hardware. It's all the same operating system. It's all the same security software. The configurations of the network infrastructure are all the same.

   ✓   Supported computer systems, operating systems, browsers, protocols, etc., are not defined. Versions should be specified, though perhaps this detail should be in a design document rather than a requirements specification.

6.10 Sample Exam Questions

To end each chapter, you can try one or more sample exam questions to reinforce your knowledge and understanding of the material and to prepare for the ISTQB Advanced Level Test Analyst exam.

1.   Which of the following types of reviews is generally the most effective at finding the greatest percentage of defects present in the object being reviewed?

   A Informal

   B Walk-through

   C Peer review

   D Inspection

2. A design specification contains the following statement:

    "A 10 MBPS or better network connection using TCP/IP provides the interface between the database server and the application server."

    Suppose that the system under test will need to transfer data blocks of up to 1 gigabyte in size in less than a minute.

    Which of the following statements best describes the likely consequences of this situation?

    A The system will suffer from usability problems.

    B The system will suffer from performance problems.

    C The system will suffer from maintainability problems.

    D This situation does not indicate any likely problems.

3. Assume you are a test analyst working on a banking project to upgrade an existing automated teller machine system to allow customers to obtain cash advances from supported credit cards. The requirements specification contains the following paragraph:

    "The system shall allow cash advances of at least 500 dollars for all supported credit cards. The correct list of supported credit cards is American Express, Visa, Japan Credit Bank, Eurocard, and MasterCard."

    Which of the following statements is true?

    A The paragraph is ambiguous in terms of supported cards.

    B The paragraph indicates potential performance problems.

    C The paragraph is unclear in terms of advance limits.

    D The paragraph indicates potential usability problems.

4. Which of the following review types involves a determination of compliance or noncompliance?

    A Audit

    B Walk-through

    C Inspection

    D Management review

7 Incident Management

"Faster/random."

> The somewhat Zen-like and uninformative complete text
> of a bug report, observed by the author and some of his
> associates on one particular project.

The seventh chapter of the Advanced syllabus is concerned with incident management. As was discussed in the Foundation syllabus, an incident has occurred anytime the actual results of a test and the expected results of that test differ. The Advanced syllabus uses IEEE 1044 standard to focus on incident lifecycles and the information testers should gather for incident reports. Chapter 7 of the Advanced syllabus has six sections:

1. Introduction
2. When Can a Defect Be Detected?
3. Defect Lifecycle
4. Defect Fields
5. Metrics and Incident Management
6. Communicating Incidents

Let's look at each section and how it relates to test management.

7.1 Introduction

Learning objectives
Only recall of content

Incident management is an essential skill for all testers. Test managers are more concerned with the process. There must be a smooth, timely flow from recognition to investigation to action to disposition. Testers are mostly concerned with accurately recording incidents and then carrying out the proper confirmation testing and regression testing during the disposition part of the process.

Testers will have a somewhat different emphasis depending on their role. Test analysts compare actual and expected behavior in terms of business and user needs. Technical test analysts evaluate behavior of the software itself and might need to apply further technical insight.

7.2   When Can a Defect Be Detected?

Learning objectives
Only recall of content

We can detect defects through static testing, which can start as soon as we have a draft requirements specification. We can detect failures, being the symptoms of defects, through dynamic testing, which can start as soon as we have an executable unit.

Testing is a filtering activity, so to achieve the highest possible quality, we should have static and dynamic test activities pervasive in the software lifecycle. In addition to filtering out defects, if we have lots of earlier filters like requirements reviews, design reviews, code reviews, code analysis, and the like, we will have early defect detection and removal. That reduces overall costs and reduces the risk of schedule slips.

When we see a failure, we should not automatically assume that this indicates a defect in the system under test. Defects can exist in tests too.

7.3   Defect Lifecycle

Learning objectives
(K4) Analyze, classify, and describe functional and non functional defects in understandable defect reports.

In figure 7-1, you see a diagram that shows the IEEE 1044 incident management lifecycle, including a mapping from IEEE 1044 that shows how typical incident

ISTQB Glossary

defect (or bug): A flaw in a component or system that can cause the component or system to fail to perform its required function, e.g., an incorrect statement or data definition. A defect, if encountered during execution, may cause a failure of the component or system.

error: A human action that produces an incorrect result.

failure: Deviation of the component or system from its expected delivery, service, or result.

incident: Any event occurring that requires investigation.

incident logging: Recording the details of any incident that occurred, e.g., during testing.

root cause analysis: An analysis technique aimed at identifying the root causes of defects. By directing corrective measures at root causes, it is hoped that the likelihood of defect recurrence will be minimized.

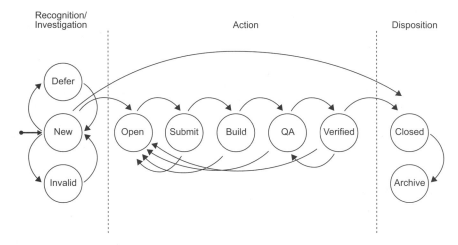

Figure 7–1 *IEEE 1044 incident management lifecycle*

report states in an incident tracking system would fit into this lifecycle. Let's look at this lifecycle.

> **ISTQB Glossary**
>
> **anomaly:** Any condition that deviates from expectation based on require-ments specifications, design documents, user documents, standards, etc., or from someone's perception or experience. Anomalies may be found during, but not limited to, reviewing, testing, analysis, compilation, or use of software products or applicable documentation.

We assume that all incidents will follow some sequence of states in their lifecy-cle, from initial recognition to ultimate disposition. Not all incidents will travel through the exact same sequence of states, as you can see from figure 7-1. The IEEE 1044 defect lifecycle consists of four steps:

■ Step 1: Recognition. Recognition occurs when we observe an anomaly, that observation being an incident, which is a potential defect. This can occur in any phase of the software lifecycle.

■ Step 2: Investigation. After recognition, investigation of the incident occurs. Investigation can reveal related issues. Investigation can propose solutions. One solution is to conclude that the incident does not arise from an actual defect; e.g., it might be a problem in the test data.

■ Step 3: Action. The results of the investigation trigger the action step. We might decide to resolve the defect. We might want to take action indicated to prevent future similar defects. If the defect is resolved, regression testing and confirmation testing must occur. Any tests that were blocked by the defect can now progress.

■ Step 4: Disposition. With action concluded, the incident moves to the disposition step. Here we are principally interested in capturing further information and moving the incident into a terminal state.

Of course, what's driving the incidents from one state to another, and thus from one step in the lifecycle to another, is what we learn about the incident. We need the states because defects are handed off from one owner to another owner, so we must capture that learning. Therefore, within each step—and indeed, embedded in each state—are three information capture activities:

■ Recording

■ Classifying

■ Identifying impact

The way this process works is shown in table 7-1.

Table 7–1 *IEEE 1044 classification process*

Step	Activities		
	Record...	Classify...	Identify impact...
1. Recognition	Include supporting data	Based on important attributes	Based on perceived impact
2. Investigation	Update and add supporting data	Update and add classification on important attributes	Update based on investigation
3. Action	Add data based on action taken	Add data based on the action taken	Update based on action
4. Disposition	Add data based on disposition	Based on disposition	Update based on disposition

During the recognition step, we will record supporting data. We will classify based on important attributes that we have observed. We will identify impact based on perceived impact, which might differ from the final impact assessment.

During the investigations step, we will update and record more supporting data. We will update and add classification information on importance based on attributes uncovered during the investigation. We will update the impact based on investigation too.

During the action step, we will record new supporting data based on action taken. We will also add classification data based on the action taken. We will update the impact based on the action too.

Finally, during the disposition step, we will record final data based on disposition. The classifications will be adjusted and finalized based on the disposition. The final impact assessment will be captured.

Notice I've been talking about data and classifications. The IEEE 1044 standard includes mandatory and optional supporting data and classifications for each activity in each step. We'll review these in the next few sections. By the way, when I say "mandatory supporting data and classifications," I mean mandatory for IEEE 1044 standard compliance.

Each of these data items and classifications is associated with a step or activity. The IEEE has assigned a two-character code in the standard: RR (recognition), IV (investigation), AC (action), IM (impact identification), and DP (disposition).

We'll go through these data items and classifications. As we do so, don't get lost in the trees and fail to see the forest. The important thing to think about is not—usually—"Is my incident management system IEEE 1044 compliant?" but rather "Might this data or classification be useful to capture?"

The following are the recognition step classifications:

- Project Activity (RR1XX): What were you doing when the incident was observed? This is a mandatory field for IEEE 1044 compliance.
- Project Phase (RR2XX): What phase was the project in (mandatory)? This will have to be tailored to your lifecycle.
- Suspected Cause (RR3XX): What do you think might be the cause (optional)? I've found that, in many cases, capturing this data can be useful for the developers, especially if you have very technical testers.
- Repeatability (RR4XX): Could you make the incident happen more than once (optional)? I have a problem with IEEE 1044 calling this optional, personally, as I think that reproducibility is an absolute must in terms of an incident report.
- Symptom (RR5XX): How did the incident manifest itself (mandatory)?
- Product Status (RR6XX): What is the usefulness of the product if the incident isn't resolved (optional)? I disagree with the optional category for this one too.

The *XX* characters at the end of the codes indicate that these are hierarchies. Subclassifications exist within each one. For example, each of the project activity choices has a specific code like RR110, RR120, etc. IEEE 1044 defines choices for these as well, but we're not going to review down to that level of detail here.

The following are the recognition step data:

- What environment were you working in when you saw the incident? You should capture product hardware, product software, database, test support software, platform, firmware, and other useful information.
- What origination details can be captured (including who was the tester)? You should capture your name, the date the incident was observed, the code or functional area, the distribution (which is the version of the test object), and contact information like email address, address, phone number, and company ID.
- At what time did you see the incident? This is operating time (i.e., time since last reboot or total uptime), wall clock time, system time, and CPU time.
- What, if any, vendor information applies? This includes company, contact name, vendor ID, expected resolution, and expected resolution date.

The following are the investigation step classifications:

- Actual Cause (IV1XX): What really caused the incident (mandatory)?
- Source (IV2XX): What was the incident's origin (mandatory)? This question involves the underlying mistake that was made.
- Type (IV3XX): What type of defect caused the failure (mandatory)? This is a question of defect taxonomy.

Remember that classifications from previous steps can be updated during this step.

The following are the investigation step data:

- What acknowledgement information can we capture? What data was received, what report number was assigned, who is the investigator, what are the estimated start and complete dates of the investigation, when (subsequently) did the actual start and complete dates of the investigation occur, how many person-hours were spent, on what date did we receive this acknowledgment, and what documents were used in the investigation?
- What verification information can we capture? What was the source of anomaly (or incident) and how did we verify the data from recognition process?

Remember that data from previous steps can be updated during this step.

The following are the action step classifications:

- Resolution (AC1XX): When and how should the incident be resolved (mandatory)?
- Corrective Action (AC2XX): What can be done to prevent such incidents in the future (optional)?

Remember that classifications from previous steps can be updated during this step.

The following are the action step data:

- What resolution identification information can we capture? What test item is to be fixed, what specific component within the item is to be fixed, how can we describe (in text) the fix, when is the planned date for action completion, who is the person assigned, what is the planned date of fix completion, or, if the fix is deferred, where is our reference or authority for that?
- What resolution action information can we capture? What is the date on which it was completed, which organization is assigned to verify resolution, and which person is assigned to verify resolution?

Remember that data from previous steps can be updated during this step.

The following are the disposition step classifications and supporting data:

- Disposition (DP1XX): How was the problem finally resolved (mandatory)?
- What anomaly (or incident) disposition information should we capture? What action was implemented, on what date was the report closed, on what date was document updating complete, when was the customer notified, and what reference document numbers might exist?
- What verification information should we capture? What is the name of the person doing the verification, on what date did the verification occur, what version and revision levels were verified, what method did we use to verify, and what is the test case we used to verify?

Remember that classifications and data from previous steps can be updated during this step.

Now, throughout the lifecycle, impact classifications are made and revised. Let's look at some of those impact classifications:

- Severity (IM1XX): What is the impact on the system (mandatory)?
- Priority (IM2XX): What is the relative importance of the incident (optional)? I disagree with this being optional. In fact, I'd say it's more important than severity in many cases.
- Customer Value (IM3XX): How does this incident affect customer(s) or market value (optional)? Again, this strikes me as essential information.
- Mission Safety (IM4XX): How does this affect mission objectives or safety (optional)? This would apply only to certain systems, of course.
- Project Schedule (IM5XX): How will resolving this incident affect the project schedule (mandatory)?
- Project Cost (IM6XX): How will resolving this incident affect the project cost (mandatory)?
- Project Risk (IM7XX): What is the project risk associated with fixing this incident (optional)? This seems like another one that should be required.
- Project Quality/Reliability (IM8XX): What is the project quality/reliability impact associated with fixing this incident (optional)? Yet another important variable.
- Societal (IM9XX): What are the societal issues associated with fixing this incident (optional)? This would apply only to certain systems.

The following are the impact data:

- What is the cost impact of this incident? That includes cost to analyze, estimated cost if the fix is done, estimated cost if the fix is not done, and other costs of resolution.

- What is the time impact of this incident? That includes estimated time required if the fix is done, estimated verification time if the fix is done, estimated time if the fix is not done, and actual implementation time.
- What is the risk of this incident? This is a text description.
- What is the schedule impact? This includes assuming the incident is resolved, assuming it's not resolved, and if it is resolved, what the actual schedule impact was.
- What is the contract change, if any?

Again, remember that these data items can be changed later in the lifecycle if required.

7.4   Defect Fields

Learning objectives
(K4) Analyze, classify, and describe functional and non functional defects in understandable defect reports.

Having looked at the fields defined in IEEE 1044, let's look at how to apply IEEE 1044, particularly how to make its lifecycle and fields map to your situation. As you saw in the previous section, IEEE 1044 specifies a set of mandatory and optional classifications and data fields. People involved with an incident report set and update those fields at various points in the incident report's lifecycle. Typically, that occurs as part of a state transition, when the report moves from one state to another. Remember that figure 7-1 showed how IEEE 1044 maps the lifecycle onto a typical incident report state transition diagram.

The companion standard to IEEE 1044, IEEE 1044.1, is about how to implement an IEEE 1044–compliant incident management system in your organization. The authors of that standard understand that different organizations have different names for incident classifications and data. So IEEE 1044.1 defines a process for mapping the IEEE terms for fields and data to the names used at a particular organization. Your organization can be compliant with the IEEE 1044 standard without having to rename classifications and data and without having to rework your incident lifecycle.

Why bother with IEEE conformance? Well, it certainly makes sense to use a consistent incident management process within your company across projects. I did an assessment for a client once where we tried to compare the quality of the software in a current project with similar software from past projects. Because the incident management processes were not the same—not just the tools, which I could have handled, but the meanings of the classifications and the data gathered—it was not possible to do this comparison. If you have IEEE conformance throughout your organization, then you can compare not only from one project to another, but also with other organizations that are also IEEE compliant.

The following is the process for applying the IEEE 1044 standard to your organization:

- Step 1. Map your current classifications to IEEE 1044 classifications. This will give you an idea of the size of the job.

- Step 2. Determine the need to conform to IEEE 1044, based on the size of the effort required. Keep in mind that conformance does not need to be an all-or-nothing proposition. You can decide to achieve conformance in certain areas, for certain classifications and data elements, but not for others.

- Step 3. Review the IEEE 1044 classifications, considering especially those classifications that are easy to gather, currently useful, or worth analyzing in the future. You'll want to have those in your system.

- Step 4. Select essential classifications for implementation.

- Step 5. Define how to use these classifications. For example, what type of analysis do you intend to do on incident data, and when? It's important to know this because your incident management process must be set up to collect the data in such a way as to be useful for these analyses and in such a way as to provide the data in time.

- Step 6. Document the categories associated with the classifications. For example, which one is a recognition category, which one is an impact category, and so forth? The less you have diverged from the IEEE 1044 standard in terms of naming, of course, the easier this will be.

- Step 7. Document the classifications and their use.

- Step 8. If you care about IEEE compliance, this is the point to document conformance or nonconformance with IEEE 1044. What value is this? Well, probably none if your incident management system is for your own use. However, if you are a software or testing services company and you intend to connect your incident management system with your clients', then IEEE compliance might provide a common point reference.

- Step 9. Define the supporting data to collect at each step.

- Step 10. Document the supporting data to be collected. Now, personally, while the IEEE 1044.1 standard puts steps 9 and 10 down here, I'd actually do these in parallel with steps 1 and 5.

- Step 11. Map the classifications and data to the states in your current incident, bug, issue, or defect tracking system. Yes, the correct name, from IEEE's point of view, is incident, because you don't know if a behavior is a bug or defect until after investigation. Really, though, call it whatever you would prefer.

- Step 12. Determine and document the process for gathering classifications and data in the incident tracking system. In other words, during what state is a classification or piece of data initially input? During what states may it be updated? During what states must it be updated? Who may or must input? Who may update? Who must update?

- Step 13. Plan for use of the information. Again, to me this is backwards in the order of things. I'd do this in parallel with step 2.

- Step 14. Provide training to users and management. Users need to know how to input and update classifications and data. Managers need to know how to use the metrics and other information from it.

So, these last couple of sections have given you some ideas on how to expand your incident management system based on IEEE 1044 compliance. However, IEEE 1044 compliance is just a means to an end. What are we trying to accomplish?

Remember that we capture all of this information in the interest of doing something with it. What we want to do immediately is to take action to resolve the incident. Incident reports should capture actionable information. An actionable incident report has the following properties:

- It is complete. It is not missing any important details.
- It is concise. It does not drone on and on about unimportant matters.
- It is accurate. It does not misdirect or misinform the reader.
- It is objective. It is based on facts, as much as possible, and it is not an attack on the developers.

In addition to taking action for the individual incident report, remember that many test metrics are derived from aggregate analysis of incident reports. This was discussed in the Foundation syllabus in the chapter about managing testing. So it's important for incident reports to capture accurate classification, risk analysis, and process improvement information.

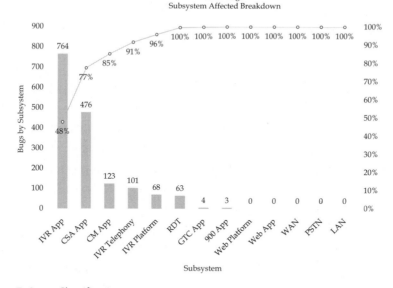

Figure 7–2   *Classification*

Figure 7-2 shows an example of using classification information to learn something interesting about a project. This Pareto chart analyzes the number and percentage of bugs associated with each major subsystem—system, really—in a large complex project. This project, called the NOP project, tied together 10 systems via a wide area network, a local area network, and the phone system to implement a large distributed entertainment application.

As you can see in figure 7-2, the interactive voice response (or IVR) application is responsible for about half of the bugs. The customer service application (or CSA) adds about 30 percent more. The rest of the applications are relatively solid. The content management (or CM) application is less than 10 percent of the bugs. The interactive voice response server's telephony and OS/hardware layers each are around 5 percent, with the remaining applications and infrastructure accounting for the other 4 percent.

7.5 Metrics and Incident Management

Learning objectives
Recall of content only

The use of the textual descriptive information in the incident reports is usually obvious to test analysts, but it's easy to get confused about the use of the classifications. I had one client tell me about spending hundreds of thousands of dollars on consulting to improve their incident tracking system to use the latest in classification schemes, orthogonal defect classification. However, they tried to save money on the project by not training people in how to use the fields, so all of the classification information was worthless!

Incident classification information needs to be seen from the immediate point of view of the project and from the long-term point of view of organizational and process improvement. From the project point of view, incident classifications should support test progress monitoring as discussed in the Foundation syllabus. Various metrics like bug cluster analysis, defect density analysis, and convergence (also called open/closed charts) are used during a project to manage defect trends and check readiness for release.

From the organization and process point of view, we want to assess how we're doing and figure out how to do better. So, incident classifications should support process improvement initiatives. We should be able to assess phase containment, which is the percentage of defects that are detected and removed in the same phase they were introduced. We should be able to assess root causes so we can reduce the total number of defects. And, we should be able to assess defect trends across projects to see where best—and worst—practices exist.

7.6 Communicating Incidents

Learning objectives
Recall of content only

Bad incident reports are a major cause of friction and poor relationships in project teams. My associates and I see it all the time. To maintain good relations in the team, keep the following in mind.

It is usually not the tester's job to apportion blame or affix fault. Avoid any statements that could be construed as accusations or blaming. Avoid comments that someone could take personally.

A good incident report should provide objective information. Stick to the facts. If you are going to make an assumption or state a theory, state your reasons for doing so. If you do decide to make such assumptions or theories, be sure to remember the first rule about not getting personal.

An incident report is usually an assertion that something is wrong. So, when you are saying that a problem exists, it helps to be right. Strive for utmost accuracy.

Finally—and this is more of a mindset but it's really an important one— start to see incident reports as a service you provide, not just to managers but also to developers. Ask developers what information you can include in your reports to help them out. You'd be surprised what a difference this can make.

Some testers get frustrated when "their" bugs don't get fixed. When we see that during an assessment, my first thought is that something is broken in the incident management process. Ideally, a bug triage or incident triage meeting occurs, involving a cross-functional group of stakeholders, to prioritize

> **ISTQB Glossary**
>
> **configuration control board** (or change control board or bug triage committee or incident triage committee): A group of people responsible for evaluating and approving or disapproving proposed changes to configuration items and for ensuring implementation of approved changes.

incidents. It's seldom good to rely on just developer or tester opinions about what should be fixed or deferred. That's not to say that developers' and testers' opinions and input doesn't count, but rather that good incident management requires careful consideration of the options for handling an incident. Few projects have the luxury of fixing every single incident that comes along.

To sum it all up, good communication and relations within the team, good defect tracking tools, and good defect triage are all important for a good incident management process. Incident management is a testing fundamental that all test analysts should master.

7.7   Incident Management Exercise

Assume that a select group of Telephone Bankers will participate in HELLO-CARMS testing as a beta test. The bankers will enter live applications from customers, but they will also capture the information and enter it into the current system afterward to ensure that no HELLOCARMS defects affect the customers. The bankers are not trained testers and are unwilling to spend time to learn testing fundamentals. So, to avoid having the bankers enter poorly written incident reports and introduce noise into the incident report metrics, management has decided that, when a banker finds a problem, they will send an email to a test analyst to enter the report.

You receive the following email from a banker describing a problem:

> "I was entering a home equity loan application for a customer with good credit. She owns a high-value house although the loan amount is not very large.

At the proper screen, HELLOCARMS popped up the "escalate to Senior Telephone Banker" message. However, I clicked continue and it allowed me to proceed, even though no Senior Telephone Bank Authorization Code had been entered.

From that point forward in this customer's application, everything behaved normally.

I had another customer with a similar application—high-value house, medium-sized loan amount—call in later that day. Again, it would let me proceed without entering the authorization code."

The exercise consists of two parts:

1. What IEEE 1044 recognition and recognition impact classification fields and data are available from this email?
2. What steps would you take to clarify this report?

The solutions are shown on the following pages.

7.8 Incident Management Exercise Debrief

First, I evaluated each of the pertinent recognition and recognition impact classifications and data fields to see if this email or other information I assume I have is presented. My analysis is shown in table 7-2.

Next, I have annotated the report with some steps I'd take to clarify it before putting it into the system. The original information is shown in italic, while my text is shown in regular font.

I was entering a home equity loan application for a customer with good credit.

I would want to find out her exact data, including income, debts, assets, credit score, etc.

She owns a high-value house although the loan amount is not very large.

I would want to find out the exact value of the house and the loan amount.

I would test various combinations of values and loan amounts to see if I could find a pattern.

Table 7–2 Incident report IEEE 1044 coverage

IEEE Information	Available?
Project Activity	Presumably, we know this for all such beta tests.
Project Phase	Presumably, we know this for all such beta tests.
Suspected Cause	Not available.
Repeatability	Available, but more isolation and replication of this issue is needed.
Symptom	Available.
Product Status	Not available, but we can presume that it's unacceptable for the product to allow the Telephone Bankers to bypass a risk management policy like this.
Environment	Presumably, we know this for all such beta tests.
Originator	Presumably given in the sender information for the email.
Time	Not available.
Vendor	Some of the vendor information we can presume to know, while the other information, such as about when they will supply a fix, is not applicable at this point.
Severity	Available.
Priority	Not available, but again we can presume this is a high priority.
Customer Value	Not available, but inferable.
Mission Safety	Not applicable.
Project Schedule	Not applicable at this point, as investigation is required.
Project Cost	Not applicable at this point, as investigation is required.
Project Risk	Not applicable at this point, as investigation is required.
Project Quality/ Reliability	Not applicable at this point, as investigation is required.
Societal	Not applicable at this point, as investigation is required.
Cost	Not applicable at this point, as investigation is required.
Time	Not applicable at this point, as investigation is required.
Risk	Not available, but again we can make some inferences and describe the risk associated with letting telephone banks bypass bank risk management policies.
Schedule	Not applicable at this point, as investigation is required.
Contract Change	Not applicable at this point, as investigation is required.

At the proper screen, HELLOCARMS popped up the "escalate to Senior Telephone Banker" message. However, I clicked continue and it allowed me to proceed, even though no Senior Telephone Bank Authorization Code had been entered.

I would want to find out if the banker entered anything at all into that field.

I would test leaving it empty, input blanks, input valid characters that were not valid authorization codes, and conduct some other checks to see whether it is ignoring the field completely.

From that point forward in this customer's application, everything behaved normally.

I would test to see whether such applications are transferred to LoDoPS or are silently discarded. If they are transferred to LoDoPS, does LoDoPS proceed or does it catch the fact that this step was missed?

I had another customer with a similar application—high-value house, medium-sized loan amount—call in later that day. Again, it would let me proceed without entering the authorization code.

Here also I would want to find out the exact details on this applicant, the property value, and the loan amount.

7.9   Sample Exam Questions

To end each chapter, you can try one or more sample exam questions to reinforce your knowledge and understanding of the material and to prepare for the ISTQB Advanced Level Test Analyst exam.

1. Assume you are a test analyst working on a banking project to upgrade an existing automated teller machine system to allow customers to obtain cash advances from supported credit cards. The requirements specification contains the following paragraph:

    The system shall allow cash advances from 20 dollars to 500 dollars, inclusively, for all supported credit cards. The correct list of supported credit cards is American Express, Visa, Japan Credit Bank, Eurocard, and MasterCard.

    You are reviewing an incident report written by one of your peers. The *steps to reproduce* section of the report contains the following statement:

    1. Inserted an American Express card into the ATM.

    2. Properly authenticated a test account with $1,000 available cash advance balance.

3. Attempted to withdraw $20 from the account.

4. Error message, "Amount requested exceeds available funds," appeared.

5. Reproduced this failure with two other accounts that also had sufficient available credit to cover a $20 withdrawal.

6. Verified that the ATM itself had sufficient cash to service the request.

7. Problem did not occur with Visa, Japan Credit Bank, Eurocard, or MasterCard.

Assume the defect report is currently in a *new* state, indicating it needs a review. Relying on the information given in this scenario and assuming that your organization follows an IEEE 1044–compliant lifecycle, which of the following statements best describes what should happen next to this report?

A Move it to an *invalid* state as it does not describe a valid defect.

B Move it to a *defer* state as it does not describe an important defect.

C Move it to an *open* state for prioritization by project stakeholders.

D Move it to a *build* state so that the tester will check the fix.

2. Continue with the scenario described in the previous question.

Assume the defect report is currently in a *new* state, indicating it needs a review. Also assume that your organization follows an IEEE 1044–compliant incident-classification scheme. Rely on the information given in this scenario. Which of the following IEEE 1044 classification fields cannot yet be classified?

A Suspected Cause

B Actual Cause

C Repeatability

D Symptom

3. Which of the following is a section included in an IEEE 829–compliant incident report?

    A Test items

    B Procedure steps

    C Location

    D Steps to reproduce

4. Which of the following shows the steps of IEEE 1044–compliant incident management in proper order?

    A Recognition, investigation, action, disposition

    B Recognition, action, investigation, disposition

    C Investigation, recognition, action, disposition

    D Recognition, investigation, removal, disposition

5. Which of the following is a classification that you would make for the first time during the investigation step of an IEEE 1044–compliant incident management process?

    A Suspected cause

    B Source

    C Resolution

    D Disposition

8 Standards and Test Process Improvement

Executive: "We are a CMM level 5 development organization. We have been accredited as CMM compliant by an SEI registrar. We follow our approved processes for all projects. "

Author: "But what if your client does not want to follow your processes. They have their own process, or they have no process and don't want any."

Executive: "But our processes are SEI approved as CMM compliant."

Author: "So what? I have clients who don't care about that. Does that mean that I should not refer those clients to your organization unless they want CMM-compliant software development?"

Executive: "Well, if your client insists that we follow their processes, then we will."

Author: "And if my client insists on no process?"

Executive: "That's okay."

An exchange between the author and an executive of a large, CMM level 5 software development organization located in India in 2001. This illustrates the point that standards and process compliance is a complicated topic, and one often used more as a marketing tool than as a process improvement technique.

The eighth chapter of the Advanced Syllabus is concerned with standards and test process improvement. The concepts in this chapter apply primarily for test managers. There are no learning objectives at any level defined for test managers in this chapter. However, as a test analyst or technical test analyst working on a test team that might be subject to standards or test process improvement efforts, it's good to be familiar with the main concepts and terms of their work. In addition, if you're studying for the ISTQB Advanced Level Test Analyst exam, remember that certain concepts related to standards are covered in the

ISTQB Glossary

Capability Maturity Model (CMM): A five-level staged framework that describes the key elements of an effective software process. The Capability Maturity Model covers best practices for planning, engineering, and managing software development and maintenance.

Capability Maturity Model Integration (CMMI): A framework that describes the key elements of an effective product development and maintenance process. The Capability Maturity Model Integration covers best practices for planning, engineering, and managing product development and maintenance. CMMI is the designated successor of the CMM.

Test Maturity Model (TMM): A five-level staged framework for test process improvement, related to the Capability Maturity Model (CMM), that describes the key elements of an effective test process.

Test Maturity Model Integration (TMMi): A five-level staged framework for test process improvement, related to the Capability Maturity Model Integration (CMMI), that describes the key elements of an effective test process.

Test Process Improvement (TPI): A continuous framework for test process improvement that describes the key elements of an effective test process, especially targeted at system testing and acceptance testing.

Foundation Syllabus and thus are examinable. So you should read chapter 8 of the Advanced Syllabus for familiarity and recall only. You should also review the standards discussed in the Foundation Syllabus, ensuring that you have mastered the learning objectives related to them.

9 Test Tools and Automation

"Rex, I found the control codes I can use to make the tape library cycle back to the first tape for the automated burn-in test."
"Really? Did the vendor tell you?"
"No, Rex, I experimented with various control codes until I found which ones would make the first tape load."
"Did you tell me you didn't think you could figure it out?"
"Yes, I did tell you that, but I figured it out."
"Greg, the next time you tell me you can't do something, I really, really won't believe you now. Have you told the vendor yet?"
"No. I was planning to call them."
"Sure, go ahead and call them, but tell them they have to pay us for it."

A discussion between the author and a senior automation
test engineer after the engineer solved a particularly
tough test automation problem.

The ninth chapter of the Advanced syllabus is concerned with test tools and automation. While the Foundation syllabus covers this topic as well, the Advanced syllabus goes beyond the Foundation material to provide a solid conceptual background for test tools and automation. In addition, the Advanced syllabus elaborates on the categorization of tools introduced in the Foundation syllabus. Chapter 9 of the Advanced syllabus has three sections:

1. Introduction
2. Test Tool Concepts
3. Test Tool Categories

Let's look at each section and how it relates to test analysis.

9.1   Introduction

Learning objectives
Only recall of content

In this chapter, we'll expand on some basic tool ideas described in the Foundation syllabus. We first address general tool concepts and then specific tools.

All testers need a basic grasp of the test tools available and what they can—and can't—do. Too often, organizations and individuals bring bad expectations to the use of test tools, usually the expectation that the choice of the right tool will solve all testing problems. That's not realistic.

The Advanced syllabus groups the tools according to role; i.e., those for test managers, those for test analysts, and those for technical test analysts. Of course, some tools have broader use, across multiple roles.

9.2   Test Tool Concepts

Learning objectives
(K2) Compare the elements and aspects of each of the following test tool concepts: benefits and risks; test tool strategies; tool integration; automation languages; test oracles; tool deployment; open source tools; tool development; and tool classification.

Test tools can be very useful, and, indeed, some are essential. It's hard to imagine a test project that involves more than two or three people getting along without some incident tracking system. Generally, test tools can improve efficiency and accuracy of testing. However, you have to carefully select, implement, and use the tools to receive the benefits.

While we often think of test automation as meaning automation of test execution, we can automate other parts of the test process as well. However, it's probably true that most of the test automation that happens involves attempts to automate tasks that are tedious or difficult to do manually, such as regression testing and performance testing.

Getting the full benefit from test tools involves not only careful selection and implementation, but also careful ongoing management. You should plan to use configuration management for test tools, test scripts, test data, and other test tool items and remember to link version numbers of tests and test tools with the version numbers of the items tested with them. You should also plan to create a proper architecture for your test automation system. Too often as a consultant and practitioner I've seen test teams saddle themselves with constraints due to poor design decisions made at the outset of automation.

A good architecture supports another important aspect of good automation, which is creating and maintaining libraries of tests. With consistent decisions in place about size of test cases, naming conventions for test cases and test data, interactions with the test environment, and such, you can create a set of reusable test building blocks with your tools. You'll need a library in which to store those.

Automated tests are programs for testing other programs. So, like any program, the level of complexity and the time required to learn it often means that you'll want to have some documentation in place about how it works, why it is like it is, and so forth. This doesn't have to be fancy, but most automated test systems of any complexity need it.

Finally, remember to plan for expansion and maintenance. Failure to think ahead, particularly in terms of how the tests can be maintained, is probably the biggest single cause of test automation failure.

Let's examine these issues in more depth, starting with the business case for automated testing. Remember, test automation should occur only when there's a strong business case for it, usually one that involves shrinking the test execution period, reducing the overall test effort, or covering additional quality risks. When we talk about these benefits, notice that they are benefits compared to the duration, effort, or coverage we would have with manual testing. A return on investment has to be considered in terms of comparison to other alternatives.

9.2.1 Test Automation Costs

In any business case, we have to consider costs, risks, and benefits. Let's start with the costs. We can think of costs in terms of initial costs and recurring costs. Initial costs include the following:

- Evaluating and selecting the right tool. Many companies try to shortcut this and they pay the price later, so don't succumb to the temptation.
- Purchasing the tool, or adapting an open source tool, or developing your own tool.
- Learning the tool and how to use it properly. This includes all costs of intra-organizational knowledge transfer and knowledge building, including designing and documenting the test automation architecture.
- Integrating the tool with your existing test process, other test tools, and your team.

Recurring costs include the following:

- Maintaining the tool and the test scripts. This issue of test script durability—how long a script lasts before it has to be updated—is huge. Make sure you design your test system architecture to minimize this cost, or to put it the other way, to maximize test durability.
- Ongoing license fees.
- Support fees for the tool.
- Ongoing training costs; e.g., for new staff that come on board or tool upgrades.
- Porting the tests to new platforms.
- Extending the coverage to new features and applications.
- Dealing with issues that arise in terms of tool availability, constraints, and dependencies.
- Instituting continuous quality improvement for your test scripts. Again, it's a natural temptation to skip this, but with a disparate team of people doing test automation, to do so means that the tool usage and scripts will evolve in incompatible ways and your reuse opportunities will plummet. Again, trust me on this, I saw a client waste well over $250,000 and miss a project deadline because they had two automation people creating what was substantially the same tool.

In the Foundation syllabus there was a recommendation to use pilot projects to introduce automation. That's a great idea. However, keep in mind that pilot projects based on business cases will often miss important recurring costs, especially maintenance.

We can also think of costs in terms of fixed costs and variable costs. Fixed costs are those that we incur no matter how many test cases we want to automate. Tool purchase, training, and licenses are primarily fixed costs. Variable costs are those that vary depending on the number of tests we have. Test script development, test data development, and the like are primarily variable costs.

9.2.2 Test Automation Risks

You should also consider risks. In addition to those covered in the Foundation syllabus, consider these additional risks:

- Your existing manual testing could be incomplete or incorrect. If you use that as a basis for your automated tests, guess what, you're just doing the wrong thing faster! You need to double-check manual test cases, data, and scripts before automating because it's more expensive to fix them later.
- You produce brittle, hard-to-maintain test scripts, test frameworks, and test data that frequently need updates when the software under test changes. This is the classic test automation bugaboo. Careful design of maintainable, robust, modular test automation frameworks, design for test script and data reuse, and other techniques can reduce the likelihood of this happening. If it does happen, it's a test automation project killer, guaranteed, because the test maintenance work will soon consume all resources available for test automation, bringing progress in automation coverage to a standstill.
- You experience an overall drop in defect detection effectiveness because everyone is fixated with running the scripted, invariable, no-human-in-the-loop automated tests. Automate tests are great at building confidence, managing regression risks, and repeating tests the same way, every time. However, the natural exploration that occurs when people run test cases doesn't happen with scripts. You need to ensure that an adequate mix of human testing is included.

Now, as you can see all of these risks can—and should—be managed. There is no reason not to use test automation where it makes sense.

9.2.3 Test Automation Benefits

Of course, the reason we incur the costs and accept the risks is to receive benefits. What are the benefits of test automation?

First, I must emphasize that most smart test teams invest—and invest heavily—in developing automated test cases, test data, test frameworks, and other automation support items with an aim of reaping the rewards on repeatable, low-maintenance automated test execution over months and years. When I say "invest heavily," what I mean is that smart test teams do not take shortcuts during initial test automation development and rollout because they know that will reduce the benefits down the road.

Smart test teams are also judicious about which test cases they automate, picking each test case based on the benefit they expect to receive from automating it. Brain-dead approaches like trying to automate every existing manual test case usually end in well-deserved tears.

Once they're in place, we can expect well-designed, carefully chosen automated tests to run efficiently and with little effort. Because the cost and duration are low, we can run them at will, pushing up overall coverage and thus confidence upon release.

Given the size of the initial investment, you have to remember that the benefits will often take months if not years to equal the initial costs. Understand: In most cases, there is no shortcut. If you try to reduce the initial costs of development, you will create a situation where the benefits of automated test execution are zero or less than zero, and you can do the math yourself on how long it takes to reach break-even in that situation.

So, above and beyond the benefits of saved time, reduced effort, and better coverage (and thus lower risk), what else do we get from test automation done well?

For one thing, we have better predictability of test execution time. If we can start the automated test set, leave for the night, come back in the morning, and find the tests have all run, that's a very nice feeling, and management loves that kind of thing. For another thing, notice that the ability to quickly run regression and confirmation tests creates a by-product benefit. Because we can manage the risk associated with changes to the product better and faster, we can allow changes later in a project than we otherwise would. Now, that's a two-edge sword, for sure, because it can lead to recklessness, but used carefully, it's a nice capability to have for emergencies. And, because of the late and frequent changes inherent in certain lifecycle models, especially in agile and iterative lifecycles, we can find this ability to manage regression risk without ever-increasing effort essential in certain projects.

Because test automation is seen as—and really is—more challenging and more esteemed than manual testing, testers and test teams find the chance to work on automated testing rewarding.

Finally, there are certain test types that cannot be covered manually in any meaningful way, such as performance and reliability. With automation in place, we can cover those, which again reduces risk.

9.2.4 Test Automation Strategies

As I have said to clients on a number of occasions, a test tool by itself is not a test automation strategy. Let me give you a non software example of this.

Where I currently live, in central Texas, we have these huge, unsightly juniper bushes that people call—for some reason—cedars. They are not cedars. Cedars are noble, upright, useful trees. These juniper bushes are nothing but overgrown gin factories, and when they pollinate in the winter every single one of the three to four million noses in central Texas starts to run.

My family lives on 11 acres—about 4 hectares—of property. We are surrounded by junipers. My wife and I want to get rid of them. However, going to Home Depot and buying a chain saw is not a strategy for clearing 11 acres of junipers, some of which are twice as tall as I am. A chain saw is one of a number of useful tactics involved in clearing 11 acres of junipers, but a strategy involves picking where to start, knowing which junipers require a tractor and which I can deal with using a chain saw, planning for keeping the junipers down, figuring out disposal of the cut junipers, and the like.

So, here are some strategies for test automation. Most importantly, automate for the long term. Build a maintainable automated test system. Automate only automatable tests. Automatable tests can run unattended and do not require human judgment during test execution to interpret the results. Automate those tests and tasks that would be error prone if done by a person. This includes not only regression testing—which is certainly a high-value target for automation—but also creating and loading test data. Only automate those test suites and even test cases within test suites where there's a business case. That means you have to have some idea of how many times you'll repeat the test case between now and the retirement of the application under test.

Even though most automated tests involve deliberate, careful, significant effort, be ready to take advantage of easy automation wins where you find them. Pick the low-hanging fruit. For example, if you find that you can use a freeware scripting language to exercise your application in a loop in a way that's likely to reveal reliability problems, do it.

That said, be careful with your test tool portfolio, both freeware and commercial. It's easy to have a portfolio get out of control, especially if everyone downloads their own favorite freeware test tool. Have a careful process for evaluating and selecting test tools and don't deviate from that process.

Finally, to enable reuse and consistency of automation, make sure to provide guidelines for how to get tools, how to select tests to automate, how to write maintainable scripts, and the like.

9.2.5 Test Tool Integration and Scripting

Test tools can and should be made to work together to solve complex test automation projects. We'll see an example of what I mean by that a little later.

Many organizations use multiple test and development tools. They could have a static analysis and unit test tool, a test results reporting tool, a test data tool, a configuration management tool, an incident management tool, and a graphical user interface test execution tool. Such organizations have a need—though sometimes a need they are unaware of—to integrate all the test results into the test management tool and add traceability from the tests to the requirements or risks they cover. In such situations, try to integrate tools and get them to exchange information.

Just because you bought a single vendor's test tool suite doesn't necessarily mean they will integrate. Such suites should, though, and you shouldn't buy ones that don't. If you can't get a fully integrated set of tools, you might have to integrate them yourselves. The extent of effort you put into doing this should be balanced against the costs and risks associated with moving the information around manually. Lately, there have been many advances in integrated development environments. We testers can hope that this presages similar integration for test tools in the future.

Most test automation tools—at least those for execution—have the ability to use scripting languages. Typically, we are going to write the testing framework in these scripts and then use data or keywords in flat files, XML files, or databases to drive the tests. This supports maintainability.

During chapter 4, you'll remember that we grappled with this issue of combinatorial explosions in testing. Manual testing doesn't deal well with combinatorial tests, as we are overwhelmed by the effort. However, using scripting languages, we can often create tests that can cover more combinations than we could manually.

Some tools also provide the ability to go directly to an application's API. For example, some test tools can talk directly to the web server at the HTTP and HTTPS interfaces rather than pushing test input through the browser.

Scripting languages and their capabilities vary widely. Some scripting languages are like general-purpose programming languages. Others are domain specific, like TTCN-3. Some are not domain specific but have features that have made them popular in certain domains, like TCL in the telephony and embedded systems worlds.

Not all tools cost money—at least to buy. Some you download off the Internet and some you build yourself. In terms of open source test tools, there are lots of them. As with commercial software, the quality varies considerably. I've used some very solid open source test tools, and I've heard some stories about real garbage. Even if an open source tool costs nothing to buy, it will cost time and effort to learn, use, and maintain. So evaluate open source tools just as you would commercial tools—rigorously and against your systems, not by running a canned demo. Remember, the canned demo will almost always work and establishes nothing more than basic platform compatibility.

In addition to quality considerations, with open source tools that have certain types of licenses, such as the Creative Commons and GNU Public License, you might be forced to share enhancements you create. Your company's management will want to know about that if it's going to happen.

If you can't find an open-source or commercial tool, you can always build your own. Plenty of people do that. However, it's often a very expensive way to go. Also, because one or two people often develop these as a side activity, there's a high risk that when the tool developer leaves, the tool is dead. Make sure that custom tools are documented.

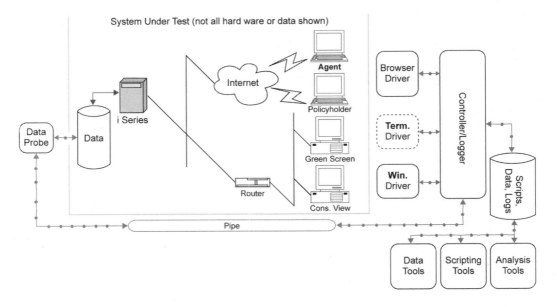

Test System (software components = boxes, data flows = dotted lines)

Figure 9–1   *Integrated test architecture*

Finally, a caution: When testing safety-critical systems, regulations might require the certification of the tools used to test them. This could preclude the use of custom and open source tools for testing such systems.

Let's look at an example of an integrated test system architecture, shown in figure 9-1. This is an automated test system for an insurance company. The system under test—or, more properly, the system of systems under test—is shown in the middle.

On the front end are three main interface types: browsers, legacy UNIX-based green screen applications, and a newer Windows-based Consolidated View. The front-end applications communicate through the insurance company's network infrastructure, and through the Internet, to the iSeries server at the back end. The iSeries, as you might imagine for a well-established regional insurance company, manages a very large repository of customers, policies, claim history, accounts payable, accounts receivable, and the like.

On the right side of the figure, you see the main elements of the test automation system. For each of the three interface types, we need a driver that will allow us to submit inputs and observe responses. The terminal driver is shown in a dotted line because there was some question initially about whether that would be needed. The controller/logger piece uses the drivers to make tests happen, based on a repository of scripts, and it logs results of the tests. The test data and scripts are created using tools as well, and the test log analysis is performed with a tool.

Notice that all of these elements on the right side of the figure could be present in a single, integrated tool. However, this is a test system design figure, so we leave out the question of implementation details now. Best practice tells us to design what you need first, then find tools that can support it rather than letting the tools dictate how you design your tests. Trust me on this one, too, as I have the scars to prove it! If you let the tools drive the testing, you can end up not testing important things.

This brings us to the left side and bottom of the figure. In many complex applications, the action on the screens is just a small piece of what goes on. What really matters is data transformations, data storage, data deletion, and other data operations. So, to know whether a test passed or failed, we need to check the data. The data probe allows us to do this.

The pipe is a construct for passing requests to the data probe from the controller and for the data probe to return the results. For example, if starting a particular transaction should add 100 records to a table, then the controller uses one of the applications to start the transaction—through a Windows interface via the Windows driver, say—and then has the data probe watch for 100 records being added. See, it could be that the screen messages report success, but only 90 records are added. So, we need a way to catch those kinds of bugs, and this design does that for us.

In all likelihood, the tool or tools used to implement the right-hand side of this figure would be one or two commercial or freeware tools, integrated together. The data probe and pipe would probably be custom developed.

9.2.6   Test Tool Classification

Throughout this book, we've been looking at taxonomies of various kinds. In the next section, we'll go through various tools, organized by a particular taxonomy. However, let's close this section by looking at various ways we could classify tools.

In the Foundation syllabus, we grouped tools by the test activity they supported. We can also group tools by the level of testing they support; e.g., unit test tools, integration test tools, system test tools. This strikes me as quite a weak way, given the potential for reuse.

We can group tools by the types of defects we are looking for with them. Alternatively, we can group tools by the type of test techniques they support. For example, we saw pairwise and classification tree tools earlier in this course.

We can group tools by the purpose of tool, such as the activities and tasks within the fundamental test process that the tool supports. Or, we can group tools by the application domain they are used to test, which is most useful for domain-specific rather than general-purpose test tools. We can group tools based on how they are applied.

9.3   Test Tool Categories

Learning objectives

(K2) Summarize the test tool categories by objectives, intended use, strengths, risks, and examples.

(K2) Map the tools of the tool categories to different levels and types of testing.

In contrast to the alternative classifications just discussed, we can group tools based on the user, which is how we'll do it in this section. In our discussion about tools and their classifications, keep in mind that I'm augmenting the tools categories introduced in the Foundation syllabus, along with introducing new tools categories. So, you'll need to refer to the Foundation syllabus as well as the Advanced syllabus for general information concerning the other tool categories not included in this section.

9.3.1   Test Management Tools

Test management tools are, naturally, used to manage testing. Because testing generates information, there's a lot of information to manage, including the following:

> **ISTQB Glossary**
>
> **test management tool:** A tool that provides support to the test management and control part of a test process. It often has several capabilities, such as testware management, scheduling of tests, the logging of results, progress tracking, incident management, and test reporting.

- Tracing test artifacts to the test basis, such as requirements, risks, etc.
- Capturing test environment data for complicated environments.
- Tracking of concurrent test execution, including when tests are running in different test environments at multiple sites.
- Tracking various test-related metrics such as the time and effort required to execute test cases, test suites, regression test sets, and other test-process-describing metrics; the number of test cases, test scripts, test environments, and so forth; the pass/fail rates for tests; the number of blocked test cases (along with the blocking conditions); the trends in various metrics like bug find/fix rates; the number and status of requirements; and the relationships and traceability between test scripts, test designs, and so forth.
- Test management tools often have certain organizing concepts embedded in them, which they will manage. They can serve as both the central repository and driver of test cases and other test artifacts. They can organize test conditions and test environments. They can store and group tests cases for regression suites and test sessions. They can handle logging and failure information and provide instructions for environment restart and reinitialization.

Test management tools are used by test managers, test analysts, and technical test analysts. These tools are useful throughout the project lifecycle.

9.3.2 Test Execution Tools

Used properly, test execution tools should reduce costs, increase coverage, and/or make tests more repeatable. Because of the large amount of effort and tedium, test execution tools are often used to automate regression tests.

Most test execution tools work by executing a set of instructions written in a scripting language, which is just a programming language, customized for the tool. The tool usually provides a precise ability to drive key presses and mouse actions, along with inspection of the graphical user interface or some other interface. That can lead to brittleness of the test scripts and expected results.

The scripts can be recorded using capture playback facilities or constructed like a real application. You can use capture playback for tracing the path of exploratory or other nonscripted testing, but the resultant scripts and expected results are very difficult to maintain.

Test execution tools use a comparator to compare the expected results—which were usually captured during some previous test run—with the actual results. Usually these comparators can be instructed to avoid comparing fields that will vary, like dates and times.

Test automation scripts constructed like real programs tend to be built of libraries of functions or actions, which are then driven by tables of keywords or data. The keyword approach is called keyword-driven or action-word-driven test automation. The separation of the data from the scripts can overcome the maintainability problems created by capture playback.

Poor skills in programming and bad design of automation architecture can cause failure of test automation. There's also a need for careful management. And, because the test execution scripts are programs, we need to remember to test them.

Let's look more closely at this idea of keyword-driven or action-word-driven test automation. To be more specific, keywords will represent some business interaction with the system. For example, we could have a keyword for "cancel order" that would result in a whole workflow that made that happen. We can then string together keywords to create test procedures, which can correspond to a use case or a whole end-to-end scenario. Inside, the keyword is implemented as an executable test script or scripts using whatever tool was chosen. The scripts are modular. Sophisticated programming skills are required to implement such a framework.[1]

While expensive up front due to the cost of creating the framework, this approach offers a number of advantages. First, domain experts, based on their

---

1. For a further discussion, see Hans Buwalda, *Integrated Test Design and Automation*.

> **ISTQB Glossary**
>
> **keyword-driven testing:** A scripting technique that uses data files to contain not only test data and expected results, but also keywords related to the application being tested. The keywords are interpreted by special supporting scripts that are called by the control script for the test.
>
> **test execution tool:** A type of test tool that is able to execute other software using an automated test script, e.g., capture/playback.
>
> **test oracle:** A source to determine expected results to compare with the actual result of the software under test. An oracle may be the existing system (for a benchmark), a user manual, or an individual's specialized knowledge, but it should not be the code. [Author's note: A test oracle can be manual, such as a requirements specification, or it can be automated, such as a legacy system or competitor's system.]

understanding of the system, can define keywords. So the tests can be written based on a user's view of the system, not the tool's or the test automator's view.

Once the framework is in place, domain experts, using the keywords along with data they define, can write the test cases themselves. Once the test cases are done, anyone can run them. No real expertise is required, unless a test fails. In that case, the domain expert might need to isolate the failure to see if the problem is the system under test or—as is always possible—the test framework.

The modular scripts and test cases are easier to maintain than other, more linear approaches to automation. If one screen changes, there is usually just a single, reused script that must be updated.

The test specifications are independent of implementation, so you could port them to another implementation of the framework. We actually had a system like this years ago, where we tested various versions of a query tool that ran on about a dozen operating systems with three frameworks. It took a while to learn how to program the framework so it looked the same to the tests, but once we figured it out, we had no trouble moving the tests around.

Test execution tools are mostly used by test analysts and technical test analysts, who can use them during any test level as part of test execution for that level. Keyword test development is mostly done by domain experts and test analysts, though technical test analysts create the frameworks. The testers and domain experts can perform test execution via keyword-based tests during any test level as part of test execution for that level, but it happens most typically during system and acceptance test.

9.3.3   Debugging, Troubleshooting, Fault Seeding, and Injection Tools

Debugging and troubleshooting tools can help us narrow down the area where a bug lives. In some cases, as with user interface bugs, the bug's location is obvious, but in other cases the bug can be a long way from the symptom. Debugging tools can include logs, traces, and simulated environments.

Debuggers have the ability to allow a programmer to execute programs line by line, watching for unexpected control or data flows. They can halt the program at any program statement, if the programmer has a hunch about where the bug lives or wants to check some variables at the point. Debuggers can set flags on and examine program variables.

As mentioned in the Foundation syllabus, debugging is related to testing but it is not testing. Similarly, debugging tools are related to testing but they are not testing tools.

Fault seeding and fault injection are different but related techniques. Fault seeding uses a compiler-like tool to put bugs into the program. This is typically done to check the ability of a set of tests to find such bugs. Of course, the modified version of the program with the bugs is not retained as production code! This is also sometimes called mutation testing. I've never seen this actually done.

Fault injection is usually about injecting bad data or events at an interface. For example, I have a tool that allows me to randomly corrupt file contents. Notice that this is something that Whittaker's attack technique, covered in chapter 4, discusses.

Debugging, troubleshooting, fault seeding, and fault injection tools are mainly used by technical test analysts. Technical test analysts can use these tools at any point in the lifecycle once code exists.

9.3.4   Static and Dynamic Analysis Tools

Static analysis tools, which automate some parts of the static testing process, can be useful throughout the lifecycle. They provide warnings about potential

> **ISTQB Glossary**
>
> **debugging tool:** A tool used by programmers to reproduce failures, investigate the state of programs, and find the corresponding defect. Debuggers enable programmers to execute programs step by step, to halt a program at any program statement, and to set and examine program variables.
>
> **fault seeding tool:** A tool for seeding (i.e., intentionally inserting) faults in a component or system.
>
> **static analyzer:** A tool that carries out static analysis.
>
> static analysis: Analysis of software artifacts, e.g., requirements or code, carried out without execution of these software artifacts.

problems with code, requirements, etc. For example, a code analysis tool will flag dangerous or insecure constructs. Running a spelling and grammar checker on a requirements specification can reveal too high a difficulty level.

The usual problem we've had when using these tools for clients is the number of false positives. In this case, a false positive is a potential problem that does not actually cause any damage. The number of false positives on an existing code base can be huge, as many as one for every 5 or 10 lines of code. There are various strategies for working around this, like only using the tool on new and changed modules of code. Fortunately, vendors recognize this problem and are working to fix it.

Let's look at an example of static analysis and text execution tools in action. Figure 9-2 shows a testing framework my associates and I built for a client. This tool provided automated static analysis and unit, component, and integration testing, using both commercial and open source tools. The best way to read this figure is clockwise starting at the bottom left. Let's see how this worked.

The individual programmers worked on their own PCs, creating unit, component, and integration tests for their code as they built it. They ran the unit tests locally using JUnit. At the end of each day, they checked their work into Perforce, the configuration management system, but that code was labeled as "not ready for the build" until it was approved.

Once the unit tests passed, the programmer would have their code and unit tests reviewed by the lead programmer in their group. (Yes, that's a bit more

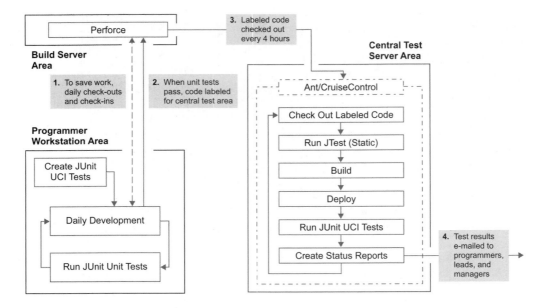

Figure 9–2   *Static analysis and unit test execution*

informal of a review process than I would have preferred, but it was all we could convince them to do.) If the review was a success, the code and tests were then checked into Perforce labeled as "ready for the build."

Now, the central test server had a script running on it that checked for new "ready for build"–labeled code every four hours. If it found some, it would initiate a new test run. That test run consisted of two parts. The first was a static test using the JTest tool from Parasoft. Next, a full dynamic test running all the unit, component, and integration tests in the repository. Once the test run completed, the results were emailed and posted on the intranet.

I think this approach is clever and one just about every development organization should try to adopt. Notice that the very activity that increases regression risk—checking in new or changed code—also triggers the actions that will reduce that regression risk.[2]

Dynamic analysis tools provide runtime information on the state of the executing software. They can pinpoint a number of problems that are hard to

---

2. You can find the complete article on this case study, "Mission Made Possible," on the RBCS website at www.rbcs-us.com.

> **ISTQB Glossary**
>
> **dynamic analysis tool:** A tool that provides runtime information on the state of the software code. These tools are most commonly used to identify unassigned pointers, check pointer arithmetic, and monitor the allocation, use, and de-allocation of memory and flag memory leaks.

find in static analysis and hard to isolate in dynamic testing. These tools include evaluating pointer use, but perhaps memory leak detection is the most common example. Memory leaks are particularly likely in programming languages like C and C++ where the programmer manages memory directly—because they sometimes mismanage it!

Static and dynamic analysis tools are mostly used by technical test analysts. Technical test analysts can use static analysis tools at any point in the lifecycle once the work product to be analyzed exists. They can use dynamic analysis tools during any test level as part of test execution for that level.

9.3.5 Performance Test Tools

Performance test tools typically consist of two major elements. One is a load generator. The other is a measurement and analysis component. The load generator executes a script, which implements an operational profile. You should remember the concept from chapter 5. Sometimes these scripts are captured, though my experience is that they more typically are created. The script needs to be able to throw at the system under test whatever kind of data the system needs to accept.

When a mix of scripts is run under most performance testing tools, a complex mixture of simulated or virtual users can be pounding on the system simultaneously. In many cases, the tools are not pounding directly on the user interface but rather on a communication interface such as HTTP or HTTPS. While this is happening, the measurement component is gathering metrics. The following are typical metrics:

- Numbers of simulated users
- Number and type of transactions generated by the simulated users
- Response times to particular transaction requests made by the users

> **ISTQB Glossary**
>
> **performance testing tool:** A tool to support performance testing and that usually has two main facilities: load generation and test transaction measurement. Load generation can simulate either multiple users or high volumes of input data. During execution, response time measurements are taken from selected transactions and these are logged. Performance testing tools normally provide reports based on test logs and graphs of load against response times.

Based on these metrics, we can create various reports, including graphs of load against response times.

Performance testing is a complicated activity. There are a number of important factors to consider:

■ Do you have sufficient hardware and network bandwidth on the load-generator host required to generate the loads? I have seen load generators saturate before the system under test did, which defeats the purpose.

■ Is the tool you intend to use compatible with the communications protocol used by the system under test? Can the tool simulate everything you need to simulate?

■ Does the tool have sufficient flexibility and capability to allow you to create and run the different operational profiles?

■ Are the monitoring, analysis, and reporting facilities that you need available?

While simple load generators for reliability testing are commonly built in-house, performance test tools are typically purchased or open source versions used. The real tricky part—and where most of the work will be should you decide to build your own performance testing tool—is in the measurement and analysis piece. When my associates and I have had to build performance testing tools, that was usually the hardest part.

Let me mention something at this point that you should keep in mind. Many performance-related defects are design problems. I have seen late discovery of serious performance problems doom a project. So, when performance is a key quality risk, be sure to use modeling and unit testing to performance-test critical components rather than waiting for system tests.

Let's look at an example here, this time for performance testing using integrated tools. I've mentioned the wide area network IVR server project earlier in this book. In the center of figure 9-3, you see the architecture of that system. We have the wide area network of IVR servers to the right side, the support content management and customer service application servers in the center, and the customer service agent desktops at the left.

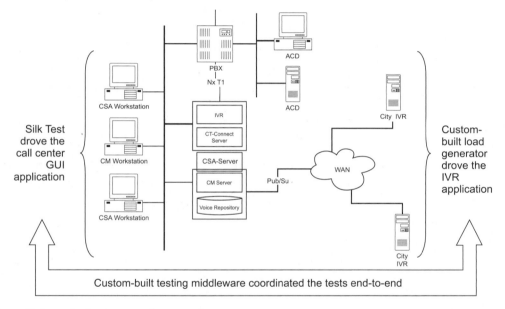

Figure 9–3 *Performance testing example*

If someone pressed 0 while on the IVR, the system was supposed to transfer them via voice over IP through the network to a waiting agent. At the same time that the agent answered the phone, that agent was supposed to see, popping up on his screen, all the profile information in the system about the user he was about to talk with. That had to work reliably, and it had to work even if the server was loaded down.

So, we needed a way to do end-to-end performance testing. We had a load generator that could create calls on the IVR side. The load generator was

ISTQB Glossary

hyperlink test tools: Not defined in the ISTQB glossary.

scripted, so we could include 0 in some of those scripts. The load generator was also able to coordinate, through custom middleware, with QA Partner (now called SilkTest), which was driving and watching the screens. We could actually time the transaction, from pressing 0 on the IVR to seeing the screen pop on the customer service agent's desktop. We would run a bunch of these transactions, capture the transit time, and log that information for later analysis.

Performance test tools are typically used by technical test analysts. Technical test analysts can use these tools during any test level as part of test execution for that level, but it happens most typically during system and acceptance test.

9.3.6   Web Testing Tools

Web tools are another common type of test tool. One common use of these tools is to scan a website for broken or missing hyperlinks. Some tools will also provide a graph of the link tree, the size and speed of downloads, hits, and other metrics. Some tools will do a form of static analysis on the HTML to check for conformance to standards.

Web tools are used mostly by test analysts and technical test analysts. They can use these tools at any point in the lifecycle once the web site to be analyzed exists.

9.3.7   Simulators and Emulators

Simulators, as those of you who have watched any movies about space flight know, provide a way to test in an artificial environment. We might want to do this because some of the code or some other part of the system is unavailable. We might want to do this because the real system is too expensive to use in testing. We might want to do this because testing in the real system is unsafe. For example, aircraft, spacecraft, and nuclear control software is usually tested in simulators before being deployed. I suppose you could say that the deployment constitutes the first test in the real environment.

> **ISTQB Glossary**
>
> **emulator:** A device, computer program, or system that accepts the same inputs and produces the same outputs as a given system.
>
> **simulator:** A device, computer program, or system used during testing that behaves or operates like a given system when provided with a set of controlled inputs.

Some simulators can be sophisticated, able to inject faults, produce reproducible pseudo-random data streams, and the like. My experience with testing in simulators has been, no matter how good, there were always things we found when we went onto the real hardware. Timing problems and resource constraints and dependencies in particular are tricky to simulate.

An emulator is a type of simulator where software mimics hardware. My first encounter with an emulator was in my assembly language course in my first year of computer science at UCLA. Rather than allow us to write real assembly language that ran on their multiuser VAX machines—they were smart enough not to let us do that, as we would have killed those machines for sure!—they provided us with an emulator that looked like a dedicated assemble-and-test environment for our programs.

The potential advantage of an emulator is the kinds of elaborate testing that can be done—at least if the emulator includes it. The one UCLA gave us didn't have a lot of fancy support for testing, as it was mainly designed to prevent us from getting direct access to the VAX hardware. A well-designed emulator, created to support testing, could allow for tracing, debugging, recording, and other kinds of "watching the program run from underneath" activities that would be impossible in a real system.

Test analysts and technical test analysts, depending on the type of emulation required, use these tools. They can use these tools during any test level as part of test execution for that level, but these tools are most typically used during early test levels when the item simulated or emulated is unavailable.

9.4 Sample Exam Questions

To end each chapter, you can try one or more sample exam questions to reinforce your knowledge and understanding of the material and to prepare for the ISTQB Advanced Level Test Analyst exam.

1. Which of the following is an example of an automated test oracle?

    A A legacy system

    B Manual calculation of results

    C A requirements specification

    D A comparator

2. Assume you are a test analyst working on a banking project to upgrade an existing automated teller machine system to allow customers to obtain cash advances from supported credit cards.

    When the user first inserts a valid credit card type, the system considers the user to be in the *unauthenticated* state. Prior to requesting a cash advance, though, the user must enter the *authenticated* state. The user authenticates by entering the proper personal identification number (PIN).

    The system should be able to support up to 1,000 authentication transactions in process at one time. It should be able to complete authentication of a user within two seconds.

    Which of the following test tool types is most likely to be useful for this testing?

    A Static analysis tools

    B Performance test tools

    C Dynamic analysis tools

    D Web test tools

3. Assume a project is following a sequential lifecycle model. Which of the following gives an example of applying a static analysis tool at the earliest possible point in the project?

    A Grammatical analysis of a requirements specification

    B Performance simulation of the network and database design

    C Security risk analysis of the application code and database design

    D Automated unit testing with J-Unit test frameworks

10 People Skills and Team Composition

"You lose."

U.S. President Calvin Coolidge, demonstrating his
laconic communication style in replying to a woman who
told him that she had bet she could get him to say more
than two words to her.

The 10th chapter of the Advanced syllabus is concerned with people skills and
test team composition. The chapter starts with the skills of the individual tester,
then moves to internal and external test team dynamics. It concludes with discussions of motivating testers and test teams and with communicating testing
results. Chapter 10 of the Advanced Syllabus has six sections:

1. Introduction
2. Individual Skills
3. Test Team Dynamics
4. Fitting Testing within an Organization
5. Motivation
6. Communication

Most of these sections are primarily the domain of test managers. However, let's
look at each section, particularly the section on communication, and how it
relates to test analysis.

10.1 Introduction

Learning objectives
Recall of content only

This chapter is focused primarily on test management topics related to managing a test team. Thus, it is mainly the purview of Advanced Test Manager exam candidates. Because this book is for test analysts, most of our coverage in this chapter is simple recall.

However, it is important for all testers to be mindful of their relationships while doing test work. How effectively you communicate with your peers will influence your success as a tester. Of course, you should also be sure to improve your hard skills over time so that you become a better tester.

10.2 Individual Skills

Learning objectives
Recall of content only

The concepts in this section apply primarily for test managers. There are no learning objectives defined for test analysts in this section. In the course of studying for the exam, read this section in chapter 10 of the Advanced syllabus for general recall and familiarity only.

10.3 Test Team Dynamics

Learning objectives
Recall of content only

The concepts in this section apply primarily for test managers. There are no learning objectives defined for test analysts in this section. In the course of studying for the exam, read this section in chapter 10 of the Advanced syllabus for general recall and familiarity only.

> **ISTQB Glossary**
>
> **independence of testing:** Separation of responsibilities, which encourages the accomplishment of objective testing.

10.4 Fitting Testing within an Organization

Learning objectives
Recall of content only

The concepts in this section apply primarily for test managers. There are no learning objectives defined for test analysts in this section. In the course of studying for the exam, read this section in chapter 10 of the Advanced syllabus for general recall and familiarity only.

10.5 Motivation

Learning objectives
Recall of content only

The concepts in this section apply primarily for test managers. There are no learning objectives defined for test analysts in this section. In the course of studying for the exam, read this section in chapter 10 of the Advanced syllabus for general recall and familiarity only.

10.6 Communication

Learning objectives
(K2) Describe by example professional, objective, and effective communication in a project from the tester perspective, considering risks and opportunities.

There are three levels of communication for most test teams:

- First, we communicate, mostly internally but also with others, about the documentation of test products. This includes discussions of test strategies, test plans, test cases, test summary reports, and defect reports.

- Second, we communicate feedback on reviewed documents, typically on a peer level both inside and outside the test group. This includes discussions about requirements, functional specifications, use cases, and unit test documentation.

- Third, we communicate as part of information gathering and dissemination. This can include not just peer level communications, but communications to managers, users, and other project stakeholders. It can be sensitive, as when test results are not encouraging for project success.

It's important to remember that both internal and external communications affect the professionalism of test analysts.

Effective communication assists you in achieving your objectives as a test analyst, while ineffective communication will hinder you. It's important to be professional, objective, and effective. You want each communication you have, both inside and outside the test team, to build and maintain respect for the test team. When communicating about test results, giving feedback on issues with documents, or delivering any other potentially touchy news, make sure to use diplomacy.

It's easy to get caught up in emotions at work, especially during test execution when things are often stressful. Remember to focus on achieving test objectives. Remember also that you want to see the quality of products and processes improved. Don't engage in communication that is contrary to those goals.

It's also easy to communicate as if you were communicating with yourself or someone like you. In other words, we testers often speak in a sort of shorthand about very fine-grained details of our work and findings, and with a certain degree of skepticism. When talking to fellow testers, this is fine. However, you have to remember to tailor communication for the target audience. When talking to users, project team members, management, external test groups, and customers, you need to think carefully about how you are communicating, what you are communicating, and whether your communications support your goals.

As a test manager, I have seen a single thoughtless email, bug report, or hallway conversation do a great deal of damage to my test team's reputation and credibility. So even with all the other work you have to do, remember to think about your communications.[1]

I have spent a couple of hours reviewing the current status of the site and the acceptance test. Please see attaches [documents] with deferred bug reports and [test status]...for pass 2.

The following issues are must-fix to move forward with Deployment:

○ Consistency of meeages and UI (for examples, see bug 85, 91, 92, 95, 97)

○ Newsletter link...not in place as agreed (see bug 98)

○ Identification and resolution of internal dead links (see bug 103)

While some of this issues might strike the casual reader as picayune, please understand that our target customers...are sensitive to any errors...

In the interests of moving forward and having this critical marketing collateral in place...I have agreed to defer a number of bugs from pass 1 either failed verification testing or which related advertised product features [the vendor] retroactively and unilaterally withdrew... Please note that deferral ofthese bugs does not indicate acceptance by RBCS of the disposition of those bugs for all time.

Finally, please note that there were eighteen (18) new bug reports filed during the second pass.

Figure 10–1   *Acceptance test status email*

Here's an example of test communication, shown in figure 10-1. This is an excerpt of an email to a vendor about the results of acceptance testing our new website. The first paragraph is to communicate that this is a carefully thought-out analysis, not just one of the dozens of "fired-off" emails someone is likely to get. The message is, "Pay attention to this email, please, because I did." This paragraph also refers the reader to further details in the attached document.

The second paragraph—including the bulleted list and closing sentence—summarizes what needs to be done to complete the acceptance testing and move into deployment. The third paragraph clarifies the meaning of the

---

1. You can find an excellent discussion of people issues in testing in Judy McKay's *Managing the Testing People*.

deferral of certain bugs. I wanted to make sure that I was not waiving any legal rights RBCS had to insist on these problems being fixed later. The final paragraph is a subtle—I hope—hint that we were disappointed to be still finding problems.

Now, this type of email is appropriate for me to send as a customer to a vendor, explaining test results. Would you send it to your development colleagues? Probably not. The important point here is that every word and every sentence of that email had a communication objective.

10.7 Sample Exam Questions

To end each chapter, you can try one or more sample exam questions to reinforce your knowledge and understanding of the material and to prepare for the ISTQB Advanced Level Test Analyst exam.

1. Assume you are a test analyst working on a banking project to upgrade an existing automated teller machine system to allow customers to obtain cash advances from supported credit cards. Earlier in the project, you were unable to obtain a list of the supported credit cards, which at that time was an action that was not included in the requirements specification. Which of the following is an example of a good way to communicate that problem in an email?

    A "Until I receive a complete list of supported credit card types, no progress on test design can occur."

    B "When will it be possible for us to know which specific credit card types will be supported? Test design is impeded by a lack of clarity here."

    C "Here we go again. The requirements specification is incomplete and ambiguous."

    D Do not communicate the problem; just log the delaying effect of the information problem and be ready to explain the delays to management when they ask.

11 Preparing for the Exam

"Because I am hard, you will not like me. But the more that you hate me, the more you will learn."

Senior Drill Instructor to U.S. Marine boot camp attendees,
in Stanley Kubrick's Vietnam film, *Full Metal Jacket*

The 11th chapter of this book is concerned with topics that you need to know in order to prepare for the ISTQB Advanced Level Test Analyst exam. The chapter starts with a discussion of the ISTQB Advanced Level Test Analyst learning objectives, which are the basis of the exams.

Chapter 11 of this book has two sections:

1. Learning objectives
2. ISTQB Advanced exams

If you are not interested in taking the ISTQB Advanced Level Test Analyst exam, this chapter might not be pertinent for you.

11.1 Learning Objectives

Each of the Advanced syllabus exams is based on learning objectives. A learning objective states what you should be able to do prior to taking an Advanced exam. Each Advanced exam has its own set of learning objectives. I listed the learning objectives for the Advanced Test Analyst exam at the beginning of each section in each chapter.

The learning objectives are at four levels of increasing difficulty. Exam questions will be structured so that you must have achieved these learning objectives to determine the correct answers for the questions. The exams will cover the more basic levels of remembrance and understanding implicitly as part of the more sophisticated levels of application and analysis. For example, to answer a question about how to create a test plan, you will have to remember and understand the IEEE 829 test plan template. So, unlike the Foundation exam, where simple remembrance and understanding often suffice to determine the correct answer, on an Advanced exam, you will have to apply or analyze the facts that you remember and understand in order to determine the correct answer.

Let's take a closer look at the four levels of learning objectives you will encounter on the Advanced exams. The tags K1, K2, K3, and K4 are used to indicate these four levels, so remember those tags as you review the Advanced syllabus.

11.1.1 Level 1: Remember (K1)

At this lowest level of learning, the exam will expect that you can recognize, remember, and recall a term or concept. Watch for keywords such as *remember, recall, recognize,* and *know.* Again, this level of learning is likely to be implicit within a higher-level question.

For example, you should be able to recognize the definition of "failure" as follows:

- "Nondelivery of service to an end user or any other stakeholder"
- "Actual deviation of the component or system from its expected delivery, service, or result"

This means that you should be able to remember the ISTQB glossary definitions of terms used in the ISTQB Advanced syllabus and also standards like ISO 9126 and IEEE 829 that are referenced in the Advanced syllabus. Expect this level of learning to be required for questions focused on higher levels of learning like K3 and K4.

11.1.2 Level 2: Understand (K2)

At this second level of learning, the exam will expect that you can select the reasons or explanations for statements related to the topic and can summarize, differentiate, classify, and give examples. This learning objective applies to facts, so you should be able to compare the meanings of terms. You should also be able to understand testing concepts. In addition, you should be able to understand test procedure, such as explaining the sequence of tasks. Watch for keywords such as *summarize, classify, compare, map, contrast, exemplify, interpret, translate, represent, infer, conclude,* and *categorize.*

For example, you should be able to explain why the reason tests should be designed as early as possible:

- To find defects when they are cheaper to remove
- To find the most important defects first

You should also be able to explain the similarities and differences between integration and system testing:

- Similarities: Testing more than one component, and testing non functional aspects.
- Differences: Integration testing concentrates on interfaces and interactions, while system testing concentrates on whole-system aspects, such as end-to-end processing.

This means that you should be able to understand the ISTQB glossary terms used in the ISTQB Advanced syllabus, and the proper use of standards like ISO 9126 and IEEE 829 that are referenced in the Advanced syllabus. Expect this level of learning to be required for questions focused on higher levels of learning like K3 and K4.

11.1.3 Level 3: Apply (K3)

At this third level of learning, the exam will expect that you can select the correct application of a concept or technique and apply it to a given context. This level is normally applicable to procedural knowledge. At K3, you don't need to expect to evaluate a software application or create a testing model for a given software application. If the syllabus gives a model, the coverage requirements for that model, and the procedural steps to create test cases from a model in the Advanced syllabus, then you are dealing with a K3 learning objective. Watch for keywords such as *implement, execute, use, follow a procedure,* and *apply a procedure.*

For example, you should be able to do the following:

- Identify boundary values for valid and invalid equivalence partitions.
- Use the generic procedure for test case creation to select the test cases from a given state transition diagram (and a set of test cases) in order to cover all transitions.

This means that you should be able to apply the techniques described in the ISTQB Advanced syllabus to specific exam questions. Expect this level of learning to include lower levels of learning like K1 and K2.

11.1.4 Level 4: Analyze (K4)

At this fourth level of learning, the exam will expect that you can separate information related to a procedure or technique into its constituent parts for better understanding and can distinguish between facts and inferences. A typical exam question at this level will require you to analyze a document, software, or project situation and propose appropriate actions to solve a problem or complete a task. Watch for keywords such as *analyze, differentiate, select, structure, focus, attribute, deconstruct, evaluate, judge, monitor, coordinate, create, synthesize, generate, hypothesize, plan, design, construct,* and *produce.*

For example, you should be able to do the following:

- Analyze product risks and propose preventive and corrective mitigation activities.
- Describe which portions of an incident report are factual and which are inferred from results.

This means that you should be able to analyze the techniques and concepts described in the ISTQB Advanced syllabus in order to answer specific exam questions. Expect this level of learning to include lower levels of learning like K1, K2, and perhaps even K3.

11.1.5 Where Did These Levels of Learning Objectives Come From?

If you are curious about how this taxonomy and these levels of learning objectives came to be in the Foundation and Advanced syllabi, then you'll want to refer to Bloom's taxonomy of learning objectives, defined in the 1950s. It's fairly standard educational fare, though you probably haven't encountered it unless you've been involved in teaching training courses.

As a practical matter, I recommend thinking about the levels this way:

- K1 requires the ability to remember basic facts, techniques, and standards, though you might not understand what they mean.
- K2 requires the ability to understand the facts, techniques, and standards and how they interrelate, though you might not be able to apply them to your projects.
- K3 requires the ability to apply facts, techniques, and standards to your projects, though you might not be able to adapt them or select the most appropriate ones for your project.
- K4 requires the ability to analyze facts, techniques, and standards as they might apply to your projects and adapt them or select the most appropriate ones for your projects.

As you can see, there is an upward progression of ability that adheres to each increasing level of learning. Much of the focus at the Advanced level is on application and analysis.

11.2 ISTQB Advanced Exams

Like the Foundation exam, the Advanced exams are multiple choice exams. Multiple choice questions consist of three main parts. The first part is the stem, which is the body of the question. The stem may include a figure or table as well as text. The second part is the distracters, which are choices that are wrong. If you don't have a full understanding of the learning objectives that the question covers, you might believe that the distracters are reasonable choices. The third part is the answer or answers, which are choices that are correct.

If you sailed through the Foundation exam, you might think that you'll manage to do the same with the Advanced exams. That's unlikely. Unlike the Foundation exam, the Advanced exams are heavily focused on questions derived from K3 and K4 level learning objectives. In other words, the ability to apply and to analyze ideas dominates the exams. K1 and K2 level learning objectives, which make up the bulk of the Foundation exam, are only covered implicitly within the higher-level questions.

For example, the Foundation exam might typically include a question like this:

Which of the following is a major section of an IEEE 829 compliant test plan?

A Test items

B Probe effect

C Purpose

D Expected results

The answer is A, while B, C, and D are distracters. All that is required here is to recall the major sections of the IEEE 829 templates. Only A is found in the test plan, while C and D are in the test procedure specification and the test case specification, respectively. B is an ISTQB glossary term. As you can see, it's all simple recall.

Recall is useful, especially when first learning a subject. However, the ability to recall facts does not make you an expert, any more than my ability to recall song lyrics from the 1970s qualifies me to work as the lead singer for the band AC/DC.

On the Advanced exam, you might find a question like this:

Consider the following excerpt from the Test Items section of a test plan.

During System Test execution, the configuration management team shall deliver test releases to the test team every Monday morning by 9:00 a.m. Each test release shall include a test item transmittal report. The test item transmittal report will describe the results of the automated build and smoke test associated with the release. Upon receipt of the test release, if the smoke test was successful, the test manager will install it in the test lab. Testing will commence on Monday morning once the new weekly release is installed.

Should the test team not receive a test release, or if the smoke test results are negative, or if the release will not install, or should the release arrive without a transmittal report, the test manager shall immediately contact the configuration management team manager. If the problem is not resolved within one hour, the test manager shall notify the project manager and continue testing against the previous week's release, if possible. If the test release fails installation, additionally the test analyst who attempted the installation shall file an incident report.

Assume that you are working as the test manager on this project. Suppose that you have received two working, installable, testable releases so far. On Monday of the third week, you do not receive the test release.

Which of the following courses of action is consistent with the test plan?

A Filing an incident report describing the time and date at which you first noticed the missing test release

B Creating a test procedure specification that describes how to install a test release

C Sending an SMS text to the configuration management team manager

D Sending an email to the project manager and the configuration management team manager

The answer is C. A, B, and D are distracters. A is wrong because it is not that the release didn't install, it's that it didn't even arrive. B is wrong because, while such a test procedure might be useful for installation testing, it has nothing to do with the escalation process described in the test plan. C is consistent with the test plan. D is not consistent with the test plan because the spirit of the one-hour delay described in the test plan excerpt is that the configuration management team manager should have a chance to resolve the problem before the project manager is engaged. In addition, when time is of the essence, email is not a good escalation technique.

As you can see, this kind of question requires analysis of a situation. Yes, it helps to know what the IEEE 829 templates such as the test plan, incident report, test item transmittal report, and test procedure specification contain. In fact, you'll probably get lost in the terminology if you don't know the standard. However, simply knowing the IEEE 829 standard will not allow you to get the right answer on this question except by chance.

11.2.1 Scenario-Based Questions

Further complicating this situation is the fact that many exam questions will actually consider a scenario. In scenario-based questions, the exam will describe a set of circumstances. It will then present you with a sequence of two, three, or even more questions.

For example, the questions about the scenario of the test plan excerpt and the missing test release might continue with another pair of questions:

> Assume that on Monday afternoon you finally receive a test release. When your lead test analyst attempts to install it, the database configuration scripts included in the installation terminate in midstream. An error message is presented on the database server in Cyrillic script, though the chosen language is U.S. English. At that point, the database tables are corrupted and any attempt to use the application under test results in various database connection error messages (which are at least presented in U.S. English).
>
> Consider the following possible actions:
>
> I   Notifying the configuration management team manager
>
> II   Notifying the project manager
>
> III   Filing an incident report
>
> IV   Attempting to repeat the installation
>
> V   Suspending testing
>
> VI   Continuing testing
>
> Which of the following sequence of actions is in the correct order, is the most reasonable, and is most consistent with the intent of the test plan?
>
> A I, II, V
>
> B V, I, IV, III, I
>
> C VI, II, I, III, IV
>
> D II, I, V

The answer is B, while A, C, and D are distracters. A is wrong because there is no incident report filed, which is required by the test plan when the installation fails. C is wrong because meaningful testing cannot continue against the corrupted database, because the project manager is notified before the configuration management team manager, and because the incident report is filed before an attempt to reproduce the failure has occurred. D is wrong because the project manager is notified before the configuration management team manager and because no incident report is filed.

As you can see, with a scenario-based question it's very important that you study the scenario carefully before trying to answer the questions that relate to it. If you misunderstand the scenario—perhaps due to a rushed reading of it—you can anticipate missing most, if not all, of the questions related to it.

Let me go back to this question of learning objectives for a moment. I said that the exam covers K1 and K2 learning objectives—those requiring recall and understanding, respectively—as part of a higher-level K3 or K4 question. There's an added complication with K1 learning objectives: They are not explicitly defined. The entire syllabus, including glossary terms used and standards referenced, is implicitly covered by K1 learning objectives. Here is an excerpt from the Advanced syllabus:

> This syllabus' content, terms and the major elements (purposes) of all standards listed shall at least be remembered (K1), even if not explicitly mentioned in the learning objectives.

So, you'll want to read the Advanced syllabus carefully, a number of times, as you are studying for the Advanced exam.

Not only should you read the Advanced syllabus, but you'll need to go back and refresh yourself on the Foundation. Again, an excerpt from the Advanced syllabus:

> All Advanced Certificate examinations must be based on this syllabus and on the Foundation Level syllabus. Answers to examination questions may require the use of material based on more than one section of this and the Foundation Level syllabus. All sections of this and the Foundation Level syllabus are examinable.

Notice that the second sentence in the preceding paragraph means that a question can conceivably cross-reference two or three sections of the Advanced syllabus or cross-reference a section of the Advanced syllabus with the Foundation syllabus. So, it would be smart to take a sample Foundation exam and reread the Foundation syllabus as part of studying for the Advanced exam.

11.2.2 On the Evolution of the Exams

The structure of the Advanced exams is in flux and might not be completely and universally determined until the end of 2009. Even once the ISTQB Advanced Exam Guidelines are finalized, note that there is a somewhat insidious paragraph tucked away in the Advanced syllabus that reads as follows:

> The format of the examination is defined by the Advanced Exam Guidelines of the ISTQB. Individual Member Boards may adopt other examination schemes if desired.

I have written this chapter in large part based on the draft ISTQB Advanced Exam Guidelines. I assume that most ISTQB national boards and exam boards will choose to follow those. However, it is permitted, based on this paragraph in the Advanced syllabus, for exams to be created by some boards that differ from the ISTQB Exam Guidelines and thus what is described in this chapter. You'll want to check with the national board or exam board providing your exam to be sure. They should post on their website the version of the ISTQB Advanced Exam Guidelines they used to create their exam.

Okay, having read this, you might be panicking. Don't! Remember, the exam is meant to test your achievement of the learning objectives in the Advanced syllabus. This book contains solid features to help you do that, including the following:

- Did you work through all the exercises in the book? If so, then you have a solid grasp on the most difficult learning objectives, the K3 and K4 objectives. If not, then go back and do so now.
- Did you work through all the sample exam questions in the book? If so, then you have tried a sample exam question for most of the learning objectives in the syllabus. If not, then go back and do so now.
- Did you read the ISTQB glossary term definitions where they occurred in the chapters? If so, then you are familiar with these terms. If not, then return to the ISTQB glossary now and review those terms.
- Did you read every chapter of this book and the entire ISTQB Advanced syllabus? If so, then you know the material in the ISTQB Advanced syllabus. If not, then review the ISTQB Advanced syllabus and reread those sections

of this book that correspond to the parts of the syllabus you find most confusing.

I can't guarantee that you will pass the exam. However, if you have taken advantage of the learning opportunities created by this book, by the ISTQB glossary, and by the ISTQB Advanced syllabus, you will be in good shape for the exam.

Good luck to you when you take the exam, and the best of success when you apply the ideas in the Advanced syllabus to your next testing project.

Bibliography

Advanced Syllabus Referenced Standards

British Computer Society. BS 7925-2 (1998), Software Component Testing.

Institute of Electrical and Electronics Engineers. IEEE Standard 829 (1998/ 2007), IEEE Standard for Software Test Documentation.

Institute of Electrical and Electronics Engineers. IEEE Standard 1028 (1997), IEEE Standard for Software Reviews.

Institute of Electrical and Electronics Engineers. IEEE Standard 1044 (1993), IEEE Standard Classification for Software Anomalies.

International Standards Organization. ISO/IEC 9126-1:2001, Software Engineering – Software Product Quality.

International Software Testing Qualifications Board. ISTQB Glossary (2007), ISTQB Glossary of terms used in Software Testing, Version 2.0.

US Federal Aviation Administration. DO-178B/ED-12B, Software Considerations in Airborne Systems and Equipment Certification.

Advanced Syllabus Referenced Books

Beizer, Boris. *Black-Box Testing*. Wiley, 1995.

Black, Rex. *Managing the Testing Process (Second Edition)*. Wiley, 2002.

Black, Rex. *Critical Testing Processes*. Addison-Wesley, 2003.

Black, Rex. *Pragmatic Software Testing*. Wiley, 2007.

Buwalda, Hans. *Integrated Test Design and Automation*. Addison-Wesley, 2001.

Burnstein, Ilene. *Practical Software Testing*. Springer, 2003.

Copeland, Lee. *A Practitioner's Guide to Software Test Design*. Artech House, 2003.

Craig, Rick, and Stefan Jaskiel. *Systematic Software Testing*. Artech House, 2002.

Gerrard, Paul, and Neil Thompson. *Risk-Based e-Business Testing*. Artech House, 2002.

Gilb, Tom, and Dorothy Graham. *Software Inspection*. Addison-Wesley, 1993.

Graham, Dorothy, Erik van Veenendaal, Isabel Evans, and Rex Black. *Foundations of Software Testing*. Thomson Learning, 2007.

Grochmann, M. "Test Case Design Using Classification Trees." Conference Proceedings of STAR 1994.

Jorgensen, Paul. *Software Testing: A Craftsman's Approach (Second Edition)*. CRC Press, 2002.

Kaner, Cem, James Bach, and Bret Pettichord. *Lessons Learned in Software Testing*. Wiley, 2002.

Koomen, Tim, and Martin Pol. *Test Process Improvement*. Addison-Wesley, 1999.

Myers, Glenford. *The Art of Software Testing*. Wiley, 1979.

Pol, Martin, Ruud Teunissen, and Erik van Veenendaal. *Software Testing: A Guide to the T-map Approach*. Addison-Wesley, 2002.

Splaine, Steven, and Stefan Jaskiel. *The Web-Testing Handbook*. STQE Publishing, 2001.

Stamatis, D. H. *Failure Mode and Effect Analysis*. ASQ Press, 1995.

van Veenendaal, Erik, ed. *The Testing Practitioner*. UTN Publishing, 2002.

Whittaker, James. *How to Break Software*. Addison-Wesley, 2003.

Whittaker, James, and Herbert Thompson. *How to Break Software Security*. Addison-Wesley, 2004.

Wiegers, Karl. *Software Requirements (Second Edition)*. Microsoft Press, 2003.[1]

Other Referenced Books

Beizer, Boris. *Software System Testing and Quality Assurance.* Van Nostrand Reinhold, 1984.

Beizer, Boris. *Software Test Techniques, 2e.* Van Nostrand Reinhold, 1990.

Jones, Capers. *Software Assessments, Benchmarks, and Best Practices.* Addison-Wesley Professional, 2000.

Koomen, Tim, et al. *TMap Next.* UTN Publishers, 2006.

McKay, Judy. *Managing the Test People.* Rocky Nook, Inc., 2007.

Nielsen, Jakob. *Usability Engineering.* Academic Press, 1993.

Tufte, Edward. *The Graphical Display of Quantitative Information, 2e.* Graphics Press, 2001.

Tufte, Edward. *Visual Explanations.* Graphics Press, 1997.

Tufte, Edward. *Envisioning Information.* Graphics Press, 1990.

White, Gregory, et al. *Security+ Certification.* Osborne, 2003.

Other References

Holmes, Jeff. "Identifying Code-Inspection Improvements Using Statistical Black Belt Techniques." *Software Quality Professional*, December 2003, Volume 6, Number 1.

Black, Rex, and Greg Kubaczkowski. "Mission Made Possible." *Software Testing and Quality Engineering*, July/August 2002, Volume 4, Issue 4.

dictionary.com, for standard English words.

---

1. In an omission, this book is not included in the Advanced Syllabus bibliography but it is referenced in the Advanced Syllabus text. Therefore, I have included it here.

RBCS

TIME TESTED.
TESTING IMPROVED.
www.RBCS-US.com

HELLOCARMS
The Next Generation of Home Equity Lending

System Requirements Document

Table of Contents

II   Versioning

Ver.	Date	Author	Description	Approval By/On
0.1	Nov 1, 2007	Rex Black	First Draft	
0.2	Dec 15, 2007	Rex Black	Second Draft	
0.5	Jan 1, 2008	Rex Black	Third Draft	

III   Glossary

Term[1]	Definition
Home Equity	The difference between a home's fair market value and the unpaid balance of the mortgage and any other debt secured by the home. A homeowner can increase their home equity by reducing the unpaid balance of the mortgage and any other debt secured by the home. Home equity can also increase if the property appreciates in value. A homeowner can borrow against home equity using *home equity loans*, *home equity lines of credit*, and *reverse mortgages* (see below).
Secured Loan	Any loan where the borrower uses an asset as collateral for the loan. The loan is secured by the collateral in that the borrower can make a legal claim on the collateral if the borrower fails to repay the loan.
Home Equity Loan	A lump sum of money, disbursed at the initiation of the loan and lent to the homeowner at interest. A home equity loan is a secured loan, secured by the equity in the borrower's home.
Home Equity Line of Credit	A variable amount of money with a prearranged maximum amount, available for withdrawal by the homeowner on an as-needed basis and lent to the homeowner at interest. A home equity line of credit allows the homeowner to take out, as needed, a secured loan, secured by the equity in the borrower's home.
Mortgage	A legal agreement by which a sum of money is lent for the purpose of buying property and against which property the loan is secured.
Reverse Mortgage	A mortgage in which a homeowner borrows money in the form of regular payments which are charged against the equity of the home, typically with the goal of using the equity in the home as a form of retirement fund. A reverse mortgage results in the homeowner taking out a regularly increasing secured loan, secured by the equity in the borrower's home.

1. *These definitions are adapted from www.dictionary.com.*

000 Introduction

The Home Equity Loan, Line-of-Credit, and Reverse Mortgage System (HELLOCARMS), as to be deployed in the first release, allows Globobank Telephone Bankers in the Globobank Fairbanks call center to accept applications for home equity products (loans, lines of credit, and reverse mortgages) from customers. The second release will allow applications over the Internet, including from Globobank business partners as well as customers themselves.

At a high level, the system is configured as shown in Figure 1.

The HELLOCARMS application itself is a group of Java programs and assorted interfacing glue that run on the Web server. The Database server provides storage as the Application is processed, while the Application server offloads gateway activities to the clients from the Web server.

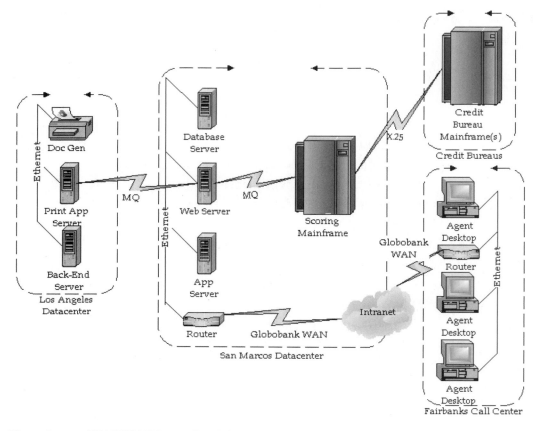

Figure 1   *HELLOCARMS System (First Release)*

001 Informal Use Case

The following informal use case applies for typical transactions in the HELLO-CARMS System:

1. A Globobank Telephone Banker in a Globobank Call Center receives a phone call from a Customer.

2. The Telephone Banker interviews the Customer, entering information into the HELLOCARMS System through a Web browser interface on their Desktop. If the Customer is requesting a large loan or borrowing against a high-value property, the Telephone Banker escalates the application to a Senior Telephone Banker who decides whether to proceed with the application.

3. Once the Telephone Banker has gathered the information from the Customer, the HELLOCARMS System determines the credit-worthiness of the Customer using the Scoring Mainframe.

4. Based on all of the Customer information, the HELLOCARMS System displays various Home Equity Products (if any) that the Telephone Banker can offer to the customer.

5. If the Customer chooses one of these Products, the Telephone Banker will conditionally confirm the Product.

6. The interview ends. The Telephone Banker directs the HELLOCARMS System to transmit the loan information to the Loan Document Printing System (LoDoPS) in the Los Angeles Datacenter for origination.

7. The HELLOCARMS System receives an update from the LoDoPS System when the following events occur:

    a LoDoPS System sends documents to customer.

    b Globobank Loan Servicing Center receives signed documents from customer; and, c Globobank Loan Servicing Center sends a check or other materials as appropriate to the Customer's product selection.

Once the Globobank Loan Servicing Center has sent the funds or other materials to the Customer, HELLOCARMS processing on the application is complete, and the system will not track subsequent loan-related activities for this Customer.

Once HELLOCARMS processing on an application is complete, HELLOCARMS shall archive the application and all information associated with it. This applies whether the application was declined by the bank, cancelled by the customer, or ultimately converted into an active loan/line of credit/reverse mortgage.

003   Scope

The scope of the HELLOCARMS project includes:

- Selecting a COTS solution from a field of five vendors.
- Working with the selected application vendor to modify the solution to meet Globobank's requirements.
- Providing a browser-based front end for loan processing access from the Internet, existing Globobank call centers, outsourced (non-Globobank) call centers, retail banking centers, and brokers. However, the HELLOCARMS first release will only provide access from a Globobank call center (specifically Fairbanks).
- Developing an interface to Globobank's existing Scoring Mainframe for scoring a customer based on their loan application and HELLOCARMS features.
- Developing an interface to use Globobank's existing underwriting and origination system, Loan Document Printing System (LoDoPS), for document preparation. This interface allows the HELLOCARMS system, after assisting the customer with product selection and providing preliminary approval to the customer, to forward the preapproved application (for a loan, line of credit, or reverse mortgage) to the LoDoPS and to subsequently track the application's movement through to the servicing system.
- Receiving customer-related data from the Globobank Rainmaker Borrower Qualification Winnow (GloboRainBQW) system to generate outbound offers to potential (but not current) Globobank customers via phone, email, and paper mail.

004   System Business Benefits

The business benefits associated with the HELLOCARMS include:

- Automating a currently manual process, and allowing loan inquiries and applications from the Internet and via call center personnel (both from the current call centers and potentially from outsourced call centers, retail banking centers, and loan brokers).
- Decreasing the time to process the front-end portion of a loan from approximately 30 minutes to 5 minutes. This will allow Globobank's Consumer Products Division to dramatically increase the volumes of loans processed to meet its business plan.
- Reducing the level of skill required for the Telephone Banker to process a loan application, because the HELLOCARMS will select the product, decide whether the applicant is qualified, suggest alternative loan products, and provide a script for the Telephone Banker to follow.
- Providing online application status and loan tracking through the origination and document preparation process. This will allow Telephone Banker to rapidly and accurately respond to customer inquiries during the processing of their application.
- Providing the capability to process all products in a single environment.
- Providing a consistent way to make decisions about whether to offer loan products to customers, and if so, what loan products to offer customers, reducing processing and sales errors.
- Allowing Internet-based customers (in subsequent releases) to access Globobank products, select the preferred product, and receive a tentative loan approval within seconds.

The goal of the HELLOCARMS System's business sponsors is to provide these benefits for approximately 85% of the customer inquiries, with 15% or fewer inquiries escalate to a Senior Telephone Banker for specialized processing.

010   Functional System Requirements

The capability of the system to provide functions which meet stated and implied needs when the software is used under specified conditions.

ID	Description	Priority*
010-010	*Suitability*	
010-010-010	Allow Telephone Bankers to take applications for home equity loans, lines of credit, and reverse mortgages.	1
010-010-020	Provide screens and scripts to support Call Center personnel in completing loan applications.	1
010-010-030	If the customer does not provide a "How Did You Hear About Us" identifier code, collect the lead information during application processing via a drop-down menu, with well-defined lead source categories.	2
010-010-040	Provide data validation, including the use of appropriate user interface (field) controls as well as back-end data validation. Field validation details are described in a separate document.	1
010-010-050	Display existing debts to enable retirement of selected debts for debt consolidation. Pass selected debts to be retired to LoDoPS as stipulations.	1
010-010-060	Allow Telephone Bankers and other Globobank telemarketers and partners to access incomplete or interrupted applications.	2
010-010-070	Ask each applicant whether there is an existing relationship with Globobank; e.g., any checking or savings accounts. Send existing Globobank customer relationship information to the Globobank Loan Applications Data Store (GLADS).	2
010-010-080	Maintain application status from initiation through to rejection, decline, or acceptance (and, if accepted, to delivery of funds).	2
010-010-090	Allow user to abort an application. Provide an abort function on all screens.	3

Table continues

ID	Description	Priority*
010-010-100	Allow user to indicate on a separate screen which, if any, are existing debts that the customer will retire using the funds for which the customer is applying. Allow user the option to exclude specific debts and to include specific debts. For debts to be retired, send a stipulation to LoDoPS that specifies which debts that the customer must pay with loan proceeds.	3
010-010-110	Exclude a debt's monthly payment from the debt ratio if the customer requests the debt to be paid off.	3
010-010-120	Provide a means of requesting an existing application by customer identification number if a customer does not have their loan identifier.	4
010-010-130	Direct the Telephone Banker to transfer the call to a Senior Telephone Banker if an application has a loan amount greater than $500,000; such loans require additional management approval.	1
010-010-140	Direct the Telephone Banker to transfer the call to a Senior Telephone Banker if an application concerns a property with value greater than $1,000,000; such applications require additional management approval.	2
010-010-150	Provide inbound and outbound telemarketing support for all States, Provinces, and Countries in which Globobank operates.	2
010-010-160	Support brokers and other business partners by providing limited partner-specific screens, logos, interfaces, and branding.	2
010-010-170	Support the submission of applications via the Internet, which includes the capability of untrained users to properly enter applications.	3
010-010-180	Provide features and screens that support the operations of Globobank's retail branches.	4
010-010-190	Support the marketing, sales, and processing of home equity applications.	1
010-010-200	Support the marketing, sales, and processing of home equity line of credit applications.	2
010-010-210	Support the marketing, sales, and processing of home equity reverse mortgage applications.	3
010-010-220	Support the marketing, sales, and processing of applications for combinations of financial products (e.g., home equity and credit cards).	4

Table continues

ID	Description	Priority*
010-010-230	Support the marketing, sales, and processing of applications for original mortgages.	5
010-010-240	Support the marketing, sales, and processing of preapproved applications.	4
010-010-250	Support flexible pricing schemes including introductory pricing, short-term pricing, and others.	5
010-020	*Accuracy*	
010-020-010	Determine the various loans, lines of credit, and/or reverse mortgages for which a customer qualifies, and present these options for the customer to evaluate, with calculated costs and terms. Make qualification decisions in accordance with Globobank credit policies.	1
010-020-020	Determine customer qualifications according to property risk, credit score, loan-to-property-value ratio, and debt-to-income ratio, based on information received from the Scoring Mainframe.	1
010-020-030	During the application process, estimate the monthly payments based on the application information provided by the customer, and include the estimated payment as a debt in the debt-to-income calculation for credit scoring.	2
010-020-040	Add a loan fee based on property type: • 1.5% for rental properties (duplex, apartment, and vacation) • 2.5% for commercial properties. • 3.5% for condominiums or cooperatives. • 4.5% for undeveloped property. Do not add a loan fee for the other supported property type, residential single family dwelling.	3
010-020-050	Capture all government retirement fund income(s) (e.g., Social Security in United States) as net amounts, but convert those incomes to gross income(s) in the interface to LoDoPS. [Note: This is because most government retirement income is not subject to taxes, but gross income is used in debt-to-income calculations.]	1
010-020-060	Capture the length of time (rounded to the nearest month) that the customer has received additional income (other than salary, bonuses, and retirement), if any.	3
010-030	*Interoperability*	
010-030-010	If the customer provides a "How Did You Hear About Us" identifier code during the application process, retrieve customer information from GloboRainBQW.	2

Table continues

ID	Description	Priority[*]
010-030-020	Accept joint applications (e.g., partners, spouses, relatives, etc.) and score all applicants using the Scoring Mainframe.	1
010-030-030	Direct Scoring Mainframe to remove duplicate credit information from joint applicant credit reports.	2
010-030-040	Allow user to indicate on a separate screen which, if any, are existing debts that the customer will retire using the funds for which the customer is applying. Allow user the option to exclude specific debts and to include specific debts. For debts to be retired, send a stipulation to LoDoPS that specifies which debts that the customer must pay with loan proceeds.	1
010-030-060	If the Scoring Mainframe does not show a foreclosure or bankruptcy discharge date and the Customer indicates that the foreclosure or bankruptcy is discharged, continue processing the application, and direct the Telephone Banker to ask the applicant to provide proof of discharge in paperwork sent to LoDoPS.	3
010-030-070	Allow user to indicate on a separate screen which, if any, are existing debts that the customer will retire using the funds for which the customer is applying. Allow user the option to exclude specific debts and to include specific debts. For debts to be retired, send a stipulation to LoDoPS that specifies which debts that the customer must pay with loan proceeds.	3
010-030-080	Capture all government retirement fund income(s) (e.g., Social Security in United States) as net amounts, but convert those incomes to gross income(s) in the interface to LoDoPS. [Note: This is because most government retirement income is not subject to taxes, but gross income is used in debt-to-income calculations.]	1
010-030-090	Pass application information to the Scoring Mainframe.	1
010-030-100	Receive scoring and decision information back from the Scoring Mainframe.	1
010-030-110	If the Scoring Mainframe is down, queue application information requests.	2
010-030-120	Initiate the origination process by sending the approved loan to LoDoPS.	2
010-030-130	Pass all declined applications to LoDoPS.	2
010-030-140	Receive LoDoPS feedback on the status of applications.	2
010-030-145	Receive changes to loan information made in LoDoPS (e.g., loan amount, rate, etc.).	2

Table continues

ID	Description	Priority*
010-030-150	Support computer-telephony integration to provide customized marketing and sales support for inbound telemarketing campaigns and branded business partners.	4
010-040	*Security*	
010-040-010	Support agreed-upon security requirements (encryption, firewalls, etc.).	2
010-040-020	Track "Created By" and "Last Changed By" audit trail information for each application.	1
010-040-030	Allow outsourced telemarketers to see the credit tier but disallow them from seeing the actual credit score of applicants.	2
010-040-040	Support the submission of applications via the Internet, providing security against unintentional and intentional security attacks.	2
010-040-050	Allow Internet users to browse potential loans without requiring such users to divulge personal information such as name, government identifying numbers, etc. until the latest feasible point in the application process.	4
010-040-060	Support fraud detection for processing of all financial applications.	1
010-050	*Compliance (functionality standards/laws/regs)*	
	[To be determined in a subsequent revision]	

* Priorities are:

1   Very high
2   High
3   Medium
4   Low
5   Very Low

020   Reliability System Requirements

The capability of the system to maintain a specified level of performance when used under specified conditions.

ID	Description	Priority
020-010	*Maturity*	
	[To be determined in a subsequent revision]	
020-020	*Fault-tolerance*	
	[To be determined in a subsequent revision]	
020-030	*Recoverability*	
	[To be determined in a subsequent revision]	
020-040	*Compliance (reliability standards/laws/regs)*	
	[To be determined in a subsequent revision]	

030   Usability System Requirements

The capability of the system to be understood, learned, used, and attractive to the user and the call center agents when used under specified conditions.

ID	Description	Priority
030-010	*Understandability*	
030-010-010	Support the submission of applications via the Internet, including the capability for untrained users to properly enter applications.	2
	[More to be determined in a subsequent revision]	
030-020	*Learnability*	
	[To be determined in a subsequent revision]	
030-030	*Operability*	
030-030-010	Provide for complete customization of the user interface and all user user-supplied documents for business partners, including private branding of the sales and marketing information and all closing documents.	3
	[More to be determined in a subsequent revision]	
030-040	*Attractiveness*	
	[To be determined in a subsequent revision]	
030-050	*Compliance (usability standards)*	
030-050-010	Comply with local handicap-access laws.	5

040   Efficiency System Requirements

The capability of the system to provide appropriate performance, relative to the amount of resources used under stated conditions.

ID	Description	Priority
040-010	*Time behavior*	
040-010-010	Provide the user with screen-to-screen response time of one second or less. This requirement should be measured from the time the screen request enters the application system until the screen response departs the application server; i.e., do not include network transmission delays.	2
040-010-020	Provide an approval or decline for applications within 5 minutes of application submittal.	2
040-010-030	Originate the loan, including the disbursal of funds, within one hour.	3
	[More to be determined in a subsequent revision]	
040-020	*Resource utilization*	
040-020-010	Handle up to 2,000 applications per hour.	2
040-020-020	Handle up to 4,000 applications per hour.	3
040-020-030	Support a peak of 4,000 simultaneous (concurrent) application submissions.	4
040-020-040	Support a total volume of 1.2 million approved applications for the initial year of operation.	2
040-020-050	Support a total volume of 7.2 million applications during the initial year of operation.	2
040-020-060	Support a total volume of 2.4 million conditionally approved applications for the initial year of operation.	2
	[More to be determined in a subsequent revision]]	
040-030	*Compliance (performance standards)*	
	[To be determined in a subsequent revision]	

050 Maintainability System Requirements

The capability of the system to be modified. Modifications may include corrections, improvement, or adaptations of the software changes in environments and in requirements and functional specifications.

ID	Description	Priority
050-010	*Analyzability*	
	[To be determined in a subsequent revision]	
050-020	*Changeability*	
	[To be determined in a subsequent revision]	
040-030	Compliance (performance standards)	
	[To be determined in a subsequent revision]	

060   Portability System Requirements

The capability of the system to be transferred from one environment to another.

ID	Description	Priority
060-010	*Adaptability*	
	[To be determined in a subsequent revision]	
060-020	*Installability*	
	[To be determined in a subsequent revision]	
060-030	*Co-existence*	
060-030-010	Should not interact in any nonspecified way with any other applications in the Globobank call centers or data centers.	1
	[More to be determined in a subsequent revision]	
060-040	*Replaceability*	
	Not applicable	
060-050	*Compliance*	
	[To be determined in a subsequent revision]	

A   Acknowledgement

This document is based on an actual project. RBCS would like to thank their client, who wishes to remain unnamed, for their permission to adapt and publish anonymous portions of various project documents.

Answers to Sample Questions

Chapter 1

1	C, D
2	C

Chapter 2

1	B, D
2	A
3	B
4	D

Chapter 3

1	D
2	B
3	A

Chapter 4

1	D
2	C
3	B
4	A
5	C
6	D
7	C
8	A
9	A

10	D
11	B
12	A
13	B
14	C
15	B
16	D
17	B
18	A
19	C
20	A
21	C
22	B
23	C
24	B
25	B

Chapter 5

1	D
2	A
3	B
4	C
5	C

Chapter 6

1	D
2	B
3	C
4	A

Chapter 7

1	C
2	B
3	D
4	A
5	B

Chapter 9

1	A
2	B
3	A

Chapter 10

1	B

Index

Advanced Software Testing—Vol. 1

Guide to the ISTQB Advanced Certification as an Advanced Test Analyst

Rex Black

This book is written for the test analyst who wants to achieve advanced skills in test analysis, design, and execution. With a hands-on, exercise-rich approach, this book teaches you how to define and carry out the tasks required to put a test strategy into action.

Learn how to analyze the system, taking into account the user's quality expectations. Additionally, learn how to evaluate system requirements as part of formal and informal reviews, using an understanding of the business domain to determine requirement validity. You will be able to analyze, design, implement, and execute tests, using risk considerations to determine the appropriate effort and priority for tests. You will also learn how to report on testing progress and provide evidence to support your evaluations of system quality.

This book will also help you prepare for the ISTQB (International Software Testing Qualifications Board) Advanced Test Analyst exam. Included are sample exam q[...] appropriate level of difficult[...]

learning objectives covered by the ISTQB Advanced Level syllabus. The ISTQB certification program is the leading software tester certification program in the world. With about 100,000 certificate holders and a global presence in 50 countries, you can be confident in the value and international stature that the Advanced Test Analyst certificate can offer you.

With a quarter-century of software and systems engineering experience, author Rex Black is President of RBCS, a leader in software, hardware, and systems testing, and is the most prolific author practicing in the field of software testing today. He is President of the ISTQB and is a Director of the American Software Testing Qualifications Board (ASTQB).

Related books:
Vol. 2: ISTQB Advanced Test Manager
(ISBN 978-1-933952-36-9)
Vol. 3: ISTQB Advanced Technical Test Analyst
[IS]BN 978-1-933952-39-0)

ISBN: 978-1-933952-19-2
US $ 49.95
CAN $ 49.95

9 781933 952192